D0842169

A WORLD ON FILM

By Stanley Kauffmann

Novels

The Hidden Hero
The Tightrope
A Change of Climate
Man of the World

Children's Play

Bobino

Criticism

A World on Film
On Books (in preparation)

A World on Film

CRITICISM AND COMMENT

BY Stanley Kauffmann

HARPER & ROW, PUBLISHERS

NEW YORK

FIRST EDITION

LIBRARY OF CONGRESS CATALOG CARD NUMBER: 66-15733

C-Q

To
Robert Evett
Gilbert A. Harrison
and
F. R. Ruskin
of *The New Republic*

Since he began reviewing movies for *The New Republic* eight years ago, Stanley Kauffmann has become recognized as America's leading film critic. During the same period film as an art acquired a large and enthusiastic following, and indeed, as Kauffmann says, a "film generation" came into being.

No previous decade has seen so many good films from such varied sources—from Antonioni's avant-garde works to the finest Hollywood musical, *West Side Story;* from Kurosawa's Japan through the 20th-century America of *Dr. Strangelove* to the *dolce* London of *Darling*. It has been Kauffmann's strength to distinguish in these films the lasting from the ephemeral, and the truly original from the merely faddish.

A good movie critic must dissect each picture into its many components—camera work, script, direction, acting, editing.

CONTINUED ON BACK FLAP

0566

this book, explains the rise of the film to its present pre-eminent position and tries to gauge the direction of the cinema of the future.

STANLEY KAUFFMANN was born in New York and is a graduate of New York University's College of Fine Arts. He spent a number of years as actor and stage manager in a repertory company, has published one-act plays, and had several long plays produced in summer theaters. He has directed in theater and radio, written seven novels, and spent some years as a book publisher's editor. In addition to writing his regular film criticism in *The New Republic,* Mr. Kauffmann conducted a program called "The Art of Film" on WNDT, the New York City educational television station. For his film criticism, Mr. Kauffmann has been made an Honorary Fellow of Morse College of Yale University.

Mr. Kauffmann is now drama critic of the *New York Times*.

Contents

Preface

This book is a selection of criticism and articles written between early 1958 and late 1965 while I was the regular film critic of *The New Republic*. Many of the reviews have been edited slightly for this volume, but where an opinion needed to be substantially altered or amplified, it has been done in a postscript. Most of the material comes from *The New Republic;* the exceptions are noted.

About the arrangement: There are some groupings by subject and some by country of origin (which is not always the nationality of the director). But this does not mean that, for example, every mention of adaptation is in the adaptation section, only those reviews in which that topic is emphasized; and in the subject groups, there are films that would otherwise have been under national headings. Within each section the order is chronological except that, when a director first appears, all other reviews of his work then follow before we go on to the first appearance of the next director. In the Acting and Adaptation sections, the same procedure is used for actors and authors. Consequently, there is an occasional reference to a film that is reviewed later in the book, but most of these titles are now familiar to many, and this grouping by artists within sections seemed preferable to strict chronological order because of the added associative value.

This is not to imply that there was a plan, from the beginning, behind these independently written items; yet there is one unifying element of which I have long been happily aware. I discovered early the special pleasures and benefits of writing regularly for a group of demanding readers. The continuity generates a relationship both with them and with one's critical self, past and future, that cannot be reached through occasional criticism—like, for instance, most of the literary criticism in this country. I cannot imagine a more stimulating life for a critic of new works than to be able to address regularly a group of the best readers he can conceive of and to be given a free hand in doing it. This volume has been dedicated to editorial friends at *The New Republic,* and that is small enough thanks; it ought also to be dedicated to the magazine's readers. Whatever the book contains that is worth preservation owes much to a sense of their presence and interest.

S. K.

January, 1966

PART I

SUBJECTS

War

During, After, Before

Grand Illusion (July 27, 1959)

Jean Renoir's masterpiece, *Grand Illusion,* is now being revived, and to see it again is to discover how much we ourselves have changed. Can 1937, when it was made, really have been so long ago? Brotherhood, peace, the waste of war—how clear and final those issues once were. How poignant this film makes them seem today, when every political utterance reminds us that tension is a constant in international affairs, that disarmament (for all the polite gestures made toward it) is about as tenable a concept as Moral Rearmament, that—peace to the idea of world peace—all we can hope for at present is nonwar through Gargantuan deterrents.

Couched in terms of individual confrontation—a man with a man, rather than bloc against bloc or two hemispheres competing for outer space—*Grand Illusion* remains a towering film. By now it has attained the state of all good art that has lived some time among men: it moves us more than ever because it no longer surprises us. The blinding of Oedipus, the suicide of Anna Karenina—we know they are coming and thus are additionally moved. The Athenians used old stories for their tragedies because their plays were presented at religious festivals, and to be able to foresee the end of the protagonist's life gave the audience a taste of what it was like to be a god. In this film Rauffenstein and de Boieldieu and Maréchal are fated in our eyes, and from a temporary Olympus we can watch an era end.

For, of the two principal themes in the film, that one has present currency. The futility of war is no longer so manageable an issue; we are now in a struggle for survival of the species, not peace between

3

countries. But this film, better than any I know, dramatizes the end of an era: the world of the Christian gentleman, the Europe of church and class that had governed Western history after the fall of Rome. Another world, in growth since the Reformation, is on the rise: the humanist, temporal, democratic world. It is in the First War that the two worlds pass, one declining and the other ascendant; and in this film we can see them pass.

Those of us who happen to be neither aristocrats nor devout Christians can still perceive the loss that is eulogized here. It is scarcely sentimental to recognize virtues in an opponent. The end of honor, dying all about us, and the protracted death of God (as Nietzsche predicted) are, it seems, the concomitants of modern evolution. But the loss of the nobility of one and the comfort of the other is no less disconcerting because, in the process, we also mitigate injustice and oppression and restriction of the mind.

Again this film reminds us how little shock there was in the Second War. The Hitlerian atrocities that preceded it and the two bombs that ended it were new experiences for the world. But the war *qua* war could not shock us greatly. Ypres and the Somme had long before destroyed pretty patriotism and the scarlet soldiery that went home with romantic scars to make the ladies gasp. By 1939 we were used to the idea of war as butchery, scientific and huge; there were no brave, lilting songs of the Second War to turn to ashes in our mouths. The millions bayoneted and blown to pieces twenty-five years earlier were too vividly remembered.

Still, even as late as 1937, it seemed a valid argument against war that a Frenchman and a German were both human beings who could, if permitted, discover their common humanity. Today we concede that fact readily; but over us all hangs the immense, iron Nevertheless. . . .

This latest viewing confirms how richly characterized and finely wrought *Grand Illusion* is. Though it is long and meaty, it is an aggregate of understatements, not explications. Example: the lonesome silence that descends on the prisoners preparing for the camp show when one of their number appears for the first time in female wig and dress. Or the scene in which Gabin, raving after solitary confinement, rushes out of his cell. A lesser director would have followed him into the corridor and shown him being subdued; Renoir has us wait with his patient, round-shouldered guard until Gabin is carried back in. Or Fresnay's death scene. Von Stroheim converses briefly with him at his bedside, then goes over and takes a drink. The nurse calls him softly. Von Stroheim hesitates, then takes another drink. (It is the second drink that makes the scene.) Then he turns and goes to the nurse. She looks at her watch and jots down the time on her chart, then clamps off the infusion tube. We have not seen Fresnay die, but we have felt it.

It is a beautiful work, now doubly sad. It is strange that, except for parts of *The River,* Renoir's subsequent work has not come near it.

The Elusive Corporal   (March 9, 1963)

Jean Renoir has made almost forty films in forty years, among which are the undisputed masterpiece, *Grand Illusion,* and a disputed one, *Rules of the Game.* In this long career he has sometimes returned to themes treated earlier (*La Chienne,* 1931 and 1945). In *The Elusive Corporal,* he returns to the material of *Grand Illusion*—French prisoners of war in German hands. But there is a difference—a greater one, he states, than that this is a later war.

The earlier picture, he says, showed international class unities that transcended nationalisms, whereas the new one is about the solidarity of men—Frenchmen—facing a common ordeal. "To the men of *Grand Illusion* the enemy invasion did not mean the end of their way of life; they were rooted on solid ground. But today's people move through quicksand, in a world that is in transition."

Renoir's statement implies that social structure is a stronger framework for behavior than national feeling—a tenable viewpoint, I think. His conclusion apparently is that, although conflicts in order (1914) could be expressed in serious drama, conflicts in social anarchy (1940) lead to disinvolved, ironic comedy. The tone of his film—in its treatment of fake French heroics, true French heroism, German smarminess and German brutality—is that of Marcel Aymé's stories of the Occupation.

A young French corporal meets a couple of old pals when they are all captured in 1940. The story follows the corporal as, with and without his pals, he makes a series of unsuccessful attempts to es-

cape, loses heart, is reheartened by the daughter of a German lady-
dentist who treats him, at last escapes, and reaches Paris. Despite its
reminders of *Grand Illusion* and Cayatte's *Tomorrow Is My Turn,*
the film is a scherzo on heartbreak and decline. This seeming paradox
is made possible partly because of Jean-Pierre Cassel's performance
as the corporal, but it is principally accountable, of course, to Renoir.
Comedy is, in one sense, a matter of selection; you can include comic
elements in tragedy but not vice versa. Thus, when Cassel is trapped
in a railroad station and a German soldier fires at him, the shot
misses; and it is amusing to see another man grab his leg and howl.
Renoir has eliminated the serious possibilities—for example, Cassel's
being killed or the other man's being shot in the stomach. What he
chooses is true enough but it keeps us and the hero peripheral: observers rather than sufferers. Grim circumstances befall the hero but
never irretrievably. The figurative bullets either wound him slightly or
hit others, some of whom are quite unrelated to him; even then they
never really kill. The one exception is an episode that is both out of
key and intrinsically false—a friend's suicidal act of atonement.

Scene after scene (with the exception noted) is accomplished with
Renoir's dependable delicacy, tacit chuckle, muted love. The film is
so full of excellences (as when the boot-licking French sergeant discovers the corporal's escape clothes and is self-shamed into silence)
that it is a retroactive surprise to find that the whole lacks impact.

This, I think, is precisely because Renoir's theme, stated above, is
not in it. No theme is in it. What the film comes down to is a series of
fine and less fine scenes. *Grand Illusion* moved inexorably on thematic rails; but neither implicitly nor explicitly is this true of *The
Elusive Corporal.* In any large sense it accomplishes little. It is a
collection of wartime adventures that could be expanded or reduced;
it has no inevitable form. And the motions of the story relate only to
the story—certainly not to the theme Renoir says he was trying to
dramatize. This film could have been set in World War I; *Grand
Illusion* could not have been set in World War II.

Cassel's performance is embodied delight, mercurial and sure. He
is the Harlequin of our day. In this later film he adds both a few
somber shades and a suggestion of Buster Keaton. When he strides
out in the civilian clothes the girl has found for his escape—bowler
and double-breasted overcoat—his intense seriousness is as hilarious
as Buster's would have been. Cassel's range is not yet remarkably

wide, but he is unique—a dancer-actor with the invincible charm of a young man who has an appropriately high regard for his own gifts. In her few scenes Conny Froboess, the German girl, quickly develops reticent, sexy pathos.

Pursuit of the Graf Spee; The Enemy Below   (March 3, 1958)

For jolts to preconceptions let us be grateful. Two naval films of World War II are announced; one is English, a Michael Powell-Emeric Pressburger production with Anthony Quayle, John Gregson, and Peter Finch; the other is a Hollywood picture with Robert Mitchum directed by Dick Powell. We know immediately, we think, which film we can expect little of. How healthily surprising to be wrong—to find that the first picture, *Pursuit of the Graf Spee,* is almost unrelievedly dreadful and the second, *The Enemy Below,* is compact, competently written, ably acted.

It is difficult to understand how English film-makers could have done thus badly with material so apt to their gifts as the triumph over the German pocket battleship in 1939. But their script sounds as if it had been culled from Broadway revue sketches lampooning pukka sahibs; the color scenes of battle look stagy and hand-tinted; and the acting, which is generally astounding in its ineffectiveness, occasionally becomes ludicrous. Peter Finch is vacuous as the German commander Langsdorff, John Gregson is self-consciously brave as a British captain, and Anthony Quayle, as the British commodore, plays for the camera and microphone as if he were doing *Oedipus* outdoors. The scenes in Montevideo with scantily clad girls on shore watching the harbor are exactly the sort of thing that tickles Bloomsbury and Chelsea about Hollywood.

The Enemy Below pits an American destroyer captain against a German U-boat captain in a South Atlantic duel. Sheer excitement is distilled by the acute camera work, the literate dialogue by Wendell Mayes (whose screenplay is based on Commander D. A. Rayner's novel), and the solid performances of Curt Jurgens and, if you please, Robert Mitchum. Jurgens has already demonstrated that he is a forceful actor; Mitchum probably owes a debt here to his director, Dick Powell. All of them are indebted to the script, which gives them interesting, character-creative things to say and do. The ending—in which the American captain personally rescues the German captain— inflates credibility close to the bursting point, but it never quite bursts.

What makes these two pictures worth discussion, beyond the intrinsic values of the American film, is, first of all, the fact that they were made. Their virtually simultaneous appearances help to signify a new era in the movies' attitude toward our enemies of World War II, who are here portrayed as worthy of understanding and some sympathy. This was inevitable and presumably desirable; it was certainly predictable. During the last two years Americans have bought millions of paper-bound copies of war books, mostly nonfiction and most of them retailing war experience from the enemy viewpoint. Curiosity about what the enemy was thinking and feeling is natural and is now being satisfied.

However, while the books generally give us the answers straight and undiluted, both these films handle such matters if not in distorted form then highly selectively. Neither of the German commanders in these pictures is a Nazi. Finch, as Langsdorff, is noncommittal on the subject; we note only that he returns Nazi salutes with conventional salutes. Jurgens is quite vocal about it and hates the ardent Nazi on his U-boat. Both commanders are crammed to the teeth with naval etiquette and respect for the enemy's bravery. (The British attack on the Graf Spee interrupts a Christmas celebration that the captain has arranged for his British prisoners.)

It would be silly to doubt either the punctilio of some German officers or the fact that some of them were anti-Nazi, but there is considerable evidence that this was not the unvarying rule. After a war one wants enemies revealed as the human beings they were, not as the faceless threats they had to be considered during the war if one was to fight them; but if it is pretended—in films or elsewhere—that most of Hitler's commanders were cavaliers *au fond* whose sympathies lay essentially with ours, mockery compounds itself.

These films raise two further noteworthy matters. The past few months have brought us four pictures that, with differing success, deal with the waste and tragedy of war: the two discussed above, *The Bridge on the River Kwai,* and *Paths of Glory.* This trend is especially interesting in an age committed to, nominally, cold war. It is remarkable that film producers felt sufficiently confident of public

response to antiwar sentiments to risk heavy investments on them—
and have been proved right.

Equally interesting is the fact that the first three of these pictures
are stories at the command level. The conflicts and defeats and triumphs are all in the senior officers' realm. The fundamental appeal of
both the naval pictures is that of the joust; they are knightly encounters, except that here the steeds are intricate vessels with crews of
from dozens to hundreds. Moreover, these pictures make clear that
the only place in which war is still a matter for warriors is at the point
of high command, that to be anything less is to be an assembly-line
mechanic or a cog in a unit, very possibly brave but not necessarily
soldierly.

At the same time that these pictures deprecate war, they dramatize
why it has always appealed to some intelligent and capable men. In a
sense these films are backward looks at probably the last major war
with opportunities for the exercise of the martial ideals of honor and
chivalry. The most thorough pacifist can feel a twinge at that thought
when he faces the prospect of electronically controlled warfare. These
films raise a question about the military man, not the stupid sadist or
civilian misfit but the man of the breed of General Marshall. Patriotic
motives and international exigencies bind him to his duties, but one
wonders what he thinks of his calling in an age where manly virtue is
less important than engineering skill.

We are told that the invention of radar before the snorkel is what
defeated the U-boats, not naval skill per se: that if German nuclear
and rocketry scientists had made faster progress, the war would have
taken a different course despite all that armies could do. It is ironic to
think, as these films imply, that a physicist who may have the temperament of a nervous nursemaid now takes precedence in war over the
proud captains. Our era is witnessing the acceleration of a change in
the ancient profession of arms so drastic as to mean its demise in
anything like its old form. Pictures like *The Enemy Below* may become sentimental souvenirs of the days when the bloody business of
war had something attractive in it for at least some men.

On the Beach   (December 14, 1959)

Shortly before his death in 1946, H. G. Wells reportedly composed his own epitaph: "God damn you all; I told you so." Indeed he did tell us, and since then there have been many others, their number increased by the atomic atmosphere, to point out that our present road leads to the abyss. Still we cling to the road, fenced in principally by stupid pride and proud stupidity. "Better death than dishonor," the maiden used to proclaim in old plays, but it was her death or her dishonor. If she jumped out the window, she didn't take nine-tenths of the human race with her.

The latest warning about the consequences of atomic war—and without question the one that will be seen by most people—is Stanley Kramer's film of Nevil Shute's best-selling novel *On the Beach*. The book has frightened hundreds of thousands, the film will frighten millions—in a good cause. In such a cause, possibly the most urgent in history, is it relevant to criticize the artistic merits of the effort? Yes.

Anatole France's juggler paid his tribute to Mary by performing his act—the best tribute he could give. Shute, a skillful romancer, paid his tribute to the great issue of his time by spinning a skillful romance about it. Neither with the juggler nor with Shute did the gravity of the occasion raise the intrinsic quality of the tribute. John Paxton's screenplay merely condenses the novel, and Kramer has directed with a mixture of high seriousness and sentimentality. All these men mean generally well and, to a degree, have done well; but until the Bomb actually does go off, there will still be a difference between art and *Kitsch*. Perhaps even after.

The scene is Australia after atomic war has taken place in northern latitudes. Now the Australian people are simply waiting for the radiant dust to be borne southward toward them; under sentence of death, they live out their last months. To them comes an American submarine, last survivor of our Navy, which subsequently makes an exploratory cruise to northern waters only to find desolation from Alaska down. The submarine returns to Australia to confirm the death sentence. There is a neatly balanced group of characters: the American commander; a rootless, unhappy beauty; a gallant fellow hopelessly in love with her; a young couple with a baby. One could concede the neatness of balance of the cast if the suspicion of soap-opera cross section were not re-enforced by the vacuousness of much of the writing, by the clichés and contrivances.

Kramer's direction, too, is severely tainted—disappointingly inferior to *The Defiant Ones*. He does excellent things like an auto race whose drivers don't care if they are killed, chilling scenes of people lining up politely for suicide pills, Salvation Army rallies calling for repentance with gradually diminishing crowds. (The last of these is absolutely deserted, with a banner reading "There Is Still Time—Brother.") But he freights his film with trite trash like the heroine's visit to the submarine with sailors ogling her (right out of any old Ann Sheridan picture); with middle-brow artistic effects (sun dancing on water behind a kiss or slow circling by the camera of another kiss); and with love and family scenes that are sheer woman's-magazine. When the film hews close to its theme, it is effective and valuable; when it deals with its characters as characters, it is often phony. Just when we are gripped by horror, along comes a pure Hollywood touch to remind us that what we are seeing is only a movie.

Nor is Kramer substantially aided by his cast. Gregory Peck, the submarine commander, embodies Gordon Craig's ideal of an actor: an *Übermarionette*, wooden to the core. Anthony Perkins, the young husband, continues to ravage his talent by giving us cute mannerisms practiced before a mirror instead of the authentic acting of which he is capable. Donna Anderson, his wife, is unremarkable. Fred Astaire, in his first nonmusical role as the hopeless lover, is still an attractive fellow but a wretched actor. One can endure Astaire's unconvincing readings and slightly embarrassed butterfly presence when one knows that he is only filling in the gaps between songs and marvelous dances. Here, stripped of that subconscious assurance, we are forced to put more strain on his power of conviction than it can bear.

A pleasant surprise in the cast is Ava Gardner, who captures considerable of the hunger and self-disgust of the heartsick drunk she plays.

It is worth noting that in an extraordinary business deal unrelated to the recent official exchange of films between the US and the USSR, the Soviets have contracted to show *On the Beach* in the immediate future. The subtitles will be provided here, and the Russians have agreed not to alter them. These facts may indicate a wish on the Russians' part to portray this country as something other than a warmonger. And from the political propaganda view, this use of the picture is an admirable feather in Kramer's well-plumed cap. But utility is a treacherous standard in art; so is such a consideration as Kramer's courage in making this picture. After the propaganda value and the producer's courage are weighed, the film must stand or fall by its effect on the viewer, whether he is American or Russian or Tasmanian; and that effect, as detailed above, is seriously qualified by mediocrities of writing, acting, and direction. Kramer, like the rest of us, doesn't want the world to be blown up; but he doesn't want to lose money saying so. The mold is iron, but the content has a lot of gelatin in it.

Perhaps in his caution, too, he is like the rest of us. We don't want destruction, but we don't want to lose anything in order to prevent it. So, in the end, this film is more of a microcosm of our parlous state than it intended to be.

Judgment at Nuremberg   (December 11, 1961)

Stanley Kramer is one of the rare Hollywood producers interested in social-political subjects (the Scopes trial, the nuclear threat), and some believe that by tackling such subjects he earns at least partial remission from criticism. (How much? 20 per cent off for effort?) I was castigated for my review of On the Beach, with the implication that anyone who found faults in the film was antipeace. Prepared now to be thought pro-Nazi, I have to point out that Kramer is simply one more "spectacular" producer who treats social-political matters with the same Hollywood Apparat as if he were making a damp domestic drama: star-studded casts, irrespective of aptness for role; ingenuity to keep the script within mass-digestion limits; and "big-studio" camera treatment of important players. (See the first shot of Judy Garland.)

Judgment at Nuremberg deals with the trial of four Nazi judges in 1947. What is the idea content for which Kramer is to be hailed? Typical of the whole script is its treatment of the former Minister of Justice (Burt Lancaster), so we can concentrate on him. He is a reputedly brilliant jurist, a proud man who despises his three dock companions and who haughtily rejects the authority of the American court. He sits mute through the trial—building up, we are led to believe, to a statement of the attractions of the Nazi system for many educated Germans, plus a statement either of stubborn unregeneracy or of articulate disillusion. What we get finally is a pallid little aria of repentance: a long fuse and no explosion. Worse, we are left wondering why he became a Nazi; how he squared this with the principles in the books he had written previously; why he changed; and why, in the light of his behavior, he considered himself superior to his fellow accused. We are told that during the Third Reich he despised Hitler personally and once called him a bourgeois; this, too, is unaccommodated in the character we see. We are given no more than a flashy presentation of what a clever TV-type writer thinks is an "off-beat" Nazi—all initial shock value with no intellectual or dramatic fulfillment.

The defense lawyer (Maximilian Schell), who thinks that confession by Nazis will leave Germany abject and without self-respect, quotes various compliments to Hitler before the war, including that of Churchill. (He might also have included Lloyd George.) These provocative statements are whisked through in a show of candor, unanswered by the prosecution, not even mined for their true value to the defense. The prosecutor (Richard Widmark), who has been investigating Nazis for some time and is supposed to be knowledgeable about them, is still naïve enough to be puzzled—when he looks around a beer hall—that these friendly, singing people could have been Nazis.

And the chief judge (Spencer Tracy), after much taciturn consideration, delivers a verdict of simple detestation of Nazis which (quite apart from the fact that one may agree with it) could have been made before the first witness was sworn. This is the film in little: a brave show of political and moral surgery that goes no further than laying out the instruments; a series of superficial explorations leading back to undisturbed preconceptions.

Let us charitably pass over the "human interest" stuffing in the recesses of the trial: the judges and their wives right off the hook in the stock-character closet; Tracy's friendship with a German general's widow (Marlene Dietrich) who says that when the Allies hanged her husband, she learned what hate was. (She would have felt better, she says, if they had shot him. We latter-day clods will never appreciate patrician honor.) There is also a feeble attempt to pump up some drama with army pressure on the prosecutor to go easy. He is told that to punish Nazis is to help Communists. This late-entry theme is left unresolved dramatically and unexplored intellectually.

Tracy has a long but poor part, consisting of gavel-rapping, small courtesies, and one large speech; nothing much can be done with it except to supply presence, which he has. Widmark continues to savage his roles like a half-starved bloodhound. Miss Dietrich is very carefully photographed in a very wooden performance. Schell, if he will fall out of love with his quick sweet smile, can be a good actor. Lancaster cannot. Made up like a college boy for an old man's role, he plays it to fit.

"Guest" appearances, as witnesses, are made by Montgomery Clift and Judy Garland in small parts designed to be show stoppers. Clift, as a weak-minded victim of Nazi sterilization, is much too conscious of having a small effective part to be effective in it. Miss Garland plays a woman who, as a girl, was befriended by an old Jew who was tried on the false charge of having sexual relations with her. Miss Garland is a popular singer with a fanatical following. The attempt to treat her here as a great actress who has graciously condescended to a minor role is inappropriate.

Kramer, zoom lens in hand, has directed the film with a mixture of hollow gravity and mild commercial competence.

Questions of German responsibility for Nazi action, of Allied legal right to try a conquered nation, of individual guilt in a military state —these worrisome and important matters are all flirted with. If only Kramer, the Coast's "serious" producer, would leave serious subjects alone. Better no one in Hollywood dealing with them than glossy, paltering films like this one.

Dr. Strangelove   (February 1, 1964)

Stanley Kubrick's film *Dr. Strangelove* is the best American picture that I can remember since Chaplin's *Monsieur Verdoux* and Huston's *Treasure of the Sierra Madre* (both 1947). The screenplay is by Kubrick, Terry Southern (whose touch is tartly manifest), and Peter George, and is derived from George's novel *Red Alert* (originally published as *Two Hours to Doom* by "Peter Bryant"), which had roughly the same plot basis as *Fail-Safe* and had it earlier. A nuclear attack is accidentally launched on Russia; in order to avert retaliation and total war, the American President calls the Soviet Premier to warn him that the unintended attack is coming and to help him destroy the US planes. But one plane gets through, drops its megaton message, and detonates the Soviet Doomsday Machine, a thermonuclear device which, once triggered, cannot be untriggered and which will blanket the earth with radioactive material for ninety-three years. This film is a comedy.

A comedy, not a satire. Satire, in Fowler's good definition, is aimed at amendment. It is written by men about men for the improvement of their world. *Dr. Strangelove* has been made, quintessentially, from the viewpoint of another race on another planet or in another universe, observing how mankind, its reflexes scored in its nervous system and its mind entangled in orthodoxies, insisted on destroying itself. The film, therefore, does not hope to alter men; it is simply a (distant?) future report on what happened; as recounted by Mark Twain's Satan to a moderately interested Lord or by an amused scout to Hardy's President of the Immortals. It is so truthful a film, so unsparing, so hopeless in the last pit-bottom depths of that word, that the very blackness has a kind of shine. It is to the vestige or promise of the Olympian in us that it speaks, and it is that possibly saving remnant in us that it makes laugh.

Thus the comedy, which might also be called *Whatever Happened to Man?*, is that, as we watch man's fate overtake him and vice versa, we note his ingenuity (very cute), his irrationality (incredible), his idealism (pathetic). Tragedy might have been possible in this history of his if perfection had been possible in his future, but the point seems to be that this is "the promised end." There is nothing to prevent the film's being seen as a cautionary tale; still its subject matter is the so-far incurable in us. The text might have been taken from Shaw's Devil in *Man and Superman*:

The power that governs the earth is not the power of Life but of Death; and the inner need that has nerved Life to the effort of organizing itself into the human being is not the need for higher life but for a more efficient engine of destruction.

This is not a film to please Peace Marchers or Nuclear Disarmers. It does not tell what we must do to be saved. Nor is it a comfort for those who find smug superiority in irony: from the juvenile insipidities of Carl Foreman on film to the obscenity-decked verbal cartoons of Lenny Bruce in night clubs. This film says, "Ban the bomb and they'll find another way. The real Doomsday Machine is men."

The story takes place in three principal settings. (The college-humor proper names that follow are not, in my view, attempts to amuse; they are indications of amusement—derogations rather than jokes.) These settings are: the office of General Jack D. Ripper, Commander of Burpelson Air Base; the Pentagon War Room with a conference headed by President Merkin Muffley (erotica students, observe) and Chief of Staff "Buck" Turgidson (observe again), attended by the Russian Ambassador and a top US scientific advisor, Dr. Strangelove, a cripple in a wheel chair whose name originally was Dr. Merkwuerdigichliebe and who has the accent to prove it. The third setting is the interior of the one plane that, maimed, fights through to drop a bomb under the command of Major "King" Kong, a Texan to end all Texans, which—along with many others—he does. General Ripper is a kind of triple-distilled Bircher, convinced of a Communist plot to take over the country as proved by fluoridation of water. He feels that our government is laggard, that his only recourse is to launch an attack by his own group, thus forcing the US inevitably to implement the attack and thus making himself a maligned but justified savior of all things decent. On his staff is a British exchange officer, Captain Mandrake, who quickly sees that Ripper has gone mad and tries to wheedle out of him the recall code for the planes. Meanwhile, under direct presidential order, other US troops are storming the air base to capture Ripper. He commits suicide before they break in. Mandrake then puzzles out the proper code from some pet phrases of the General and telephones them to the Pentagon—with the reluctant permission of his captor, Colonel "Bat" Guano—in time to have all but one of the planes recalled.

The film bristles along on sharp points before, during, and after the events above. The President's homey telephone conversations with Premier Kissoff; the Russian Ambassador's mania for espionage with tiny cameras; Turgidson's automatic joy that one of his planes has broken through the Russian defenses; the navigator carefully correcting an error in his log as the wounded plane approaches its goal and certain end. All these are inescapably (it seems) hilarious and all are further proof, to cite Shaw's Devil again, of man's chief inventions:

. . . of the sword and gun; above all, of justice, duty, patriotism and all the other isms by which even those who are clever enough to be humanely disposed are persuaded to become the most destructive of all destroyers.

Kubrick's films up to now have given strong evidence of his incisiveness, his mordant humor, his felicitous eye, his cool maneuver of dramatic impact. The script of *Paths of Glory* (1957) had all the simplistic and banal antiwar propaganda that *Dr. Strangelove* transcends, but it was executed with ruthless, vivid immediacy. *Spartacus* (1960) was the best of the post-television film spectacles, an entertaining, if mindless, show with many well-done scenes, intimate and panoramic. *Lolita* (1962) was tantalizingly unsatisfactory, but in such sequences as the opening murder, it predicted the qualities that have now suavely exploded in his new film. *Dr. Strangelove* is, first and foremost, absolutely unflinching: relentlessly perceptive of human beings to the point of inhumanity. In technique, it understates provocatively and comments by apposition. Kubrick's precise use of camera angles, his uncanny sense of lighting, his punctuation with close-ups and occasionally with zoom shots, all galvanize the picture into macabre yet witty reality.

There are shortcomings. The casting of Sterling Hayden as Ripper was, in a way, too right. The rest of the cast, because they are comedians, comment on their parts as they play them. Hayden, evidently humorless, presents Ripper the only way he can: as deadly realistically as he would in any Stanley Kramer antiwar film. If George C. Scott, who is excellent as Turgidson, had played Ripper, the fanatic would have been flayed as well as portrayed. Even Keenan Wynn, nicely deadpan as Guano, could have improved the part. Hayden's chief asset is that he looks exactly right—like a famous reactionary columnist, in fact.

Peter Sellers plays three roles, Mandrake, Muffley, and the title role, and differentiates them miraculously. His RAF-type is renowned and here is extremely subtly rendered. His American and German accents are familiar from *Lolita* and again are frighteningly accurate. Strangelove is viciously complete; but the well-meaning President lacks points of character geography, and might have been improved with specific references to latter-day presidents and public figures.

The "newsreel" shots of the US soldiers attacking the US base seem out of place, not so much because the comedy is chilled by the sight of actual deaths but because individual deaths are on too small a scale for this comedy. The bomber crew are somewhat incongruously "straight" as against their somewhat cartoon commander. The mushroom explosions at the end, over a chorus of *We'll Meet Again*, go on about twice as long as necessary.

But all these defects only keep the film from perfection, not from power or from blow-torch assault.

In its mode it stands alone, too much so, among recent American films. In the American novel, recent work by Terry Southern himself, Joseph Heller, J. P. Donleavy, and Elliott Baker is creating a kind of modern Swiftian tradition. (An antecedent not lost in this film: the plane's first target is "Laputa.") But *Dr. Strangelove* is not eminent merely because of the flatness of surrounding movie country—it is a fine achievement: a fiery laugh at those humans down there, parochially self-righteous and self-condemned.

I see that I have omitted to mention the picture's full title. It is *Dr. Strangelove: or How I Learned to Stop Worrying and Love the Bomb*.

(March 21, 1964)

As expected, controversy about *Dr. Strangelove* has arisen here and abroad. To those who do not find it funny or artistically fine, I can offer only condolences and my best wishes for speedy reincarnation. To those who claim that its content is too ridiculous for credibility, I recommend the newspapers. In the same week in which the US takes economic action against nations who trade with Cuba because Castro is spreading Soviet Communism, we also sell a huge lot of wheat to Soviet Russia. Were those actions determined by Stanley Kubrick and Terry Southern or Johnson and Rusk?

But the most resounding answer to the claim that the film's parody is baseless is contained in Lewis Mumford's letter in the March 1, 1964, *New York Times*. I quote two passages for those who may have missed this important letter:

Dr. Strangelove would be a silly, ineffective picture if its purpose were to ridicule the characters of our military and political leaders by showing them as clownish monsters—stupid, psychotic, obsessed. For we know that most of them are in fact intelligent, devoted men, with only a normal proneness to suspicion, pride, and error. What has masked the hideous nature of our demoralized strategy of total extermination is just the fact that it has been the work of otherwise well-balanced, responsible men, beginning with Henry L. Stimson.

What the wacky characters in *Dr. Strangelove* are saying is precisely what needs to be said: this nightmare eventuality that we have concocted for our children is nothing but a crazy fantasy, by nature as horribly crippled and dehumanized as Dr. Strangelove himself. It is not this film that is sick: what is sick is our supposedly moral, democratic country which allowed this policy to be formulated and implemented without even the pretense of open public debate.

This film is the first break in the catatonic cold war trance that has so long held our country in its rigid grip.

If that is anti-American, it is also anti-British, anti-French, anti-Russian, anti-Chinese—anti all obsolescent political solipsisms. Mr. Mumford's letter is one more item in our long debt to this civilized and civilizing man.

POSTSCRIPT. There were further objections, from observers more enlightened than those to whom Mr. Mumford was replying. These objections were generally of three kinds: Kubrick's ideas were too simple ("pop nihilism" was one critical phrase), his targets were too easy, and he used some glib character stereotypes. The first comment made an unwarranted assumption about this kind of art, whose function is to flay with derision. What depth have the political or social ideas in, say, Brecht's *A Man's a Man?* The chief criteria are the aim of the work and the quality of execution. The aim of *Dr. Strangelove* is salutary, I think, and its execution first class. To the second objection, events themselves keep proposing an answer. The recent conduct of international affairs has, in some respects, outdone broad political cartoon. To insist on more subtlety in this respect than is evident in President Muffley or General Turgidson is to insist on a depth—for the sake of one's own intellectual dignity—that simply is not reflected in the facts. As for the third objection, which usually centered on the use of a German as the scientific evil genius and a Texan as the action-happy pilot, doubtless there is in life more variety than any one selection could satisfy; but Kubrick's selection does not strain credibility.

Most serious objections to this film seem to me not so much criticism as an indication of the need for more films in similar vein.

Spectacles

The spectacular film is not a new invention. Italians made the first Quo Vadis *in 1912, and in 1926 Abel Gance, the French director, made* Napoleon *to be shown on three screens side by side. In its early days the film was anxious to display a scope superior to the stage and to lure patrons from the theater. Since World War II the spectacle industry, always alive, has surged again as a measure against television. With the exception of the first film that follows, these are some of the results.*

Ivan the Terrible, Part II; Ben-Hur (December 28, 1959)

Two costume epics, currently on view, have equal though different saddening side effects. The first of these is one of the legends of the cinema world, Part Two of Eisenstein's *Ivan the Terrible,* completed in 1946, which many of us never expected to see. (The projected Part Three we certainly won't see. Four reels of it are rumored to have been completed before he died, but they have disappeared.)

This Eisenstein film—part black-and-white, part in color—is thin in story and dilates its few climaxes. It tells of Ivan's return from voluntary exile, his quarrel with the church, his stand against the boyars, and the trick by which he makes a would-be assassin kill a pretender to the throne. The hour and forty minutes that this takes could have been reduced almost to half by another director. It is easy to be bored by this *Ivan;* any clever suspense picture or musical is more consistently entertaining. But what we are given in this film is texture—of a unique and wonderfully rich kind—as if we were being

20

shown yards of gorgeous material not fully fashioned into usable garments, rather than neatly tailored.

Eisenstein saw, like no other director. His scenes, every one of them, are composed like gnomic statements. "This," he seems to say, "is the quintessence of a Russian sixteenth-century cathedral, or of boyardom, or of ancient Muscovite greed." With his camera, he can dramatize a nose, a ruff, a goblet, a barbarously beringed finger, and make it tell you something historical and sociological and human.

Yet he is not a mere director of photography. Objects, costumes, doors, walls, light and shadow are constituents of his drama, but he is primarily a director of actors. (His career began in the theater.) The common criticism of this and the earlier *Ivan* is that they are operatic. I'd like to live long enough to see an opera so well acted. The real point, the paradox, is that in *Alexander Nevsky* and even more in the *Ivan* films, Eisenstein attempted to combine a style of acting that is diametrically opposed to the conventions and scope of the cinema with the very best use of the camera that has ever been made. It is complained of the later Shaw that he wrote untheatrical plays when he was, in fact, extending theatrical methods. Eisenstein had not abandoned the film for wooden posture and display; he was trying to enrich it by adding to the best of its elements the best of another theater: combining the large-scale abstraction of romantic acting with the agility and intimacy of the camera. The fusion is far from a complete success, but it is the attempt that gives these films their texture.

The grotesqueries are numerous. Reactions are italicized. People turn and stare off wide-eyed before they answer the simplest questions; no one moves forward without first taking a little backward step to launch himself. It is all highly artificial, yet the artificiality is so magnificently sustained that the film achieves the *sine qua non* of high art: a silent countermelody, more important than what is being given voice. Beneath the sporadically interesting surface, we can feel life burning. We are sometimes bored, but we are always convinced.

Nikolai Cherkassov, one of the finest actors ever to appear on the screen, is again Ivan and gives a performance easy of discount by the petty-minded but full of treasures for those unafraid of size. Those mincing French mimes with their Pierrots and wind-tossed lovers might well learn from the robust way that Cherkassov and his fellows use their bodies to inform us. The miraculous cameramen are, as in

scenes are the worst. We get lines like "Spartacus, put me down—
I'm going to have a baby."

Olivier, as the rich Crassus, gives an impeccably patrician performance that fits a certain aloof element in his personality. Laughton
is less offensive than he has been in years as the republican Gracchus.
Ustinov, as a slave dealer, revels in his familiar vein of conscious
chicanery, with speech and gestures made up of broken arcs—matters
started and self-interrupted. Jean Simmons does her pretty best with a
nervously written part. Kirk Douglas, the Spartacus, is very near the
top of his form, which is powerful indeed, holding himself in check
for his big moments and creating the sense of an obscure man
touched capriciously by fate.

Because of the nature of this film, Stanley Kubrick's direction will
probably be underrated, but by and large he has done a penetrating
and imaginative piece of work. His intimate scenes are well composed, deftly turned inside out (so to speak) to reveal their contents;
and his large scenes show a large eye. The battles, which are stunning, resemble their daddy, *Alexander Nevsky,* but that is an admirable sire. Clean, swift editing—most of the time—keeps the film lean-
ing forward.

Spartacus cannot in any sense other than the technical be taken
seriously. Basically it depends for its life on your willingness to let it
exist. But if you do, you can enjoy it, for a lot of first-rate professionals have pooled their abilities to put on a first-rate circus.

Lawrence of Arabia   (January 12, 1963)

What *is* there about T. E. Lawrence? Other war heroes have
been intelligent and sensitive, have written well about their exploits,
yet none exerts his pull on intellectuals and artists. Part of the reason,
probably, is that he is the man of action that the intellectual would be
if he had to be and could be; part that his character is a continually
tempting and frustrating riddle; part that he is a symbolically
archetypal modern man. About this last, in a comprehensive and
comprehending essay in the current *Hudson Review,* Irving Howe
writes: "What finally draws one to Lawrence, making him seem not
merely an exceptional figure but a representative man of our century,

is his courage and vulnerability in bearing the burden of consciousness." Lawrence faced some of the great emptinesses of our age and
had them dramatized for him in the vast physical emptiness of the
desert. His Arabian career is a Melville allegory, with sand instead of
sea; Bedouins instead of sailors; a goal of victory, instead of a white
whale, to wreck him when he reached it.

Now Robert Bolt, the accomplished author of *A Man for All Seasons,* has attempted to read the Lawrence riddle. For Sam Spiegel and
David Lean, the producer and director, he has written a screenplay
which, with intermission, runs over four hours. Despite this length,
Bolt deals only with the Arabian career—the material of *Seven Pillars of Wisdom.* He takes Lawrence from January, 1917, when he is
map-making for British Intelligence in Cairo, to the capture of
Damascus in October, 1918, after which he is sent home. Bolt's
Lawrence is a wryly supercilious, brave, and thoughtful man, bound
on a rack of duty and happily bound there, who finds in killing a
reality more terrible than he had hoped for and finds in successful
leadership a wine somewhat too strong for him. Before his campaigns
are over, he knows that soldiers are the fools of other men and of
history and that idealistic soldiers are the worst fools. At the end he
seems haunted by the realization that he has subconsciously known
all the time that the Arab Revolt would be bilked and that he had
pushed this knowledge aside in order to have the fun (his own word)
of it all; that the price of this fun is the loss of his taste for life.

I shall not detail liberties that Bolt has taken with *Seven Pillars.*
Obviously compression and selection were necessary; some chronological rearrangement and coloration can be ascribed to dramatic
license. Bolt's dialogue is generally lively, precise, evocative—several
light-years above the usual original screenplay. But after we have
allowed for license and have appreciated the dialogue, we cannot
blink the script's shortcomings. We never know, to begin with, why
the inept, dreamy map-maker is chosen for the Arab expedition;
something is said much later about his skill in languages, but it is
insufficient. At intermission point, knowing that the film is restricted
to Arabia, we feel there is little to anticipate other than more of what
we have already seen: battles, vistas, camel charges (and we are
right). The second long interview with Allenby, in which the General
appeals to Lawrence to return to the front because he has a great
man's destiny, is sticky. Some of the Auda Abu Tayi scenes are

transmutations of "noble red man" material from better westerns.

More important, the famous episode of Lawrence's homosexual humiliation by the Turks is badly skimped—symbolized by a lascivious pinch, a flogging, and his being thrown out into the mud. Terence Rattigan hung his whole play *Ross* from this episode, which was another kind of imbalance. But Lawrence did say of the experience: "That night the citadel of my integrity had been irrevocably lost." In the film the episode is unreadable except to the initiate and is not used as a focal point for the strong sexual element—of an averse, puritanical kind—in Lawrence.

Further, in terms of full character presentation, it was crippling to confine the script to the Arabian campaigns. The picture holds to them because it wants to exploit action in wide-screen color; but it would have been much more satisfactory if it had condensed some of the derring-do, omitted some, and given us samples of his subsequent activities: his role at the Peace Conference; his literary ambitions and achievements; his hair shirt, and pseudonymous re-enlistments as a private. (Under the opening credits we see the fatal motorcycle accident, but it is not clear how long a postwar time had elapsed or what he had been doing; the sequence is unrelated and pointless except to show that he was worth a posthumous bust in St. Paul's.) To confine an exploration of Lawrence's character to war is as incomplete as it would be with, say, Ulysses S. Grant.

All that noted, it is pleasant to acknowledge that, in most of its execution, the picture is stunning. I have never had a greater feeling of being so thoroughly immersed in a film's atmosphere and of having this immersion compensate to a high degree for faults. F. A. Young's camera work is much more than the lavish color photography I expected; it acts on the viewer to re-enforce the temper and tenor of the story, creating a mystique of its own through its vastness, variety, frightening grandeur. Young also tosses off some virtuoso feats: e.g., the gradual resolution of a molten rider approaching through shimmering heat, a number of scenes shot directly into a metallic sun. It is impossible to imagine this film apart from its photography.

The acting, too, is so rich as to elevate the film intrinsically. Peter O'Toole makes his screen debut as Lawrence after a relatively brief but intense English stage career that included three major Shakespearean roles at Stratford. From the start there is the impact of a genuinely theatrical personality; this is amplified by an attractive voice, subtly incisive readings, an interesting, expressive face—a face that is strong yet, in a valuable sense, feminine. There is never a moment's doubt with O'Toole that Lawrence is the extraordinary man he is made out to be. No, that is too negative; O'Toole is so good that, throughout the film, we feel that the script is catching up with his complexities.

As Feisal, Alec Guinness comports himself with easy dignity. Anthony Quinn—hook-nosed to match the Kennington portrait—has vigorous conviction as Auda despite his American accent. Jack Hawkins, as Allenby, leavens authority with a touch of pomp, and Anthony Quayle is sturdily ingratiating as a ruddy, roast-beef colonel. Playing a diplomat, Claude Rains, always fine and now a vintage actor, is simply not on the screen long enough to suit us. Arthur Kennedy deals competently with the crass part of the American correspondent who publicizes Lawrence (the name has been changed). A leading Egyptian actor named Omar Sharif, who looks like a serious Terry-Thomas, is glowingly noble as Sherif Ali.

David Lean's direction has had to blend two modes: intimate, delicate, subjective material, and tremendous effects—battles, camel charges, train explosions—in the De Mille tradition as refined by John Ford. For the most part, he guides the film firmly and feelingly in both veins. Some of the intimate scenes drag toward the end; some of the "big" scenes show a tendency to overexploit the Arabian locations. But there are very few directors who could handle both veins (as Lean also did in *Bridge on the River Kwai*) with such relative success.

All the more pity that after the care expended on this film, the result was smeared with a musical score—played thunderously—right out of an Ali Baba movie with Yvonne de Carlo. Perhaps it cannot be excised, but is it too late to have it toned down a bit?

The picture's fundamental fault is a failure of courage; to take a chance on *not* being a spectacular, *not* putting in all the battles possible, *not* seasoning with "sure" scenes; to care only for a try at the truth about Lawrence. But if finally it is not first-rate, it is at least the first spectacular for adults, with a fascinating subject, much good writing, excellent acting, and visual experiences that almost touch the other senses.

The Greatest Story Ever Told   (March 6, 1965)

Sometimes I am more relieved than at other times that I am not a Christian; these occasions include the experience of most films about Jesus. I was again glad of my graceless state, which freed me from at least one kind of offense, all through the latest, longest, most lavish solecism, *The Greatest Story Ever Told*. A sociologist might find an interesting correlation between a decline in religious influence and the increase in religious films. Possibly it is no coincidence that recent years, which are festooned with such ethical garlands as Bobby Baker's doings and mass cheating at the Air Force Academy, have seen large audiences flocking to *The Ten Commandments, Ben-Hur, King of Kings*. One emptiness recognizes another.

Many years and, of course, many millions went into this latest opus. George Stevens, "in creative association with Carl Sandburg," produced and directed and was coauthor of the screenplay. In my view Stevens is the most overrated craftsman in American film history, but some of his pictures have been competent entertainments—*Shane,* for example. No more than three minutes of this new film have elapsed before we suspect that Stevens' name and fame have been purchased by the Hallmark Greeting Card Company and that what we are looking at is really a lengthy catalogue of Christmas cards for 1965—for those Who Care Enough to Send the Very Best. All the side lighting (dawn or sunset), back lighting (halo effects), picturesque groupings, and soda-fountain colors seem inspired by the soggiest nineteenth-century religious chromos; any self-respecting Victorian household would have been proud, sir, to hang any still from this film in its parlor.

To suit the syrup-dimmed eye that envisioned this film, the pace is funereal (this is taken to be synonymous with "religious"), the acting is generally adenoidal and sententious. Most of these characters seem well aware that they are in the Greatest Story. Here, we feel, is a Baptist with a nice camera sense, a Pilate who washes his hands because the Gospels record it and he must fulfill the prescription.

There are two exceptions to the generally bad acting. One is Claude Rains as the sick old Herod who slaughters the innocents. His part is small. The other is Max von Sydow, the Swedish actor who has been seen here in several Bergman films. His part is large.

(Jesus.) Von Sydow has a beautiful face and voice, with just sufficient tinge of foreign accent in his speech to set him apart nicely from
the commonplace. He has brought all the freshening force of imagination and talent at his command to the dreadful task of playing Jesus,
but he cannot overcome the handicaps of the picture's pace, the bad
dramaturgy, the vulgar colors and compositions. Nevertheless, the
only moments that come close to the true power of the story are von
Sydow's speaking of a few lines here and there; "I am the Resurrec-
tion and the Life," or the Seven Last Words, which suggest the melancholy caverns of Haydn's music on the subject.

Music. There is some *religioso* sobbing and tootling from the
studio pen of Alfred Newman, with assistance—although Maestro
Newman does not share the credit—from Handel (*Hallelujah
Chorus*) and Verdi (*Requiem*). Speaking of collaboration, let us note
that the screenplay is based on both Testaments (Revised Standard
Version, not King James), plus a book by Fulton Oursler and "other
writings by Henry Denker." Probably it is from the latter sages,
rather than the former, that this picture derives its tone of being all
things to all men. As Dwight Macdonald pointed out about an earlier
film crucifixion of the Christ story, it is impossible to tell here that
Caiaphas and the Sanhedrin were Jews.

The film runs (if that is the word) four hours, plus intermission,
and in the large cast are many famous actors, some of whom play
very small parts. This leads to a sport we may call "actor-spotting"
—recognizing the actor or actress who may be speeding past in wig
and costume with only a few lines. There is nothing wrong with this
sport except that, particularly for the quick small roles, producers
ought to pick actors without the letter "s" in their names. When John
the Baptist first appears, "Charlton Heston" gets whispered all
through the theater; or in smaller parts, it's "Sal Mineo" or "Shelley
Winters" or "Donald Pleasence." The effect is like a thousand simultaneous gas leaks. I prefer the effect when John Wayne walks
through, as a centurion, and the audience murmurs his name—
without an "s"—a large moan, like a dinosaur giving birth.

Since much fuss has been made about the location shooting for this
film (in John Ford's Utah country), I must emphasize that I have
rarely seen so many patently phony process shots in one picture; bad
attempts to match painted backgrounds with real locations. Even at
the technical level, the film is far from first class.

At last year's Venice Festival we were shown *The Gospel According to Saint Matthew,* made by the Communist poet and film director Pier Paolo Pasolini. I hope very much that this "cinema-verité" version of the story is brought here. Whatever its shortcomings, it is a film made for the reason that makes any art work on this subject valid; love for Jesus as man or Man. This elephantine Stevens bore is just one more corporate enterprise, with a ledger that has a long entry in the debit column and is now hoping to balance its books. If there is a hell, surely it is not for us humble, harmless atheists but for the merchandising Christians like George Stevens and his "creative associate" Carl Sandburg.

Acting

The chief attraction in the film of Irwin Shaw's novel *The Young Lions* is Marlon Brando's performance as a German soldier. Brando's career has now reached the point where, in itself, it clearly merits serious discussion, but first let us consider this most recent film of his as a whole.

Shaw's overlong, occasionally moving but glib novel juxtaposed two cultures, American and German, ostensibly to show that, although dictatorships have a head start of fanatic discipline and idealism in any conflict, democracy—despite its religious and racial dissensions, its delays and laxness—must always blunder through to eventual triumph. This seems a sentimental and fallacious view, discounting, as it does, economic and manpower resources, geographical disposition, military and scientific skill, and simple luck; but the screenplay by Edward Anhalt contrives to sentimentalize it further.

Christian Diestl, the German, is no longer a man brutalized by Nazism; he is a sensitive soul who is increasingly revolted by war. (Brando himself is said to have insisted on this alteration.) Diestl's story thus ceases to be that of German youth gulled by false politics; he could be a Brazilian or Siamese soldier sickened by slaughter. More or less as in the novel, the American Jew, Ackerman, wins the respect of his company with his fists, but now the kindly old colonel punishes the naughty captain who permitted the persecution. The chromium-plated intellectual, Whitacre, becomes a Bing-Crosby-type ambler, sporadically plagued by guilt about his selfishness.

Ackerman is played by the gifted Montgomery Clift, and here an

31

unpleasant truth must be stated. Reportedly, Clift has recently had extensive plastic surgery performed on his face because of a motor accident. The change is startlingly apparent, but what is worse, the surgery seems to have left much of his face immobilized. This is undoubtedly horrible for him, but it is not something that can be politely overlooked in a profession which consists principally of displaying your face and asking the public to react to it.

Whitacre is played by Dean Martin as part of the current wave of using vaudevillians as actors, in which everyone from dear Ed Wynn to the less dear Red Buttons has taken to the drama. Once in a while this recurrent craze produces a remarkable result (Walter Huston came from vaudeville); such a result is not yet apparent in the current cycle.

Under Edward Dmytryk's direction the film weaves, moderately skillfully, the stories of the two Americans and the German until their paths cross outside a concentration camp at the war's end. There the nervous, cowardly Whitacre shoots the unarmed Diestl. The film's basic flaw is in the assumption that by combining three stories that would otherwise be commonplace, you will produce an epic; and the finish crowns its superficiality with pointlessness. Some of the scenes are good set pieces, but we soon sense that the film's honesty and intelligence are thin. It becomes just another mildly competent war picture, more complicated than most. Yet it is worth seeing because of Brando's performance.

I have had a chance to watch Brando's career from its beginning because he made his professional debut in a children's play of mine at the Adelphi Theater in New York in 1944. His role consisted of being hit on the head and falling down; but he managed to find a way of falling down that, without being obtrusive, was individual. After this, although already in his early twenties, he gave a remarkable performance as the young son in short pants in *I Remember Mama*. He brought a doggedly sophisticated Broadway audience to its feet in a small part in *Truckline Café*. As Marchbanks in one of Katharine Cornell's revivals of *Candida* he sounded like a cab driver and moved like a third baseman but still had some touching moments. In the first production of *A Streetcar Named Desire* he found the leading role that established his kingdom.

Since then he has repeated that part on film and has made his way thoughtfully and fiercely through a wide range of screen roles; the paraplegic in *The Men,* the satirizable but unforgettable cyclist in *The Wild Ones,* Zapata in *Viva Zapata!,* Antony in *Julius Caesar,* the poetical brute in *On the Waterfront,* the gambler in *Guys and Dolls,* Napoleon in *Desirée,* Sakini in *Teahouse of the August Moon* (I didn't see the last two named), the Virginian soldier in *Sayonara,* and the German in the present film. The list of parts, from Shakespeare to prime musical comedy, is in itself a comment. These performances were by no means equally good, but they provide us with a body of work about which some statements can be made.

The first is that he is overwhelmingly the outstanding creative artist among contemporary American film actors. Kirk Douglas can sometimes match him in force but lacks his subtlety and pathos; Burt Lancaster has comparable ambition but small talent. Brando begins with a good actor's instrument—his body. Not a huge man, he is both solid and lithe. We are all perhaps too much aware of the effect of his chest through a torn undershirt; but more to the point, he seems to carry in him a silently humming dynamo of energy, bridled and instantly ready. Whenever he moves, something seems to impend. There is in acting, indisputably, an element that is often called star quality; partly it is this constant hint of possible lightning.

His face is enormously more expressive than one expects. It is not the soulful mask of a Barrault or Fresnay, yet it has more than the forceful masculinity of a Gabin. Even his somewhat gross mouth, its worst feature, can become sensitive, not with fancy make-up and lighting but by the artist's method: imaginative suggestion. His voice has been adequate to almost everything he has asked of it. He has worked toward more delicate vocal colors and his command constantly increases.

Actors, even more than most artists, are restricted by their personalities, but Brando strives to expand as far as possible, to use himself in playing other people rather than to bring those people to himself. In *The Young Lions,* for instance, we can see at once that he has caught perfectly the stiff cordiality, the slightly declamatory speech, the somewhat angular movements, the charm and the consciousness of charm that create another man—Diestl—for us. Yet, with that paradox which is part of the fascination of acting, he is also always unmistakably Brando, not some flavorless hack with wig and putty nose and laboriously disguised voice.

Brando has evolved a personal style that relies largely on understatement and the liberal use of pauses. Often the effect is heartbreaking; remember the poignancy he gave the vapid monosyllable "Wow" in *On the Waterfront* when he learned that his brother was threatening his life. Occasionally the style lapses out of meaning into mannerism; some of *Sayonara* could have used compression. But in essence he reflects in his style—as actors often do—a prevalent artistic vein of his day. Kemble exemplified the classic, elegant eighteenth century, Kean the wild, torrential romantics of the early nineteenth century, Irving the elaborate majesty of the late Victorians. I compare Brando with these luminaries only to draw a parallel. He is a taciturn realist; an epitome not of that joyous realistic revolution which swept away the humbug that obscured the contours of the world but of the generation born into realism which has seen its world with harsh clarity, whose work is to reconcile itself to that world's revealed boundaries and to find its triumphs inwardly.

It will be interesting to see which way Brando goes (he is not likely to stand still): whether he continues to explore methods of underplaying or whether, without losing his personal quality, he will attempt explicit, "larger" parts. The future is open to him for he has the most enviable combination: enormous talent and enormous box-office power. He can have his almost unlimited pick of the world's literature past and to come.

Five years ago I wrote that by reason of the ease with which he could punch us effectively but inartistically in the solar plexus he stood in danger of becoming a histrionic Mickey Spillane. I think he is past that danger. He now has the opportunity to be the first American film actor to achieve greatness.

One-eyed Jacks   (April 3, 1961)

Marlon Brando, the best American film actor, has now directed his first film—a Technicolor western called *One-eyed Jacks,* in which he plays the leading role. Because of the many fingers in any film-making pie, it is hard to know precisely how responsible a new director is for a picture. But making allowance for maximum assistance, one can still say that Brando shows a vigorous directorial tal-

ent. The camerman couldn't have selected all the shots; the editor
didn't direct the actors and knit the scenes internally.

This film is so extraordinarily good in several elements that it
raises the paradoxical question of why it was made. Many serious
actors have done at least one western no matter how remote from
their métiers (Cagney, Bogart, Clift); it was presumably inevitable
that Brando would eventually tip his sombrero to the cinema gods.
But this film isn't sufficiently meaty or novel to explain why Brando
chose it as his first directorial-acting effort. It is only an exercise, well
accomplished; not anything like the films he could and possibly will
make.

That consideration aside, there is almost nothing left to offer but
praise. The story is classic: the old western motif of revenge. Brando
and Karl Malden are American bandits in Mexico in the eighties and
are trapped in the mountains by the *rurales*. Malden goes for horses
and doesn't return; Brando surrenders and serves five years on a
Sonora chain gang, sustained only by hatred of the double-crosser.
Then he goes gunning for Malden who has since become a sheriff in
California and has married a Mexican woman with a teen-age daughter.

The cat-and-mouse game between avenger and prey is well, if predictably, played out. Many plot conventions are observed. Brando
seduces the stepdaughter in order to hurt Malden and ends up in love
with the girl. An egregious bully of a jailer gets his comeuppance.
There is even that most pat of patsies, the bit actor brought in to be
caddish and get killed in order to show the hero's essentially noble
nature and physical prowess. (Here it is a noisy lout who abuses a
tart in a saloon.) I'm afraid there is even the scene where the hero,
with jaw set, is lashed with a mule whip across his bare back, fainting
before he permits himself to cry out.

Yet it is never boring. Partly this is because, although some motivations are jostled about and the ending is hastily hemstitched, the
dialogue by Guy Trosper and Calder Willingham keeps generally
clear of the corn. Secondly, the viewer's eye is constantly being re-
warded by scenes like the capture in the barren Sonora hills, the
gorgeous chases along the Pacific shore (horses against the sea), and
the Chinese fishing village near Monterey where Brando hides out.
But chiefly the film's quality comes from its performances.

Previously Malden has often seemed more vocal than genuine, one of those actors who, like the early Laughton, trade on their lack of physical attraction. ("If such an unhandsome man has such a big part, he must be a good actor" seems to be the audience assumption on which he has relied.) Here, however, his performance is built on character instead of external effect, and there is much less of the mirror sense of Malden watching Malden. He has used careful architecture to violence rather than quick jumps to noise. As his daughter, Pina Pellicer doesn't trade solely on the winsomeness of a Spanish accent; she conveys the somewhat pathetic surrender of an inexperienced girl to overwhelming physical attraction, combined with her conviction that if she falls in love with a man there must be something good in him. This conviction—half poetry, half egotism—has its effect on the man, as it sometimes does even in nonfiction.

But the film's foundation is Brando as the Rio Kid. He creates a life lived close to the edge of life, whose fabric is elemental emotion and frontier skill (handiness with a gun, with a horse). There is no moment when we doubt that, to a man reared in a raw world, this life and those skills are as complex and desirable as those of any modern executive reared in suburbia. In short, he makes the basis and goals of Rio's life seem, within the framework, reasonable. That reality of being, fired with Brando's innate emotional charge, thrusts this picture into motion from its opening moment.

He is an actor whose very shoulders seem to speak, to suggest a sense of energy always about to explode—in affection or attack: a frame packed with theatrical power. His voice is still limited, but he knows how to capitalize on its limitations. His face is smashed-brutish or authentically beautiful, depending simply on how he wants it to look.

Parodies of Brando have become a staple of night-club comics, usually based on the contemporary ruffians he has played so memorably that they have become archetypal social statements. The parodists ignore his Okinawan, German, Mexican, Deep Southerner (among others), none of which was merely The Wild One with an accent. I have just seen, belatedly, Teahouse of the August Moon, and I don't know another American film actor who could range from Zapata and Antony to Sakini, right down to the comic articulation of the legs.

Volcanic emotion, reliable technique, imaginative versatility, slashing personality. With all of these, where will Brando go? Prophecy is the critic's gallows, and I am not searching for the steps. Brando may waste himself as foolishly as he did in *The Fugitive Kind* (where he himself caricatured Kowalski). But the risks of prophecy must not prevent my saying that his future has the farthest artistic horizon of any American film actor—indeed, of *any* English-speaking actor of his generation that I know except Christopher Plummer and Colleen Dewhurst. And now he proves to be a highly competent director!

In spite of the commercial tangle of our film-making, in spite of the visible and invisible pressures our society puts on an actor, especially a star, one can say of Brando what can be said at present of no other American actor: his future—brilliant or prosaic—depends only on himself.

The Ugly American   (April 20, 1963)

In *The Ugly American,* whose screenplay is considerably re-arranged from the Lederer-Burdick novel, Marlon Brando plays an ambassador newly sent out to Sarkhan, a fictitious country with recognizable elements of Laos and Vietnam. He is also meant as our representative in a second sense because, through him, we are to learn a few simple truths: It is not necessarily a proof of Communism in a foreigner to disagree violently with American policy, particularly in his own country; American blindness to this fact has driven many people, particularly Asians, toward Communism. The novel also made much of the inadequacies of the US Foreign Service. Here, except for a cartoon-crude Embassy press officer, the burden is borne by the Ambassador. Even though he has an old friend in a popular Sark-hanese leader, he has to discover how remote he has been from understanding.

The several lessons of the film are unexceptionable, if elementary; and its final irony is apt. Stewart Stern's script is passably con-structed, despite a clumsy two-part reunion sequence between Brando and his old buddy and a sprinkling of the usual domestic scenes between the Ambassador and his wife in which she says, "Darling, you must rest," etc., etc., etc. The Eastman Color, as always, looks washed out compared with Technicolor. Pat Hingle and Jocelyn Brando play an American couple; he is building the highway that is the *casus belli* of the film, she runs a children's clinic. Hingle is his customary homespun self and Miss Brando is better than you might expect a star's sister to be. Eiji Okada, the lover in *Hiroshima, Mon Amour,* plays the local leader, and although he has a devilish time making his English clear, he works up very considerable power. There is feline charm in Kukrit Pramoj, a Thai publisher and former government minister, who appears as the Sarkhanese Premier. George Englund's direction is pedestrian.

Apart from the picture's laudable political points, its most interesting element is Brando's performance. Once again—unlike other American stars—he has insisted on trying a role different from his past ones. It is not a part of any depth, but it is unlike anything he has done, and equipped with slender mustache and pipe and moderately refined speech, he strides chestily into it to create in us yet again a basic dissatisfaction—a dissatisfaction that is the result of his uniqueness. Here is an actor of undeniable fiery talent, strong personality, a hunger for seriousness, and all we keep thinking is, "Not yet, not yet."

It is the very fact of his moving performances in the past, even of his failures like *Mutiny on the Bounty,* that makes us feel that he is not what he ought to be, that makes us expect more of Brando than of just any run-of-the-mill giant star. We can still hope that Brando will flare into genuine importance. We can doubt that this will lie in devotion to the possibly old-fashioned idea of external range: Change of aspect and accent from Okinawan guide to Southern army officer to English lord. Nor does it necessarily lie in devotion to Good Causes, like the subject of *The Ugly American.* Brando could be the leading actor of a new theater in this country, a new film. (In a sensible world, in an unconstricted picture, he should have played the police chief in *The Balcony.*) Instead of choosing parts along which he gropes for occasional chances to cut loose, he needs parts in which the authors have cut loose to begin with. There seems to be a theater/film building up in Europe and, belatedly, in this country of which he might be the prime protagonist. Perhaps that is his road to fulfillment instead of mimicking, in somewhat hamstrung fashion, the career motions of eminent actors of the past. Perhaps he is indeed the quintessential American actor of our time, still snared in outmoded theatrical concepts which are further entangled with the pseudoquality of Hollywood "superior" pictures. If this is true, his is not a career but a case history.

The Reluctant Debutante   (September 8, 1958)

If there is anything in the theater more delightful than an exquisitely beautiful woman with a hilarious gift for comedy—which is to define Kay Kendall—it is probably too potent for public safety. Possibly a partial explanation of the strong effect is that the smug male ego is overwhelmed by the idea of a stunning woman being able to do anything extremely well, but there is also something especially charming and subtly sexual in the fact that she can, of all things, make you laugh.

The Reluctant Debutante, in which Miss Kendall and her husband Rex Harrison appear, was written by William Douglas Home from his play of the same name and is, as a script, worth only the briefest summary. The stars play the English father and stepmother of a teenage girl whom they try to launch in London society. She was reared in the States and is recalcitrant. After various misadventures, festooned with generally amusing dialogue, the girl escapes a pudding-ish Guards officer and is united with a good Amurrican (who turns out to be a duke). It is dexterously directed by Vincente Minnelli, and the excellent Metrocolor suggests that color films may be better off with controllable interiors than in dreaming over landscapes. Miss Kendall's Balmain gowns will make the stodgiest fogy gasp.

From the moment her crescent-moon nose comes through the door into her husband's office, we are in Miss Kendall's power. Her slightly crazy *ambiance,* her luscious voice and speech, the very delicacy of the bones of her wrists and hands, all these serve one of the theater's prime and serious functions: to give the audience someone to fall in love with. She is, moreover, a highly skilled professional, with more accent on the physical than one usually finds in comediennes. One sequence in this picture is the funniest single bit of comic action I have ever seen performed by a woman. One morning after a late night she comes hazily floating out of her bedroom in a negligee, and as she decends the three steps into the drawing room, she discovers an unexpected guest at the breakfast table. She just keeps descending until she is sitting on the steps. Please believe that, in describing it, I have not spoiled it for you.

The subject of Rex Harrison always makes me a little sad. I think he has one of the finest contemporary acting talents and I also think

that, in considerable degree, he is wasting it. What superb performances he gave in *Major Barbara, The Notorious Gentleman,* and
Anna and the King of Siam (in which he left the subsequent Yul
Brynner somewhere west of Suez). In the theater his Henry the
Eighth in Maxwell Anderson's *Anne of the Thousand Days* lifted that
leaden play up from the floor by sheer artistic will and imagination; in
spotty comedies like *Bell, Book and Candle* and *Love of Four Colo-
nels* he still found ways to spin scintillating lacework across the
stage.

But time gallops, and he has not yet measured himself against the
parts of which he is capable. Where is he now? Still imprisoned, after
two years, in a behemoth hit (currently at Drury Lane). True, it is a
sort of Shaw and a good show, but when will he be free of it? And
what will follow it? He has sufficient box-office appeal to do anything
he chooses in the theater and almost equivalent appeal at the movie
box office. Here is a man who could stand with Olivier and Gielgud
but who takes few steps to get there. If only he were as ambitious for
himself as his admirers are for him. Meanwhile, if he is to continue
in this vein, using only the top third of his remarkable voice and the
top tenth of his talent, one hopes he will guard against laugh-getting
mannerisms like perplexed rubbings of his brow and breaking his
voice upward.

Still this trifling picture is a treat for those interested in acting. We
tend these days to take the value of a film or play from its literary or
idea value, discounting the performances in it. I certainly am not
plumping for a return to the standards of the nineteenth century,
when acting was all and which, in the hundred years from the retire-
ment of Sheridan to the arrival of Shaw, produced scarcely one play
in English worth remembering. But acting is an art with its own
aesthetics and its own rewards, and it can exercise its magic, if it has
to, on the flimsiest of bases. The two principal performances in this
film are well worth seeing.

The daughter and the young man are played by Sandra Dee and
John Saxon, who can be praised only for their nerve in displaying
their ineptitude in such company.

My Fair Lady   (November 14, 1964)

The film of *My Fair Lady* is worth every penny of the $17 million it reportedly cost because it preserves Rex Harrison's performance. Whatever one thinks of the musical, of the very idea of the musical, his performance is clearly a flower of artistic elegance with its roots in three-hundred-year-old comic styles, a miracle of ease that results from a lifetime's training of talents. One had only to see others in this part to see (a) imitators of him; (b) actors who had stepped into it rather than grown into it, relying mostly on superficial suavities. Harrison is so rich in the role that, even in this musicalized version of Higgins, he gives us a small intellectual-social history.

This is not to delimit him to comedy; no one familiar with his career would believe it. But even in serious roles, his methods derive from his comedy perceptions and techniques (as is true of Guinness, as is not true of Olivier). For this reason he is par excellence a Shaw actor, and it is an artistic crime that, besides his Cusins of some years back, we have not had his Tanner, his Ridgeon and a non-Mankiewicz Caesar.

Among the others in the cast the two eminent performances are Mona Washbourne's housekeeper, starchy enough to be a comic comment without verging on caricature, and Gladys Cooper's Mrs. Higgins, giving us in a smaller role a smaller measure of Harrison's qualities. Audrey Hepburn, as Liza, is frequently appealing and is never downright poor; but she has long been accustomed to tailormade roles and she tries to tailor Liza to herself as she goes. It is one thing for an actress to infuse a role with her personality, quite another to make the role a showcase for a personality. Miss Hepburn often tries to supply what her fans expect.

Her initial cockney accent is insecure. When Harrison reads her lines from phonetic transcription, he sounds the way she ought to have sounded. Also, when her songs occur, it is not always unnoticeable that another voice takes over for her.

Cecil Beaton, that transmigrated Yellow Book soul, has designed gorgeous costumes—clothes that make metaphor out of mode. His scenery is less successful. The outdoor sets contrast a somewhat stagy feeling with the interiors which are realistically noodled within an inch of their inhabitants' lives. George Cukor's direction is like a rich gravy poured over everything, not remotely as delicately right as the Asquith-Howard *Pygmalion*. It is at its worst in the heavy handling of Stanley Holloway's musical numbers. Presumably, too, Cukor is responsible for miscasting Wilfred Hyde White, a good actor, as Pickering, who should be more staunch, blunt, courtly. Was John Williams not available?

The songs by Alan Jay Lerner and Frederick Loewe, excepting the servants' banal "Poor Professor Higgins" litany, still sound pretty and clever. Lerner's screenplay spells out the last bit of suggestive transition that his stage version had retained.

Despite all reservations expressed, I must make clear that this fantastically successful show has been converted into a generally entertaining film. But—as against the play from which it was taken—the word "great" has, as usual, been too generously applied. Only Harrison's performance deserves the highest praise. His first name has never seemed more apt.

My Uncle, Mr. Hulot   (December 8, 1958)

One of the latter-day staples of the "art" movie houses is Jacques Tati's 1953 film, *Mr. Hulot's Holiday*. Its revivals attract large audiences, many of whom apparently know it by heart; the laughter of the *aficionado* who is seeing a film for the third or fourth time has its own possessive quality. Tati has now released *My Uncle, Mr. Hulot,* and it seems to me that the faults that marred the first film have proliferated in the second.

Certain achievements must be credited to Tati, which explain his hard-core devotees. He is the only performer I know of in sound films (possibly excepting Cantinflas) who is attempting to recapture the immensely more imaginative and abstract comedy of silent days. As his own director, he has extraordinary visual taste and a strong sense of design; some of the shots in this new film are as startling as salon photographs or French posters. As coauthor of his own script, he shows powers of invention and distillation. But for myself, I kept feeling all through Hulot 1, which I saw again recently, that I ought to be laughing more than I was, and with Hulot 2, I was for long stretches quite bored.

The chief trouble with Mr. Hulot is that he has no more character than a circus clown, and his films do not tell stories about him, they merely accrete scenes in which he appears. But, oddly, many of the scenes that amused me most in these two films didn't even concern him—scenes like the confusion on the train platforms at the very opening of No. 1 or a game that some boys play in No. 2. (They hide behind a fence, and one of them whistles when someone walks by; if the passer-by turns his head as he walks and collides with the lamppost on the corner, the boy who whistled scores a point.)

No. 1 told of Hulot's various contretemps at a seaside resort, after which he simply got in his beetle-car and went home. In No. 2 he is the bumbling brother-in-law of a rich industrialist. Hulot lives in the garret of a quaint old house while his sister and her husband live in a large modern house which is dizzyingly mechanized—top, bottom, and outside. Their young son is fonder of his grasshopper uncle than he is of his efficient father. Thus we have the familiar argument of the superiority of the curlicue to the clean angle, of comfortable disorder to oppressive antisepsis, and (I suppose) of the soul to the brain. It is *Modern Times* and *A Nous la Liberté* warmed over, but not quite.

The picture ends with the departure of Hulot as father and son are brought together by the father's learning to be peccably human. But Hulot has not brought them together; he is unaware, seemingly, of any trouble between them—indeed, unaware of anything in the world around him. He does not (as Chaplin did) express antipathy to an enslaving system. On his two expeditions into offices, he is anxious to serve but is swamped with accident; at the film's end he leaves on another job, still anxious to serve. For all we know, Hulot is eager to make good and have a push-button house just like his brother-in-law's.

Hulot is used by Tati, as actor and director, as a creature of silhouettes; there is never a close-up of him, and his facial expressions count for little. Crippled for us both as character and personality, Hulot is further hampered not only by a lack of story but by the picture's lack of focus on him, as well as by the way he is allowed to leak into it at the beginning and out of it at the end. The film is about ten minutes along before we meet him, he shares screen time fairly evenly with his relatives throughout (which may be generous but is poor art), and a couple of minutes before the end, he simply leaves the picture, he doesn't exit. The laws of the theater are not academic;

they grow out of audience need. Tati violates them and leaves us unsatisfied.

As writer, Tati is fertile but not thorough. Effects are repeated without variation. For example, there is a street cleaner who turns from conversation to sweep away rubbish, only to turn back for another comment just before his brush moves. The first and second times, it's funny; we can predict it thereafter, and it is never worked into Hulot's adventures (as Keaton or Langdon would have done).

All through the picture there are unfulfilled ideas. The rich couple have invited guests, and when the buzzer sounds, the husband pushes the button on the veranda that releases the front gate. In a long shot we see the newcomer in what looks like a fez, seemingly holding out a rug. The husband tells the rug peddler to leave, but he peddler remains in the gateway, gesticulating. This is continued for about thirty seconds, then it's discovered that the peddler is in fact the lady from next door in smart cloche and large shawl, and all we can think is, "Why did she stand so long in the gateway?" Chaplin would have had the angry husband tell the peddler to leave, the husband would then have gone about his business, and the wife would have discovered the error and apologized and invited the neighbor in, the husband would have returned to see the supposed peddler in his garden (back view, legs concealed by hedge) and would have gone up and kicked him in the seat. Thus the initial comic situation would have been developed and concluded. As is, it's just an idea— fizzled.

Only two strands are woven to a conclusion: the whistle-and-collision gag, which accidentally unites father and son, and the theme of the concierge's teen-age daughter, who adores Hulot. Every morning as she waits by the door for a sight of him, he touches her nose affectionately. At the end, when he's leaving, she appears in long hair, tight dress, and high-heeled shoes—transformed. He is embarrassed, and touches her mother's nose, instead. More of this, more of progress, would have eliminated the episodic lumpiness of the film and might have made it a comedy of exceptional quality.

Tati is a composer of striking pictures, a perceiver of the potentially comic in the everyday, a performer with a witty style. But, even more with the second Hulot picture than with the first, I found myself wishing that he would now make a finished work out of the stimulating notes he has jotted down on film.

The Horse's Mouth   (December 15, 1958)

Anyone who has tried it knows the surest way to outrage a painter: ask him what he thinks of the portrayals of painters in novels, plays, and films. *Lust for Life,* novel or film, is a certain foam-producer, but even Maugham and Zola do not satisfy the painter. He may never be satisfied, for the fundamental reason that the mind that translates life into words is organized differently from the mind that translates it into colors and shapes—not only differently but basically irreconcilably as any editor who deals with designers about book jackets has learned.

Still, possibly out of envy, writers continue to try to understand the painting process from the inside out. The most celebrated example in this generation is Joyce Cary's novel *The Horse's Mouth,* the latter life and wryly difficult times of a ribald contemporary English painter named Gully Jimson. Perhaps derived in part from the gruff Turner and the salty Augustus John, Jimson conveyed to many readers (always excepting painters) what it is like to spend your life battling or ignoring or laughing at a world intrinsically uninterested in painting.

The last thing the book suggested was that it would make a film, and the appearance of the film confirms that reaction. The picture, in good Technicolor, has been done with taste and intelligence and it presents an excellent performance by Alec Guinness, but it is unsuccessful. Could it have been anything else? The novel, in staccato, seemingly random form, gives us episodes, reflections, aversions, and predilections that combine to make a portrait of a character who, as such, would appeal to any actor. And Guinness, who wrote his own adaption, knows as well as anybody that a portrait is not a play and has attempted to transmute the novel into dramatic form. But it remains immutable. The script is only a rag bag of adventures, some of them quite funny, a few of them touching, but all of them, it seems to me, worried by the necessity of being dramatic and by the incomplete effort to achieve this. The strain, on Writer Guinness' part, to render Cary's study in *motion,* leads to excesses; for example, the sequence in which Jimson and his friends take over the Beeders' luxurious apartment is pushed to incredible extremes in order to give the camera something extraordinary to record. A hunger for pace leads to a breathless inconclusiveness; we never learn, for instance, how the Beeders reconciled themselves to the damage of their apartment.

Out of this welter of enforced activity and splintery ends emerges Actor Guinness' performance. If Writer G. has not fashioned an organic screenplay, he has at least hewn out a fine, flashy part for himself. Actor G.'s Jimson is a superb creation, a wonderfully cranky, disillusioned enthusiast who knows that the battle lines are drawn forever, that the artist is always on the ostensibly losing side but only ostensibly, and who wouldn't change sides for anything. With a hitchy, little jerky stride, a shrewd, measuring eye, and a gravelly, gin-soaked voice, Jimson enters full-blown—through a prison gate, incidentally. Guinness doesn't proceed to create him for us; as with the best acting, Jimson *is,* from the moment he appears. We know immediately that he is a human being with a history, who was miseducated and re-educated, who aspires, gets knocked, and reaspires, whose soul soars and whose clothes probably stink. He has existed, for sixty years or so; his entrance is merely the point at which we pick him up.

By now, of course, Guinness has something extra assisting him when he steps before us; in addition to his present work, we are aware—consciously or otherwise—of the difference between his newest part and his past creations. Not many contemporary actors, even good ones, are capable of or are allowed to demonstrate comparable versatility. Jimson is enhanced by our remembrance of the Colonel in *The Bridge on the River Kwai,* Fagin, *The Lavender Hill Mob,* the entire family Guinness played in *Kind Hearts and Coronets.* Against that background we admire him additionally.

Guinness' endowment and career have, I think, shortcomings. He doesn't have in him the depths of hell into which the Cardinal in *The Prisoner* should have descended. Occasionally he attempts exercises in public; he should have kept *Father Brown* for his friends. He has virtually no sex appeal, which fact vitiated *The Captain's Paradise.* Still he has a wide range, and he obviously conceives of the actor in the delightful old-fashioned sense: as a man who enacts many different kinds of people.

Kay Walsh is first-rate as Coker, Jimson's plain, puritanical but devoted friend. Renee Houston, the queen of the English music halls, plays Sarah Monday, Jimson's ex-wife, and wins us like a music-hall performer—by the ability to project an engaging personality rather than by acting skill. The paintings that are supposedly Jimson's were made by the English artist John Bratby, and if they are somewhat less sensual than we might have expected Jimson's to be, they are suitably anarchic and forceful.

Some Came Running   (January 12, 1959)

The film of James Jones' elephantine novel *Some Came Running* takes over two and a half hours of our time, unjustifiably; but it does raise an interesting collateral subject. First, let us settle that the story is the (presumably) quasi-autobiographical account of an ex-soldier and ex-writer, his return to his Midwestern birthplace, his catalytic effect on staid citizens, and his resumption of writing. Nothing in this script becomes it like our leaving it.

But the film raises the matter of the acting success of personalities like Frank Sinatra and Dean Martin. This success exemplifies a trend which need not be viewed with alarm but should at least be viewed. Sinatra is the hero of this picture and Martin his gambler friend.

It is generally known that Sinatra was waning in popularity as a singer when he was given a role in the film of Jones' first novel and launched himself on an acting career. Martin, also a singer, split with his night-club partner and has become an actor. The question raised by these successful second careers is: how come? Is acting so easy that experienced entertainers can always turn to it when club bookings fall off? Or have these men talents that have blossomed late?

In my view, they have not. The entertainer who tries and succeeds at acting is not a new phenomenon. In our time the pattern was set by Bing Crosby, and these men follow in his sauntering steps. Crosby moved from songs interspersed with wisecracks to comedy with incidental songs to drama with or without songs. For many, he proved that he could act. For me, he proved something quite different: that complete self-confidence and an acute sense of timing will see an experienced performer through a tailor-made part and will give him the gloss of having acted.

Sinatra began his second career with the knowledge that millions of people had found him good to look at (even if in a different job) and with a skill at banter derived from floor-show quipping. These would have been sufficient to get him by (they are all that Martin has); he could stand in front of a camera with aplomb and exchange lines in a scene the way he used to exchange cracks with a TV announcer or an MC. Additionally, Sinatra has an emotional quality that Martin lacks.

But the emotion displayed by Sinatra, one feels, is always Sinatra's emotion, not the character's. (The drug addict's shivering in *The Man with the Golden Arm* is a trick that anyone could learn in five minutes.) This is not a tribute to his ability but to his script writers. He simply behaves in any part as he would behave in life.

Admittedly, Sinatra scores some effects. But I enjoy them the way I occasionally enjoy his singing. The analogy between his singing and his acting is reasonably complete. There is little technique in either: only a small, innate gift and a poise that enables his pleasant self to affect us. If it were possible to see Sinatra in Brando's role in *On the Waterfront,* it would clarify the difference between mere simulation and creative acting.

The Crosby school is hugely popular for another reason: it satisfies a social hunger which it has in part created. Millions of American youths want, apparently, to be casual, loose-limbed in walk and spirit, mellow-voiced in an offhand style, pursued by ladies but cool with them, not pugnacious but handy with their fists, not soft but susceptible of being touched to finer issues—and always in contemporary argot. The adolescent dream image changes continually through history: the knight, the beau, the Victorian idealist. Today for many it is the Bing-Frank-Dean figure. No difficulty ruffles him, he is deep in an undemonstrative way, and he has a terse boff line for every occasion.

A female member of this school is Shirley MacLaine who plays a warmhearted chippy in the film. Most of her work is done for her by her overdressing (which, in turn, is overdone) and by our preconceptions of the part; but she supplies just enough small-scale naturalness —with what might be called parlor presence rather than theatrical personality—to fill in the outlines.

A paradoxical embarrassment of the picture is that a genuinely good actor gives a poor performance. Arthur Kennedy, who plays Sinatra's brother, has long since proved his quality, but here he is like a good singer who, as happens to the best of them, starts an aria off pitch and struggles to get back through the whole piece. Kennedy seems conscious somehow that he hasn't got the thing right and this makes him strive harder and harder, but it is never under control. One keeps wishing he could go back and start over.

The Nun's Story   (June 29, 1959)

One of the fascinating and unresolvable questions about acting is the relationship between the person of the actor and his art. Since he is his own instrument, he is like a violinist who can never change violins. More, he is like a novelist who must be personally acceptable to you before you can admire his books.

However, along with its drawbacks, this condition sometimes has special rewards for actor and audiences. Audrey Hepburn is a good young actress—limpid, compassionate, intelligent, and attractively dignified. She has generally been equal in talent and technique to what she has been asked to do. But her performance as Sister Luke in *The Nun's Story* is better than her sheer ability, as such, could make it: because her person is so right for the part. After she has done all she can do with knowledge and design, her beauty speaks for her.

Obviously, all actresses capitalize on their looks, whether they rely as heavily on their charms as Marilyn Monroe must or whether, like Kay Kendall, the good looks simply serve as a charming setting for their talents. But the effect in this part is extraordinary because of the uniquely appropriate quality of Miss Hepburn's beauty and the remarkable way it serves as an intensifying glass for the inner travail she is trying to convey. Besides, the nun's coif concentrates our attention so compellingly on her countenance that her face becomes the principal theater of this drama. The point at which physical attributes take over from controllable skills cannot be located to exactness, but certainly there are moments when the mere line of her cheek or the composure of her brow is effective *for her role*.

Readers of the best-selling book will recall that it is the story of a girl who joins a nursing order of nuns and after some years of work, principally at a hospital in the Congo, discovers that she is first a nurse and only second a religious—if at all—and so leaves the order. From the moment we see Miss Hepburn standing on a bridge in her native Bruges, on her way to give up the world at nineteen, the right note is sounded. We follow her through this two-and-a-half-hour picture as one follows a lantern on a journey. We watch her mature with virtually no help from make-up and certainly none from costume and hairdo; it is all internal. Equally so, her struggle and growing resolve. In the last scene, after she has changed back into secular clothes, she walks out the door, down a long cobbled street, hesitates at the crossing, then turns the corner—all in absolute silence, no swelling music on the sound track, just the concluding motion of the drama.

It is her performance—of increasing spirituality and decreasing religiosity—that holds this long picture together; for the film, in sum, is not as good as she is in it. It includes bits and scraps as if it wanted to pay at least token obeisance to as much of the book as possible. Thus there is about it an occasional indication of cutting-room harassment.

Given the sometimes patchy script, Fred Zinnemann has directed with enormous skill and conviction. The chief technical problem was the matter of time lapses, since the picture covers a number of years in a number of places. In the attempt to give the film shape and flow—without clichés like falling pages of calendars—Zinnemann has been largely successful. Sequence by sequence he has handled his material penetratingly. Almost the whole first hour is taken up with the rituals of admission to the order, and Zinnemann gives this section the reality of a documentary without losing the feeling of subjective experience.

He also handles his actors very well, very interestingly. Peter Finch (in his best screen performance, as the Congo surgeon) makes his first entrance walking away from the camera. We are told who he is but do not meet him until later. He makes his last exit (as we watch with Sister Luke from a departing train) walking away from the station in the receding distance, going back into his own cycle of existence. We feel with Sister Luke that we have encountered by chance the path of an appealing human being, joined it temporarily, then diverged as patterns of obligation demanded.

The scenes between these two reflect more than perfect taste, they are directed and played with power. We know very well that the surgeon is in love with Sister Luke and that he is further distilling the conflicting essences within her; but nothing overt is ever done or said about it. Thus their time together and their parting are all the more affecting.

In the large and good supporting cast, Dame Edith Evans is outstanding as the head of the order. She is an actress whose face serves her, in its way, in similar manner to Miss Hepburn's. It is the face of holiness, of a woman who long ago left physical life and exists in a kind of visible disembodiment. As two other sisters, Mildred Dunnock and Patricia Collinge are like accompanying and harmonious chimes.

So much of this film is Catholic in detail as well as in theme that the non-Catholic may at first be estranged, almost repelled by it. The idea of the cloister is inevitably a repellent one to those who believe that earthly life is the purpose and value of earthly existence. But the film's strength, sustained by Miss Hepburn's performance, is such that even the unconvinced will feel a tug of envy for those who have found the assurances which he can never accept. And that, after all, is the point of Sister Luke's story.

I'm All Right, Jack   (May 30, 1960)

The influx of English films starring Peter Sellers poses a question that hasn't required much consideration since the rise of Peter Ustinov. What is the difference between a comic performer and a comic actor? All terms of discussion in this area have been debased in the twentieth century's flood of publicity and advertising about films, radio, and television. For example, the word "comedian," once used to mean an actor in comedies, now denotes Berle and Benny. But one definition that might help to clarify the matter is that a performer is a person who does things to make you laugh; an actor creates a character at whose actions and utterances you laugh.

One can readily see the difference between Bob Hope and Rex Harrison, but what of Ustinov and Sellers? Don't they put on wigs and mustaches and assume accents? Why are they not actors, too? Admittedly, the distinction becomes more subtle when one leaves the realm of microphone joke tellers, but subtle though it is, it exists. In any comic appearance of Ustinov's, I have always been more conscious of his effort to make me laugh than of his creation of character, no matter how polished his reproduction of speech and mannerism. Sellers, who is much less of a personality than Ustinov, seems more interested in acting; at least he seems aware that he ought to be acting. But for me the result remains one of surface effects, astonishingly clever, often very funny, but still a collection of surfaces. With both men, I always feel as if I had just attended a party where they had rocked the company with comic turns.

Is the distinction cited above worth making? If one laughs (as I certainly have often done at both), is the distinction a semantic trifle? The question answers itself when one sees true comic acting like Alec Guinness' Gully Jimson. Indeed the answer makes the question necessary. The difference in depth and vitality, in every intent, shows us that with Ustinov and Sellers our good will has in a sense been betrayed, our attention has been misdirected. With Guinness it is taken to the core and enriched before it is returned; with the entertainer it is merely reflected off a dazzling exterior.

If you set aside your conjecture of what Guinness would have done with the part, you can easily be amused by Sellers as a shop steward in *I'm All Right, Jack*. He has caught to perfection the accent and smugness of the son of working-class parents who has elevated himself via council schools and workers' club self-education; and Sellers' costumer, make-up man, and script writers have supplied him with the proper accouterments and materials. All that is missing is our conviction that Fred Kite, the steward, really exists, that what we see is anything more than Sellers doing a flawless take-off.

The film itself, which also stars Ian Carmichael and Terry-Thomas, two old antagonists, is a consistently diverting lampoon of the new Britain, the postwar labor paradise, where union strength can now allow moral malpractices to flourish almost as grandly as in this country. (Indeed, the picture is one more instance of time lag between the two countries; we have had these evils for years, although —significantly—Hollywood has not yet dared to lampoon them.) If Carmichael and Terry-Thomas are restricted in range, they are nevertheless comic actors of extraordinary skill, with finesse far beyond that of the mimetically accomplished Sellers. As a well-intentioned Oxonian in the ranks of labor and a blowsy ex-officer turned personnel manager, they harass each other entertainingly.

Management, too, comes in for its share of satire, and the film takes pains to balance the shortcomings and merits of both sides. But there is a historical point here. Long ago Bernard Shaw, hardly a reactionary, wrote that trade unionism would be the capitalism of the working class. This is a comedy about the new conflict—between two kinds of capitalists.

It Started in Naples; Let's Make Love   (October 3, 1960)

As they do with governments, countries usually get the film stars they deserve. Marilyn Monroe and Sophia Loren, each of whom now appears in a comedy well tailored for her, are good examples. To see both in one week, as I did, is inescapably to compare them not only as women and actresses but as national evocations. Although each lady has a big international audience, each seems to represent what her compatriots, male and female, consider desirable in women.

Miss Loren, as she often tells us in her American films with flashing eyes and hand flung toward heaven, is "Eetahlian." Which is not to say that you can see anyone like her in Italy. But she embodies what might be called the travel-poster virtues. In her, as in the travel literature, no defects are apparent.

In Miss Loren there is no murderous hate of the poor by the rich, no time-hallowed vulgarity, no neurotically exaggerated fear of sickness and death. What is Sophia, who is she? She is sunlight, she is hearty warmth, she is great contentment with Simple Things, she is song and laughing dance, she is free-hearted love that yet is never depraved. The wonder is that, although she could not possibly exist, there she is: existing. She is not fake.

On the other hand no one can ever believe that Miss Monroe really exists. She is a figment, carefully synthesized by her own shrewd mind and those of her advisers. And it is curious that while Miss Loren embodies Italian strengths, Miss Monroe seems to have been devised to embody American weaknesses. No flawless Juno this, but, in the tradition of Jean Harlow, lots of flesh and not too fussy. A hushed, unreal voice made for dark back seats of cars. Not a mate but a protectorate. A girl to wheedle up against you and ask for expensive things—so that you'll go out to be a success in life. There is some self-mockery, but it is always implicit mockery of you, too, for being fascinated by her.

Of course she is no more a complete picture, in her negative way, of American womanhood than Miss Loren, in a positive way, is of *Italia femminile.* But with Miss Monroe, the account need not be balanced by listing the American woman's virtues. Every male reader must be aware of them, if not married to them. And no female reader needs reminding.

As to their performances, ease and abandon are the keynotes of Miss Loren's, caution and studied effect are the notes of Miss Monroe's. Miss Loren is a large, excellently proportioned woman with a face of *farouche* beauty and with Etruscan eyes. She is an actress of respectable competence and, in comedy, is distinguished by her explosive high spirits. She makes you feel that she loves being large, beautiful, and in the movies, that she loves the men who want her and the women who admire her. You are convinced that if they fished her out of a swamp and shoved her in front of a camera, she would photograph with the same electric beauty. Her two songs in this picture are less songs than romps. Hollywood has corseted her figuratively and literally, but the happy animal still breaks loose.

Miss Monroe, however, is an actress of abysmally little talent. She exudes an air of caution and contrivance, of concern with angles and lighting, with retakes, coaching, souping up of the baseless voice by vigilant engineers. She seems all put together; but one of the secrets of her success is that—to counteract this synthetic feeling— the character that she and her advisers have chosen to create is a rather sloppy girl. She is not a heavy vamp; she is an innocent trollop who seemingly doesn't know as she walks toward you that her pneumatic equipment is jiggling wildly 'neath the cardigan; and so she is often entertaining. But she is rarely credible, even in her "serious" performances like that in *Bus Stop,* and her effect is aided by the consciousness of extrinsic publicity that the audience brings with it.

As to their new films, they are both based on comic ideas dug up from the grave but fairly well revived. Miss Loren's *It Started in Naples* is about an American man and an Italian woman brought together by mutual concern for a child. The Technicolor shows us ageless Naples and Capri and aging Clark Gable. Happily Vittorio De Sica is on hand, as a lawyer, to grace the picture. Melville Shavelson's direction is far from flawless; Miss Loren's first entrance and the final scene could have been much better staged and photographed. But if you can abide Gable, and evidently millions can, you can have a good nonsensical time at the film.

Miss Monroe's comedy is based on the idea (in 1960!) of a billionaire concealing his identity and wealth in order to woo a poor girl. In this case she is a singer in an off-Broadway revue (more lavish here, of course, than some Broadway shows), and he gets a job in the cast to be near her. The film's chief attraction is Yves Montand, the billionaire. His face is craggy, his manner self-confident, strong, humorous, his talents many and appealing. Let the faithful pray that he won't allow himself to be "packaged," that he won't have a few of his qualities emphasized, wrapped in cellophane, and merchandised in a series of similar pictures; in short, that he will insist on playing a range of parts to the fullest of his ability and personality.

George Cukor has directed in his plush, experienced way, but comedy is not his genius. Billy Wilder would have got more out of the scene in which the girl discovers who the man is. The film is not as consistently entertaining as Miss Loren's and has little of the infectious quality. And the script includes the Oldest Living Joke:

"Boy, call me a taxi."

"O.K., you're a taxi."

But it makes Miss Monroe pleasantly available to her fans, and it presents Mr. Montand. The scene in which Milton Berle teaches him how to be a comic is first-rate knockabout fun.

Marilyn (August 3, 1963)

The pathos of Marilyn Monroe's death was made more painful by the threnodic balderdash printed about her in serious journals. At any given moment a few popular performers become darlings of the intellectuals who see artistry in them beyond the general estimate. Miss Monroe had the dubious fortune to be one of these, and the high-flying flapdoodle soared even higher at her death. All that was missing was a repetition from Lee Strasberg, America's pre-eminent theatrical teacher, of his statement that she was a great actress.

Twentieth Century–Fox, for which she did most of her work, has now issued a feature-length film called Marilyn, consisting of excerpts from fifteen of the pictures she made for that company. There is a ridiculous commentary, appropriately delivered by Rock Hudson, but the picture is nonetheless interesting. It dramatizes two elements in her life: the development of her *persona* by a corps of specialists and her own development as a performer. The first excerpt shows her as a member of a small chorus in *A Ticket to Tomahawk* (1949), and while Hudson tells how she stood out even then, we find ourselves wondering why anyone paid any attention to her. There is no excerpt from the film in which she first did attract attention—*The Asphalt Jungle*—because it was made by another company. But she was coached and coachable and we can see her responding to it through the decade while, simultaneously, the personality is tested and confirmed. The best excerpt included is from *The Seven Year Itch,* directed by Billy Wilder, but her best performance—in Wilder's *Some Like It Hot*—is not sampled here because it too was done for another company. We do, however, see how she learned to sock out musical numbers and to mimic. In *Bus Stop* she gave a good imitation of Kim Stanley's performance in the Broadway production. The final shots are her hair and costume tests from her unfinished last picture, and they show her at her most attractive.

It would be silly to swing to the other extreme of the critical pendulum and assert that Miss Monroe had no special appeal and capability. If mere studio synthesis and pectoral display could make stars, Jayne Mansfield would be as successful as Miss Monroe, which she is not. Jane Russell is closer to physical perfection than Miss Monroe was, and has an adequate singing voice, but in their duet from *Gentlemen Prefer Blondes,* Miss Russell recedes. Miss Monroe had a special sex appeal, not of the bedroom but of the drive-in; and she had humorous, transparent mock-innocence. Skillful coaches and directors made a professional performer out of what would otherwise have been an amateur imitator of professional performers. As for her sad death, it tells us nothing we did not already know about Hollywood and American culture.

The Hustler; Paris Blues   (October 9, 1961)

Two concurrent films present the happy task of discussing Paul Newman. This young American actor started under the handicap of some physical and temperamental resemblance to Marlon Brando and has played many parts in which it was easy to envision Brando. There was an initial impression that he had been brought out as a cut-rate Brando, available to the producers who couldn't get the original.

It did not take long to dispel this impression. Film performances such as those in *The Long Hot Summer, Cat on a Hot Tin Roof,* and (much of) *Exodus,* his Broadway performance in *Sweet Bird of Youth,* and now these two films reconfirm—as the airlines say—his sound skill, plentiful talent, his personal note. Those who, out of artistic antiquarianism, maintain that acting is impossible in pictures, that technicians always do it all for the actor, are invited to watch the picnic scene in *The Hustler,* in which Newman, as a wizard pool player, explains to his girl the thrill that he gets out of winning. If that scene is not finely tuned acting—well understood, carefully planned, technically primed, then set ablaze with talent—the acting world is a lot poorer than even my conservative estimate.

The Hustler and *Paris Blues* give Newman two versions of the same part: a young man with a gift, whose principal virtue is his devotion to that gift, and to whom love means chains.

In the first he is a pool hustler: an expert who makes a living by concealing his skill in pool until he has drawn commonplace players into betting heavily and then wins carefully so as not to reveal that they have been hoodwinked. The script of *The Hustler,* by Sydney Carroll and Robert Rossen, from Walter Tevis' novel, strains hard to give an air of menace and criminality to the pool hall. When the film started (really started, after the pretitles teaser), I thought it was building to a knife fight, at least, not a pool game.

The theme is hand-me-down Hemingway. A young man shoots pool clean, true, brave, and he wants to stay that way; but the non-heroic world drives him into the clutches of a gambler. The gambler is the somewhat incredible cause of the death of the player's girl, who loved him and is the first he has truly loved. To honor her, the player comes back and beats the champ who had earlier beaten him, then walks out into the night.

Besides the pseudomenace, the script is full of pseudomeaning. (S. J. Perelman could amuse himself by translating it into the bridge or chess world.) But the execution of the script is extraordinarily good. Rossen, the coauthor, has directed with a sure, economical hand. Newman is first-rate. As his neurotic, lame girl, Piper Laurie has a part rather obscurely explained but which fits her like a chic strait jacket. Miss Laurie's powers are all interior-directed. She embodies Method views of Stanislavsky, Freud, and Sociology 22 (Mon., Wed., Fri.–1:30-3 P.M.). This is not to mock her; all these qualities suit her part here, and she gives it movingly anguished touches. But, at present, acting consists for her of taking lines and emotions apart in public. As soon as the audience becomes more important to her than acting "problems," as soon as continuous projection becomes her chief aim, she may be a good actress indeed.

George C. Scott—except for some moments toward the end when the script forces him to be false—gives his most credible performance to date as the gambler: some well-knit, nonegocentric acting. Rossen has skillfully handled Jackie Gleason, as a pool shark. Gleason does not act, he poses for a number of pictures which are well arranged by Rossen. It is the best use of a manikin by a director since Kazan photographed Burl Ives as Big Daddy.

Paris Blues has a rewarding idea buried in it, but it does not involve Newman's part. Four writers have adapted Harold Flender's novel, whose sole asset was the idea they have minimized: An American Negro jazz musician, living happily in Paris, falls in love with an American Negro teacher vacationing there. She wants to return to the United States and help to improve Negroes' future; he wants to stay in Paris and be happy now. The plot has been inflated to give them each a white friend, and the romance between the white pair has taken over, reducing the racial subject to a couple of squabble scenes.

Martin Ritt's direction, in the intense realistic vein of Rossen's, is inferior to it. The patchwork part keeps Newman's trombone player from being as good as his pool player, but it has many effective moments. Joanne Woodward, as his girl, is a capable actress who would be better if she mastered one technical matter: breathing. Her voice is insufficiently supported and sometimes drones out before she reaches the end of a line.

Sidney Poitier, whose story this ought to be, is superb. What this magnificently endowed man does with this tritely written role deserves more attention than present space allows. Diahann Carroll, the beautiful popular singer, plays his girl (sans music) with great personal appeal but not much else. Louis Armstrong makes a boisterously welcome appearance, and the film is kind enough to "introduce" Serge Reggiani, an actor who has been a fixture of French films for about two decades.

The Chapman Report; Period of Adjustment

(November 24, 1962)

Whatever the state of acting is in the English-speaking world, the state of its appreciation is low. A century ago audiences had a primary interest in acting, not in plays; in our times the primary interest has swung from actor to dramatist. In art, as elsewhere, everything has a price. If audiences' taste in plays will no longer endure trumpery virtuoso showpieces like *The Bride of Lammermoor* and *The Fool's Revenge,* they no longer get the brilliancies of Irving's and Booth's performances in them—actors whose careers were at least partially the result of contemporary interest in acting. (Audiences are still interested in singers' performances, and some nineteenth-century brummagem still flourishes in operatic contexts that give singers good opportunities. The two plays above are the bases of *Lucia* and *Rigoletto.*)

In the brief history of the film, the predominant emphases in production have been on the mythic qualities of stardom per se and on direction. Because of the delights of the former, irrelevant to art, and the accomplishments of the latter, film audiences—even less than theater audiences—are little concerned with the nature and quality of acting. Besides, those who might have developed taste in the matter have been deterred by certain beliefs: that film acting is only a diluted form of stage acting; or that it is always mere "behaving" (which it often merely is); or that stars are only personalities whose "performances" are supplied by technicians (which, again, is often true); or that genuine acting is impossible without a live audience. Professionals also add that no line of established roles is open to the film actor (except in Japan, where classics are continually remade) and there is no chance in films to refine a performance through repetition and study.

All these points are arguable: stage and film acting are, I think, arts with almost as many dissimilarities as mutualities, and although stage acting came first, they are not arbitrarily to be ranked One and Two because of this fact any more than the contemporary theater and contemporary film can be thus ranked. We all know that there are untalented stars whose careers depend on their personalities and the kindness of technicians, but we also know from experience that, although genuine film acting perhaps ought theoretically not to exist, it demonstrably does; and the "live audience" belief has at least as much basis in nostalgic sentiment and actors' vanity as it has in art. (If it were really valid, why would it not apply equally to musicians when recording?) But the net effect of these beliefs cannot be argued: people with taste in other fields have little taste or even interest in subject of film acting. This is not to imply that they have much taste or interest in stage acting, but it is cerainly less in films.

It is thus possible for actors to perform for years in films, to be famous, without having their artistic qualities properly valued. To name one such example, Jean Simmons. Now a new talent is rising—Jane Fonda. Her light is hardly under a bushel, but as far as adequate appreciation is concerned, she might as well be another Sandra Dee. I have now seen Miss Fonda in three films. In all of them she gives performances that are not only fundamentally different from one another but are conceived without acting cliché and are executed with skill. Through them all can be heard, figuratively, the hum of that magnetism without which acting intelligence and technique are admirable but cold.

In *Walk on the Wild Side,* a film beneath comment, Miss Fonda played a girl of the road, vicious, foxy, tough. Now she has two new films. In *The Chapman Report,* which (to put it in a phrase) is not up to the level of the novel, she plays a frigid young middle-class widow. The girl's pathological fear of sex, exacerbated by her hunger for love, is expressed in neurotic outbursts that cut to the emotional quick, with a truth too good for the material. In Tennessee Williams' comedy *Period of Adjustment,* which is amusing enough, Miss Fonda plays a nervous Southern bride, anxious in more than one sense. Her comic touch is as sure as her serious one. Besides the gift of timing, she has what lies below all comedy: confidence in one's perception of the humorous—where it begins and, especially, where it ends. Her performance is full of delights, like the moment when the desolate bride telephones her father long-distance and her tears flood out as she manages to gasp: "Precious Daddy!"

It would be unfair to Miss Fonda and the reader to skimp her sex appeal. She has plenty. Not conventionally pretty, she has the kind of blunt startling features and generous mouth that can be charged with passion or the cartoon of passion as she chooses. Her slim, tall figure has thoroughbred gawky grace. Her voice is attractive and versatile; her ear for inflections is secure.

What lies ahead of this appealing and gifted young actress in our theater and film world? Does she stand a chance of fulfillment, or is she condemned—more by our environment than by managers—to more success? With good parts in good plays and films, she could develop into a first-rate artist. Meanwhile it would be a pity if her gifts were not fully appreciated in these lesser, though large, roles.

Toys in the Attic   (August 17, 1963)

Toys in the Attic, a terrible picture, raises two matters worth discussing. It is another example of the occasional phenomenon—the film that exposes the inflated reputation of a play. Lillian Hellman is the most overrated American dramatist of the century because she has chosen serious subjects and has plated a serious-seeming covering over generally hokey melodrama. Here she has no subject. None. She has grasped at several en route; repressed incest, true love despised, persistent immaturity, race prejudice, the grind of greed, and others. But her grasp has been weak as they floated by, and they do not save her play from drowning. Often (*The Children's Hour, The Little Foxes, Watch on the Rhine*) the underpinning of nineteenth-century Sardoodledom has compensated theatrically for her pretensions to depth. But here the device of Julian's sudden wealth and sudden collapse is simply too familiar to affect us. All writers who have used that device since *Juno and the Paycock* ought to have left it alone.

Second, the performances of the two sisters, by Geraldine Page and Wendy Hiller, make an illuminating comparison. Miss Page, an actress of amply demonstrated talent, is one of the best practitioners of the Actors Studio Method. One can see how she has delved into "life logic," examined motives, summoned sense memory—all to some good. The very intensity of her devotion to the Method, of her preparations, has some effect despite her mouth-twistings, despite her "relating" to objects (halting a line and changing its inflection as she picks up a shopping bag or a loving cup). Truth is her watchword; but next to Miss Hiller she looks like the archetype of Artificiality. For Miss Hiller is—to the audience, at least—a disciple of no method. Blessed with a radiance that in itself gives her beauty and a voice that only has to be heard to compel, Miss Hiller acts with a simplicity of technique, a nonexaltation of it, a closeness to her subject that allows no cracks to gleam between her and the character. Miss Page is a gifted, well-trained performer obviously responding to her trainer—herself. Miss Hiller's acting is a perfect infusion of the character with the appropriate elements of her own voice, personality, being. Her performance is at least as carefully planned as Miss Page's yet not ostentatiously so. Not to try to assess who has "more" talent, I think the difference is one of sequence: Miss Page wants you to admire Miss Page playing Carrie with emotional truth. Miss Hiller wants you to be moved by Anna; then, if you care to realize who made the magic, she would be pleased.

The casting of Dean Martin, the night-club singer and comic, as Julian, is an offense to Miss Page, Miss Hiller, and us.

Gone Are the Days   (September 28, 1963)

Gone Are the Days is a sporadically engaging, sometimes quite funny curiosity. It is based on the play *Purlie Victorious* by Ossie Davis, the Negro actor, and he plays the leading role, as he did in the theater. The purpose is to cartoon race prejudice, using the instruments of old-fashioned plotty melodrama and stock Southern plantation characters. Sometimes it gets tedious, particularly when it loses its parody vein—like the tree-house dialogue between Davis and the owner's son. But the idea of making stereotyped conceptions ridiculous by overstereotyping them takes imagination and, at this moment, daring. Ruby Dee is winsomely wide-eyed as the pure heroine. Godfrey Cambridge presents a burlesque of Stepin Fetchit so intense that it should make us all ashamed to look at another comic Negro servant; and Sorrell Booke does the best parody of a Southern planter since Frank Morgan played *The Pride of the Claghornes* in the Kaufman-Schwartz revue *The Band Wagon*. Davis has written himself a perfectly snug part as the ambitious preacher. His ringing, swinging exhortations are delivered with ripeness and force and with the propensity to burst into song in the middle of rhetoric that seems the heritage of everyone but "white Protestants of Northern European extraction." (The wording of a proscriptive sign I once saw on a Southern swimming pool.) Davis and company deserved a more resourceful director than Nicholas Webster.

Becket   (March 14, 1964)

Peter O'Toole and Richard Burton in a film of *Becket*? A prospect of interest. On the basis of his performance as T. E. Lawrence, O'Toole promises well as the high-living, luxury-loving chancellor who is suddenly touched to priestly ascetism. Burton, who has often portrayed the somewhat angry reveler, should do well as the warrior-king who had boyish adoration, then boyish enmity, for his friend.

Lo, however, the roles, and logical expectation, have been reversed. It is Burton as Archbishop, O'Toole as King. The expected casting might have resulted in a richer picture, but this approach has its rewards. Burton, when perceptibly awake, conveys something of the soiled profligate purging himself. O'Toole's performance is sometimes lurid and occasionally merely loud, but it is never technically strained and it has fire. He has the vocal and emotional range to fulfill large designs. The shortcomings here are in the extremities of his design.

As for Anouilh's play, which Edward Anhalt has simply snipped and basted for the screen, it is a boulevard craftsman's smart contraption out of history. Factually, its dramatic license approaches licentiousness. Becket was not a Saxon but a Norman. (He was, however, London-born and was the first Englishman, in that sense, to hold high office after the Conquest.) He was fifteen years older than Henry, not his fellow youth. The play does not hint that Henry was, as Trevelyan says, among those few English monarchs who have done great and lasting work, a man with "a clerkly mind trained in the best European learning of his day." To inaccuracy must be added anachronistic flavor; many of Henry's *mots* sound more Right Bank than regal.

The story's attraction for dramatists is understandable. T. S. Eliot's *Murder in the Cathedral* is the best-known instance; Tennyson also wrote a verse drama on the subject, which, with permission that the laureate granted on his deathbed, Henry Irving successfully adapted for the stage. The change in Becket's character, particularly against the background of his relation to the King, is enticing material. Though Anouilh has seen it only as opportunities for *coups de théâtre,* nevertheless the power of the central event cannot be entirely shackled by artifice, however shiny. Becket is an inevitably fascinating figure, this roistering chancellor who found in God the love he had been seeking unsuccessfully in beds and bottles, to whom the new rigors of priesthood were almost shamefully easy. Anouilh does not come near to emcompassing the theme, but he is deft enough to make his version of it dramatically viable.

In the small role of the King of France, John Gielgud is a master on a buskin holiday. (Anouilh omits to mention that Henry was King of as much of what we call France as the French King was. Henry was not, essentially, an English King; he probably regarded England as the least important of his domains.) Donald Wolfit, with wonderful old theatrical face and voice, is on hand as a bulldog bishop. Peter Glenville, who directed the Broadway version, also directs the film and at least is prevented by the second medium from certain coynesses of pseudoimagination.

Whole Actors, Please   (*Theatre Arts,* October 1961)

When the sound film came out in 1927, the late Sir Thomas Beecham allegedly exploded: "Now there's *no* place where one can go and hear nothing." It turned out to be worse than that, for dialogue divided an art that had been as supranational as music into numerous national arts.

Two very different methods were soon devised to overcome the language barrier: subtitles and postrecorded translated dialogue, called dubbing. Each method has its intolerant partisans. I am an intolerant partisan of subtitles.

The long debate as to which is better has lately flared again. This debate concerns any intelligent person who likes films, because (a shameful fact but true) the majority of interesting films come from abroad. Thus this is more than a parochial professional question; it involves the satisfaction of the best film audience.

To help crystallize my reasons, let me state what I take to be the produbbers' arguments, from past writings by Bosley Crowther and others who feel as he does, and reply to them. Let us establish two ground rules. I am comparing only good dubbing with good subtitling; no one on either side defends bad work. And I am talking about an audience that does not understand foreign languages, which includes me.

Now to the arguments.

1. Subtitles are visually annoying.

This is irrefutable, but we are dealing with a choice between two annoyances, two substitutes. Both are lame; the only question is, which is less lame. No viewer enjoys seeing words printed across a lady's bosom or across the Japanese countryside, but many of us would much rather put up with that annoyance than be cheated of the voices of the actors we are watching and of the sound of their language. That seems to us a considerably greater annoyance.

If dubbing had been adopted universally when it was invented (1931), I would never have heard the voices of Vittorio De Sica in *Bread, Love and Dreams,* Françoise Rosay in *Carnival in Flanders,* or Victor Sjöström in *Wild Strawberries,* to name three out of thousands. That is a quite genuinely dreadful thought to me and, surely, to others who esteem acting as a potent art.

Further, the very sound of a foreign language is an important ingredient in the flavor of a foreign film—it helps to create the work's atmosphere and define its world. Subconsciously, at least, the produbbers recognize this fact because most of them want dubbing to be done in accented English. This hybrid position admits that foreign sound is part of the effect of the film, and that purely American sounds are inappropriate. But consider the logic of stripping off a French sound track so that an American can speak in English the words of a Frenchman in France, giving the Frenchman a foreign accent in his own country to make him sound like a native. It is, of course, an old theatrical convention, but it has always been irrational and it is here unnecessary.

Professor Robert Gessner contends that a subtitle is "aesthetically disastrous" to a pictorial composition. It is certainly not aesthetically helpful; but the totality of an acted film is sight *and* sound and a device that helps us to retain both seems to me aesthetically preferable by far. Perhaps a way can be found to print subtitles on a black band added to the bottom of the frame. That would be both more legible and less hurtful than the present method.

But even the present method is much less annoying than watching dubbed versions, and being constantly aware that every word you hear was not uttered by the person who seems to be speaking it; that you are being tendered a silent-film performance plus a radio performance by someone else.

2. Dubbing and postrecording are usual in making most foreign films, anyway.

True. In most foreign (and many domestic) films, dialogue is often recorded after filming, generally because the place or manner of filming is unsuitable for recording. It is also true that in some foreign films, especially Italian ones, different actors are used from the start for the vocal parts. One Italian beauty whose career is now over was never actually heard by the public; another who is now being launched is beginning the same way.

But the vast majority of actors who are *actors* do their own recording. Although an actor may record his dialogue later, it is still his performance, the one that was in his mind when he did the things visible on the screen. It is difficult to imagine that serious actors (and it is their work we are interested in safeguarding) would spend their careers allowing their lines to be spoken by others in their own languages. Occasionally a good actor makes a film in a foreign country and allows his lines to be dubbed in the foreign language, but the better he is and the better known he is, the less likely it is to happen and the less satisfactory when it does happen. Anyone familiar with Katina Paxinou, for example, cannot help being disturbed by the Italian voice used for her in the subtitled "original" Italian version of *Rocco and His Brothers*.

There exists a kind of mechanic's mentality that sees film-making as an international switching yard where different strips of dialogue can be hitched to a film for export. For thirty years American film companies have been doing that with films they send abroad. Admittedly it is a neat, electronically facile idea, but it disregards completely the wholeness of acting, the pride of the serious actor, and the interests of the serious audience.

3. Fuller translations can be used with dubbing than with subtitles.

Obviously dubbing allows more words to be used, and skill in lip synchronization is constantly improving, both as to matching and to ease. But this argument misses the real point. Of all the art forms employing spoken or written language, film is the only one that can be presented in another country *without translation*. To look at a Russian edition of *War and Peace* with interleaved English synopses would be nonsense because the novel depends solely on language. To watch *Alexander Nevsky* with subtitles is to be able to follow a performance in Russian. There is, inevitably, some loss; nevertheless (this is worth repeating) subtitles make it possible *to follow a Russian performance in Russian.* It is this unique boon that the dubbers would destroy, replacing it with the translation that is essential elsewhere and inessential here.

And when subtitles are as good as those by Noelle Gillmor (*Hiroshima, Mon Amour*) and Rose Sokol (*The Joker*), pith and character are amply conveyed.

4. *Virtually every country except the United States and the British Commonwealth has always seen imported films in dubbed versions.*

Yes, and what are they like? I have seen American films dubbed into Italian and Spanish, and although I am not competent to comment on the translations, I can certify that those audiences have a distorted idea of the personalities and abilities of James Cagney, Edward G. Robinson, and Orson Welles.

The United States and the British Commonwealth are also virtually the only places where operas are presented in their original languages. On this subject Harold C. Schonberg wrote earlier this year in the *New York Times*: "If translation involves a loss in purely musical values—and it has to—then what the opera-in-English people want to do has its immoral aspects. Instead of wanting to bring people up to the level of music, they are demanding that music be brought down to the level of the people."

For "musical values" and "opera," read "acting values" and "film," and the statement applies here.

5. *Dubbed films will attract larger audiences than subtitled films.*

Further in his article Mr. Schonberg said: "[The translators'] idea is to get people into the opera houses by offering inducements and bribery. Anything goes. Too many people today are making a living by showing the public how to evade its mental responsibilities. Simplifications, popularizations, condensations—anything but the real thing."

A few months ago I might have paraphrased this by saying it is artistically blasphemous to tamper with *L'Avventura* in order to attract Sinatra fans. That is still true, but another factor has entered the argument. Federico Fellini's *La Dolce Vita,* with subtitles, is an immense success not only in New York but—at this writing—in eight other American cities. It is probably the most successful foreign-language film ever shown here, and its press agents state that there are no plans to release a dubbed version.

The truth seems to be that subtitles will not keep an apposite audience away from a good foreign film. Nor will an inferior foreign film (excepting sex bombs and epics like *Hercules*) substantially increase its chances by being dubbed. Indeed, there is evidence that dubbing may discourage part of the audience that a foreign film might otherwise attract; and it is incontrovertible that subtitling is profitable or it would long ago have ceased.

6. *Some foreign directors approve of the dubbing of their films for export.*

Let us take Fellini as a case in point, Miss Gillmor, the expert subtitler who is now a believer in dubbing and who had Fellini's blessing for the American *Dolce Vita* dubbing, wrote an article for the *New York Times* about his keen support. John Francis Lane, who was Fellini's choice to prepare the British version of the film, wrote a similar article for the British magazine *Films and Filming.* I don't know whether a dubbed version has been, or will be, released in Britain, but after the success of the subtitled version here, we have not seen any insistence by Fellini that the present film be withdrawn and that a dubbed version replace it. Since he is an artist, one must infer that he is artistically satisfied with the subtitled version or he would not have permitted it in the first place; and that his approval of dubbing—so enthusiastically reported by Miss Gillmor and Mr. Lane —was a realistic appraisal of nonartistic and, in the event, nonreal facts.

Proponents of dubbing frequently dub their opponents "intellectuals" or "aesthetes" or "purists" (a species of name-calling that fits Mr. Schonberg's description of their counterparts in opera). I can only wish it were true. If a man becomes a purist simply because he prefers a device that enables him to enjoy films in languages he doesn't understand and to enjoy foreign actors' whole performances, then obviously there are hundreds of thousands of purists in this country.

But it was not purism that, up to now, kept this country relatively free of dubbing; it was economics. Most pictures shown in foreign countries are American, and, almost from the advent of sound, were dubbed to ensure mass audiences abroad. However, few pictures shown here are foreign, and few of those few are intended for mass audiences, so subtitling—the cheaper process—was employed. For me and for many others, this was a happy circumstance. It enabled us to go to theaters full of actors' voices from all over the world, and to understand them. Now we are told that we must lose these advantages because the mechanics of dubbing has improved.

Well, it's an ill wind. If the dubbers prevail, their success will be one of the few things that reconcile me to middle age. At least by being born when I was, I will have had thirty-odd years of foreign films as foreign films. But I shudder for my film-going future, and for generations yet unbored.

Adaptations

The history of the film is, in enormous measure, a history of adaptations of material from other sources. This is for several reasons: the maw of film production that cannot be fed entirely with original scripts; the fact that the film was invented long after a treasury of fiction and drama had come into being; the film's power as further exploiter of successful and/or good new works of fiction or drama. It is true that, much of the time, most first-rank directors use material written by themselves or others directly for the screen. (An international poll of 117 film historians in 1958 chose the twelve "best" films ever made, and only three of them were adaptations— von Stroheim's Greed, *Pudovkin's* Mother, *and De Sica's* Bicycle Thief.) *Yet even in serious films the amount of adaptation is large. To underscore this activity I have selected here some reviews of films that were adapted from well-known (English-language) works of fiction or drama. The section closes with the review of an adaptation from a stage musical.*

Desire Under the Elms   (April 7, 1958)

That great actress, Margaret Anglin, who died recently at eighty-one, told me once the story of her first meeting with Eugene O'Neill. In the mid-nineties she was engaged as the ingenue in the company of James O'Neill, the dramatist's actor-father, and one day after a matinee Mrs. O'Neill came backstage to visit her, bringing young Eugene, aged about seven. The ladies embraced, and then Miss

70

Anglin noticed the boy lingering bashfully in the doorway. "Come in, little boy," she said. "Don't be afraid. I won't kiss you." Young Eugene glowered up from under dark brows and said, "You might."

Gnomic reductions of complicated souls are notoriously unreliable, but the film of *Desire Under the Elms* recalled that anecdote vividly to mind. There is plenty of kissing in it, without hesitancy; but an inherent fear of joy, a conviction that pleasure must be paid for, haunts the story. The play intends to pluck out the dry demon of puritanism that it may shrivel in the sunlight, but underneath this, one feels a conviction that even this excision will not improve matters much. In a quite literal sense, life will always be one damned thing after another.

The story takes place in New England in 1850. (The film, inexplicably, makes it 1840, so that the references to the discovery of gold in California sound odd.) Ephraim Cabot, a gnarled old farmer who is twice a widower, with two sons by his first wife and one by his second, brings home a third wife. On the day she arrives, the two older sons leave for California, financed by the youngest son, Eben, who has stolen the money from his father's buried hoard to get rid of them, so that he can inherit the farm alone. The new wife is much younger than her husband; she and her stepson Eben fall in love. Eventually she is delivered of a boy who Ephraim joyously and falsely believes is his. A quarrel between father and son leads to a quarrel between Eben and the wife. He claims that she tricked him into making love to her because the old man couldn't and she wanted an heir for the farm. To prove this is untrue, she murders the baby. First, Eben is repelled from her; then he returns to stand trial with her for infanticide, to share the moral responsibility.

This is strong stuff, but that never daunted O'Neill. In a letter to George Jean Nathan about this play, he wrote: "Its poetical vision illuminating even the most sordid and mean blind alleys of life—that is my justification as a dramatist!" What is curious is that, in spite of its violent materials, the work is now so largely unmoving. There are several reasons for this, I believe, some of them mentioned below, but partly it may be because the American puritan strain against which O'Neill was inveighing has gone underground, as it were, and has taken other forms. The flinty, avaricious New England God-fearer is no longer a puritanical symbol for our times; he has been replaced by the advertising man tormented by a sense of wasted life into alcoholism. The transmutation tends to make these O'Neill characters of more historical than emotional interest.

Then, too, the construction of the play after the baby's birth is so contrived that it draws attention to itself. Why should Eben immediately believe his father's story about Anna instead of her version? Why should she keep silent about her plan to murder the baby? Why, after being revolted by her crime, should Eben change so quickly and come back to accompany her to prison?

However, in spite of these points, this film would affect us more if it were better acted. The best work is done by Sophia Loren as the young wife, who in this version is an Italian, not a New Englander. Miss Loren, breath-stoppingly beautiful, is quite convincing as a woman who has been used harshly by men and who means to be revenged on the world through this marriage but who is confounded by falling in love. Under Delbert Mann's direction, Miss Loren gives considerable evidence of development as an actress.

As the two older sons, Frank Overton and Pernell Roberts are fine. Both of these actors are well known in the theater: Overton is now performing capably in a Broadway play, and Roberts is remembered for an unconventional but frequently effective Petruchio last year. In this film they give trenchant portrayals with a good sense of period and style.

It is in the two principal male performances that the picture falters badly. Anthony Perkins has by now established that he is a young actor of talent, but he is miscast here. He lacks the rancor and weight for Eben. His immaturity is especially evident in the love scenes with Miss Loren. I expected her to brush him aside with the back of her hand.

Burl Ives, as Ephraim, attempts to perpetuate the myth that he is an actor. This pleasant folk singer was utilized ingeniously by Elia Kazan in the Broadway production of *Cat on a Hot Tin Roof;* by getting Ives to stand still most of the time and, presumably, by spoon-feeding him readings (he has never spoken lines so well since), Kazan was able to use the singer's bulk and presence to give the illusion of force. Less capable directors have not been able to equal Kazan's achievements. In this film Ives' eyes are dead and meaningless throughout, and his voice, as is often the case with a singer's speaking voice, is severely limited in range. His attempts, as Ephraim, to dominate his household are superficial, laid on muscularly; they do not grow out of a genuine actor's powers of creation and projection. Only in the frenetic dance to celebrate his son's birth, where athleticism masks the flaws, does Ives achieve some flavor of this self-appointed protagonist of God, antagonist of man.

Irwin Shaw's screenplay makes few alterations in the original drama. He brings Ephraim home unexpectedly one day to create suspense in the illicit love affair; he leaves Eben's theft of his father's money undiscovered; he brings back the two older sons from California, rich and married, to gloat over their father. The chief alteration is in making the young wife a foreigner, but "there is example for't." O'Neill himself prepared a screen treatment in which he not only made the wife a Hungarian, he prettied up the story, which Shaw does not.

In fact the screenplay is so good that it illustrates a recurring paradox in recent films made from famous works. This script, like that of *A Farewell to Arms* and (with a few reservations) *The Sun Also Rises,* is a remarkably faithful transcription of its source. Yet in these pictures the impact of the O'Neill and Hemingway works has been lost.

The chief reason is the casting. Every time they speak, Jennifer Jones and Rock Hudson, of *A Farewell to Arms,* destroy not only their own credibility but that of everything that has been built up around them by others. Tyrone Power and Ava Gardner, of *The Sun Also Rises,* sound like nothing but movie stars, no matter how earnestly they try to act. In the O'Neill film Anthony Perkins, who needs appropriate roles, and Burl Ives, who needs vocational guidance, fail the script.

In this last picture there is an added reason for failure, the same problem that the film of *Death of a Salesman* presented a few years back. Both of these pictures, though adapted with devotion, were made from plays so intrinsically theatrical that they cannot be successfully rendered in any other medium. Their theater form is part of their being; film does not liberate them, it dissipates them.

Still, the prime reason for the failure of the Hemingway and O'Neill pictures remains the casting. It is an irony that, as screen adaptions have improved, the economic position of the movies has become so grave that producers must continue to use box-office names in these better scripts, even when they are as wildly incompetent as Rock Hudson. Has Hollywood grown up too late? Producers now take their responsibilities as adapters more seriously, but have movies declined so far in popular favor that they must sacrifice this lately won seriousness to financial survival?

Long Day's Journey Into Night   (September 24, 1962)

Eugene O'Neill's *Long Day's Journey Into Night* is the full statement of the early autobiography that he had disguised and used partially in several plays. *Beyond the Horizon* (1918) is about two brothers, one of whom is tubercular; the doomed couple in *All God's Chillun Got Wings* (1923) have his parents' first names; other plays contain further references and derivations. In 1941 O'Neill was at last able to write it all out nakedly (though not for production in his lifetime)—all contained in an August day in 1912 at the summer home of the Tyrones, a day during which the parents and their two sons are flayed open to reveal their hate and need of one another.

After O'Neill's tortuous peregrination to this play, it is interesting that he was not factually accurate about his past. There is no artistic reason, of course, why he had to be, but the alterations and omissions are revealing. Some examples: the father is berated for his stinginess about the house and about the care of his younger son's illness; but the New London house cost James O'Neill $40,000, a ducal sum in those days, and the record of his spending on the boy's illness contradicts the latter charge. The play disregards the fact that the younger son (the author—called Edmund here) had already been married and was a father; or that the older son was absent in a sanitarium for alcoholics when the doctor confirmed that Edmund had tuberculosis; or that the mother had been through the traumatic experience of a breast operation for cancer.

It is notable, too, that all the family except Edmund have grievous character flaws. James is a miser and egotist. Mary is a morphine addict. Jamie is a boozer and corrupter. But Edmund has no faults. He is that classic attractive figure, the consumptive young poet. It could easily be argued that *Long Day's Journey* is a work of self-defense, with the facts of O'Neill's life given incompletely and with some warped emphases in order to justify his dissipated life; that he thought he *had* to lead a wild life, like Baudelaire and Strindberg, in order to be an artist, and wrote this play as *ex post facto* vindication for his acting-out of an attitude.

But whether or not this is true, the work has strength. To me, it is not, as Mary McCarthy called it, "the greatest realistic drama since Ibsen" (thus dismissing Hauptmann, late Tolstoy, early O'Casey), but it is a large dramatic engine whose components are carefully assembled before your eyes and which grinds its way to its conclusion with the inexorability that is the mark of the totally committed artist. Few would call O'Neill a *writer* of the first rank or a thinker of any consequence or an illuminator of the soul to an unusual degree; but he was here so tenaciously dedicated to a revelation of his truth that the play generates authority even when it is not completely compelling.

And now this extremely long, one-set drama has been placed on film. Why? Among the praised plays of this century, is there one less suitable for filming? The project seems to be the work of what can be called the TV mind. One of the chief "serious" functions of television has been the adaptation of plays of merit, lopping and cramming them into fixed time and limited space, for which the carpenters expect gratitude because TV has brought Something Good to a vast public. Ely Landau and Sidney Lumet, producer and director of this picture, who are well known for their "good works" in television, have now brought Something Good to films, and in the transposition have converted a theatrically viable play with tedious stretches into a turgid film with affecting episodes.

About 95 per cent of the original script has been retained, and, inevitably, there is power in its moments of highest intensity, which would hold us even as a phonograph recording or a chalk talk. But in the main, when this version must live or languish as a film, it languishes. This theatrical whale has been stranded on the beach of another medium; it is robbed of whatever grace and integral movement it had in its natural element and is left with only its size and some hints of majesty to impress us.

Since the play is essentially unadaptable to film and, anyway, since no real adaptation has been attempted, Lumet has tried to supply the missing cinema motions with movement of the camera. This not only fails, it is frequently intrusive. His work with the actors is much more successful.

As the father, Ralph Richardson provides a sound performance, instead of the affected distortion that he often palms off as originality. One cannot quite believe that his face ever set feminine hearts aflutter or that he is more than occasionally Irish (when he remembers the brogue); but he drives hard and honestly for the center of this warped, grandiloquent man.

Katharine Hepburn, as his wife, brings understanding and artistic plan to the part. She is simply miscast. Besides looking too young to be the mother of Jason Robards, Jr., her personality and temperament do not encompass this Irish-American woman whose religious-chromo dreams have wrecked her life. (For it is not cheap doctoring or an uncongenial theatrical life that have made Mary Tyrone a drug addict; it is her guilt at having betrayed a nun's vocation.) The whole tenor of Miss Hepburn's being—her Yankee accent itself—is unsympathetic to this lace-curtain part. An actress of lesser talent and perception, better suited to the role, might have had greater effect.

Robards has already been saluted, deservedly, for his performance on Broadway of the sardonic, sporadically remorseful Jamie. He repeats and deepens it here. Edmund is played by Dean Stockwell, an actor with an only partially mobile face and negligible emotional power.

None of them is helped by a blatant, one-level soundtrack, incongruous piano music, or (particularly at the end) by low-grade high jinks in the photography.

God's Little Acre   (June 30, 1958)

Erskine Caldwell stated in a recent interview (*Newsweek,* June 2) that he has had no disagreement with his movie-making partners about what was omitted from the film of *God's Little Acre.* To insist that he ought to have protested is perhaps a little like Abbot telling Costello, "I'm not going to let that guy insult you. You go right over there and sock him." Still one has only to reread the novel to suspect that Caldwell is more tired today than he was in 1933, in more ways than one.

The enormous special reputation of the novel and its fantastic sales—particularly in millions of paper-bound copies—tend to obscure the fact that it is an estimable book, moving, funny, spare.

Readers accustomed to the blaze of Caldwell's popularity may not recall that he started as the most earnest of little-magazine writers and became one of the late Maxwell Perkins' protégés. He was a regional novelist of the Southern poor in the days before it was necessarily profitable. He has lost neither his skill nor his sincerity; his trouble is that he has had very little new to say after his first four or five books (he has published thirty-four), so that we have come to regard him as the source of a staple product rather than a literary creator.

But neither its fantastic success nor his subsequent self-imitation can vitiate his achievement in this early book. It is one of the few modern novels I know that cut cleanly to the core of a ludicrous-tragic situation and can make you roar with laughter, not after but at the same time that they wring your heart. It is possibly too heavy-handedly symbolic: Ty Ty's pursuit of the nonexistent gold (the irretrievable past) and Will's struggle to turn on the power in the factory (the common man's fight to control his destiny) are such neat devices that they obtrude somewhat between us and the matters they represent. But the book stands another reading better than many other proletarian novels of the thirties, most of which are interesting today only as historical documents. *God's Little Acre* is still affecting because Caldwell's first interest was the people in a situation, not the situation or its causes and cures. A case might be made that the book's perennial popularity is a kind of proof that sex alone will not sell books. Sexier books than this one are available, but they lack its clear, almost abstracted reality and its drama.

The film, directed by Anthony Mann from Philip Yordan's screenplay, skimps the proletarian aspects of the book and treats the sex in that censored, suggestive fashion which takes it out of the blood stream of the characters and makes it a matter of Hollywood bosoms and fake fire. Of course no movie could live up to the book's sexy reputation, but the nadir of silliness is reached when, one moonlight night, bare-chested Will leans against a wall of the house and reaches around the corner to knead the hand of Griselda who leans against the other wall in her slip.

However, as with several recent films from books and plays of stature, there have been intelligences and talents involved in the compromises, so the picture is not without some striking merits. Chief among these is Robert Ryan's performance of Ty Ty. Ryan makes him a vigorous and arresting patriarch. Grizzled, crease-necked, in-domitable and loving, he might be a Calabrian peasant or an Austra-lian aborigine, the head of any simple clan who in his thick-fingered way is trying to claw a path through which his children may follow. The scene in which Ty Ty, struck down by one son, grovels, gnawing at the dirt, while another son hugs him, assuring him of love, is a kind of scene infrequently attempted in a Hollywood film, and is memor-able.

Another success, both more modest and more surprising, is Buddy Hackett's performance of Pluto Swint. He is not the lard-bellied, grotesque lover of the novel; he looks more like a beady-eyed platy-pus. Still, though too young and spry, Hackett conveys pathetically his long-suffering love for Darlin' Jill.

In his interview Caldwell said, "I'm delighted with the perform-ances because most of the cast are from the theater and are unspoiled by movie-making techniques." This is confusing because the two best performances, cited above, are given by a man known principally for his film work (Ryan) and a man recruited from the stage (Hackett). It is further confusing because the two worst performances—which are fatal to the picture—are given by a film actor (Aldo Ray) and a stage personality (Tina Louise). As Will, Ray is merely a husky-voiced, tubby lump, devoid of the quality of the folk hero, the Peo-ple's Man, that Caldwell gave him. As Griselda, Miss Louise is not permitted to disclose fully the only assets of which she gives any evidence.

Mann has directed the film with a keen eye for dramatic and pictorial composition. An excellent cameraman, Ernest Haller, has achieved some lovely shadings in black and white and some telling effects in depth. The music by Elmer Bernstein is as poor as the photography is good. It always begins with an intrusive ballad vamp, and—no fault of the composer's—it always enters at the same level of volume as the dialogue.

Caldwell said further in his interview that he prefers this movie to the one of *Tobacco Road*. A happy ending was put on the latter which he thought quite unnecessary. Does he think the happy ending of this film is necessary? To see the holes in the fields filled in and Ty Ty plowing again, to see Pluto elected sheriff and Darlin' Jill chirping down the walk to greet him, to see Buck and Griselda blissfully reconciled, will undoubtedly please those who sit nervously through a picture in the fear that it may leave them disturbed; but these changes though patched on with slick, opportunistic logic are perhaps more necessary to Caldwell and his producers than to other admirers of the novel.

Cat on a Hot Tin Roof   (September 29, 1958)

When Vittorio De Sica was asked why so many of his films deal with adultery, he is said to have replied, "But if you take adultery out of the lives of the *bourgeoisie,* what drama is left?" It is perhaps this belief that has impelled Tennessee Williams into the areas that his art inhabits. He has recognized that most of contemporary life offers limited dramatic opportunity; he is not content to reshuffle the cards in adultery cribbage; so he has left "normal" life to investigate the highly neurotic, the unrepressed, the violent, and the grimy. It is the continuing problem of the contemporary writer who looks for great emotional issues to move him greatly. The anguish of the advertising executive struggling to keep his job is anguish indeed, but its possibilities in art are not large scale. The writer who wants to "let go" has figuratively to leave the urban and suburban and either go abroad, go into the past, or go into those few pockets of elemental emotional life left in this country. Certainly there is an artistic function in representing gray-flannel life; but not all artists are interested in it, and those who have done it may long for larger, stronger drama.

Thus, I think, Williams arrives at his undershirted brutes who rape deranged sisters-in-law and his sensitive poets seized and eaten by ravenous Latin-American children. What keeps most of his work out of the swamp of sensationalism is his gift for evocative dialogue, his ability to give his plays a garment of poetic rhapsody (while he is, in fact, constructing as craftily as Sardou), and his quick sympathy for buried emotional horror which he can often convey piercingly. But there are risks in this vein. It tends to rely on the exclusively visceral effect, it can linger so long over animalistic characters that they become repellent rather than moving, and unwavering devotion to it makes us suspect the author of exploiting the lurid rather than seeking raw emotion. All these risks are realized in *Cat on a Hot Tin*

Roof, which I think is Williams' least worthy long play to date. It seems to me to abuse a license he has earned by past work, like a planter despoiling his own fields; it lacks resonance beneath its action; its writing is sometimes stilted, some of its motivations are insufficient, and its resolution is feeble.

These faults are all italicized in the current film of the play, which manages to add one more fault. In the script by Richard Brooks and James Poe, the matter of the son's imputed homosexuality is watered down by an explanation of a special friendship with his dead teammate so complicated and cautious that one wonders how the actors kept straight faces. (The effect of this dilution is somewhat as if *Othello* were played as written except that Iago reports that Cassio has danced with Desdemona, not slept with her.) But most of the elements are unchanged: Big Daddy's illusory escape from cancer and his resolve to enjoy life, punctured by the truth of his condition; Maggie's desperate love for the unresponsive Brick; Gooper, his wife and brood, showering affection on Big Daddy and Mama in the hope of controlling the estate.

The film will undoubtedly be popular because of a sexual frankness remarkable in American movies—for example, Big Mama pounds the bed to indicate to her daughter-in-law the place where marriages fail; but artistically it arrives at even less point than the play, the change in Brick toward Maggie is even less convincing, and the sweet adjustment of Big Daddy to his sentence is spurious.

Brooks, who also directed, has shoved the action around the big house in an obvious manner, presumably to demonstrate the advantages of films over the restrictions of one stage set. He has allowed the Gooper brood to caricature their adulation of Big Daddy so wildly that, against his attempts to create hard reality in other scenes, it is as if cartoon sequences had been woven into the film. His one accomplishment is with Elizabeth Taylor as Maggie. The lovely Miss Taylor lacks the inner fire from which all else grows and without which nothing can really live; but she is a diligent pupil and, with Brooks' help, has worked so hard that she gives a certain surface to her performance.

Of course there will be some who, impressed by the difference between Miss Taylor in this picture and in the past, will conclude that she reveals unsuspected talent. But virtually any movie hopeful capable of inducing hysterics, feather-bedded by the film devices of re-

recording, camera angles, and clever cutting, could be made to seem equally impressive.

This contrasts with Paul Newman's performance of Brick, which is genuinely creative—the kind of acting in which buried smoldering is made manifest and in which the thought processes *between* lines are clear and interesting. It is almost impertinent to praise Judith Anderson as silly, warmhearted Big Mama; she affords us an example of transformation by art.

When Burl Ives played Big Daddy on Broadway, his widely hailed portrayal seemed to me merely the ingenious use of his presence by the director. From it, however, Ives has learned enough to make a career for himself; he is currently repeating that portrayal not only in this film but as a Texas beef baron in *The Big Country* and a Florida gang chief in *Wind Across the Everglades,* in each case a lusty, life-loving tyrant. May one suggest that three times is enough? Ives, to this viewer, is simply an outsize man with a moderately effectual personality, not an actor. Like Napoleon's army, he has traveled on his stomach. His performance, like his theatrical person and like Williams' play, is imposing bulk without much content.

Suddenly, Last Summer   (January 18, 1960)

In his life of Rossini, Stendhal says that only a man capable of making a fool of himself for love can have the power to understand fine art. One might adapt this to read: "Only the man capable of fine art has the courage to make a fool of himself over something he loves"; and then apply it to *Suddenly, Last Summer* by Tennessee Williams. This is basically a foolish, unrewarding work, but it could not have been conceived or written except by a dramatist of extraordinary talent. What has happened presumably is that Williams has in this piece plunged so far into its nether reaches after an idea that he has lost his sense of relevancy. Instead of showing us horror and suffering as related to the streams of possible or desirable life, he has created an exercise in Grand Guignol.

To make it worse, he has plunged with such blind fervor that he has not composed a good Guignol. It is thin and distended, and although the dialogue is in aptness and figuration beyond the reach of almost any other contemporary American dramatist, the result is static—even more so than in most plays which consist of the gradual revelation of events that occurred before the curtain rose. The film script is simply an arbitrarily prolonged question to which we are finally given an answer.

The question is: what has unsettled young Catherine Holly's mind and why is her aunt anxious to have a lobotomy performed on her so that she will not remember the cause? The doctor who is being urged to operate, by imploration and professional pressure, soon becomes a sort of private eye trying to solve his "case," rather than a physician intent on cure. Even the last scene, in which all the principals are gathered and Catherine finally is able to tell the truth, is like the obligatory scene in most mysteries where the detective assembles all the suspects and finally unmasks the criminal.

The film is further handicapped because censorship lets it only hint at the point on which it depends; a confrontation of the fact of the homosexuality of a young man (dead before the film begins) and the devious way in which he has made his mother and his cousin serve it. We are given, instead, circumlocutions both about this and the bizarre death to which his homosexuality brought him.

As the rich aunt, who makes her first entrance and last exit in a facilely symbolic openwork elevator in her mansion, Katharine Hepburn gives a trenchant performance in a part not quite worth the conviction she lends it. Elizabeth Taylor, as carefully directed as she was in *Cat on a Hot Tin Roof,* is sometimes vital and at the very end strikes a spark or two. Montgomery Clift, as the young doctor, is present a good deal of the time, but his contribution is small. Clift had, in earlier days, a certain fine-drawn tremulousness, limited but sometimes quite moving. It has gone; and his present effect, I'm afraid, is that of a husk that once contained a small kernel.

Joseph L. Mankiewicz's direction is adept in technical cinema terms; he knows how to handle a camera, he understands cutting and tempo. But his whole labor in this instance is to give screen life to a story that fights it every inch of the way. He is driven to such cheap B-picture effects as using close-ups of demented people in an asylum to scare us. But one can sympathize with his desperation to find some way of making this film come visually alive.

The Fugitive Kind   (May 2, 1960)

Is there a future for Tennessee Williams? Or is there nothing ahead of him but his past? His second film of the season, *The Fugitive Kind*, raises more than a suspicion of bankruptcy of material, of his feeding on himself.

This picture is based on his play *Orpheus Descending*, a revision of his earliest full-length play *Battle of Angels*, which closed on its try-out tour about twenty years ago. Like all of his long plays—if you remember *The Glass Menagerie*, *A Streetcar Named Desire*, *Summer and Smoke*, *Camino Real*, *The Rose Tattoo*, *Cat on a Hot Tin Roof*, and *Sweet Bird of Youth*—this one too is about a search for free, full emotional life. A vagabond guitar player, disgusted with his futile existence, drifts into a small Southern town, gets a job clerking, and hopes to live simply and fully. But his animal musk undoes him. He is pursued by a rich young hellion who wants to drown her frustrated idealism in his embrace; he stirs the senses of the Italian wife of his employer; and he even provokes religious visions in the sheriff's wife. At last the men of the town eliminate him.

This film derived from Williams' first play has the same theme as his latest play: the world forces a young man of extraordinary sexual power to live by that power and then punishes him for doing so. It is as though in these two works Williams has circumscribed his subcontinent of exploration.

The question that this new film raises for us vis-à-vis Williams is: how long can you and I go on being represented by riffraff? When Williams first appeared, he seared his audience because his milieu was a novel semiunderworld and because the currency of that world (not of all the South but of his South) was violence and sex. Our urbane theater, except in murder mysteries and sheer melodrama, takes a long time to get down to these elemental theatrical forces, if it ever gets to them at all. But Williams *began* with them and clothed them in considerable poignancy and poetic figuration, both of language and symbolic action. By now, however, his almost unvaried return to the same seamy arena, at the same cultural level (no matter how much money his people have), begins to make us restive.

Kowalski and Mangicavallo in their undershirts were virtually irresistible. They represented qualities in us—without equivocation—

that were starved for externalization in art. But they keep coming back in Williams' work, and the more often they return, the more apparent it becomes that there is more in us than there is in them. Lurid colors, the feral slash, are always welcome in the theater both because they are constants in life and because they are where the theater has its root. But a writer who is limited to those elements is not made for the long journey. His new work begins to remind you of his past work; and, what is in a way worse, he himself begins to be conscious of this and strives to give deeper "meaning" to the use of more or less the same material. In this film and in *Sweet Bird,* Williams feels it necessary to deliver precise messages about the most important things in life. They are, says he, to live and to love. But how long can we find rewards in a writer—no matter how gifted—for whom "live" and "love" mean to copulate?

Sweet Bird and his last film *Suddenly, Last Summer* were both hugely successful, in my view, because Williams' name has become a trade-mark of sweaty sexuality wrapped in perfumed poesy. There is enough "art" about the efforts to assure the pop-eyed playgoer that he is not a mere sensation seeker; how could he be happier? It is in neither my province nor my power to predict success so I can't say whether this new film will draw crowds. But Williams may be turning into a theatrical Erskine Caldwell—whose novels continue to make mountains of money long after they ceased to be good because his name is a guarantee of mattressy sex. One hoped—and still hopes—for more from Williams. There was ample cause to believe that he would grow along Strindbergian, even Chekhovian lines. There is cause now to fear that he is trapped by the facility with which he can rework the same vein—possibly convinced that by refusing to move into new areas he is being true to himself—and that he is also trapped, perhaps unconsciously and insidiously, by the public's present image of him.

The repetitious effect of the film is enhanced by the presence of Marlon Brando in the leading role. His performance of Kowalski in *Streetcar* was archetypal in the Williams canon. To be fair, this new role is quite different from Kowalski in aspiration, but it is so similar in diction and status that Brando, like Williams, seems to be deriving from his own past work. The result is such a caricature—with overdone pauses, brute-brow fumbling for the right word, apelike hand groping for truth—that the artist that Brando may become may some day buy up all the prints of this film and burn them.

Anna Magnani does her best to fill the role of the storekeeper's wife with reality, but the part is porous imitation; as fast as she pours honesty in, it runs out. Williams gives her a few catch phrases to prove that she is a full-blooded, earthy woman ("the wine garden of my father"—"there is life in my body"), but they ring hollow in their pseudoelemental way.

Joanne Woodward, too, suffers from comparison with herself. She has played this part (the headstrong Southern girl) several times before. Miss Woodward is a good young actress, but she is powerless against the empty pretentiousness of the role and against the fact that, in a short fifteen years or so, much of this material and method has moved from immediacy and truth to theatrical cliché.

Sidney Lumet, the director, is usually at least clever at least part of the time—an acquisitive magpie who has picked up, along with tin-selly trash, a few small gems. This time he brings us nothing but bits of colored glass. The less-than-perfect mantle of Elia Kazan is here draped on considerably narrower shoulders. The finale: Miss Magnani, pregnant by Brando, is shot by her husband, who is dying of cancer. Meanwhile the new wing of the store—a pretty confectionery which she built to revive the spirit of her father's wine garden—is blazing furiously, deliberately fired by her husband. And while Miss Woodward stands on the sidelines screaming his name, Brando is forced back into the blaze by the streams of two fire hoses played on him by vindictive friends of the cuckold.

Let the description serve as its own comment.

Sweet Bird of Youth   (April 16, 1962)

Except for its first act, which was raffishly funny, *Sweet Bird of Youth* was an embarrassment on the stage. Whatever one might say against Williams' previous work, it had been the antithesis of the plotty and the laboriously social-conscious. This play hung its denouement on a twist (the film star's discovery, through a phone call, that her supposed flop was a big hit) whose flimsiness would have bothered Norman Krasna; and its political subplot was full of sophomoric thought and language that betrayed Williams' discomfort in this area.

In the film, the play's faults are underscored by Richard Brooks, the

director-adapter, and are now visible to the purblind. Paul Newman
and Geraldine Page, repeating their stage roles, get excellent value
out of the *humour noir* of the bedroom scenes, but their performances
are again shaken apart by the plot desperation of the play.

Brooks has also contributed some false touches of his own. In the
play the modern Micaela had to be operated on (and sterilized)
because of a venereal disease given her by the hero; later, the hero is
castrated by her brother and his pals. Brooks has "licked" these
elements—for the film's family audience, no doubt—by changing the
first item to an abortion and (although he retains all the dialogue that
leads up to it) by substituting for castration one blow across the
hero's face. "Now no girl will ever love you," says the girl's brother;
whereupon the girl promptly goes off with the hero. Brooks' bone-
headedness is further documented in a scene on the front porch of the
hotel. TV men and carpenters are preparing for a political rally; in
their midst Miss Page and Newman have a loud emotional scene. Not
one of the technicians ever turns to look at them.

POSTSCRIPT. The initial question in the review of *The Fugitive Kind*
seems to have been answered. The Williams cycle—at least of what is
now recognizable as the Williams "kind" of play—seems to have
concluded: the play of the sex-freebooter hero or of sex-sensation
dynamics, redolent with the sweet-rank odor of rotting flowers. This
cycle and the public appetite for it seem to have been coterminous.
For about twenty years after the early forties there was an audience
for these theatrical distillations of Faulkner-cum-Freud. The phrase is
not to deny Williams' genuine and trenchant dramatic powers; one
has only to consider hothouse forcings like the works of William Inge
and Paul Bowles and Speed Lamkin to appreciate that Williams is
authentically gifted. But underneath the excellent acting parts and the
glandular poignancies, there seemed to be a conscious steamy merchandising. Like most merchandising, it subsisted on vogue, and thus,
as it exploited its market, destroyed it. *The Glass Menagerie,* an
unsensational play, still has appeal; *A Streetcar Named Desire* is
already a quasi museum piece.

The audience has had what it wanted from Williams. This does not
mean that he reached the utmost limits of shock and that they are
now bored; those limits keep changing and anyway audiences like
to be taken to them again and again. But styles and flavors can grow

wearisome, and *Night of the Iguana* (as film) proves that Williams' late admixture of religion and religious symbolism cannot freshen his style. Sophistication, in both good and deplorable senses, is growing in America. Through this century the dashing lover, as romantic theatrical image, was replaced by the stalwart idealist, and he was replaced by the free fornicator who seemed infinitely more realistic— indeed, more truly poetic with Laurentian wise-blood lyricism. Now, though intercourse does not appear to be passé, sex as salvation or as ultimate honesty or even as poetry has a hint of lavender sachet about it. This remoteness is emphasized when the characters are lower-class Southerners.

It may be that the Negro revolution has made it difficult for a writer to use such a Southerner, at present, as a hero image of any kind. Certainly it is possible that, for an audience of an increasingly high educational level, the use of the "natural" man as surrogate becomes more and more patently artificial. Theater writing of the near future (which is relevant to this section on adaptations as a source of films) seems to be moving toward a higher social class among white characters and to be drawing its working-class or "natural" characters more and more from Negroes and Puerto Ricans, as they advance into public eye and conscience. Sexuality becomes an instrument of more and more complicated social and religious problems, not in itself a declaration of truth and freedom. Increasingly it is related to a consciousness of the larger agonies and vacancies—in themselves agonizing—of our time.

It would be pleasant to be faced with a good new Williams play as contravention of the above; good art, of whatever kind, is more important than critical projection. But at the moment it seems as if such a play would have to be conceived differently from the Williams mode of the past.

The Old Man and the Sea   (October 6, 1958)

The appearance of the film version of *The Old Man and the Sea* reminded me that Ernest Hemingway, probably the best-known and surely the most influential of all American novelists, has written only one novel with an American setting. Many of his short stories, of course, take place here, but only *To Have and Have Not* among his novels is set (in part) in America. Also, although there are many American men in his books, all his novels except that one have exotic heroines.

These facts are more than curiosities, I believe—they are revealing. In discussing Tennessee Williams recently, I suggested that it may be the lack of large-scale emotional material in conventional American life that has driven him to the neurotic fringes of society. A similar sense that his dramatic scope could not be thoroughly tried by the American scene may have sent Hemingway—not, in his case, to neurotica—to foreign countries. Foreign heroines followed logically. Besides, they have ready-made mystery and romance; and an ultra-masculine, realistic, rhinoceros-hunting author is interested in women principally as romantic images.

Every strength has an attendant possible weakness. If Hemingway found large themes for his large talent, he succumbed to a certain travel snobbism. (You there in Omaha, don't you wish you were here with me in this Paris *bistro* or Pamplona *cantina?* Here, I toss you a few foreign phrases and names of wines and streets to dream with.) In addition, his alien view has led him to overvalue certain discoveries. For instance, in Spanish one does indeed say "thou" to friends and one speaks of "the Tigers of Detroit," but Spanish-speaking people don't think that remarkable. We don't often find those forms in good translations of Spanish works; the translator tries to render another language truly (to use one of Hemingway's pet words) in English. Hemingway, however, taken with the novelty of the forms and the thrill of being away from home, "thou's" us and insists on a diminishingly effective pseudo-Biblical simplicity. At bottom, there is in this a wide-eyed juvenile wonder combined with a professional's glee at finding a pocket of quaint material to mine.

Hemingway's short novel *The Old Man and the Sea* is a good example of his virtues and faults. The story itself is straight, clean, heroic, and ironic. A man journeys out on the faceless sea (a capsule Ahab), fights, wins, then loses: but really wins because he has had the courage to fight and to lose. Fine. But through the story Hemingway, both the Wide-eyed and the Gleeful Exploiter, comes peeping in too often. The sense of contrition before simplicity, plus the pervasive feeling that the author is a man with motorcars and lawyers who is "getting back to fundamentals," is damaging to the art of the piece.

It is remarkable how these virtues and faults are paralleled in the film of *The Old Man*. The director (John Sturges) and the screen adapter (Peter Viertel) have hewn faithfully to the story line. This is feasible even though the drama is largely internal because much of the Old Man's inner conflict is given voice on the sound track—by Spencer Tracy who plays the part. Moreover, a great deal of the papier-mâché peasant grandeur has been shorn away by the necessity for condensation. But it has been replaced by Tracy's papier-mâché performance.

Tracy has had a long career in films as a kind of American Jean Gabin; and although his work has degenerated somewhat into mannerism, a slow-blinking, taciturn competence that is by now predictable and slightly boring, still he has often been highly effective. But his performance in this film demonstrates that he has made his reputation in very carefully fitted roles and that he is not, in the best sense, an actor at all; he is a "behaver." He has spent his life behaving credibly in front of a camera, and if that is not a small achievement, neither is it a great one.

As the Old Man, his hair has been clipped and dyed white, he has put on pajamalike Cuban clothes and he walks about barefoot, but he carries with him always fifty films in which he tipped his fedora back and was urbanely sage. This is not to say that an actor is condemned to a small field because he has made his mark in it; but Tracy has very little as a performer besides the ability to market his personality. It is not the Old Man's personality; and as we often feel impatience in the book with an author who has knowingly "gone simple," so with Tracy we feel that at any moment, having tired of the masquerade, he may reach into the bottom of his boat, pick up a radiophone and summon his motor cruiser. He has not even taken the trouble to adapt his speech to the part. In his casual American accent, the short declarative sentences frequently sound incongruous. This is the closest to a one-man cast that I can remember seeing, so it is easy to understand why a huge box-office name was sought for the part. But, despite the film's merits, the producer has insured his venture at the price of a central failure.

James Wong Howe's color photography of the sea is excellent; outstanding among numerous beautiful scenes is one of a fleet of small fishing boats starting out just before dawn, each with a lantern on its mast. Some of the special effects are poor; it is obvious when a

studio close-up has been superimposed on a location shot. Sturges'
direction is only fair. Perhaps no director could have had much effect
on Tracy, but Sturges has contributed a few heavy-handed touches of
his own. The dream scenes of the African coast are needlessly literal,
and a really egregious blunder is the moment when the weary Old
Man, bearing his mast on his shoulder, trudges up the street and
stumbles to his knees before a church door. I almost heard a voice
whisper: "Get it? Station of the Cross!!"

The Doctor's Dilemma   (December 29, 1958)

The producer who attempts to adapt a Shaw play for films
soon realizes, if he is perceptive, that it is impossible; he must allow
Shaw to adapt the film form to his play. For Shaw is a dramatist in
the classical tradition: almost everything in his plays happens through
the words. (Or, as actors say, "He must be played *on* the lines, not
between them.") Now language is, if not the enemy, at least the
burden of the motion picture. In good pictures the words are good,
but the picture does not rely on them in the way that Shaw or Shakespeare or Marlowe relied on them. Admittedly, in plays as well as
films, one wants not a single word more than necessary; but language is central to the classical theater, and to the film it is supple-
mentary.

It is therefore suicidal, for a Shaw film, to start by seeing how
many words you can leave out. You must leave in as much as possible. Work for visual variety with camera angles, if you like, and
divide acts so that parts of them are played in different places, but
broadly speaking you must set out boldly to break the movie world's
rules; you must make a filmed play, not a film, or you will end up
with little of either. You cannot adapt a great dramatist's work to
another form because if he was truly great, he has built the work into
the form and vice versa. (How thoroughly Olivier's *Hamlet* film
demonstrated this.) When you make your Shaw film, use the best
camera crew and cutter you can get, but place your chief bet on
Shaw. He can write better than the best cameraman can photograph.

The film of *The Doctor's Dilemma* makes almost all the elemental mistakes. It can be recommended guardedly because of some factors cited below, but Anatole de Grunwald, the producer and adapter, has committed the error of errors: he has tried to movie-ize the play. He has sliced the script to the bone and beyond; and because he has not condensed proportionately, he has distorted the story and theme. For what he has taken away of Shaw's play, he tries to compensate by giving us some shots of Harley Street, old motor cars, a quarrel with a butcher, a Hampstead pawnshop. It is, mildly speaking, an unfair exchange.

I don't suggest that every word of the play should or could have been retained. I'm not shocked by, for instance, the moving of the Jennifer-Ridgeon scene at the end of Act III from the artist's studio to Ridgeon's house. But the general implication of this script is that if only poor old Shaw had had MGM around when he was writing this play, they could have shown him how to save time; and if only he could have written directly for films instead of the miserably limited theater, he would himself have done things like bringing in the recovered Blenkinsop at the end and having the dead artist speak on the sound track to his wife.

When Shaw was himself on hand during the filming of *Pygmalion, Major Barbara,* and *Caesar and Cleopatra,* he supplied extra material as a kind of lubrication to slide the camera from one place to another. De Grunwald lacked that advantage, and it must be admitted that, in his inserted scenes, he has at least had the courtesy to use no dialogue at all or to use lines lifted from other places in the play. But here again, in my view, he has erred; instead of trying to write Shaw scenes without Shaw, he should have plumped heavily for making the most of the Shaw scenes he had.

Yet even this maimed script could have been much more effective if it had been directed by someone who understands the Shaw style. Anthony Asquith, a competent film hand per se, does not. He was codirector with Leslie Howard of the fine *Pygmalion* film, but does one remember from it the close-ups and angles and inserts, or does one remember Howard's long warning to Eliza ending "The angels will weep for you," Wilfred Lawson's bardic dustman, Wendy Hiller turning on Higgins with her soft, heart-rending "Oh, you are a devil"? In other words, does one remember the film devices or the performing of Shaw?

Asquith has not had a good actor-director's collaboration this time.

What he has done is to hire the best cast he could find and to say, in effect, "Look, chaps, I'm going to be terribly busy with camera set-ups. I'll just have to leave the lines to you." The result is that we see a number of good actors fending for themselves, with no sense of over-all scene structure and with much left unrealized in each of their parts. Felix Aylmer, who could have been a prime Paddy Cullen, is funeral-paced and sloughs off the crusty humor. Alastair Sim, though not a favorite o fmine (he always has a faint air of the don sporting, the professor in the faculty-club play), could have been incisive as Walpole. John Robinson, who is equipped for Ridgeon, could have fulfilled the role as far as the adaptation allows. Only Robert Morley, perfectly cast as B.B. and knowledgeable about Shaw, gets consider-able out of his part. Schutzmacher, whose flavor contributed so much to the play's world, has been completely deleted.

The pleasant surprises of the film are Dirk Bogarde as Dubedat and Leslie Caron as Jennifer (here made Ginevra and a Breton). Bogarde achieves a lissomeness and a cool, diabolic honesty which I had not expected; and the adenoidal veil which has often come between his voice and us is rent by conviction here. He has been cheated of his grand climactic credo; the film, frightened of large utterance, simply has him murmur "Michelangelo . . . Rembrandt . . . Velasquez" and another phrase or two, then he dies. He is thus also cheated of his wonderful dying line, reported by Walpole: "He wants to know is the newspaperman here." De Grunwald has corrected Shaw's lapse in characterization.

Miss Caron is by no means ideal for Jennifer; she is more a kitten than a young priestess. But she persuades us of her utter devotion to her husband as man and genius, and her playing of the death scene is irresistible. The script cheats her, too; she is robbed, along with Ridgeon, of the meat of Act V in which the doctor admits that he allowed her husband to die, she is touched by his candor and states her faith in her dead husband and his obedience to him through remarriage. The script omits Ridgeon's reaction to the news of her remarriage, the crucial line: "Then I have committed a purely disin-terested murder"; and thus we are nicely protected from Shaw's truth.

Cecil Beaton, who understands Victorian-Edwardian costume so well, has little scope in this film, but he has clothed Miss Caron perfectly. She looks as if she had been dressed by her husband, a penniless artist who knows her good points and has roamed around the studio picking up a piece of cloth here, a shawl and a hat there. The result is pure Bohemia.

The Sound and the Fury   (March 16, 1959)

A recurrent debate about criticism of films and plays is whether adaptations ought to be considered in relation to their originals or as entities in themselves. Where the original is a work of little importance or reputation, the question can be begged. Otherwise, in my view, reference to the original is unavoidable. Imagine going to see a film advertised as Chekhov's *Sea Gull* and finding that in it Trigorin has been made a Mongol (to suit a Mongolian star), that he does not seduce Nina but has taken a Daddy Longlegs interest in her which blossoms into cozy marriage, and that the character of Konstantine has been excised.

Far-fetched as that sounds, it is a fair analogy with what has been done in the film of Faulkner's *The Sound and the Fury*. Quentin (Caddy's brother) has been completely eliminated, along with about half the novel. Jason has been made a Cajun to fit Yul Brynner's accent. He is no longer Caddy's brother; he is the son of Father Compson's second wife by her previous marriage. Thus there is no blood relationship between him and the younger Quentin (Caddy's daughter), and the antagonism between them can blossom into love and probably marriage. This from a novel which Irving Howe calls one of the three or four twentieth-century works of prose fiction in which the impact of tragedy is felt and sustained, a novel which ends with Quentin's flight with a carnival showman and the certainty that, whatever happens to her, the Compson family is doomed.

Make every allowance for the legitimate needs of screen adaptation. Even then, if words mean anything at all, how can this occasionally touching movie of a declining family's regeneration be called a film of Faulkner's work—a book which (to quote Howe again) records "the fall of a house, the death of a society"? If black is white and right is left, which way is up?

An editorial in the current *Esquire* suggests a double standard for criticizing films made from novels: that reviewers should treat such

films as complete in themselves because most people haven't read the
originals and a review that points out divergences is only spoiling
their fun. It is a stirring little crusade for the sacredness of ignorance,
and if only our culture can continue to keep most people from reading books, it may prevail.

But let us temporarily adopt *Esquire*'s suggestion. This film, then,
was made by the same producer and director (Jerry Wald and Martin
Ritt) who made an earlier Faulkner derivative, *The Long Hot Summer*. It has the same false Technicolor prettiness, the same generally
competent direction. Joanne Woodward, who was in the other film,
gives us more of the same quite good performance of a young Southern girl of independent spirit. Ethel Waters is comforting as Dilsey.
Yul Brynner does his too-often-seen best as Jason. John Beal is
pathetic as the sodden brother, Howard—a character invented for the
film, presumably to take up some of the slack caused by dropping
(the older) Quentin.

But the only really interesting performance is the Caddy of Margaret Leighton. Miss Leighton seems somewhat worried by the Southern accent, as if she had to carry a bothersome parcel while performing, but she is an artist whose neurotic palette is perfectly suited to
the role. Her smallest move is charged with purebred emotion; she can
make us feel, in a poignant way, the very fineness of her bones.

Within its own context, the script has inconsistencies and loose
ends. How does Jason, who boasts that he is the family mainstay,
support them after he hits his employer Earl Snopes? What happened
to Quentin's resentment of Caddy because of her mother's reluctance
to defend her? Why did Jason tear furiously after the thieving Quentin and her lover only to tell her that she could do what she chose
and then leave her? These questions are posed by the script, not the
novel.

Still it must be admitted that the screen writers have nibbled
around busily enough in the book to come up with a script of superficial intelligence which contains some good scenes. Most of the sequences with the idiot Benjy (Jack Warden) are effective; several of
Miss Woodward's and Miss Leighton's scenes are well composed. But
they seem pages from a family album, not elements of a unified
progressive drama. The net result of the film, aside from its final note
of optimism, is of a sprawling, occasionally gripping fourth carbon
copy of Chekhov in Dixie—just another ambling "study" of Southern
social disintegration and transition.

What is missing? If *Esquire* will pardon us, Faulkner is missing. The gigantic, death-destined tension is missing. So the point of the work—the force that knits the pieces fiercely together and hurls them forward—is missing. The effect of the film is like hearing snatches of a symphony through closed concert-hall doors.

In the same issue of *Esquire,* Wald is quoted as saying: "Mass audiences are hep now. There are 25 million college graduates." He must be banking on a belief—possibly well founded—that few of them have read one of the most highly regarded of all American novels and that those few won't care about its perversion. "I'm gonna do Lawrence's *Sons and Lovers* next," he says, "and I just bought *Winesburg.*" He adds that he also has an option on *Ulysses.*

Why not? With the technique of evisceration and trimming and substitute stuffing that he has perfected, he can make a good neighborhood movie out of any book he chooses. How about Nietzsche's *Beyond Good and Evil?* Gad, what a title!

Middle of the Night (June 8, 1959)

There must be many still alive who remember the great days of television. Back in the early fifties, hardly a Sunday went by without its article on the dramatic renaissance that was taking place in the land. The theory went that, if any medium demanded so much material, it must produce at least a small number of fine works. All we had to do was wait; among the TV oysters there were bound to be some pearls.

Those of us who doubted were called cynical or blind, but we thought there were factors that made the theory dubious. Commercial sponsorship afflicts the field doubly: editorially (references to Buchenwald's gas ovens are eliminated because the sponsor is the American Gas Association!); and because its interest is not intrinsic, it is based on the effect of the plays as advertisements. (There are fewer serious dramatic programs on TV now not because there are fewer writers but because plays weren't selling cars and cigarettes.)

In those distant days of the TV dramatic boom, the picture companies, nervously competing, rushed to buy successful TV scripts—so that if you missed a much-discussed play in your living room, you could probably see it around the corner at the Bijou ten months later. That parade, too, has dwindled; but these remarks are prompted by the film of Paddy Chayefsky's *Middle of the Night,* which was born on TV and has already had another incarnation in the theater. To me this is the best of the TV transformations into film, far more effective than the grubbily patronizing *Marty* or the dramatically fallacious *Twelve Angry Men.*

The Chayefsky school of TV writing tends to dwell on the small moment in the small life, as if the author's mind were cramped by the narrow screen into concentration on naturalistic minutiae. Crises are often built of accumulated naggings rather than large conflicting forces. But despite its naturalistic texture, the Chayefsky school is a romantic one—in the sense that all art can be viewed as either classic or romantic. The former states the universal and through it tries to reach the particular, the latter states the particular and tries to reach the universal. The Chayefskians pose a small instance and try to reach larger implications through it.

Too often they have merely stated the instance and not evoked the widespread implications. But *Middle of the Night,* though lapped in verism, goes on to touch a universal quick nerve. It has all the trappings of stenographic dialogue and repertorial detail, it has the usual air of emasculated Odets (that is, social drama without social purpose); but the subject matter is larger than humdrum life, and both major characters rise to it.

It is a story of love in a man who knows he ought not to be in love, that the facts of his life are not congenial to that love. Age is one barrier; devolving from that, the knowledge that he is deliberately cultivating the girl's pity and admiration into passion is another; consciousness of selfishness and future disaster is still another.

Fredric March plays the fifty-six-year-old New York garment manufacturer, a widower, who falls in love with his secretary, twenty-four, a divorcée. What starts out as a friendship soon becomes an affair, then an engagement. The engagement is fractured by a quarrel, engendered not so much by his jealousy as by his fear of jealousy; this is capped by a visit of her former husband in which she learns that she is still physically attracted to him.

As I remember this TV play, the girl chooses the older man at last because his humanity and maturity have spoiled her for mere raw young sex. In the film this good point is subordinated to March's decision (prompted by his partner's suicide attempt) to embrace whatever he can get of love in his remaining years without complaint. This altered emphasis puts the reunion in the man's hands, which is perhaps where the chivalrous film public wants it to be.

March is a fine and constantly growing actor, and there is nothing wrong with him in the part except that he ought not to be in it. In a film that is so finicky about accurate details of setting and speech, it is difficult to accept him as a denizen of Seventh Avenue. The phraseology and the milieu simply do not fit him.

The secretary is Kim Novak. Her character is an easily recognizable one in our society: the unhappy girl who doesn't really know why she's unhappy, what she's looking for or capable of. Miss Novak approximates some of its self-impatience and misunderstood hungers moderately well.

Several contemporary playwrights—Chayefsky and William Inge, for example—frequently use a device they derive from the Russian masters. The minor characters sound certain notes which we know are not their real notes, and each one, as if it were his constitutional right, gets his scene in which to reveal his true self. Martin Balsam as March's son-in-law, Joan Copeland as his daughter, and Albert Dekker as his partner do well in their big scenes.

Delbert Mann's direction is well attuned to this low-level-with-one-outbreak kind of writing. He can keep the commonplaces interesting or amusing, and he certainly deserves credit for what he has done with Miss Novak.

Sons and Lovers   (August 29, 1960)

With the film of *Sons and Lovers* the question arises again: for whom are the films of fine novels made?

Obviously, adaptation must occur in an almost biological sense. The book must be anatomized and reassembled so as to produce the same effect in a different medium; to the degree that this second life is achieved, the adaptation is successful. But for whom is it done? Those who care for the novel can rarely be fully satisfied. The primary matter of time prevents it; other considerations aside, it would take many hours to get on the screen the full range of even an average-length novel. And to those who don't know or care about the book, the film is frequently unsatisfactory in a different way; for the screen-writers are to some degree hobbled by the book and cannot follow their best cinematic instincts.

The Lawrence film is an example of the latter dilemma. Gavin Lambert and T. E. B. Clarke tried to bring cinematic order out of the lifelike novelistic sprawling growth of the book, rearranging, con-densing, expanding with a minimum of prettifying. (Mrs. Morel's cancer does, however, become heart trouble.) But throughout we seem to hear the screen writers saying: "If only we could let go. If only we weren't bound by this book or by reasonable extrapolations from it. What a *film* we could make of these materials, instead of a series of illustrated scenes from a novel."

A rule of thumb can be induced. If we exclude trash, then the further down the scale from greatness toward competence that our original novel lies, the more likely it is to be successfully adapted for the screen; for it is less likely to be dependent on its original form for its effect. (Margaret Kennedy says: "In a great work of art the medium is so wedded to the subject that it becomes impossible to think of them apart. To take the *writing* out of a great novel is to run the risk of emptying out the baby with the bath.")

What then can be said about the present film? The best one can promise those who like the book is that they will probably not be greatly disturbed by the adaptation and will see some elements cap-ably dramatized. Other viewers will find it an intelligently written, seriously ambitious film in which the hero seems in the middle to forget the things that bothered him at the beginning, only to remem-ber them again at the end; in which the matters he claims to have learned are not quite clear and don't seem to arise entirely out of what has happened to him.

By far the most fully realized theme in the film—a measure of both its success and failure—is the relationship between Paul's father and mother. We get a piercing sense of a life in which two people can quarrel savagely, yet still return to each other accepting the quarrels as part of their marriage—and all to the incomprehension of their son who thinks a blow taken means a blow given and that his mother ought to leave; who, for all his love of his mother, is shut out of her sexual life and cannot understand her as a woman.

Trevor Howard plays Walter Morel excellently: rock-voiced,

brusque, clumsily well-meaning, a rooster gone middle-aged and drunk. Wendy Hiller, winning actress though she is, simply seems too young to be the mother of all those grown sons in that rough and trying home. And her tenderness and beauty emphasize the Oedipal relationship with Paul in the wrong way.

Mary Ure is appealing as Clara Dawes although she never really burns. Heather Sears loses her virginity again, as Miriam, in a scene handled very much like the one in *Room at the Top* where it happened the first time. Miss Sears has a certain eupeptic charm, but she is not convincing as a farmer's daughter or a religiously inhibited girl.

Dean Stockwell (the Paul) is the only American in the cast. He works hard on his accent, and plays straightforwardly and, one might say, studiously. But his voice tends to the monotonous, and he is not quite capable of conveying the wellspring of everything questing and baffled and impatient that Lawrence means this youth to be. Stockwell says more than he contrives to make us believe.

Possibly because Lawrence is John Braine's literary grandfather, Jack Cardiff has directed this film in a matter generally reminiscent of *Room at the Top*. There is the same subtly stark black-and-white photography, the same swift juxtaposition of Midlands grime with physical intimacy—as if to suggest the struggle to keep the individual cleanly passionate amidst the soot and grayness.

The Misfits   (February 20, 1961)

Arthur Miller, in his plays, has done some representative worrying for all of us about certain defects and defeats in contemporary life. Now he has broken a five-year silence with a screenplay based on his short story *The Misfits* in which he expresses further concern.

The premise is promising: a Chicago girl goes to Reno for a divorce, and there meets three Western men. She is desperate for reliable human relationships, they are in a last-ditch fight against the diminution of large-scale life. She lives with one of them, then the other two pursue her; after a mustang-hunting expedition which acts as a touchstone, she elects to remain with the first man.

The screenplay is, in idea and much of its execution, several uni-
verses above most American films, but *The Misfits* is unsuccessful
both in its treatment of its subject and as a use of the film form; and
it is a cheerless task, because of respect for Miller and agreement
with his concerns, to examine the reasons. The film moves with
Roslyn, the girl: she is one of the two chief searchers for truth and
she is the cause of the revelation of truth to Gay, her lover. But what
does her search consist of? In the beginning we are shown a highly
insecure, neurotic girl. ("The trouble is I'm always back where I
started" . . . "Maybe you're not supposed to believe anything people
say. Maybe it's not even fair to them," etc.) Then, although she has
just told Gay she doesn't feel "that way" about him, she moves in
with him; and the first time they are visited by their friends, one of
them tells her "You found yourself, haven't you?" and the other says,
"You have the gift of life." Where did she get it? From then on this
girl, but lately nervous and restless, is treated as the Eternal Feminine, in tune with the universe ("hooked in" with the stars). What
produced this fantastic change? A few weeks of bliss with Gay? Can
Miller seriously believe that?

And how does she effect a resolution in Gay? Through her extreme
revulsion against pain—specifically against hunting. She won't let him
kill a rabbit (although she never bats an eye when he tells her that
their friend Guido goes eagle-killing in his plane); and on the horse-
hunting trip, when she learns that the mustangs are to be killed for
dog food, she becomes so frenzied that Gay gives up the hunt and
hunting and decides to change his mode of living. But how has this
made him realize that the straitening of contemporary life is inevitable? He has known for some time that mustang-hunting is less than it
was when he first did it to get stock for breeding and riding. Her
hysteria is not persuasive as a reason for his seeing these facts more
clearly. She would presumably have been equally hysterical in 1850 if
he had been killing deer to feed himself and her. Her outburst is
unrelated to the modern debasement of his mustanging, as such.

The author seems bemused by Roslyn, rather than perceptive
about her. She is a night-club performer, who had an unsettled childhood and now makes her living by scantily clad "interpretive" dancing. We have no reason to believe her more than a goodhearted,
highly sentimental showgirl, like hundreds of others, but the longer
Miller looks at her, the more rich and mysterious qualities he sees in
her. It is something like a man becoming infatuated with an attractive

but undistinguished girl and, out of a sense of guilt, investing her with qualities that no one else can see.

This infatuation leads to some embarrassingly bathetic instances in her dialogue. "Birds must be brave to live out here. Especially at night . . ." Or when the drunken Guido starts working on his unfinished house in the middle of the night: "He's just trying to say hello. . . ." Or, after an emotional scene, looking at the sky, "Help."

Miller has often had surprising lumps in his generally true dialogue. (In *Death of a Salesman* the vernacular Biff apologizes to his mother: "I've been remiss.") Here the mixture is as before. There is much acute and vivid writing; a phone call to his mother by Perce, the third man, is a brilliant character sketch. Then we get literary utterances like Guido's "We're all blind bombardiers. . . . Droppin' a bomb is like tellin' a lie—makes everything so quiet afterwards."

In form this screenplay is basically uncomfortable because Miller is a theater writer who has a generally orthodox and socially utilitarian view of theatrical art. Dialectical dialogue is its blood stream. It is an honorable tradition, and *The Crucible* ornaments it; but it is not film writing. Miller knows this and has tried to compensate for the verbal quality by including some graphic visual elements, like the rodeo and the hunt. But essentially the story is "talked out." Indeed, these uncommonly loquacious Westerners almost seem to be competing for the girl by offering her their troubled souls. And when Gay and Roslyn go off together at the end, we get a fast, almost synoptic talking-into-final-shape of the theme. This ending, after all the candid confrontation of harsh facts in our world, is as suddenly and incredibly "up-beat" as anything by the late Oscar Hammerstein.

John Huston's direction is his best in years, well knit and hard, at times even recalling *The Treasure of Sierra Madre*. Too bad that his camera occasionally peers lubriciously down the girl's bodice or elsewhere to remind us that Roslyn is really Marilyn Monroe.

Miss Monroe, complete with hushed, monotonous voice and with eye make-up even after a night in the mountains, copes more successfully with the neurotic than with the "elemental" qualities in her part. But at her best we sense that she has been coached and primed in thirty-second segments, which wouldn't matter if we weren't aware of it. Her hysterical scene near the end will seem virtuoso acting to those who are overwhelmed by the fact that she has been induced to shout.

In his last film Clark Gable has his best part since Rhett Butler and demonstrates why, although he was a transparently mechanical actor, he was a world-bestriding star. He radiates likable, decent-roguish masculinity.

Eli Wallach, as Guido the ex-Army pilot, sounds less bronco-hunter than Bronx. There is something vulgar in this effective actor's reliance on vulgarity as a métier. Montgomery Clift, who was last seen as a Westerner (unconvincingly) in *Red River,* here brings life to Perce, the battered young exile, who has nothing to live on but his willingness to get thrown off bucking horses.

A View from the Bridge   (*Show,* January, 1962)

A man strives with fate, seeking knowledge of the high gods, but his very ambition and his flaws pull him down. This is the quality of tragedy; and tragedy is Arthur Miller's ambition. But the curious fact is that this quality is more to be found in his career than in his plays. He is himself, in his artistic life, a twentieth-century tragic agonist.

From the beginning of his serious work, with *All My Sons,* it was plain that Miller had committed himself to the furthest goals and was making the biggest bet a writer can make with his life. Underneath the lumpy Brooklyn idiom masquerading as "general" English, underneath the slavish Ibsenism, a note began to sound. It was the indefinable but unmistaken note with which a dramatist says: "I am not trying merely to entertain or be affecting, to create fat little hits. I am setting out for the highest peak."

Plenty of new dramatists sound, or try to sound, this note: toward most of them, one can feel only compassion or irritation. But, unsatisfactory as *All My Sons* was, it had enough in it to tease the hopeful, to nourish the possibility that the imitativeness and awkwardness might be shucked, that the author might stand free to wrestle the angels and win some victories for all of us.

The next play, *Death of a Salesman,* more than confirmed the hope. A peculiar point about this play is that its adverse criticism—of which it has had a good deal—is markedly *ex post facto.* Not many of its severest critics deny being moved by it. They can criticize its fuzziness of theme: Is it antisuccess? Or is it that Willy has sought success ineptly? They can note that its hero is, in effect, dead at the opening and that the play is one long autopsy. These matters are more than academic quibbles—they relate to Miller's essential clarity. But the play bristles with spears of pathos that no critical shield can deflect.

Excepting his adaptation of *An Enemy of the People,* his next play came four years later: *The Crucible,* in many ways his best work. He found a congenial subject nicely enclosed in the past, shaped it conventionally well, and drove it to its point. (Is life worth losing for beliefs that end with life? If not, if people are not willing to die for beliefs, what *is* a belief?)

One relevant concern for admirers of Miller was that *The Crucible* had taken so long to appear. A young man ought to pour; his curiosities and angers are like a pack of eager hounds and—equally important—he has abundant energy to deal with what they bring him. But Miller had taken four years to write *The Crucible.* After two more years, he produced *A Memory of Two Mondays* and *A View from the Bridge,* the first a moderately interesting autobiographical sketch, the other discussed below. In the seven years since then, he has written one screenplay.

Quantity is not the sole criterion here, or Owen Davis would be the prime dramatist in American history. But the sparseness of Miller's output—three plays, two short plays, one screenplay, and some short stories and essays, in fifteen years—relates to the shortcomings of the plays themselves. And from the plays, as well as from statements he has made, one can infer something about the difficulties he has in working.

In the deepest sense, Miller's crisis is religious. Set in a solid Greek or Jewish or Christian or Marxist cosmos, with the terrain open and the compass steady, with hope clear and anguish purposeful, he could live to make dramas out of his life, dramas meaningful to his fellows and constructive of his society. Instead, he finds himself in a world with a wispy ethos and a dim cosmology, where there is no common soundboard of aspiration around him to echo his words, no grand, austere design against which his characters can measure themselves. A desolate world in which to look for tragic art; and some of that desolation must necessarily be in himself.

He was a youth in the Depression and grew up an acolyte of social justice. (His behavior before the Congressional committee that inves-

tigated his early beliefs was probably the most dignified of any witness in that committee's long, inglorious record.) As with so many
others, his social-political beliefs have failed to sustain him, and he
finds himself a god-hungry man without a god. He still has in him
the fever of large issues; he shows no interest in plays, however fine,
about domestic triangles or sensitive adolescents. He wants to create
works every one of which is, by implication, about everything. But he
cannot find enduring moral scenery or the large emotions possible
only in a world with some sort of faith.

In seeming desperation, then, he grabs material that is available
and tries to make it large. The unhappiest result of this was *The
Misfits,* the screenplay in which he tried to impose a *Götterdäm-
merung* on the doings of a mustang hunter and a stripteaser. He
seemed increasingly to recognize the thematic hollowness, trying to
compensate with verbal decoration, and the result was a tiny, in-
securely motivated story burdened with some of the most top-heavy
language ever to be heard from the screen.

This desperation of his, one infers, arises from a feeling that here
he is with vision and ability but the time is out of joint, as if he were a
sculptor stranded on an island with only a few scraps of marble.
Perhaps it was this desperation that also made him reach for the
material of *A View from the Bridge,* which now reaches us as a
motion picture.

The story deals with Eddie Carbone, a Brooklyn longshoreman
who is unconsciously in love with the niece he has reared. Into his
house come two brothers, illegal immigrants, Marco and Rodolpho.
The niece falls in love with Rodolpho; and Eddie, tormented but
unable to admit even to himself his quasi-incestuous love, reports the
illegal immigrants to the authorities and is killed by Marco.

It is a story with about the inherent profundity of *Cavalleria Rusti-
cana,* another tale of Sicilian fatalism and fatality. Its drama derives
from Eddie's subconscious insistence on catastrophe while we sit
clucking as if we were watching a man drive ninety miles an hour on
a slippery road. But it can be nothing more than a bloody accident,
not a harrowing tragedy, because of Eddie's character. Perhaps it is
vestigial snobbery to say that tragedy can happen only to princes; but
the play proves that tragedy cannot happen to longshoremen unless
they are epic longshoremen.

To provide a classic flavor, Miller gave the play an unadorned, straightforward shape, and he used a one-man chorus, the lawyer, to address us and to explain the tragic content, to try to kindle Athenian terror where we might feel only police-news sensation. Elements like Eddie's kissing the boy and the inevitability of the killing are certainly questionable, but at least Miller fitted the length to the subject. He kept it short, direct: a swift arrow-flight from bow to target.

In the film, the length has been almost doubled. Norman Rosten, the adapter, has not enriched the story with other strands; he has padded what was there with dockside scenes, lovers wandering through the Automat, a protracted final street fight like a John Wayne shoot-out. Eddie's murder has been changed to suicide, presumably so that nice Marco won't end up in the electric chair. The lawyer's choric function is gone. The original may have been an unsuccessful tragedy; the film is clear-cut melodrama—much too clearly cut.

Some of it is moving because of the acting. Eddie is Raf Vallone, whose taut face and charged body are dramatic even in repose—an actor capable of reaching into himself and bringing up a dripping handful of raw feeling. He is handicapped here by his English, with which he is highly uncomfortable, and the lines themselves sound wrong in his mouth. They were designed for a glib Italian-American. ("It gives me the willies"; "I'm the patsy.") These locutions are out of place in the mouth of a man who can hardly form English words at all. But Vallone's power frequently burns through the language barrier.

Carol Lawrence is direct and responsive as the niece. Jean Sorel, although he too suffers from language difficulties, is both delicately appealing and manly as her lover. Marco is Raymond Pellegrin, whose homely-beautiful face puts a thousand years of European suffering behind each simple line. The lawyer is Morris Carnovsky, an actor who is sometimes substantial and sometimes vapid. Here he was caught on the downgrade.

About Maureen Stapleton, who plays Eddie's wife, there are two schools of thought, and I belong to both of them. She is an actress of talent and honesty, and she is also a peddler of artificial honesty, sometimes manufacturing it for us right before our eyes. When she allows us to forget about Maureen Stapleton's ruthless refusal to be phony, she can cut to the quick of a scene.

Miller has been worst served by his director, Sidney Lumet, a man of much technical skill and excessive cleverness. He can make a film move swiftly, but when he comes to important points he hammers them. His lack of taste, I believe, is close to a lack of character. He is so anxious to be thought ingenious that he cannot trust his talent to function unharried. When Eddie and his wife discuss their marital rift in their bedroom, we see them in a mirror, and on the dressing table before them is their wedding picture. The camera holds and holds and holds on it. What might have been a subtle, telling point is destroyed because Lumet has fastened his teeth in it. When Marco gets revenge on Eddie, by lifting a chair from floor level, we know how he feels, how Eddie feels; but Lumet has to insert a reverse shot from high above, looking down over the chair to Eddie's face—to spoil Pellegrin's acting with a camera caper. When Eddie makes the informing phone call, the phone booth is in the foreground and we see him walk toward it from far across the street. It is meant to be a Via Dolorosa, but because the symbols are so patent, it is simply a long wait. After the killing, the device is reused—the lawyer makes the same long trek to a phone in the foreground. I assume there is supposed to be an ironic echo. But all we feel is Lumet groping for a final chord, a way to "get off."

Miller has had consistently bad luck with the films made from his plays. *All My Sons* had Burt Lancaster in it. *Death of a Salesman* was ineffectual on film because its time-shifts with light, which were poetic in the theater, seemed shabby in a medium that can dissolve time and space so easily; the play's effect depends largely on its form. *The Crucible* came to us from France with about the authenticity that an American film of Sartre might have for the French. Now *A View from the Bridge,* which could have been a terse shocker, has been puffed and bloated until, in the second half, even its good cast cannot interest us any longer in its battered, repetitive story.

The artistic failure of the film is not, of course, Miller's responsibility. The play's small treasure has been dissipated; for, with all its defects, it at least moved onto the stage, told its story, and left. There were glimpses of size in it, of a kind to make us feel that the author's failure to achieve tragedy with it was not entirely his fault. His shackles are, to some degree, the shackles of our time.

This is not a premature obituary notice. All men of good will can wish only well for a humane artist of good will. But Miller's artistic life—disconnected from a society that defies connection, searching for a temple it can serve—is a truer tragedy than any he has yet written.

The Innocents (January 8, 1962)

On Thursday, January 10, 1895, Henry James spent the evening with the Archbishop of Canterbury, who told him a ghost story. "It is all obscure and imperfect," wrote James in his notebook, ". . . but there is a suggestion of strangely gruesome effect in it." He clarified and perfected it, and it became *The Turn of the Screw*.

In the original anecdote, it is patent that the ghosts *are* ghosts who appear to the children. In his famous essay *The Ambiguity of Henry James,* Edmund Wilson advanced the possibility that the story is a sexual allegory, the ghosts being figments imagined by the repressed governess. If this is the case, it is doubly Freudian because James created the allegory unconsciously (just as the Ernest Jones interpretation of *Hamlet,* if valid, is doubly Freudian. Obviously, neither Shakespeare nor James—at that date—could have deliberately created a Freudian allegory; it would have to have been done through the subconscious.) Much of the theory rings true: the governess talks about the effect of her one meeting with her handsome employer, and the ghosts may be her projected wish to create a situation in which she will meet the uncle again. Still there are elements (like her knowledge of Quint's appearance) that will not fit the Freudian notion.

Now we are engaged in a small civil war, testing whether that notion can long endure. Truman Capote's screenplay—called, like William Archibald's theater dramatization, *The Innocents*—comes down strongly on the Freudian side. There are voices on the sound track heard only by Miss Giddons (and us), there are apparitions seen only by her (and us), after the boy dies she kisses him tenderly on the lips. Yet even here there are contradictions, such as the teardrop that Miss Jessel leaves on the schoolroom desk.

The film will not settle this controversy, but it does settle that there is only one way in which James' story can be well dramatized: not for stage or television or screen but as a radio play. This is for two reasons. The ghosts are much less effective when seen than when described; and a radio play can confine itself to the highlights, as James does. The film has particular trouble with passages *between* the manifestations, the living-out of the daily lives. We keep thinking: Why isn't Miss Giddons frightened all the time? How can she carry on a normal life between the ghosts' appearances? How can she sit down to table in this house and eat? How often can she

settle down comfortably with a book only to be surprised by apparitions? It is this awkwardness—which James avoided by keeping
mainly to the visitations—that gnaws at the credibility and the horror of the film. Additionally, the picture's tension depends on the
governess' role, and, unavoidably, it is insufficient. She has only one
mode of action: to try to make the children admit that they see the
figures; so the part is, literally, monotonous.

Jack Clayton, who directed *Room at the Top* so admirably, has
had less success here. In atmosphere he has hit off neither the effect
of an eerie house nor the equally frightening effect of terror in a
lovely place; he strives for a mixture of the two that infrequently
succeeds. Once in a while there is a blatant ghost-story shock but
never the feeling of soul-sickening evil that James wanted.

Clayton's most disappointing work is with the actors. Deborah
Kerr does her best, which is good, with the governess, and Megs
Jenkins has warmth as Mrs. Grose, but Clayton's ear seems to have
gone dull. He lets them play much too slowly and, in many scenes, on
the same vocal level, one of them entering on the note on which the
other stopped. He has handled the boy (Martin Stephens) fairly well,
but the girl (Pamela Franklin) has not responded. And he has miscast Michael Redgrave as the uncle, a part which calls for a vivid
brush stroke of the genteel and the romantic, neither of which is a
Redgrave quality. Imagine Laurence Olivier in the role.

All Fall Down   (April 23, 1962)

James Leo Herlihy's novel *All Fall Down,* which has now
been filmed, is a superior example of the American breed of adolescent fiction out of Sherwood Anderson by Salinger. The book fulfills
sensitively the obligations of the form; discovery of the self in the
universe, first love, first sex; but it goes past most similar books to
deal with the monstrous neurosis of an older brother and the muted
frustrations and sorrows of the narrator's parents.

The story, which is told mainly by the teen-age Clint, concerns his
father and mother, Ralph and Annabelle, and himself, and the relation of all three of them with the older son, Berry-berry. The latter
is a handsome vagabond who lives by his wits and his magnetism for

women, who comes home on a visit, nearly falls in love with a girl named Echo O'Brien, and makes her pregnant. Echo, realizing that he can never really love her or in fact anybody, kills herself. Clint, who has an adolescent crush on her and has overheard her last talk with Berry-berry, almost kills his brother. In the crisis Clint discovers that Berry-berry's glamorous wandering life, studded with women, is based on a hyperdeveloped Oedipal feeling, on a "hatred" of Annabelle that has driven him to hate and hurt all women. By this discovery Clint is freed of bondage to his older brother, freed of imitation of his anarchy. Berry-berry continues to wander and unravel; Clint is going to have a healthy life.

The film, adapted by William Inge and directed by John Frankenheimer, is, in large part, a delicate empathetic transcription. All the scenes in the Willart home are done with fluency and a truth that is more than veracity of detail, that projects contradictions of character and the piteous inability to communicate within the four walls of one home. Father and mother and two sons seem to us lonely and, to some degree, lovable, and each is imprisoned by the malformations and impositions of ego. We think: "If only they knew each other as well as we know them. If only they could speak to each other as clearly as they speak to us." This, of course, is a considerable tribute to all the artists concerned.

When the film leaves the Willart home to explore Berry-berry's life, it loses its texture and forsakes truth for fake realism. The scenes in the Florida jail, in strip-joints and bars, with avid lonesome women, are full of movie hand-me-downs: sweat, dark glasses, cruelly frank lighting, sordidness drooled over and treasured. These scenes have not been invented by the film-makers; they are all in the novel—in fact, there are others that have been omitted from the film. (For examples, Clint's first sexual experience and the fact that his brother is marketing whores.) But Inge's screenplay takes these elements out of the oblique, out of Clint's first romanticized view of them, and puts them in the foreground in the same plane with the other elements of the story. In the novel they are glimpses of harsh reality we get through Clint's immature eyes; in the film they have been yanked forward and exploited in a commonplace sensational way. Understandably, Inge and Frankenheimer wanted to dramatize important elements, rather than narrate them; but it might have been possible to do it through Clint's perspective rather than M. Spillane's.

Still, the forced hothouse steaminess of those scenes cannot obliterate the moving, exasperating honesty of all else in the film. There is even a split in Frankenheimer's direction; the striving for effect in the "tough" scenes is dropped for simplicity and sympathy in the scenes with the family and Echo. The dialogue—mostly Herlihy's—is pithy and nuttily idiomatic; the acting, with one exception, is unusually good.

The key performance is Angela Lansbury's as Annabelle. It can best be described with the grocer's lines about his wife in Shaw's *Getting Married:*

She's a born wife and mother. That's why my children all ran away from home. . . . She's a sensitive, affectionate, anxious soul; and she was never brought up to know what freedom is to some people. You see, family life is all the life she knows; she's like a bird born in a cage, that would die if you let it loose in the woods.

Miss Lansbury paints a brilliant tragicomic portrait of a mother who does all the right things—with disastrous results.

Karl Malden, who is acquiring restraint and, with it, some depth, makes a touching failure of the father—financially secure but inwardly dissatisfied, adoring of his sons but baffled by them, understanding of his wife but shackled by her. Eva Marie Saint is lovely and Fitzgeraldian as the (to Clint) wildly glamorous Echo, who has waited a long time to give herself to a man, makes her bet, and then—by her own code—pays when she loses.

Warren Beatty, whose two previous film appearances were at best promising, fares much better with the restless bored Berry-berry, who is bedeviled by his ostensible hatred of his mother, and is seduced by his powers of seduction. Physically, Beatty has the requisite magnetism; emotionally, he has the coiled-snake tension of black lower-middle-class frustration. What he needs now, as actor, is to develop a more reliable voice, with a wider range.

The one weakness in the cast is Brandon de Wilde, as Clint. De Wilde has, inevitably, lost the precociousness he had as a child actor in *The Member of the Wedding* and has not replaced it with basic credibility or even ease, let alone any indications of talent or technique. He is a pleasant, fresh youth, not much more.

Herlihy's novel, although it resolved finally to the same matter of Berry-berry's atypically extreme neurosis, was always moving because it was always essentially Clint's story. The film, by becoming equally Berry-berry's story, becomes partially clinical and at times makes us spectators instead of participants. Nevertheless its home scenes convey forcefully the sense of family life's affection and destruction, of both prison and the lost paradise.

Lolita (July 2, 1962)

"If you want to make a movie out of my book," says Humbert Humbert, "have one of these faces gently melt into my own, while I look." He is referring to the photographs in some Wanted posters. Now his advice has, essentially, been followed—with slight alteration; the film-makers have melted another face into Humbert's: a blend of sorrow and sympathy. Instead of H.H., the gonad nomad, he is now a trusty, tristful Tristan.

Assume, for the moment, that the screen adapter of *Lolita* is named John Smith. Smith recognizes that the novel is a poem of love, desire, horror and ridicule. The ecstasies of these emotions, like any ecstasy, have not bothered to keep within the traffic lines of convention; they have been controlled only so far as to be fixed in art. It is Smith's job to push this large work through the narrow entrance to Movieland. He is clever enough to see that he need not chop off much or grind it down. All he has to do is to extract some of the center and the outer edges will automatically shrink.

Smith then proceeds to his taxidermy, taking out entrails, putting in stuffing, reducing but retaining lifelike semblance. From Lolita he takes her nymphet precocity; he changes her from twelve to an unspecified midadolescent age, fifteen or so (a bigger jump than from fifteen to thirty). Thus he eliminates Humbert's sexual particularity and makes him more like the usual middle-aged fool. From Humbert he takes, too, all fire, the flaring-up at the merest touch of the beloved, and casts him as a knight-at-arms palely loitering. With the censorable elements "licked," Smith proceeds to beef up the drama. Instead of trying murder with pills, he lets Humbert nearly shoot Charlotte. He deviates from the sole, solipsist viewpoint of the book to give Charlotte a little scene with her first husband's ashes and Quilty a little scene with a hotel clerk. (To please the two stars?)

When Humbert learns that Lolita has been abducted from the hospital, Smith has him throw such a tantrum that he has to be pinned to the floor and threatened with a strait jacket. And Smith suggests a couple of close-ups of his tormented face as he lies there so that we can sympathize with his pain. Who says this story has no heart?

Smith then cuts out the pursuit of the chameleon Quilty as he had previously cut all of Humbert's antecedents (so that we never know who Humbert is or how he got that way or what way it is that he got). He puts in some funny business with a folding cot; he transposes the climactic murder of Quilty to the beginning. What matter that its humorous quality is thus incomprehensible and that the progress of the book is mutilated? It's an attention-grabber. Smith can now be happy; he has squeezed the book through the sound-stage door.

Smith is in fact Vladimir Nabokov, who himself adapted his novel for the screen. What this implies about our culture is sad. This genius (no milder term will fit) could not be "bought." Far from truckling to popularity in his books, he has made it clear that the reader must come to him; he is interested only in those who are willing and able. Others can, if they choose, read *Lolita* for its sexual passages (and be disappointed) or, like Orville Prescott and George Steiner, can dismiss *Pale Fire* as a boring literary prank. It is clear that Nabokov respects the novel. It is equally clear that he does not respect the film—at least as it is used in America. In the first he is content with nothing less than Nabokov in full; but to insist on this in films (we can infer) would be like insisting on Aristotelian form in musical comedy. He has given to films the *Lolita* that, presumably, he thinks the medium deserves.

The fact that the film was executed according to this view dismally confirms his judgment. There are flashes in it of the original. Scalpels gleam in the dialogue from time to time. Several of the scenes with Charlotte, the visit to Dolly Schiller, the murder scene, all have flavor. But instead of a prodigious madman's flaming autobiography in love, we get in sum a rather soggy odyssey of a rueful, obsessed mature man, a diluted *Blue Angel* with a teenage temptress instead of a tart.

Some elements are far above ordinary. As Humbert, James Mason gives his best performance since *Odd Man Out*. Peter Sellers is staggeringly accurate as the American Quilty and Quilty-as-a-German. In accent parts he still gives the feeling of a brilliant mimic rather than an actor; he always seems to be alone, like an entertainer, no matter how many others are with him; but he is dazzling. Shelley Winters is wistful and hygienically slovenly as Charlotte. Stanley Kubrick, the director, has caught in some sequences (the murder, Humbert in the bathtub) an approximation in film style of the novel's style. And he has drawn from Sue Lyon, a somewhat matronly nymphet of fifteen, a performance that is always sound and sometimes sly. Still Kubrick has not made the *Lolita* that, say, de Broca or Truffaut could have made from the same script. It has little impudence or lyric surge or pyrotechnics.

Two facts should have been faced from the outset. (1) Even more than with most fine novels, *Lolita's* effect depends on its prose texture. (2) To "normalize" Humbert's sexual penchant and to remove indications of sexual activity from his story is not censorship but metamorphosis; it results in a different, lesser work.

One way that both these difficulties could have been met—a way perfectly suited to a first-person novel—is the method that Sacha Guitry often used: to "narrate" the film and occasionally to include the narrator narrating. This would have given the chance to use enough of the prose to convey its quality, and it would have given Humbert the chance to comment on his past actions (as he does in the novel and as Guitry did in his films). The general tone could have been: "Yes, this is what I did then and thought lovely. Dreadful, wasn't it? Still . . . it has its funny side, no?"

The temper of the original might thus have been tastefully preserved. The seal of approval of the Production Code Administration, which this version has, might not have been forthcoming, but the film would have dramatized Humbert's belief: "It is not the artistic aptitudes that are secondary sexual characters . . . it is the other way around: sex is but the ancilla of art."

The Connection   (October 27, 1962)

Jack Gelber's play *The Connection* takes place in a loft where eight addicts—white and Negro—are waiting for their "connection" (drug procurer) to arrive with their shots. Four of the eight are jazz musicians who play from time to time, and the jazz does much more than is generally recognized to provide an organic free-form feeling, to create mood, and, in a sense, to advance the play. The connection, Cowboy, arrives with a street salvationist—an old woman—whom he has brought along to divert the police. He gives them their shots; the old woman, the musicians, and one other leave. The rest tend a man who has insisted on taking too much. The torpor with which the drama opened returns as the play ends.

Like collage and assemblage in the graphic arts, like the use of typewriters and radios in music, *The Connection* attempts to blur the dividing line between life and art. The devices to accomplish this quickly wear thin because, when we go to a play, we are more interested in seeing a play than in having it proved that it is not a play. Shirley Clarke, who directed the film version, had a more difficult problem. One cannot pretend even briefly that what we see on the screen is happening *now;* it must have happened in the past and been photographed. She and Gelber have tried to overcome this obstacle by transmuting the choric commentator and photographer of the play into a film director and cameraman making a documentary—which is the film we see. The director and cameraman are present throughout, as is the consciousness of making the film; the director is persuaded eventually to sample heroin.

This elaboration of the pretense of "real" reality as against artistic reality involves a series of artifices that make the wildest fantasy seem like *verismo* by comparison. It is almost like striking a child to point out the holes in this pretense; that the sound recording, the editing, the lighting, and so on, are all studio products. The fakery of this "real" reality reaches its high point when, near the end, the camera moves slowly over the walls of the squalid room, showing cracks and dirt—all this as if it were reportage when in fact this "documentary" is documenting a designer's movie set. The climax of the sequence is a close-up of a cockroach crawling up the wall. How carefully that roach must have been nurtured by a prop man and released at just the right moment.

The body of the film, which is simply the play as flexed by Gelber, has two main aspects: it is an exercise in naturalism and it is a blow at our society, not through the Theater of the Absurd but the Theater of Revolt. Naturalism arose in the last century because artists insisted on following inner truths to their complete outward manifestations and felt conversely that to limit the reproductions of surface details was to cramp inner truth. Like all liberators, these men also liberated pests. One of the pests is the writer who is capable of little more than the reproduction of surfaces; such, in this play, is Gelber. The good naturalist treats even the most sordid details as symbols—manifestations of the life beneath the surface. Gelber thinks his work is largely done when he has assembled the surface details—the taboo language, the bursting boil, the vomit, the nose-picking. If this really is the nature of truth and if none of it must be withheld, why do he and Miss Clarke chicken out of taking us into the toilet that these characters visit?

If the Kodak made every man a Steichen, then facile naturalistic method would make every compassionate and enraged writer a Zola or Dos Passos or Dreiser. But Gelber's gift for dialogue wavers; sometimes pungent, it sometimes sounds like a clumsy translation. His characters are for the most part predictable both in who they are and what they tell us about themselves: the simplistic, goodhearted Negro; the well-read philosopher (Jewish, naturally) who has rapport with the ignorant Negro; the one rat whom all the others can hate. The sole interesting character, the owner of the apartment—named Leach!—is described as a queer who doesn't dare to be queer, but the implications of this are not clearly dramatized. And in a dismal bankruptcy declaration, Gelber uses a black-mirror image of a George Abbot running gag: a silent little man who wanders in occasionally with a portable electric phonograph, plugs it in, listens to jazz, unplugs it and leaves.

But even if Gelber had the talent to serve his purposes, what is the substance of his revolt? No reason whatsoever is given—in this naturalistic play—as to why any of these men became addicts, no antecedents or defeats are noted. A fuzzy general pathos is adumbrated once in a while ("We're all hungry for a little hope"). There is some religious satire with the salvationist, which is dull. We anticipate a reference to the Bomb, and, near the end, we get it: a mention of "those Japanese cats." *Because* this is a mixed white and Negro group, *because* they are miserable, *because* they are waiting for someone or something to relieve their misery, we must—Gelber implies—accept them as a microcosm of our society, with its central dilemmas and delusions and hunger for delusions.

Gelber trades on assumptions. Just as the lesser proletarian writers of the thirties relied on sympathy for the working class to gloss over their deficiencies, so a Revolt writer today can rely on an audience to fill in his omissions. He has only to show a group of pointless drifters, and all of us—panting for a chance to unlimber our *Weltschmerz* and hopelessness—will at once nod and murmur, "Of course. The world today." It is something like that famous convention of gag writers who need only refer to jokes by catalogue number ("221!" "935!") to put one another in stitches. Gelber gives us the skimpiest cues, and we are meant to leap into Kierkegaardian despair.

Beckett's tramps, while waiting for Godot, wormed their way into the utter sickness at heart that even the happiest of us have sometimes felt. Camus's *Caligula* is a series of stunning metaphors of the evil that pursues us until we pursue it. Genet's Blacks are retributors for our history who—we see—will be just as rotten as we are once they get the chance. Compared with these visions of hell, Gelber's play is just a sophomore's disillusion.

The film finishes with the director addressing his cameraman: "It's all over. It's all yours now." He is looking into the camera and is (ah!) really addressing us. *What* is all ours now? What we knew before, we know now. Gelber's assumption that he has brought something home to us is a kind of impertinence.

With the exception of Carl Lee as Cowboy, the cast is generally satisfactory in the scratch-and-mumble vein. The most vivid is Warren Finnerty, who makes Leach resemble a decayed Richard Widmark. Jerome Raphel, the sage Solly, is like dozens of men whom I have fled in Washington Square Park when they wanted to discuss Big Problems.

Arthur J. Ornitz shows again his fine control of realistic photography. Miss Clarke's direction tries earnestly to be imaginative and probing.

Billy Budd   (November 10, 1962)

Five months before he died in 1891, Herman Melville finished *Billy Budd,* the greatest scenario for a novel that I know. The man who had orchestrated *Moby Dick,* if he had survived (in more senses than one), could have made *Billy Budd* another marvelously thick yet lucid symphonic work, instead of leaving it a beautiful, poignant sketch. Twelve years ago Louis O. Coxe and Robert Chapman dramatized the book, fleshing it out perceptively and sympathetically where necessary. Now Peter Ustinov has written a screenplay derived from the book and the play, has directed the film, and appears as Captain Vere. In almost every way the film is a failure, and it is Ustinov's fault.

First, the script is ill proportioned; it seems one more story of naval mutiny, then suddenly develops moral ambitions. But the script might have been made to serve if the direction had been skillful. The picture is paced too slowly, is overemphatic in holding reactions (and the editing often returns us unnecessarily to Face 1 after Face 2 has reacted to something Face 1 said); there is a plethora of shots looking up through the rigging; and many of the scenes, especially the trial scenes, are stagy, cramped, and show no film sense. Yet something of the original might even have won past the incompetent direction.

The *coup de grâce* is Ustinov's performance as Vere, for *Billy Budd* is fundamentally Vere's tragedy. ("When you are on the mainyard, think of me, and pray for those who must make choices.") Instead of the strong, humane, disciplined old sea dog—the Vere that Geoffrey Keen, for example, might have played—we get a falteringly serious version of Ustinov's familiar comic bumbling act. How he could look in a mirror and cast himself as Vere is baffling. How a man with his ear could imagine that he was sounding like Vere is utterly incomprehensible. At one point he walks his quarterdeck with spectacles and book. For the right actor, this incongruous touch would have been effective in a man-of-war's captain. In Ustinov it seems so congruous that it confirms his wrongness for the part.

Presumably Terence Stamp was cast for Billy on the (correct) ground that freshness of spirit was more important than a handsome face. But Stamp simply does not generate sufficient angelic power, an aura of the unwitting moral genius. Robert Ryan, despite his American accent amidst a British cast, might have been an effective Claggart with a director who made him compress and concentrate on the point, instead of leisurely selling more of his by-now standard menace.

The worst thing about the whole venture is that it spoils the possibility of a good film of *Billy Budd* for years to come.

The Trial   (March 2, 1963)

Orson Welles' new, keenly awaited film is "based on" Kafka's *The Trial,* and the first point to consider is the phrase "based on." In film-making there are no absolutes about fidelity to originals, but the better the source is—one might even say the better known it is—the more specific the expectations are in the audience. Welles has adapted Kafka freely. But we mustn't be rigidly literary; he is a film-maker. Two questions are pertinent. Has his picture achieved, through its medium, the same substantive effect as the novel? Or, if not (and this is a big concession when the adaptation is from a work of high stature), has it achieved a cogent effect of its own?

Before we proceed to the film's dazzling virtues, let us avoid trifling suspense and answer both questions in the negative. Kafka's novel, in briefest essence, is an allegory of a man who, representing all that is pathetic in our society, accepts imputed guilt without being clearly accused and eventually accepts punishment by death. Welles' Joseph K. refuses to knuckle under, accuses his accusers of trying to make the world absurd; he not only resists execution, he kills his executioners and is in fact laughing triumphantly at the end. So much for Kafka. But the final flaw is not that the ending has been altered and the theme shunted off but that nothing has really been substituted for it. Welles has no alternative theme. He has simply taken materials that move in a certain direction and, at the last moment, has switched directions. This is not adaption to the film form, it is temporization. It looks like nothing more than the way Hollywood would crunch a difficult book.

There are other alterations that cannot be seen as true adaptation, only as pandering and tinsel decoration. Everything sexual in the book is heavily amplified and a good deal is added. Miss Bürstner, K's typist neighbor, is made a dancer-tart who lounges around in her slip with K. The wife of the court attendant kisses and bites him. His cousin's age is reduced from eighteen to fifteen and a half, and suspicions (false) about K. and her are voiced. Even Leni, the advocate's maid-mistress who is the most sexual figure in the novel, is made more sexual, is shown in her slip and with plenty of rubbings and rollings—to such a degree that her encounters with K. become events in themselves rather than a counterpoint to the theme. These injections of Dolce-Vitamins might be explained by Welles on the ground that we do not live in the 1914 of the novel's composition, that K.'s subconscious today would contain franker images, but it is curious that the sexual images are virtually the only thematic ones to be "updated." There is no reflection of other post-1914 events—the concentration camp, slave-labor camp, nuclear bomb—in connection with such elements in the story as the oppressive authority, the circular, glossy justice, the insinuating despair. No, only the sex is modernized. Thus it seems egregious show-biz—the providing of luscious roles for Jeanne Moreau, Elsa Martinelli, and Romy Schneider.

Welles himself narrates the priest's tale of the man and the gatekeeper at the very beginning, to the accompaniment of a series of drawings. (Then, as the film itself begins, he tells us that the novel is said to have the logic of a dream—perhaps the most helpful remark since Olivier introduced his *Hamlet* as the tragedy of a man who could not make up his mind.) This transposition completely vitiates the cathedral scene when it comes; it leaves the priest with nothing to do and robs the pilgrim of progress. Other scenes—an inserted episode with Miss Bürstner's lame friend dragging a trunk, Akim Tamiroff's mouthings as Block, the advocate's client-lodger—go on long past their usefulness. Locutions like "oh brother," "all that jazz," "joyboy," clash with the European look of the film. The painter Titorelli is, for no apparent reason, tinged with effeminacy. The last scene omits what is possibly the single most poignant and symbolically important touch in the novel: the figure that appears at the distant window, arms stretched toward K. as he lies waiting under the knife.

These and other alterations, insertions, dilations, weaken the film's unity and growth. Any depth it might have achieved in spite of them, any richness of spiritual exploration, is quashed by the casting of Anthony Perkins as K. Welles is notorious for his dubious casting: Tim Holt (*Magnificent Ambersons*), Jeannette Nolan (*Macbeth*), Robert Arden (*Mr. Arkadin*). It seems a persistent egotism that he can make silk out of shoddy. Perkins is his worst error to date, and, as with the upbeat ending, commercial considerations must be suspected. Not that Perkins gives—for him—a bad performance, but an even better one by him would still be out of place. Through this film peopled with strong-featured Europeans in markedly European clothes, Perkins moves in his Ivy League suits with his Ivy League face. His bashful Yankee-boy *persona* is ludicrously inappropriate as protagonist of this conflict of humanism with temporal and divine authority—a conflict seen in terms of *Mittel-Europa* through a Jewish consciousness.

What does Welles give us, then? A number of scenes that are in themselves so brilliantly imagined, so dexterously composed, so dynamically impelled that they almost attain an aesthetics of their own, as a poem may be beautiful in diction though muddy in meaning. (Like much of Dylan Thomas.) The swift weaving motion of the opening scene which in itself seems to hypnotize K.; the editing of the flogging scene; the bursting from the empty corridor into the jam-packed courtroom and the use of the huge mob like a chorus-ballet; the billowing ocean of bundled legal books and papers; the glass-paneled corridors like baroque prisons; the prying, restless, surging camera that seems at times to push Joseph K. along—the over-all quality of an eye impatient with anything but its own piercing insight, of an energy that takes a scene and breaks it open like a nut to show us what is in it—all these and more are evidences of a superb, power-ful talent. The fine sets by Jean Mandaroux are real-unreal (the rivet-studded girders recur in court and cathedral and advocate's house); the lighting—often long and horizontal—and the photography of Edmond Richard take most of the subjects by interesting surprise. Used knowingly by Welles, these elements help to give this film the feeling of the first-rate.

But it is not: because it lacks integral design and accomplishment. Kafka's or anyone else's. Welles stands where he stood, a spoiled big-baby prodigy who cannot resist showing off and who would be un-bearable except that his showing off is often so magnificent. Part of his mistake is in selecting serious material; his worst previous films were *Macbeth* and *Othello*. He needs lesser material with which to work so that his ego has no sizable competition, for he is not capable of dedicating himself to an author, he just wants chances for virtu-osity. The effect here is like turning Joan Sutherland loose in *Woz-zeck* and telling her to improvise.

Everyone interested in films has had high hopes for *The Trial*. In the twenty-two years since *Citizen Kane,* Welles had completed only eight films and none of them had been released exactly as he wished. This picture was talked of as his renascence. But it shows that he lacks the controlling artistic intelligence of an Antonioni or Kuro-sawa. Which means, ineluctably, that he has no view of life that he wants deeply to state, no vision to convey, no relation with his world of which his films are an expression. He is a scene and sequence maker, not a film-maker.

Our age believes in a new phenomenon: talent in the abstract, talent independent of works. Norman Mailer and Edward Albee, for examples, are considered first-rate writers by many, although few would claim that they have as yet written first-rate works. Welles differs in that he has created at least one work (*Kane*) unassailably of the first rank. But since then, Welles has been—and for the time being he remains—among those who would be masters if only they would make masterpieces.

(March 16, 1963)

Other reviews of Orson Welles' *The Trial* have stated that K. was dynamited at the end. As I had written that K. resists execution, kills his executioners, and is laughing triumphantly at the end, I went to see the film again. Except for the last point, I am still not sure I was wrong. Lighted dynamite is tossed into the pit where the guards have pushed K., and in a long shot we see him pick up something to toss at the guards. I assumed it was the dynamite; what else would it be? Then in a longer shot we see an explosion—not definitely in the pit; and as smoke mushrooms, the film finishes. The laugh stops with the blast, which does not prove that K. is dead. The first time I thought that he was not; now I think Welles meant it to be ambiguous. A clear view of the explosion actually in the pit or a glimpse of the surviving guards would have settled the matter. Either way, this last scene perverts Kafka, who put it unambiguously and unprefaced by any note of triumph.

The film's virtues and defects are underscored the second time. Dozens of Welles' effects are magical; but there is no line, meaning, goal. It is neither political nor religious nor Freudian symbolism (all of which the novel has been called) nor any other kind. Perkins' performance seems even more ruinous. The music sounds haphazard. The dubbing, particularly of foreign actors, is poor. I omitted to mention that Welles plays the advocate, looking like a balloon; appositely, his performance is inflated and insubstantial.

Lord of the Flies   (August 17, 1963)

In his film of *Lord of the Flies,* Peter Brook has chosen to look out of the corner of his eye at William Golding's straightforward allegory. It seems to have been made obliquely, in a kind of hurried, snatched, newsreel way, then patched together later into the best continuous film possible. For this tale of English schoolboy castaways, Brook took his boys to a Caribbean island and, in effect, turned them loose, photographing them when they were seemingly unaware. (Yet the best shot is one that is carefully staged: the entrance of the marching choristers along the edge of the sea.) Brook's approach has been tempered neorealism: put "real" boys in the "real" situation, let them feel it themselves, don't turn them into actors. Well, he hasn't. Scenes sag heavily because cues are not picked up, lines are emitted rather than spoken. As a result, characters are not defined, drama is not joined, terror is a long time in coming and is mild when it arrives. The chi-chi cinema décor—arty shots of treetops, quivering leaves, light on the water—does not indemnify.

In this free-swinging method, some swipes are bound to hit. Some of the savagery toward the end is on the Golding standard. Piggy (Hugh Edwards) tells a story about Camberly—supposedly impromptu—that is funny. James Aubrey, as Ralph, has some good boyishly manly moments. But the core of the book's meaning is lost. The title is only literal; we hear the buzz from the beginning. The key scene between Simon and the pig's head—given voice in the novel through Simon's imagination—is reduced to a series of silent close-ups. The scene is thus made meaningless.

Two additional egregious errors. The producers and director went to great pains to find a location and use a technique which, they hoped, would avert artificiality. Then they recorded the dialogue in such a way that the ear is constantly reminded of a studio; and they smeared on music, by Raymond Leppard, which—in the phoniest Hollywood tradition—predicts what is to come and attempts to raise audience temperature when the scene on screen is tepid.

The Condemned of Altona   (September 28, 1963)

With the increasing glibness of faddish liberalism, with the deep, if brief, concern with the Human Condition during creamy expense-account lunches, we get a commensurate increase of films like *Judgment at Nuremberg, A Child Is Waiting, Pressure Point, Raisin in the Sun*. Now we have the worst of the lot, artistically speaking: the film of Jean-Paul Sartre's play *The Condemned of Altona*.

The Sartre work is somewhat lumpy and long, even slightly ridiculous in its lack of embarrassment about outsize, lurid dramatic devices, but it is a whole-souled confrontation of an immense subject, with much art, large political-historical understanding, and no trace of bourgeois moralizing. To this play has come Abby Mann, the Michael Musmanno of screenwriters, and has transformed it into a pat anti-German tract. The dangers of rebuilt Germany are not slight—as Hans Morgenthau, among others, has pointed out, but if anything is likely to make us recoil in the wrong direction, it is such material as Mr. Mann's hysterical superficialities.

The story concerns a Krupplike family of shipbuilders. The older son, an ex-officer, has imprisoned himself since World War II in a windowless room of the family mansion in Altona, a suburb of Hamburg. This self-condemned man, who believes that Germany is still in postwar ruin, is the focus of the lives of his father, sister, younger brother, and sister-in-law. It would be pointless to list all Mann's alterations of Sartre, but here are indicative ones. Some major changes: the father wants the older son to take over the firm, which makes the father seem idiotic since that son is not only unprepared but clearly unbalanced; instead of their reconciliation and joint suicide, the older son kills the father and himself; the sister-in-law, instead of being a former film star who is sick of it, is a practicing actress in a Brecht troupe. (The bits of Brecht confirm that he is now chic with the middle-guard, but the renderings here will not swell his popularity.) Some major additions: the younger son, a lawyer, is first seen prosecuting anti-Jewish hoodlums; the father has an impassioned speech justifying Germany by citing barbarism in Algeria, anti-Semitism in Russia, and McCarthyism in America; in another speech he practically rubs his hands when he says that Germany will some day have the Bomb; other characters get lines like "When I see a Mercedes-Benz, I smell the stench of the gas ovens." (*There* is an utterance that will make Broadway and Beverly Hills gulp with admiration for the "integrity" of Mr. Mann.) In short, the whole script is a reduction of Sartre's complexities of truth, responsibility, and evil into simplifications of poster wickedness.

Vittorio De Sica directed and, in sheerly visual terms, handles matters extremely well. For example, he uses contrasting vis-à-vis close-ups more successfully than I had hoped to see in a wide-screen film. But on other grounds the picture gets wildly away from him. He has made the mistake of working in a language he does not really understand and has relied on a dialogue director named George Tyne who is imperceptive and, apparently, tone deaf.

Fredric March lacks Adenauer granite as the father. Sophia Loren tries earnestly but is miscast as the actress—too melony and Mediterranean and without the bitter, hard, slim-flame quality. Robert Wagner looks right as the weakling son but is also a weakling actor. The English of Françoise Prevost, the sister, and of Maximilan Schell, the prisoner, cannot be understood much of the time. When Schell can be comprehended, he gives new meaning to an old term: ham.

But the real rapine begins with the script. The major themes of our time need a new Mann Act to prevent that gentleman from transporting them across state lines for artistically immoral purposes.

Tom Jones   (October 19, 1963)

Tom Jones has been adapted for the screen by John Osborne and directed by Tony Richardson. An imposing duo, as imposition goes these days; but the Osborne-Richardson film is the product of uncertainty, nervousness, muddled method.

Before the credits, the opening of the story (the discovery of the infant in Squire Allworthy's bed) is done in mock silent-film fashion, with hurried action and printed titles—all the stock parody. Then through the film we get such a hotch-potch of trickery, japery, hustle and bustle—including stopped camera, frenzied intercutting, winks at the audience—that we become increasingly conscious that the director is worried about "getting away" with this eighteenth-century story and would use jazz or gags about Profumo if he only dared. What is even worse is the occasional intrusion of subjective technique. (Almost *every* technique intrudes occasionally; this is the worst.) Fielding's book is the first epic of the man of middle sensuality, but it is still an epic. Richardson has cut right against the large narrative line with his imitations of current continental film vogues, his nagging ambition to be taken seriously by film clubs, and his contradictory worries about holding a large audience. His work on stage and screen continues to define the incongruity between his various ambitions and his less varied abilities.

Osborne's adaptation, presumably made under the director's guidance, suits the helter-skelter, harriedly smart-aleck direction. Whether it is Osborne's doing or the editor's, no scene seems ever to finish; and a last-minute gallows rescue, possibly inspired by *The Beggar's Opera,* has been added unto Fielding.

There are some good elements, particularly the background of squalor, gluttony, filth, painted in vividly à la Fielding's friend, Hogarth. A scene in which Tom and Mrs. Waters woo by eating—gnawing and sucking meat and fruit as they leer at each other—is very funny. Walter Lassally's color photography is exquisite and is done in the prevailing nonsunny English light. Albert Finney, as Jones, enjoys himself heartily but little of a sustained performance is possible here. Susannah York has maidenly charm as Sophia, George Devine makes Squire Allworthy bearable, Hugh Griffith makes wassailing Western appropriately unbearable. Joyce Redman, too long absent, is winning as the wanton Mrs. Waters.

But desperation is writ large over this picture. One is left wondering why, if Richardson and Osborne did not really want to film the novel or were scared of it or lacked even a New Theory to impose on it, they did not leave it alone.

POSTSCRIPT. Seemingly my wonder has been substantially answered: *Tom Jones* is one of the outstanding successes, financially and to a large extent critically, of recent years. But, to me, further acquaintance does nothing for my minority report but underscore it. It still seems to me that the film depends on camera-whirling instead of imagination, brusque truncation of scenes to simulate bubbling pace, laborious uproar to suggest humor and heartiness. Fielding seems further away than ever. In my view, to argue that the film tries to reflect qualities in the novel is merely to emphasize how those qualities have been whooped-up and vulgarized, rather than artistically adapted and directed.

Some discriminating pictorial composition is more evident now (as is the use of filters to lend a romantic tone). Edith Evans should have been commended for her performance of the elder Miss Western, and George Devine deserves more than a pat for the dignity of his Allworthy. Otherwise the success of *Tom Jones* remains for me a very strong argument for the existence of Luck.

The Loved One   (October 23, 1965)

Probably the best that film-makers could have done with Evelyn Waugh's *The Loved One* was to leave it alone; but the difficulties of filming it do not excuse the barbarously botched version directed by Tony Richardson from a screenplay by Terry Southern and Christopher Isherwood. The latter's hand is not clearly evident in the script. Southern has obviously been brought in, as a result of his service on *Dr. Strangelove,* to supply material about missiles, the Air Force, and a reuse of the word "prevert." What was tonally appropriate in Kubrick's film and humorously pertinent, is distorted here into mere trend-following. Southern seems in some danger of becoming the official black-humorist to the studios.

The fuddling of the film is quickly apparent. Before the titles Dennis, the hero, is on an airliner approaching Los Angeles; the woman next to him leaves her baby with him for a moment against his will. Discomfort; fadeout. Then, under the titles, we hear *America the Beautiful.* Then, in response to the Immigration Officer's question, Dennis says he has worked as an AID—an artifical insemination donor. Within five minutes, the pattern is established: trite and heavy gags alternating with terribly strained attempts at the daring. The main question is not good or bad taste but comic sense, of which the film has little.

Changes in the original novel were inevitable, but few are successful. Most of what makes us laugh is from the original, but much of what is retained is bunglingly done (the love scene in the cemetery, the funeral ode). Most of what has been added goes quite past satire to incredibility: the characters behave so cretinously that we feel either they must be aware of the fact or they are insane. One example out of dozens: fat Mrs. Joyboy's gluttony is so overdone that we cannot believe that her son would *not* expect his girl to be disgusted. When, later, Mrs. Joyboy pulls over her refrigerator in her greed and Dennis joins her in eating the mish-mash of foods and sauces on the floor, all we are aware of is the sidelines laughter of Messrs. Richardson and Southern, congratulating themselves on their deviltry. It makes nonsense out of Dennis's character.

Or it would if, by that time, there were still any substance to destroy. All that I was able to enjoy was Jonathan Winters' dual performance as Hollywood hack and cemetery mogul and the use of Liberace as a smarmy coffin salesman. John Gielgud, who can play comedy, does not, as Sir Francis Hinsley. Rod Steiger is uncomfortable and amateurish as Mr. Joyboy; versatility is a splendid aim but here it remains only an aim. Anjanette Comer, as Miss Thanatogenos, has a whining voice and no slightest hint of acting ability. But the fundamental miscasting that ruins the film before it starts is the use of the talented American actor Robert Morse as Dennis. In *The Journal of The Loved One,* a book even more repellent than the film, Southern writes: "Many people consider it absolute folly that Richardson has picked an American to play the role. It is obviously an eccentric choice, but surely he must know what he is doing . . ." O ye of too much faith. Morse's English accent is sporadic and spurious, but what is worse, he completely lacks the upper-class air that effortlessly envelops an English gentleman even in a menial job. At the pet cemetery Morse looks as if he were working his way through Indiana U., not—as a gentleman would—as if he were quite consciously *not* slumming. An actor like James Fox in the part could not have redeemed this film but by his intrinsic quality could have given it some of the Waugh flavor—cruel wit and cool disgust—without which it is just a spineless farrago of collegiate gags.

I was in the small minority of those who disliked *Tom Jones,* in which Richardson's comic talents were hailed. This film continues his substitution of frenzy for spirit, laboriousness for Falstaffian largeness, hectic cutting for light-fingered rhythm. Perhaps in this case, without beautiful color and eighteenth-century costumes, with a largely inferior cast, it may be seen that Emperor Richardson is nearly naked.

From Russia with Love   (April 25, 1964)

The most successful film in Britain at present is *From Russia with Love,* the second James Bond adventure to reach the screen. Ian Fleming's sadistic-suave secret agent is now involved in anti-Soviet shenanigans in Istanbul, the principal girl is Russian, and of course there are other willing ladies, including gypsies. James Bond is again played by Sean Connery, and although he is not very good at it, it seems to be where he belongs. This is not true of Lotte Lenya as a tough spy and Robert Shaw (of *The Caretaker*) as a cool killer. I hope they were both paid well.

Outside of the feeling that the film seemed to end two or three times before it actually finished, only one impression remains strongly with me. All through it I seemed to hear typewriters clicking, pens squeaking, pages rustling. Somewhere at this moment (I thought) a doctoral thesis is being prepared—in contemporary lit or social psychology—on the *oeuvres* of Ian Fleming. Someone is doing a close textual analysis of them all, is making a linear comparison between the novels and the screenplays, and especially is delving for myths, for moral comment and significance. The Age of Innocence is indeed past. A writer can't even be a hack any more—according to the lights of his time—without becoming a Cultural Fact. Children as yet unborn will some day be instructed by a teacher who got his degree in Fleming.

POSTSCRIPT. Although there is not yet a doctoral thesis, the first studies of Fleming—one of them by Kingsley Amis—have now appeared.

The Luck of Ginger Coffey   (October 31, 1964)

The Luck of Ginger Coffey, adapted by Brian Moore from his own novel, is the sort of work that is vastly overpraised simply because it is not phony. In the theater and film we are all so weary of the obviously contrived and the patently false that we tend to overvalue the merely truthful. (A recent example on Broadway is Frank

Gilroy's *The Subject Was Roses*.) Moore's film is about an Irish emigré family in Montreal; and for me it contained little more than what may be called its dermatological fidelity, plus the novelties of Robert Shaw with an Irish accent and Montreal as a setting. If this were a fourth film with Shaw as an Irishman. with Montreal as a setting, and with that fidelity as its main virtue, its lack of intrinsic interest would be very much more apparent.

It has neither depth of character nor point. Shaw, as the self-deceiving, well-meaning failure, is adequate within the limits of the role, but those limits are quickly reached. We know all we ever know about Ginger within the first ten minutes or so, and that little is not rewarding. One of his limitations is that he belies what, presumably, is Moore's theme. We are purportedly dealing with a romantic, trapped and defeated by the humdrum, a man whose rosy unrealities might possibly sustain him in his native country but are inadequate in a chromium-plated bustling city. But there is a difference between romanticism and sheer stupidity. When Ginger turns down the good job with the diaper company because he relies on the newspaper editor's word to make him a reporter, he is the only one in the theater who does not foresee the consequences. He is not a luckless dreamer but a boob. His sorry state at the end is not that of a man who has won through to some painful reality but that of the rat baffled by the maze.

Irvin Kershner's direction was first notable in *The Hoodlum Priest* and makes this film supple. But the décor of grubby minor characters and grubby detail is no substitute for content. Within mortal memory such fearless detail was a promise of import; the promise has too often been broken, as it is here. Ginger Coffey is not a small contemporary hero of fate or circumstance but an essentially dull man who does not justify all the attention that this carefully made film pays him.

The Pawnbroker   (April 24, 1965)

The question of whether tragedy is possible today—especially in films—is raised again by *The Pawnbroker*, and with some seriousness; but the question itself is not consistently well stated, let alone satisfactorily answered. This film, made from the novel by the late Edward Lewis Wallant, is Sidney Lumet's best directorial effort to date; in spite of the sense—persistent in his work—that he is a collector of styles rather than a stylist, there are many passages of harsh strength, created with cinematic fluency. But the goal is titanic, nothing less than Greek agony in coat and trousers, and this is not achieved.

Sol Nazerman is a Jewish refugee from Hitler, in New York twenty years after the event, a man frozen into a carapace of loss, never far distant in his mind from the murder of his wife and children. He lives on Long Island with relatives, travels to his pawnshop in Harlem, does his business as impersonally as is humanly possible. His shop, set in racial and social turmoil meant to parallel that of Nazi Germany, is a front for a big Negro racketeer. When Sol refuses to sign some papers at the owner's orders, he is beaten. Almost simultaneously, his Puerto Rican assistant, a reformed young criminal breezily trying to learn the business, is piqued by a brusque remark of Sol's and helps some hoodlum friends to rob the shop. In a fracas the youth gets the bullet intended for Sol. That, plus the racketeer's beating ministered to break his independence, cracks Sol's shell. Through the avenue of pain, he returns to life.

If a tragic climax, a purification through death and horror, is to take us and move us, two elements, I think, are essential in a work: Its tonality must be consistently spacious, large; and, related to this, there must be no sense of manipulation to distract us from a conviction of fate. As for the former, although the over-all tone of this film is certainly grim, many of the sequences sag into exploitation of naturalistic detail. (The bed scenes between the Puerto Rican and his Negro sweetheart, a tart; the footling do-good ministrations of a spinster social worker interested in Sol; even Sol's one forensic outburst about Jewish history.) As for manipulation, it is intrusive. Sol's life is sheer stasis when we meet him, and it is put into motion by late and obvious devices. He has for some long time accepted completely his position as front man for a criminal; now, suddenly, he decides to resist because he has "discovered" that his boss owns a brothel. We are to believe that this is too much for Sol because his wife was prostituted by Germans in a concentration camp. But can we believe that Sol is so naïve that he never suspected his boss's activities? And if not, if this newly discovered parallel is too much for him, why has not the parallel between the boss's hoods and the camp guards been too much for him long before this?

Equally, the defection of the young assistant, which leads to the robbery attempt, is capricious: caused by one remark of Sol's among dozens of moody ones that he has made. Thus, instead of growth, sure and inevitable, to a tragic conclusion, we have here a *situation,* inert and undynamic, suddenly and arbitrarily wrenched into a tragic attitude and consequently unaffecting.

Rod Steiger, who plays Sol, is convincingly, continently dark in the taciturn episodes. His forte as an actor is brooding presence, implications of power. When he tries to manifest that power, in whatever vein, he often falters. Partly this is because his voice is thin in timbre and narrow in range, particularly inconsistent with his bulk. Partly it is because he is bound in the involutions of the Actors' Studio; we are aware of internal devices being used for a kind of self-flagellation which may, if all goes well, also affect us—instead of a direct actor-audience relation. The voiceless cry over the boy at the end is presumably modeled on the celebrated similar moment of Helene Weigel in the Berliner Ensemble's *Mother Courage;* but the factors in structure and performance described above make Steiger's crisis an observable picture, not an overwhelming event.

The camerawork is by the justly famous Boris Kaufman and is excellent. We can hope, however, that he will now be allowed to drop his specialty: dreamy slow-motion lyricism, which he did first for Jean Vigo in *Zéro de Conduite* (1933) and which he was brought in to supply recently in some sequences of *The World of Henry Orient.* He does it well, but he does everything well and should not be fixed with a trade-mark.

Lumet, aided immensely by Kaufman, has made much of this film graphic and incisive. He has used throughout a subliminal device: a present event or remark prompts a memory in Sol's mind—a split-second glimpse of a past horror. This is soon followed by longer and longer flashes of it until we get a flashback of some duration. (Unfortunately Steiger's face in the camp flashbacks is just as plump as in present-day Harlem.) This pattern is too often used but is nevertheless often effective. Some of Lumet's ideas are undeniably striking: the patterns of motion in the pawnshop, the touch of having the prisoners arrive at the camp in a driving rain. Yet there are only two dependable qualities in Lumet films to date: ambition and an assurance that sooner or later (admittedly here it is later) he will lose control of structure and method.

One last, difficult but relevant point. Why is Sol still so much in the grip of the past? Why is this particular survivor so specially paralyzed? Many of us have known people who have suffered similarly, suffered so grossly that the fact of life thereafter seems (to us) incredible; yet there they are living—working, quarreling, remarrying, propagating deliberately (in one case that I know) to refute the ovens. They are certainly not unmarked or forgetful; yet they are certainly not numb like Sol. I do not argue that all people must respond similarly to experience, only that, because Sol is such a remarkable exception, we miss an explanation.

The Collector   (June 19, 1965)

John Fowles' tour de force novel, *The Collector,* has been turned with considerably more force in the film version directed by William Wyler. The novel was faced with the necessity to be a novel: one felt that the author, gifted and clever, was stuck with an idea that fell between two stools: neither a short story nor a novel. (The intermediate form—the novella—is nowadays a professional nightmare. What is one to do with it? Serious magazines groan at the prospect; popular magazines have taboos of content; book publishers hum and catch the first train to their suburban homes.) The film version is ideal for Fowles' project, for it is complete without the entire second half of the book, which reviewed events that had already been seen from one viewpoint. Fowles himself seemed to sense that the second view was superfluous since he filled it with reminiscence, talk about the H-bomb and socialism, and other paddings that were hopefully disguised as relevant symbols.

An introverted young English clerk, a butterfly collector by avocation, is painfully in love with a snooty girl who does not know he is alive, a girl of a superior social and intellectual class. He wins an enormous sum in the football pools, buys a lonely country house, fits up the cellar comfortably with everything he imagines she needs (including books and clothes in her size), then kidnaps her. She expects rape or worse, and soon discovers that she is dealing with a greater complication: not violent sex but unbalanced love. For she could be raped and either released or murdered; either way it would be over. But the young man treats her with prim respect, and she fears that she will be kept there all her life. Quick with femininity, she soon discovers the range of *her* powers over *him;* and the film settles down into a contest of wits and glands.

There are only two other minor characters, and one of them—a neighbor who bumbles in—provides the one conventional suspense episode. Essentially it is a story of two people; that is the whole point. For beneath the suspense elements, the easy parallels of butter-fly and girl collecting, the easier sexual symbols of the cellar and the pinning of butterflies, there is a social drama of considerable pathos. (In the novel the young man is impotent; by removing that element, the screenplay becomes more, not less, truthful—it avoids some facile Freudianism and achieves wider humanity.) The young man is of the wrong class and education for the girl; he could never even get enough of her time so that she could really know him. In the world-as-is, his love is doomed. So, quite simply, he changes the world. With one abrupt Jehovian gesture, he completely alters the environment in which he and she exist. After he has done it, he discovers that he has banked too heavily on proximity and opportunity, on her falling in love with him. The tragedy for him is that the change of world does not alter her feelings and intensifies his.

Superficially, the story might be called a *Pygmalion* of psycho-pathology, but abnormality is only the dynamic that dramatizes it; the essential agony is common human property. Is there a man with soul so unambitious that he has never murmured: "Ah, if she only *knew* me!" And think, in reverse view, of all those tears wept into lonely girls' pillows, not through rejection but through being ignored. This affecting theme has been clarified out of Fowles' novel by the script writers, Stanley Mann and John Kohn, and makes the ending—in which impulse becomes vice—all the more ironic.

The pair are played by Terence Stamp and Samantha Eggar. Stamp, who was miscast in the title role of *Billy Budd* but who showed attractively confident appeal on Broadway last season in *Alfie,* plays the youth with a nice sense of quietness overlaying a whirring set of complexes. The saturnine normality that he brings to his bizarre behavior creates both fright and sympathy. Miss Eggar, credibly desirable, is competent as the girl and lacks only the last inch of *hauteur,* the absolutely authentic princesslike disdain to harrow the youth with despair.

Excepting the trite suspense scene, Wyler has directed with such skillful concentration on interplay that we are never conscious that this is a film sustained by two actors. Wyler takes every moment for what it is, as it comes along, and makes the most of it; it is only retrospectively that we see it is a bravura accomplishment.

The picture suffers from "overproduction." The color is completely unnecessary, and Maurice Jarre's score is, as in *Lawrence of Arabia,* heavy. Simple black-and-white and simpler music would have enriched the film as these deluxe trappings do not.

West Side Story   (October 23, 1961)

The film of *West Side Story* produces the same brilliant effect as the play. This does not mean that the stage show has merely been duplicated; on the contrary, to get the same effect, it had to be effectively translated into a second medium. Because of the quality of the original materials and of the translation, the result is the best film musical ever made.

The price of its virtue is our disappointment that it isn't even better. For something more than half the film (as with the play), everything meshes so beautifully—with a sense that all the good elements in our theatrical arts have met in the right work at the right moment—that we are led to expect cumulation and a towering conclusion. This does not happen. I left the film, as I left the Winter Garden a few years ago, feeling that I had been cheated of a potentially tremendous experience.

But if that is an inverse compliment, it is still a compliment. The film bursts into life, not merely into action, from its opening splitsecond. Done in color on an extra-wide screen, it begins with stunning helicopter shots of Manhattan which catch the dramatic aspect of the city better than any establishing shot has done before. We zoom down from the sky right to the snapping fingers of the Jets, the white street gang. From then on, the film moves into its story with two concomitant rhythms: the one within the framework of the screen (the movement of the actors) and that of the editing and montage—the juxtaposition of shots. These two powerful rhythms, powerfully employed, along with the irresistible music, take us to the center of a moment of our time.

West Side Story has been overburdened with discussion about its comment on our society. It offers no such comment. As a sociological study, it is of no use: in fact, it is somewhat facile. What it does is to utilize certain conditions artistically—a vastly different process. Through much of the work, dance and song and cinematic skill fuse into a contemporary theatrical poem.

Leonard Bernstein's marvelously apt score has been expertly conducted by Johnny Green and is richly recorded. Stephen Sondheim's lyrics—after how many hearings?—are still fresh, evocative, supple. The weakness of the film is the weakness of the show: its book. Arthur Laurents has supplied pedestrian dialogue throughout (adapted here by Ernest Lehman), and the relentless insistence on the *Romeo and Juliet* parallel, which was probably not all Laurents' decision, maims the last third. The attempt at high tragedy is simply unsuccessful. Tony and Maria are believable and interesting while the parallel with Verona stays in the realm of encounter and of sudden, perilous enchantment. But when heroic motions are imposed on the pair, for which neither their characters nor the texture of the work have prepared us, credibility thins, and we move into Hammerstein-land, where things can sometimes be theatrically effective but are of a lesser order. The artificiality of the last third and the utter falseness of the hinted reconciliation at the end are what cause the disappointment.

Readers who saw this show will, I hope, be impatient with me by now for not having mentioned Jerome Robbins. I have saved him until last because, as exceptional as Sondheim's lyrics are, as lovely as Bernstein's score is, Robbins' contribution is the keystone. Everything else exists *within* his conception. It is insufficient to say that he did the choreography for the film; the film contains his dances but it is derived from the show which he composed in movement from beginning to end. It is essentially Robbins' alchemy that *uses* Bernstein's score, *uses* the drama and color, and transmutes the fine components into an even finer art.

When the curtain rose on the play, we all knew at once that the musical theater had been touched to a new vitality. When the film begins, and the Jets move down the streets of the West Side (studio settings faultlessly blended with location shots), as they mold swagger into ballet, we know that we are not seeing "dance numbers," we are seeing street gangs for the first time *as they really are*—only we have not been able to perceive it for ourselves.

The world has been happily aware for some years that Robbins can speak of his times in the timeless language of ballet. His work in this show was one of the few glories of the postwar American theater. He has now reshaped it, moving the audience into and around the play but without losing the feeling of theatrical presentation. Robbins, listed as codirector, did not actually direct most of the film. He was removed for "perfectionism." (The charge anesthetizes comment.) Robert Wise, an uncommonly qualified director, replaced him. Two of Robbins' dancers supervised the final rehearsal of some of the dances. But all of them were engaged in recording, essentially, Robbins' work.

Of the large cast only Richard Beymer (Tony) is inadequate; his earnestness does not compensate for his lack of appeal. Natalie Wood (Maria) is nicely poignant, and Rita Moreno and George Chakiris, as the Puerto Rican lovers, give vivid performances. The singing, most of which is dubbed, is good.

But it is Robbins' vision—of city life expressed in stylized movement that sometimes flowers into dance and song—that lifts this picture high. If a time capsule is about to be buried anywhere, this film ought to be included, so that possible future generations can know how an artist of ours made our most congenial theatrical form respond to some of the beauty in our time and to the humanity in some of its ugliness.

POSTSCRIPT. From many of the intelligentsia this film brought a strong adverse reaction. To find substantial merit in *West Side Story,* the rubric ran, was to swallow Broadway liberalism and *Kitsch* and to assume that a pure, exhilarating popular-art form was all the better for Doing Good. Occasionally specific arguments were adduced, but most of them seemed to spring from an a priori conviction that such a film must be an abortion.

No one is more jealous of the purity of the popular than the intellectual. These commentators prefer musicals in which credibility of plot and quality of acting are irrelevant and beyond criticism (as they are not in *West Side Story*), which exist for their music and dance. But it is in those very terms that these pictures seem to me inferior to the Robbins-Bernstein-Sondheim work. A favorite of the popular cultists is *Singin' in the Rain* (1952), which is set in Hollywood in the first days of the sound film. It contains several bright numbers; but apart from the fact that, compared with Robbins' dancers, Gene Kelly is only a hoofer, there are dance routines in the film itself that are indistinguishable from some of its parodies of early thirties dance routines. *On their own terms* these films of the popular cultists seem inferior to this picture they deride. Even my own past favorite *Funny Face*—clever and charming as it is—simply reworks old ideas in song and dance. I cannot see why, just because *West Side Story* has a serious subject, its achievements as a musical should be slighted. Additionally, within limits, I think it did much to dramatize its subject.

In some of the flurry over this film, my review figured, and its clear reservations were usually overlooked. Some readers were bothered by my statement that Robbins showed us street gangs "as they really are." I would have thought it obvious that the phrase was not literal, that I was speaking of feelings expressed through dance, just as the *pas de deux* in *Swan Lake* is not a marriage manual but a metaphor. And now objections to the film are said to be sustained because social workers have shown it to delinquents who pronounced it unreal. I daresay that residents of Italian shantytowns would find *Miracle in Milan* unlike anything they have experienced, but would that make De Sica's metaphorical film untrue?

In the rush to prove everything about the film detestable, its score, too, was attacked. Often its weak points (the song *Maria,* for example) were taken for the whole. I note the comments on this score in *Music in a New Found Land* (1965) by Wilfrid Mellers, the musicologist-critic-composer who was the music editor of *Scrutiny.* Mellers is aware of the score's weaknesses but says: *"West Side Story* is a musical, popularly accepted as such, and easily the most distinguished, both musically and dramatically, that has yet appeared." Later: "The negative elements—the destructiveness of the gang life—are splendidly realized in balletic terms, both in the music of the Jets or New Yorkers and in that of the Sharks or Puerto Ricans."

Earlier I called *Spartacus* a trap for snobs. I venture the same opinion—for different reasons—about *West Side Story.* To repeat: *Not* as sociology nor as a new *Romeo and Juliet* but in dance, lyrics, and music—expressing the spirit of a subject—this is the best musical film that I know.

PART II

COUNTRIES

United States

The Hanging Tree; These Thousand Hills   (February 16, 1959)

Plenty has been written about westerns in terms of cultural analysis, but less has been said about them as an artistic form. Their popularity is international, their appeal is to many kinds of people—for example, from President Eisenhower to Lloyd George, who had a stock of westerns in his private film library and often read Zane Grey. The western thrives, I believe, because it is one of the few survivals of pure melodrama, and melodrama satisfies old tribal hungers. The moral issues are clear, the external motions are large, and it is the only current fictional form in which you can be pretty sure that, at the end, the villain is going to be dead: not merely spurned in love or foiled in a business deal but good and dead. It is a lovely uncivilized feeling.

Crime shows are not really comparable. In gangster films we are either treated to the fascination of evil or asked to sympathize with a social victim—quite different appeals. And police films are now so loaded with scientific apparatus—fingerprinting, stain analysis, walkie-talkies—that, as manhunts, they are like African safaris with plane and submachine gun. You have to go to nineteenth-century opera to find another such survival of large-scale melodrama. *Il Trovatore* and *La Gioconda* have preserved it in music, like a fly in amber. The western has preserved it, too, in a mythology created in the last sixty years or so.

Bernard DeVoto, in a famous essay, slashed hard at this mythology; he noted that the gun-slinging, trail-drive West had existed for a relatively short time and that most of the trappings of the conventional western were pure romance. But his historian's outrage failed

141

to reckon with the superior aesthetic power of romance over fact. In six decades there has been created a trigger-fanning Cloudcuckooland with its own ethics and realities, in which the customs and costumes of circa 1875 extend backward and forward at will. It is on this immense reservation—situated not exactly anywhere—that the authors of westerns set their works.

This is not to say that all westerns are alike. They divide sharply into inferior and superior grades. The former, in print, are pulp-magazine caliber and on film are quickies made for the Saturday afternoon trade. (There now seem to be fewer of these; the torrent of trashy TV westerns satisfies the children.) The latter—the so-called adult westerns—are represented in print by such competent storytellers as Frank Bonham and Luke Short and in films by such directors as John Ford and Howard Hawks. Better western fiction is marked usually by strong doses of Hemingwayesque style and by an attempt to give the hero some internal problem as well as an overt one, to strip him of Superman aspects, to make him, mildly, a Hamlet of the plains. In films the literary style is reproduced by means of under-stated dialogue and tight, fast cutting.

There is also a third category—what is sometimes called the western novel (emphasis on the second word). It is usually more precise historically and it may take place before the Civil War or at the turn of the century. It has two other distinguishing features: it diverges widely from the range war or lawman-outlaw or cavalry-Indians plot, and the women in it are much more important and more complicated than in the straight western. Jack Schaefer, A.B. Guthrie, and Dorothy M. Johnson are writers in this group; occasionally it produces literature, as with Walter Van Tilburg Clark and Harvey Fergusson.

Books from this third group are the sources of the two films that prompt these remarks, Miss Johnson's *The Hanging Tree* and Guthrie's *These Thousand Hills*. Both of them are set in Montana in the seventies, one in a gold camp, the other in a cow town. Neither is its author's best work, but both are better than the films that have been made from them. Both authors have been at considerable pains to reproduce an era with some care, and to avoid the character and story clichés of the inferior straight western. And in both cases the movie-makers have taken just so much of the historical milieu and the originality as would fit within the conventional framework. They have shown a nose for whatever of the tried-and-true lurks in these books and have used just enough of the books' individuality to distinguish them from the last western you saw.

The Hanging Tree has one noteworthy feature: it marks the American film debut of Maria Schell, the currently popular purveyor of Elizabeth Bergner-Luise Rainer winsomeness. Why Miss Schell chose this vehicle is baffling. Its one small effective touch is its first sight of her, after she has been lost in the wild for four days, her face baked and disfigured by the sun. But this is an achievement for the make-up man, not the actress. Gary Cooper is the gloomy doctor who nurses her back to her customary *Süssigkeit* and protects her honor from Karl Malden.

These Thousand Hills tells of a young ambitious cowhand (Don Murray) who learns that success isn't everything. Murray is acceptable but the rest of the cast, except Stuart Whitman, are abominable. And, of course, Guthrie's little homespun cautionary tale has been wrenched to provide a final banister-breaking brawl.

It doesn't seem to me superfluous to fret occasionally about the low quality of even "major" westerns. Melodrama is as valid an art form as its cognate at the other end of the spectrum, farce; and certainly no subject matter is per se better suited to films than westerns. The best westerns—*The Gunfighter* with Gregory Peck and *High Noon* with Gary Cooper (in that order, I think)—have been exciting entertainments. Even lesser ones like *Shane* and last year's neglected *Cowboy* (with the accomplished Jack Lemmon) were films that anyone who likes movies could enjoy. But these are exceptions. The overwhelming majority—even when they start promisingly—soon throw believable motivation and dialogue and story development out the ranch-house door. Before long with most westerns, if you wait around at all, it is for the glimpses of magnificent scenery and beautiful horses when the actors are not in the way.

The Roots of Heaven; The Barbarian and the Geisha
(November 3, 1958)

An unusual opportunity to appraise a director's work arises with the virtually simultaneous release of two films by John Huston,

The Roots of Heaven and *The Barbarian and the Geisha*. It turns out to be a sad occasion because neither of these pictures is good; more sadly, neither of them makes a really honest effort to be good. The first is more pretentious than the second, but essentially they are both only blockbuster packages of Technicolor.

The term "integrity," in American art, is generally taken at the low level where it merely means resistance to commercial pressure. Huston has now so far declined that it is at this minimal level that his two new films must be judged—and found wanting. Compromise set its seal on him in *Moulin Rouge,* with its confectionery *vie bohème* and its Zsa Zsa Gabor; it was evident again in *Moby Dick.* (What director of integrity would not have preferred to leave the picture unmade rather than use the wooden Gregory Peck as the titanic Ahab?) I haven't seen *Heaven Knows, Mr. Allison* because I couldn't flog myself into seeing a picture about a Marine and a nun marooned on a Pacific island; and now we have these two films, which finally rivet the collar around Huston's neck.

He has made some fine films: *The Maltese Falcon, The Asphalt Jungle, The African Queen, Beat the Devil, Treasure of the Sierra Madre* (which I saw again recently and think his best). He made an ambitious failure in *The Red Badge of Courage.* These films are, in their foundations, as far as possible from his latest, even though the new ones are varnished with experience. In a recent interview with him and his agent, Huston expatiated on his dreams and ideals and his next pictures. The agent interpolated: "On these, John will get the usual five-figure flat payment plus a substantial participation." Let's not be money-snobs; it's past question that a man can be both a true and a rich artist. But this dual interview seemed to be held with one man with a split *persona.* Huston has by now become yet another example of promise unfulfilled, a talent corrupted—not implemented —by success.

The Roots of Heaven is based on Romain Gary's allegorical novel about a man named Morel who goes to Africa to devote himself to a campaign against the slaughter of the elephant herds. Besides his affection for the great beasts, he takes them as examples of strength without aggressiveness and takes the ivory poachers and sportsmen as example of venality and viciousness. Like Budd Schulberg's recent *Wind Across the Everglades,* which deals with an Audubon Society agent's struggle to protect swamp birds, the success of the script depends on whether the surface facts can be made to deepen: whether (in this case) the elephant can be transformed from actuality to symbol: whether indeed the very word "elephant" can be stripped of its faintly comic overtone. In this the script fails, and inevitably then there is a hint of the ridiculous in the dialogue. When Morel prevents a companion from shooting an opponent of theirs, the companion asks, "Whose side are you on—ours or theirs?" and Morel replies, "Neither. I'm with the elephants." At the end, when an American press photographer suddenly sees the basic beauty of the crusade and throws away his cameras to follow Morel, he exclaims, "I'm a free American citizen. I can help save elephants, too."

The primary count against Huston is that he consented to direct this clumsy, overlong script. Its major errors of flatulence and muddy, mechanical switches of motivation are accompanied by numerous small flaws, such as the line "I don't know why I'm telling you all this" and three arbitrarily inserted disrobings of Juliette Greco. The Huston who did *Sierra Madre* would have lighted his cigar with this script. But he then goes on to compound matters by directing this bombastic and unsound screenplay in a completely pedestrian manner. We know by the end of the first two minutes that the old Huston touch is missing. The movie begins with a jerkily edited short sequence of an elephant hunt, capped with a mysterious and threatening off-screen voice, like a TV serial. Then it moves to a long shot of a hotel in Fort Lamy, and we see Miss Greco coming down the steps. From that we cut to the first of many obviously inserted close-ups, the kind of trickery that the old film-factories employed when building up a star—exactly the sort of practice whose opposite Huston used to represent.

On we go from this disappointing introduction through a film of well over two hours' length unadorned with any touch of directorial imagination except the use and overuse of one device: a character large in the foreground, at one side, past whom we see some significant action. No frames are exceptionally well composed, no sequences have the angles and editing that used to hurtle Huston pictures forward, none of it is distinguished by what used to be the Huston forte: the invention of naturalistic "business" and the seemingly accidental intrusion of the camera, which convinced us that we were getting a peep at an exciting segment of private life in a real world: like a series of animated newspaper shots. The actors are plumped down in front of the camera, speak their pieces loud and clear, and then we plod on to another scene. Missing are the sense that we are cutting to the heart of a situation and the feeling (which Toscanini's music so often gave us) that the rhythm is superbly controlled but is just this side of bursting its bonds. There is no use of the form of the film itself to comment on its subject.

And it *is* dishonest. Is it conceivable that the Huston of *The African Queen* would have permitted the shot in which Miss Greco, after days of travel by truck, after a night in a native hut and a walk through the underbrush, appears in a neatly blocked felt hat prettily tied under her chin?

As for the cast, Trevor Howard works manfully to persuade us that elephants can provide the friendship (the script's word) which human beings so badly need. Miss Greco is unimpressive. Errol Flynn repeats the performance of a drunken English ex-officer that he gave in *The Sun Also Rises*. Paul Lukas is effective in a brief appearance as an old Africa hand, and Orson Welles, unusually restrained, contributes a good sketch of a bulbous TV commentator.

In most respects *The Barbarian and the Geisha* is no better. Its story, based on the exploits of Townsend Harris, the first American consul in Japan, is less pretentious than *Roots* but has little dramatic interest. However, if you can go to it without expecting anything of what a Huston picture once was, you can see some exquisite color photography of Japan. There are sequences in it that are as lovely as any color film I have seen since the Japanese *Gate of Hell* and for the same reason: the scenery and the clothes are beautiful. But what a reason for commending a Huston film!

The color camera is not equally kind to John Wayne (Harris) who looks bruised most of the time. As the geisha who is sent to entertain him and falls fruitlessly in love with him, Eiko Ando is pretty but unmoving. Sam Jaffe, long absent from films, can do little with the "feed" part of Wayne's aide.

On rereading what I've written here, I'm convinced that it is mild compared with what the Huston of 1948 would have written about these two pictures.

The Unforgiven   (April 25, 1960)

It has become almost a ghoulish task to comment on a new
John Huston picture. The latest is called *The Unforgiven,* is set in the
Texas Panhandle in 1871, and is, in a word, ludicrous. One example:
the Indians besiege the hero's house, are temporarily driven off, and
retire over the hill to make war medicine with drums and flutes.
Thereupon Burt Lancaster says, "We'll show them!" He and his
brother carry their piano out into the front yard and Ma (Lillian
Gish) goes out and bravely plays Mozart to defy the redskins.

If one could take the film seriously, one would be disturbed by its
curious race snobbism. (The plot hinges on whether or not an
adopted daughter has Indian blood.) But it would be difficult to
criticize this hodgepodge of crudely stitched sententiousness and lame
story-conference inspirations, in which heavily emphasized early
characters disappear and late entrants suddenly loom large. The direction shows a now-pathetic flash or two of old Huston quality, but
for the most part it is feeble and disconcerted. That Huston could not
get a good performance out of Lancaster cannot be held against him,
but he has achieved what no other director has done: he has got a
bad performance out of lovely, miscast Audrey Hepburn.

Some Like It Hot   (March 30, 1959)

Between an audience and a good film a certain confidence is
quickly established. This is especially true of comedies. The first two
or three minutes are enough to tell you whether a comic film is going
to be a dud; the first eight or ten minutes are enough to establish this
confidence. In it the audience implies: "We recognize that we are in
good hands. Take over." In addition to the fun the picture provides,
there is an extra pleasure in having found a good film and knowing it
while you're enjoying it. It is staggering to contemplate how many
millions of people around the world are going to feel that way about
Some Like It Hot. This new Marilyn Monroe–Jack Lemmon–Tony
Curtis film is a lulu.

In terms of comic devices there is very little in the film that is original, but the use of the material is delightful. In Chicago, 1929, Lemmon and Curtis are indigent musicians who accidentally witness the St. Valentine's Day Massacre. The gang searches for them to kill them, and they don't even have the money to get out of town. In desperation they borrow wigs and women's clothes and, in disguise, take jobs with an all-girl band going to Florida. The singer with the band is Miss Monroe. Their male reactions to her, while frantically trying to remain disguised, and other males' reactions to them in female clothes, constitute the nub of the plot.

Lately, in the wave of sentimentality that always seems to follow success, much has been written to the effect that Miss Monroe is not merely attractive but also has gifts as a comedienne. She has few. She is not nearly as good an actress, for instance, as her Continental counterpart, Miss Bardot; she lacks the French girl's voice, verve, moderate technical proficiency, and certainly lacks her range. But by now Miss Monroe and her advisers have learned where her strengths lie, and this role is superbly designed to conceal the weaknesses and display the strengths—physical and personal. One aspect of her superiority over such pneumatic dummies as Jayne Mansfield, Anita Ekberg, and Diana Dors is that she has learned not to take sex seriously. As a performer she kids sex; and as a character, in this film, she is so humble about her attractiveness that her effect is equal parts sexual and endearing. It is rumpled, unpretentious, good-hearted sex.

Jack Lemmon is easily one of the most expert American actors of his generation. From his first films he has demonstrated technical and temperamental gifts for comedy that are extraordinary; in several recent TV appearances he has shown his ability at the dramatic. His deft, hilariously agonized performance here sets the tone for the picture. In the colloquial vein, and perhaps in others, Lemmon's future should prove interesting in the extreme.

Tony Curtis has neither the innate endowment nor, as yet, the acquired skill of Lemmon, but he has improved so enormously since his first appearance that the very fact of his improvement seems to compensate for the difference between the two men. *The Sweet Smell of Success, The Defiant Ones,* and this film represent a growth of which Curtis can be proud and to which audiences are responding.

However its three stars would probably agree that this picture owes its continuous bubble to Billy Wilder, who collaborated on the script, produced and directed. With easy mastery, he has captured much of the scuttling, broad, vaguely surrealist feeling of the best silent comedies. No one claims that pleasure is, in itself, the highest aim of comedy, but are there many people with such an abundance of completely pleasant hours in their lives that they can afford to bypass these two hours?

The Apartment   (June 27, 1960)

Jack Lemmon is the kind of problem that American films need. He is a vigorous, highly talented, and technically equipped actor with a wide emotional range. Can Hollywood supply him with material that is good enough for him? In *Some Like It Hot* he had a superb farcical part which he played superbly; now the same filmmakers, Billy Wilder and I. A. L. Diamond, have made a comedy-drama for him, *The Apartment,* with diminished success.

The part gives him isolated opportunities which he, of course, exploits to the full; but the script wanders from near-slapstick to the near-tragic; and the story is based on a tasteless gimmick. A bachelor employee of a huge corporation allows various married superiors to take their girl friends to his apartment so as to further his advance in the company. The idea of his being turned out of his bed in the middle of the night so that his boss and a bar-acquaintance may use it is of limited risibility.

You have only to see how Lemmon sustains the early harried scenes (the kind of fragile material very easy to fracture) and how he plays cards with the sick girl he loves (where he manages to tell you delicately a number of things he doesn't say) to perceive that he is a genuine actor, neither a limited trickster nor a mere personality. This picture is not good enough for him. Still, his performance makes it worth a visit. Shirley MacLaine, opposite him, has her little specialty; she can "do" small-scale, snub-nosed humor appealingly enough. But see how flat she falls when she is called on for anything else—compassion, for instance.

One, Two, Three   (December 11, 1961)

Billy Wilder's comedy *One, Two, Three*—although frequently funny—is political satire with an air of daring but without daring anything. Still, Wilder and I. A. L. Diamond, who wrote fresh dialogue for a Molnar plot, have wit; Wilder has wit as a director, too—and the technique to implement it.

The head of Coca-Cola in West Berlin (James Cagney) has—for complex amusing reasons—to convert a young East German Communist (Horst Buchholz) into a well-dressed nobleman-executive. And has to do it in a few hours. The farce is occasionally strained (a man masquerading as a girl with balloons in his bodice, and *do* Communists grab whole chickens off plates?) The trio of Russian trade delegates seem to be playing a return engagement from *Ninotchka*. But despite its disappointments, the film has an over-all intelligent energy.

Buchholz, adequate in high comedy (*Felix Krull*), has little talent for physical farce. Arlene Francis, the American's wife, is an acceptable copy of the character that was George S. Kaufman's chief bequest to our theater: the wise-cracking female chorus. Cagney is called upon to be the dynamo of the plot and never stops humming. The picture is worth seeing just to watch Cagney furiously ordering clothes, apartment, and aristocratic antecedents for the youth; or to hear him say, "The race that produced the Taj Mahal, William Shakespeare, and striped toothpaste can't be all bad."

POSTSCRIPT. Especially, but not only, because of Wilder's subsequent work—the slope through *The Apartment* and *One, Two, Three* to the flat disasters of *Irma la Douce* and *Kiss Me, Stupid*—my review of *Some Like It Hot* now seems too mild. Continuous motion is the heart of farce, a dynamics that generates laughable action after action like guppies propagating in tandem. The motion of *Some Like It Hot* is so bright and furious that it almost achieves a separate identity laughable in itself. That motion is of course not mere movement and is not unvaryingly fast; the result would be hubbub. It is not unceasingly ludicrous; the result would not be funny. But the *impression* is that it is always fast and funny.

There are some who have criticized the young men's masquerading as psychopathic transvestism. One of the burdens of our age is that it has armed the cloddish with terminology.

In the first film on which Wilder worked, *People on Sunday* (Berlin, 1929), there is a sequence in which a city couple go into the suburban woods. As they sink on to the grass in an embrace, the camera moves up, past the trees into the clouds and across the sky. As one is just about to groan, the camera completes an arc and comes down again a short distance away—on a garbage dump. It is both a comment on the couple and a twist on what was already a cinematic cliché; it is also a somewhat flashy device. Much of Wilder's career has followed from this beginning. He has been an antisentimental professional cynic—with the second-stage sentimentality of the professional cynic. As noted above, that sentimentality can prevail eventually. But once or twice in a minor artist's life an occasion may come which, by happy confluence of circumstances, seems arbitrarily to suppress his weaknesses and give unhampered play to his strengths. *Some Like It Hot* is overwhelmingly Wilder's best film so far. This fact is rueful only because his subsequent films display just enough skill to show how much is not within his control. But, at least once, all went well with him; this first-class featherweight farce is a serious achievement.

A Raisin in the Sun; Take a Giant Step   (March 20, 1961)

In a negative way *A Raisin in the Sun* and *Take a Giant Step* are milestones in the social history of the American Negro. Both films are shoddy, and the happy fact is that today there is no compunction to praise them simply because they are well-intended works by Negroes. Too much has been accomplished in the artistic life of our country by such people as James Baldwin, Ralph Ellison, Richard Wright, Gwendolyn Brooks, and Langston Hughes (to name only a few) to permit patronization of these motion pictures because they happen to be by and about Negroes.

A Raisin in the Sun is a film transcription (not really an adaptation) by Lorraine Hansberry of her successful play and is—with one exception—excellently acted. It is largely the excellence of the performance that makes it the better of these two films. As for the script itself, Miss Hansberry's dialogue is generally commonplace and occasionally ridiculous, her perception of character is on the level of Samuel French's catalogue of amateur plays, and her sense of structure is primitive.

She tells the story of a poor Chicago Negro family—matriarch, unmarried daughter, married son and wife and child—and what they do with a $10,000 insurance benefit. The son wants to open a liquor store with some friends and free himself of his humdrum chauffeur's life; his sister wants to become a doctor; the mother wants to give the family a real home. The mother outrages her son by disregarding his ambition, but after she has paid a deposit on a house and put some money away for her daughter, she gives the remainder to the son for safekeeping in order to confirm her trust in him. He then tells us at length about the rosy future he will secure for himself and all of them; however, as anyone knows who has seen a long line of plays from *Juno and the Paycock* to *Toys in the Attic,* the expectation is being grossly inflated just to be deflated. He is—of course—cheated and left penniless.

Matters are not left there. The bulk of the play is garden-variety, lower-class domestic drama. Except for the daughter's Nigerian suitor and the superficial discussion of Negro modes of thought that he provokes, this could be, up to this point, any John Golden suburban play of the twenties transferred to a Negro setting. Now the author, running out of plot and determined that her story shall not only be about Negroes but about race problems, brings us to the barricades. The house on which the mother has paid the deposit is in a white neighborhood, and predictable trouble ensues.

When the daughter-in-law said that there were no colored people in the neighborhood, my reaction was that the mother must be an idiot not to foresee trouble. I see now that the printed stage direction for the line in which she shrugs off the news is: "(Almost idiotically)."

A pussyfooting white man comes from Clyborne Park to buy them off. He is rejected angrily. But after the son has been cheated by his Negro friend, he decides to exploit the viciousness of the whites and sends for the white agent to accept the pay-off. Then—for some completely unexplained reason and after he has expatiated about how he has learned to be a "taker" in this world—he suddenly turns noble and spurns the bribe; they all go off to live in the white community and take their chances.

All this is set in a context of blatantly contrasting sudden entrances (e.g., a conservative young suitor walking in while sister and brother are dancing wildly *à la Africaine*); arbitrary, dizzyingly swift changes of subject and mood as the author struggles to knit her various plot-strands together; a series of mechanical climaxes (every scene ends with its pat little explosion); and gems of dialogue like "Now you say after me, in my mother's house there is still God." Or, "He finally come into his manhood today, didn't he? Kind of like a rainbow after the rain." Or pseudopoetic strophes like "We a people who give children life, not who destroys them." (What people *don't* give their children life?)

As the son, Sidney Poitier—tigerish, impassioned, moving with a marvelous sense of dramatic rhythm—enlarges the play; gives it an agony that is almost too big for it and stretches it at the seams. Ruby Dee is touching as the wife whose marriage and love are being corroded by her husband's frustrations. Diana Sands as the sister and Ivan Dixon as the Nigerian student are always interesting. As the mother, Claudia McNeil gives us minstrel-show faces and stock-company thunder, and, to any matriarchial dignity left in her, applies a self-conscious touch that strikes it dead.

A Raisin in the Sun is to Negroes what *The Rise of the Goldbergs* was to the Jews: a facile vaudeville of "true" characteristics intended to prove that "they" are just like us. "They" quarrel about who is going to use the bathroom first in the morning, just like us; "they" are surly before breakfast, just like us. All men are herein made brothers by the universal refusal of wives to serve anything but scrambled eggs every morning.

It is supposed to be a critic's duty to report that an audience's reaction was different from his own when that is the case. I don't recognize that duty but will nonetheless report that the huge audience around me enjoyed itself thoroughly. In fact the loudest laugh—immense and resounding—came on the line that the son addresses to the rich suitor: "Where'd you get those fagotty white shoes?" The laugh was almost equaled when he repeated the word "fagotty" a few seconds later.

I have now fulfilled my critic's duty.

Take a Giant Step (also adapted from a Broadway play) is about a Negro boy who discovers as he reaches adolescence that his white friends are abandoning him and who goes through a crisis including an innocent session with a prostitute. The concept and writing are straight out of the Golden Age of Television (1950-58) and, except

for the same Ruby Dee, it is very badly acted and directed. It is not
worth the time of anyone, Negro, white, Oriental, or otherwise.

Splendor in the Grass   (October 16, 1961)

Splendor in the Grass, a film about Midwest adolescents, was
written by William Inge, and its parallels with *Summer and Smoke*—
by Inge's master, Tennessee Williams—are interesting. This story,
too, is about a girl of the 1920's who wants a young man and who,
when he tries to make love to her, repulses him out of parentally
derived puritanism. He then turns to a loose girl, and the heroine goes
into a decline. When she comes out of it, he is married to someone
else, and she must settle for second-best.

However, the effect is less like a high-school version of Williams'
play than an Andy Hardy story with glands. The theme is exactly the
reverse of those Victorian pamphlets for youth which pointed out the
dangers of sex; Inge is preaching the dangers of abstinence. We can
only infer that all adolescents deprived of sexual intercourse go crazy.
The miseries of adolescent repression—and of adult frustration, for
that matter—are not a joke, but this film is: because of its simplistic
view of sex and life and its sententiousness.

Natalie Wood plays the girl with a small but adequate set of skills,
and Warren Beatty is unobjectionable, if not overwhelming, as the
boy. Pat Hingle, his father, presents the moneyed version of the Inge
father he played on Broadway in *Dark at the Top of the Stairs:* a
goodhearted, imperceptive, rustic extrovert.

Elia Kazan, who directed has tried to give the film power by pushing people up against each other at every possible moment and then
pushing the camera up against them. His stylistic range has been
narrowed as severely as Studio training narrows an actor, and since
he has done and redone neurotic material like this until he is clearly
weary of it, we are given a bag of stale tricks artifically steamed up to
make them seem pulsing with Truth. Kazan has stated lately that he
is through with Broadway and will reserve himself for films and the
Lincoln Center. This film is something of a gauge that reads very
close to "Empty." He may be through with Broadway for more than
the stated reasons.

America America   (January 4, 1964)

Elia Kazan's *America America* manifests why he is an out-standing director and why he is not a first-rank artist. There are so many lovely and flavorful and dramatic moments that it is a small surprise at the end to realize that the film falls flat.

The chief flaw is a recurrent one in Kazan's work on film and stage: a defective sense of proportion. He does not know when to condense and move on; if he sinks his teeth in a scene or a sequence that he enjoys, the audience can just wait around and be damned to it until he has worried the material in every way his warm invention can think of. Conversely, and possibly in reaction to this, he is sometimes so skimpy that he is unclear.

This is the story of a young Greek, an uncle of Kazan's, living in Anatolia in 1896, on fire to escape Turkish oppression and emigrate to America. His odyssey consists of his hazardous journey to Constantinople; his labors and adventures there; his eventual departure for America and his last-minute subterfuge to be admitted. But the odyssey proceeds by chunks and flashes. Kazan dwells too long on the youth's encounter with a Turkish swindler en route to the capital; takes too long with arrangements for a marriage-for-money that the youth almost contracts; and also takes too long to launch an affair with a married woman who finally pays his passage. As much as an hour of this three-hour film could helpfully be spared—by major excisions in these sequences and by many minor ones that linger over atmosphere, reactions, repeated visual patterns.

On the other hand there are several remnants left which show that snipping has already been going on. For example, a political meeting (anarchist?), ending in assassinations by Turkish police, suddenly erupts into the film without prologue. These uncertainties both about expansion and contraction, result from uncertainties of original conception, abetted by various directorial self-indulgences.

In addition, the film is afflicted with a damaging sound track. Considerable care has been taken to photograph in authentic locations; then a sound track has been tacked on that is damped with studio deadness. Besides, almost all the principal actors contribute flat American accents and voices in their Byzantine clothes and settings. Paul Mann, as the prospective father-in-law, and Linda Marsh, as his daughter, are vocally credible exceptions. Lou Antonio, as the Turkish swindler, sounds particularly false. More care about aural planes and reality, more acute vocal casting and some judicious use of accents, would have kept the sound track from reminding us constantly that it was postrecorded.

Nevertheless Kazan has made this film, which he wrote, with considerable feeling. Aided by Haskell Wexler's excellent photography and Dede Allen's technically fine editing, he has evoked period and place: the plains of Anatolia, shadowed by unfriendly mountains and less friendly Turks; the greasy bowels of Constantinople; the suffocatingly sweet Victorian furnishings of the homes of wealthy Greeks; the human stockyards of Ellis Island. Most important, Kazan has captured what was one of the dominant passions of the Western world for a hundred years and which has not been adequately rendered in films: the burning, almost manic desire to get to America. What happened after the immigrant arrived is another, more familiar story; but this passion was a dominant and crucial one for a century. Despite the film's lags and *longueurs,* Kazan conveys it; and he has chosen well in Stathis Giallelis, the young Greek who plays the leading role with the right narrow-eyed hates, suspicions, obsessions.

Forsaking, at least for a while, the artificial Sterno heat of Tennessee Williams and William Inge, Kazan has made here his most valid work since *On the Waterfront.* The latter had social-political affinities with his roots in the Group Theater in the thirties. Now, in telling of the transplanting of his family tree, he again deals with something that really moves him, that he doesn't have to sauté in a Stanislavsky-Freud chafing dish. But as *Waterfront* was betrayed by a basic moral flabbiness, so this film is crippled by a basic artistic flabbiness. All through *America America* we see opportunities that only a director of Kazan's talent could create. When it is over, we see that it was Kazan alone who fumbled them.

The Birds   (April 13, 1963)

"I wants to make your flesh creep" is the ambition both of Dickens' Fat Boy and of Alfred Hitchcock. The latter has been making pictures for almost forty years, and by a facile realism and a superficial contempt for popular ideals, he has become the film-thriller equivalent of Somerset Maugham: a successful cynic, a man who despises what the public adores just enough to titillate them and to make them pay him well for saying so.

In the country of the bland, the wan-eyed is king. In the commercial film world that lives by stroking the public and making it pay as it purrs, a man who gibes even mildly at Home and Mother seems a very daring fellow indeed. Hitchcock's films have dallied rather than dealt with political affairs, social relations, psychological problems. His reputation for bitter realism depends less on candor and penetration than on clever technique, novelty of settings, and an emotionally cool style. Nothing is more clinical than a Hitchcock sex scene, for all the ear nibbling; nothing is less excited than his camera's eye in detailing threat or murder. His detachment, his teasings about violence seem to many brutally satiric and satirically brutal; but one has only to think of Buñuel to see the difference between a thorough, society-slashing sadist and a moderated, popular merchant of *frissons*. Hitchcock's function at its fiercest (in, say, *Psycho*) has been to give Ma and Pa a naughty little shock before they go home to beer and bed.

In fact Hitchcock's record shows not only that a vein of sentiment has run through his entire career (as with Billy Wilder) but that he has made some blatantly sentimental films. (*Waltzes from Vienna, Jamaica Inn, Rebecca, Mr. and Mrs. Smith, Under Capricorn.*) Some of the soppier items have not been intended as scare pictures; his latest, *The Birds,* is intended as a thriller and is swamped in sentimental insipidity: so thoroughly swamped that the scare scenes—a few of which are very good—seem inserted from another film.

This is his third picture based on a Daphne du Maurier story (which says a good deal). The script, by Evan Hunter (which says more), is absolutely bereft of even the slick-magazine sophistication that Hitchcock's films usually have. The dialogue is stupid, the characters insufficiently developed to rank as clichés, the story incohesive. A madcap San Francisco heiress, attracted to a young lawyer, follows him to the farm where he spends weekends with his mother and sister. During the weekend, the birds of the vicinity—thousands of gulls, crows, and others—mass and attack people in the street, a farmer in his bedroom, school children coming home. Why the birds do this, why they limit it to this community, is not explained; nor is the story concluded. At the end the birds have driven the hero off his farm. What is supposed to happen next?

The scene in which hundreds of sparrows pour out of a fireplace into a small living room is a skin-crawler. An old Hitchcock ploy is replayed—threat in a bright setting. Dozens of crows flock ominously in the sunny playground as the children sing sweetly in the schoolroom. But most of the film's ominousness is silly because it is disconnected with the plot and is devoid of point.

Jessica Tandy, the mother, has one good moment—when she discovers a body and runs voicelessly out of the house and across the yard. Suzanne Pleshette as a local schoolteacher is unobjectionable. The rest of the cast are offensively bad. The crowning impertinence is the use of a girl named "Tippi" Hedren as the heiress. Hitchcock boasts that he discovered her in a TV commercial (quotation marks and all, one assumes). On the basis of this background and training we are asked to watch Miss Hedren flounder for two hours in a leading role.

Hitchcock's direction has never been so tired, so devoid even of attempts at sardonic realism. He allows his editor to bungle—for instance, cutting from a medium shot of a character to a close-up in the middle of a line. He has not even made the most of the beautiful Bodega Bay country in California where this color picture was filmed.

Except for some sharp scenes in *Psycho,* most of Hitchcock's thrillers in the past ten years or so have seemed mere pallid refurbishings of ideas he had once used freshly and frighteningly. The roof sequences in *Vertigo,* the plane chasing the man in *North by Northwest,* the macabre jokes in *The Trouble with Harry,* all struck weak echoes. *The Birds* does not even strike echoes; it is the worst thriller of his that I can remember. In the past Hitchcock has been reproved on the one hand by some moralists who consider him wicked, on the other hand he has been admired by many *cinéastes* (especially the French) who consider that he has beat the commercial film world into letting him make truly corrosive films. The only importance of *The Birds* is in substantiating that both these prior opinions are exaggerated.

Hud   (May 25, 1963)

Among American films of the last few years, *Hud* is outstanding. Its distinctions are Paul Newman's and Patricia Neal's performances, Martin Ritt's direction, James Wong Howe's camera work,
and the swift, sharp knife-play in the dialogue—by Irving Ravetch
and Harriet Frank Jr. out of a novel by Larry McMurtry.

It tells the story of Hud Bannon, a cattleman in present-day northwest Texas, who lives on his aging father's ranch along with his
youthful nephew and a thirtyish housekeeper. As work permits, Hud
hustles his Cadillac convertible from bars to bedrooms, pursuing
pleasure fairly savagely. Between him and his father is long-standing
enmity; his nephew adores him. At the end he is left alone. His father
is dead; the housekeeper, who might have loved him, is driven off by
his vicious physical assault; the nephew has lost his adoration and has
left. Hud, unrepentant, goes into the empty house, opens a bottle of
beer, and defiantly pulls down the shade of the door.

Martin Ritt, a Brooklyn boy, disproves yet again the critical fallacy
about having to be born in a place to deal well with it in art. He gives
us the size and loneliness of the country—a size only emphasized
nowadays by the puny sound of pocket transistor radios. In the middle
of its vastness, the facts of living—the chores, the food, the fun—are
depicted in telling strokes, as the story moves. A common and justified complaint about American films is that they fail to mine the
realities of American life. Ritt does much to answer that charge here.
He has rendered this facet of America in scope and in detail. He has
carefully avoided clichés about its rawness. He has not moved in like
a satirical tourist, to mock it and run; he has endeavored to understand it, to show the relation between this gaunt demanding country
and the men who live by answering its demands.

His handling of the near-rape scene shows that he has been atten-
tive to De Sica and Hitchcock, but to learn, not to imitate. His
outdoor scenes—the greased-pig contest, the shooting of the diseased
cattle, for examples—show a fine grip of the essences of action. In his
earlier films, such as two Faulkner abortions, Ritt's direction was
tainted with the superficially arty, the clever. As with Lumet, one
could see intelligence and ambition but little self of value, only self-
concern. Ritt's Hemingway film, *Adventures of a Young Man,* for all

its streaks of marshmallow, disclosed some sense of the epic, some matching of method and material. In *Hud* his techniques are so firmly in hand that he can forget about them, and he is sufficiently confident in his talent not to worry about displaying it. This film puts him in the front rank of contemporary American directors. If he lacks Stanley Kubrick's ingenuity and wit, he has passed through portentousness to some true seriousness and has transformed egotism into solid personal style.

Similarly, Newman confirms his place in the front rank of American film actors—a rank that at present contains few besides Brando, with Lemmon and Cary Grant at their best. My one reservation is that he needs to change his pace; Hud, as a role, contains too many colors similar to his roles in *The Hustler* and *Sweet Bird of Youth*. Miss Neal, with her lovely mezzo voice and, one might say, lovely mezzo eyes, gives a performance of wit, womanliness, and reticent dignity. Brandon de Wilde's part is similar to his part in *All Fall Down:* adulation that withers and leaves him free. Ritt handles him so that his personal appeal—his youthful freshness—operates on the audience, but there is no clear evidence as yet that de Wilde can really act. His eyes, for instance, are generally dead. Melvyn Douglas, the father, has presence and understanding, but his heaviness engenders a sense of a performance derived from other performances (from Charles Bickford, for one) rather than a recreation of life from life sources.

The film's faults are in the structure of its script. First, some of the small movements of the story are surprisingly trite in view of the freshness of the dialogue. Examples: the fight in the bar over the boy's flirtation is reminiscent of numerous corny westerns. Hud's responsibility for his brother's death is telegraphed early, although much hugger-mugger is wrapped around it, and it lacks any impact when it is finally explained.

More important, the script is incomplete thematically. The mutual antagonism between father and son is poorly grounded. "My mama loved me, but she died," says Hud. Why didn't his father love him, too? The accident that caused his brother's death (a stilted device, anyway) came much later.

The main point of the script, I take it, is to dramatize the slackening of discipline from one generation to the next. Hud is cynical about moral values in what he believes is a corrupted world. But there is no reason in this film for his beliefs. Everyone concerned with him behaves decently; and as for progressive deterioration, his nephew, a newer generation, is as rigorous as the old man. When the nephew leaves at the end, Hud shouts after him, "You'll find out the world is full of crap." But the only "crap" in the story is what Hud himself puts in it, and as a possibly good man warped by a warped world, his case is simply nonexistent.

Thus the script looks less like a valid drama than a vehicle for Newman, pushed and prodded to give him certain tones and opportunities. Further, it depends implicitly on a body of psychological plays and films that have preceded it, as if they carried its roots and generation, as if we were meant to recognize this character and dilemma out of equal parts of Arthur Miller, Tennessee Williams, and Inge, well stirred and set out in the Panhandle sun to boil. The film lacks its own solid, convincing *raison d'être,* so, despite its highly impressive execution, the net experience is theatrical in a derogatory sense.

Hallelujah the Hills   (January 18, 1964)

If competitive film festivals could be taken seriously, it would be a national disgrace that this country has been represented at several foreign festivals by *Hallelujah the Hills.* This purported comedy was written and directed by Adolfas Mekas, a leader in the "New American Cinema Group," usually, and more aptly, called the "Underground Cinema." Mekas is weary of commercialism, and he proves it by being unprofessional. His film is indeed free of every kind of commercial slickness; it is also free of technical competence, acting skill, wit, and invention. It is supposed, occasionally, to parody current films and film trends, but it does not seem parody to me when two young men who are running through the woods are halted by a stopped camera, and a subtitle is flashed under them reading *Breathless.* What has that to do with Godard? Why not say *The Running Man?* Or *Under the Yum Yum Tree?*

Such plot as it has (and its most attractive aspect is its cavalier treatment of plot) deals with the protracted wooing of a girl through several Vermont winters. Otherwise it is marked chiefly by zest and a desire to revolt. But it is a revolution, as H. G. Wells remarked in another context, without a competent receivership.

The Great Dictator (March 28, 1964)

The Chaplin revival series in New York has now presented *The Great Dictator,* and a chief trouble with it is the calendar. It first appeared in 1940 at the end of a decade of impotence and frustration in this country. We had sat watching the Reichstag fire, the Rhineland, Ethiopia, Spain, the Sudetenland, Poland, and all the while we had known that Hitler was wearing Chaplin's mustache, the resemblance was there, the blow was waiting to be struck. At last it came (even then it took courage on Chaplin's part to strike it); and we were anxious to overlook the film's faults. Those who argued, for instance, against the closing oration as artistically extrinsic were dismissed as irresponsible aesthetic prattlers in the face of grim dangers.

It was fitting then to applaud Chaplin; it seems fitting now, without forgetting or withdrawing that applause, to point out that this is a poor film. It is a topical picture, but I know no cosmic law that says an artist may not do topical work. Inevitably, however, what is still effective in it is least topical: the early soldier sequences with their echoes of *Shoulder Arms;* the barber's dazed dance on and off the curb when he is hit on the head; the dictator's dance with the globe; the shave timed to Brahms' Hungarian Dance No. 5.

But three aspects of the film seem not so much dated as downright bad. Recently, I saw *City Lights* again; and I noted how much of it derived from the Victorian theater and how well Chaplin had integrated those elements into the film. Nine years later, dealing with a harshly twentieth-century subject, he not only failed to integrate those old-fashioned elements, he drenched their innate sweetness with syrup. Hannah (Paulette Goddard) is first heard off-stage before she appears (spirit of Sardou!); then, with a surge of violins—the score by Music Man Meredith Willson, incidentally—the camera sweeps up the stairs to light on her sweet, carefully smudged face. Hannah throughout is a character out of *The Cherry Pickers* or *Orphans of the Storm.* All the good people are Good; and when they escape, they settle on a storybook farm where they dine on an outdoor table under a grape arbor in a picture so itchily pretty that it would give Currier the Ives.

Second, the caricature of Hitler seems, much of the time, wrongly conceived. When Chaplin exaggerates what we knew and know of Hitler, and of dictators generally, it is very funny; the opening hate speech, the snatched interludes with the painter and sculptor, the contest for dominance with Bombardone. (And the scene in which Mrs. Bombardone gets trapped in the crowd—hilarious because one always felt that this was a possibility for the undistinguished Mrs. Mussolini.) But Hynkel falling downstairs after his opening speech, the desk pens that stick, Bombardone's train stopping in the wrong place when Hynkel waits to welcome it, are not funny because they do not extend fact, they run counter to it. For example, if Bombardone's train had stopped on an exact one-millimeter hairline that had been preset, *that* would have been caricature. These false jokes simply served at the time as our outlets for frustration. We knew Hitler was not that stupid; Chaplin, on our behalf, was sticking voodoo pins in a figurine of him. Today it is not funny, and it is decayed revenge.

Third, the bit players, without exception, are dreadful. I do not mean the featured players—Henry Daniell, Billy Gilbert, Jack Oakie, Reginald Gardiner—but all the three- and four-line actors. Chaplin notoriously sloughed off the direction of actors in scenes in which he was not involved (see *The Gold Rush*); here it extends even to some actors in his own scenes. And in his first full-dialogue sound film, the bad voices and readings of his supporting cast emphasize their inadequacy. This, too, seems an inheritance of the Victorian theater in which the visiting star's legendary injunction to the local stock company, when they wanted to know about the playing of a particular scene, was simply: "Stay downstage of me and six feet away."

In poetic drama it is only the literal mind that questions the romantic premise. (How could Orlando fail to recognize Rosalind?) But with works that come closer to realism, questions of reality arise. Why had no one ever noticed the barber's resemblance to Hynkel, even in the hospital? Particularly why was it not seen at once by Schultz, his former commander, now on Hynkel's staff?

The closing oration is, of course, a separate short film tacked on to the preceding feature, but Chaplin was aware of that, and anyway that is not what is wrong with it today. It is the content of the speech that sounds false today, because its urgencies have become the truisms of politicking, have degenerated from ideals through propaganda to mere verbiage:

The good earth is rich and can provide for everyone.
The way of life can be free and beautiful.
But we have lost the way. . . .
We think too much and feel too little.
More than machinery we need humanity.

Who said it? Chaplin? Or President Johnson, or Governor Rockefeller, or Premier Khrushchev, or President Nasser? This language, quite apart from whatever truth it may contain, has become international jabberwocky, a kind of "miracle fabric" that can be stretched, cut, and fitted to any politico. We have passed, in genuinely serious political thought, from an era of positive statement into one of negative statement, when the only political utterance that can be trusted is the one that is suspicious, critical, deflationary of uplift-via-helium. Chaplin ends by telling us that "the power they took from the people will return to the people" and exhorts Hannah and us to "look up." The trumpet note of 1940 has gone embarrassingly out of key because the chord behind it has changed.

The Cool World   (May 23, 1964)

A peculiarity of the Negro Revolution is that, unlike other minority struggles, a good deal of the literature supporting the struggle has been created by members of the majority group. Persecuted religious minorities have had few sympathetic novels written about their plight by members of oppressing groups. The injustice of the homosexual's circumstances are dealt with almost exclusively by homosexuals. But many white American writers over the past century have been concerned with injustice to Negroes. In the novel the range is from Mrs. Stowe to Bucklin Moon and Lillian Smith. In the drama there are such names as Ridgely Torrence, Paul Green, Eugene O'Neill. No medals are sought or deserved for this, no redress of injustice would come about except for the efforts of Negroes themselves (just as labor conditions would never have improved, for all the bleeding hearts, without the efforts of strikers). Still, this historical anomaly exists and is worth noting in these days of promised blues for every Mr. Charlie.

The anomaly continues—in films, at least. Shirley Clarke (white) has collaborated with Carl Lee (Negro) on a script made from *The Cool World,* a novel by Warren Miller (white), and has directed and edited the film herself. Miss Clarke's first feature, *The Connection,* used material which, on screen as on stage, struck me as sophomoric and spurious, but her direction had skill and intensity. This second film is in some technical aspects less finished, but the intensity has been intensified. The picture takes us as much by fierce fundamental concern as by its art.

This is not to slight its artistic accomplishments. Miss Clarke has made her film in quasi-documentary style—what would be called neorealism if it came from abroad. She is dealing with juvenile delinquents, and all of them are played by nonactors; only the adult roles are played by professionals. Her film was made principally on location, not in studios; and, as she has said, she wanted to make The Street the protagonist. To this end she has what may be called a visual chorus—a running commentary of sniffing dogs, front-stoop conversations, quickly snatched portraits—that creates the world into and out of which her story moves. This dramatization of the environment by means of the plot, instead of vice versa, is the film's chief and fine achievement.

A fifteen-year-old boy called Duke is ambitious to buy a "piece" (a gun) from an adult racketeer named Priest, to become president of the gang to which he belongs, and to return them to active "bopping" (gang fighting) which has declined in Harlem. It is a fairly patent allegory of an attempt by Duke to attain manhood and identity in the only way accessible to him—the antisocial one. It ends with his killing a boy in a rumble and being taken off to jail by the police.

The language occasionally gets lofty. (Duke soliloquizes: "I see Death everywhere.") None of the boys, including the personable Hampton Clanton as Duke, shows much acting ability, and Miss Clarke has not been able to make many of their scenes knit internally and grow. Most sequences are rather rough building blocks that we accept for the sake of the complete structure. Technically, too, the film must be censured for its sound track, which is sometimes incomprehensible or out of synchronization or wrongly pitched for the plane of distance from the eye, and sometimes sounds like a studio instead of the street. Some of the editing is jagged and this can possibly be ascribed to desired effect, but none of the flaws of the sound track can be taken as design.

Still, after these shortcomings and a few more have been scored, *The Cool World* remains a work of notable power. The very ruthlessness of its detail, familiar though it is, keeps it from being either tractarian or, even remotely, exploitative of the situation. There is no tedious pretense that we are eavesdropping on life itself (as in *The Connection*), yet it is the impact of the factual that compensates for many of the drama's inadequacies. Beyond such bonuses as Clarence Williams' scary drug addict and the pathetic unconcern of Yolanda Rodriguez' teen-age whore, Miss Clarke has made the central image she was after: Negroes living like animals, caged by white men in a filthy zoo. One of the subtler comments is that occasionally, looking far down Fifth Avenue from the heart of Harlem, we get a glimpse of the towering Empire State.

The film does not bother with initial motivations. When we meet Duke, he is already a young criminal, and it is assumed that we understand the social pressures that have discouraged him from anything else. It is a reasonable assumption; but if one prime element is missed, it is some hint of fundamental kinship with other adolescent rebels. The world is becoming increasingly aware of increasing violence in teen-agers generally. The racial injustice that produces Negro delinquents is only one aspect of the inadequacies in us that are producing all adolescent delinquents.

The Searching Eye; IBM Film; To Be Alive!

(September 19, 1964)

There are some fifty films to be seen at the New York World's Fair; I have seen three. Saul Bass' *The Searching Eye,* made for Eastman Kodak, devotes about twenty-five minutes, through the viewpoint of a boy, to the discovery of the universe, from the minute to the celestial. Some of it is lovely; some of it is pointlessly tricky (the widening and narrowing screen); all of it is diminished by essentially trite, imitative concepts that strain unsuccessfully, on pumped poetry, to soar.

The IBM show is as emptily flashy as the Charles Eames pavilion that houses it. The audience files, on various levels, into a steeply banked tier of seats which is then pushed hydraulically up into a huge globe, after which a trap door is swung shut beneath it. This pointless ostentation matches the film that follows. On a number of different-shaped screens, and with the aid of a live interlocutor, we are then shown that an electronic computer works the same, in essence, as a hostess planning a dinner party. This is fairly cold comfort, if true.

To Be Alive!, made by Francis Thompson and Alexander Hammid for Johnson's Wax, has understandably attracted most attention at the fair. These two gifted film-makers, with extensive careers behind them, were given a free hand by their sponsor and have made an eighteen-minute work—photographed in the US, Italy, and Nigeria—whose only purpose is joy. They have used exquisite color and three separate screens—about one-foot space between them. Sometimes all three screens contain the same picture, wide, in three parts, sometimes the same picture repeated twice or more across the three screens, sometimes contrasting pictures, sometimes complementary ones. Always the process is used in service of a feeling or idea, never to draw attention to itself; and its basic accomplishment is a sense of the teeming quality of life: so much happening all at once all the time that three screens can only begin to catch part of it. A child's curiosity, a mother's awed fascination with her baby, an adolescent and a mirror, a wedding—by stating some of these commonplaces without sentimentality but with appropriate sentiment, with a conviction that life is among other things wonderful, these two humane and talented men have produced an exhilarating film. The refreshingly simple commentary is by the poet Edward Field and is spoken simply by Robert Fields; the helpful score is by Gene Forrell. I cannot quite claim that *To Be Alive!* is worth a trip from Des Moines or Duluth. But if you happen to make the mistake of attending this tawdry Midway, this architectural version of the advertising pages of *The Saturday Evening Post,* the Thompson-Hammid film will certainly save your expedition from being a total loss.

Nothing But a Man   (January 16, 1965)

Nothing But a Man is a film that exists by virtue of character reality—that of a Negro man and wife. He is a worker on a railroad section gang who comes to a small Alabama town and falls in love with a schoolteacher. Her father, a minister, has learned to accept his Uncle-Tom place in a racist milieu; she finds her solace and purpose in her work. After marriage the hero does his best to accept local conditions but inevitably runs into trouble. There is a satisfactory conclusion, which is to say it contains neither pat solutions nor ringing promises.

The dialogue, if it lacks distinction, is also free of exhortation and cliché. It sounds like people talking, not like a doughy morality play (as in the recent *One Potato, Two Potato,* a title that describes its characters perfectly). There are no surprises in the story, but there are no manipulations. The verities are made by the two principal actors, Ivan Dixon and Abbey Lincoln. Dixon is continent, strong, unhistrionically angry; the attractive Miss Lincoln radiates quiet understanding, the patience of faith.

The screenplay was written by Michael Roemer and Robert Young; Roemer directed and Young did the photography. In all departments they are intelligent and competent. Facile preachments of future brotherhood by TV dramatists, equally facile preachments of present hate by James Baldwin and LeRoi Jones have prepared the way for this modest, taking film.

Cheyenne Autumn   (January 23, 1965)

John Ford is, after Griffith, probably the American director who has won the greatest admiration among professionals abroad. This has long seemed clear, but it was confirmed for me when I asked a couple of dozen directors throughout Europe who their own favorite directors were. Ford was not only on most lists, he was often the only American. Pietro Germi, who directed *Divorce Italian Style* and *Seduced and Abandoned,* said that when he was a young man, he saw René Clair's *A Nous la Liberté* twenty-seven times and Ford's *The Informer* seventeen times. "They were my real school. They have been the two poles of my career." (Germi's early film *In the Name of the Law,* 1949, is a Fordian western set in modern Sicily; instead of a young lawman arriving in a rustler-ridden town, a young judge arrives in a Mafia-ridden town.)

I thought of Germi, and of the Yugoslav and Pole and Hungarian and others who had talked about Ford, while I sat through *Cheyenne Autumn* and felt a sadness that Ford had not intended. Any good artist with a distinctive personal style, if he lives long enough, runs the risk of having to compete not only with disciples and imitators but with his younger and fresher self. This new film seems more derived from Ford than many derivatives by others, far inferior to the pictures with which he established what may be called the sculptured western: *Stagecoach, Fort Apache, She Wore a Yellow Ribbon, Wagonmaster,* and others. These pictures dramatized cavalrymen, settlers, Indians against the differing landscapes of the West, and managed to convey something of the realistic detail of life in those days at the same time that they converted the whole West into a huge natural theater.

Cheyenne Autumn, which was "suggested" by Mari Sandoz's book, is despite its Technicolor and Panavision 70 a pallid and straitened version of the best Ford, with no new visual ideas and, what is perhaps worse, fumbling use of the old ones—with a few labored interludes in which Ford tries to intensify some facts of daily life and a few incomplete flourishes of action. The acting is bad, the dialogue trite and predictable, the pace funereal, the structure fragmented, the climaxes puny. This is the story of the brave trek of the surviving Cheyenne, against government orders, from their wretched reservation in the Southwest back to their ancestral northern home. We are supposed to have sympathy for them by the facts of their underdog situation; and we are to know the good guys from the bad guys in the story by this sympathy. The white men who kill or harry Indians most reluctantly are the best. But Ford's control of events and atmosphere is so poor that the sympathy is never really generated, and one is only impatient with Richard Widmark, the cavalry captain, for being so inefficient at his job of recapture. (Another example: we are supposed to be outraged at another captain who puts the Cheyenne in his fort's warehouse in mid-winter; it doesn't work because Ford has shown us these Indians living in much worse conditions in the snow.) The action limps badly enough, but the rapport that is essential to westerns, the identification that is their reason for being, is wavering and weak.

The cast is beyond disbelief. George O'Brien, whom I saw in my first Ford film (*The Iron Horse,* 1924), is killed off early, thus preserving for me a shred of boyhood illusion. Widmark slouches and

slumps and yawps through this postacting phase of his career. Carroll
Baker, as a Quaker teacher, sounds like a female impersonator.
James Stewart is brought in for a return vaudeville engagement, a
recent custom in Ford westerns, this time as Wyatt Earp, a character
whom Henry Fonda really played for Ford in *My Darling Clementine*
in 1946. Sal Mineo, as a proud Cheyenne brave, acts like a reject
from a road company of *West Side Story*. Karl Malden cartoons
around as a Teutonic martinet. Edward G. Robinson, as Carl Schurz,
the Secretary of the Interior, has a few scenes in which he stubs out
long, nice-looking cigars soon after lighting them. In these days of
shortage of good cigars, I was more disturbed by the reality of this
waste than by the much less real plight of the Cheyenne.

The Preminger Paradox

(New York Herald Tribune, October 17, 1965)

A one-inch item in the New York *Herald Tribune* of October
16, 1935, announced that Gilbert Miller, the theatrical producer, was
returning from Europe aboard the *Normandie* accompanied by the
Viennese director who would stage his production of *Libel,* Doctor
Otto Ludwig Praeminger *(sic).* This was probably the first time that
this director was mentioned in the American press and possibly the
last time that his name was misspelled.

Thirty years and more than twelve stage productions and twenty-
nine films later, Otto Preminger is legally and fervently American but
is still atmospherically European. Several other contradictions apply
to him and his career. His professional record is both vastly overrated
and incompletely known. He is increasingly adored by certain film
cults, who devote whole issues of journals to him, while other critics,
at least equally serious, view his work with steadily decreasing interest. He has a reputation—deserved—for intelligence and cultivation,
and another reputation—equally deserved—for shrewd exploitation
of mass tastes. He has fought courageously for the liberalization of
constricting film production codes, and he has fought this good fight
with an eye and a half on the box office. He has (I can testify) plenty
of Old World courtesy, and he is (as dozens can testify) a harsh
egotist. There are numerous stories of his high-handed behavior to

actors, there are numerous stories of his quite private philanthropies to actors. In the public eye, he has the aspect of a Prussian officer, but he was born at the opposite end of the Teutonic spectrum—a Viennese Jew.

His latest films, *The Cardinal* and *In Harm's Way,* have summoned most of these contradictions to particular inspection. In the past, much of what he has done has had a gloss of art, but these most recent films seem to have puzzled many because they have no such gloss. *The Cardinal* is a polychrome heartstring-tugger, nothing else; *In Harm's Way* is one more guts-and-glory naval saga, complete with John Wayne as a crusty commander and an ensign son who finally does him proud. Those who have thought of Preminger as a man who managed to smuggle sophisticated work past the Hollywood sentries have been going about with slightly bewildered, hurt looks. This present inquiry hopes to explain why their disappointment is not justified.

Preminger is an outstanding example of the paradox constructed principally by popular imagination. In addition to giving him success, the public has insisted on accrediting him with a stature to which, in fact, he has never asserted title. The world thinks that George Stevens, for example, is a great director because a mighty publicity machine has told them so again and again. But Preminger is cannily innocent. He has never claimed to be a great artist nor, so far as I know, allowed that claim to be made directly for him. It is the American public—stimulated by the fastidious worldliness, the accent, the Erich von Stroheim pate, the air of arrogant and nonchalant candor —who have insisted that the director of *Under Your Spell* (Hollywood, 1936) and *Beverly Hills* (Broadway, 1940) has a special aura of fine artistry. In his newspaper interviews, radio and television appearances, Preminger has done little to discourage the idea that the mantle of Max Reinhardt rests upon him, but it is only his personality, not any specific claims of his, that have encouraged the idea.

Reinhardt was Preminger's idol, mentor, and first theatrical employer; and it is his shade, even for those who never heard of him, that still hovers effectively above Preminger; for although Preminger does not in any way approach him in quality or ambition (nor does he claim it), it is as a quasi-scion of Reinhardt's that he was launched in this country, and it was the projection and maintenance of that image that helped his career to flourish. (Those in a position to know have hinted that even Preminger's drawling speech and nasal voice are derivative of Reinhardt.)

The association between the two began in 1923 when Preminger was seventeen. He was the son of Dr. Marc Preminger, a Viennese lawyer, and was intended by his father for the bar. Reinhardt had recently opened the refurbished Theater in der Josefstadt, an exquisite rococo jewel box of a playhouse, and the younger Preminger, law-bound but stage-struck, applied for an acting audition there. After some months he was granted a hearing, and passed. His father permitted him to pursue acting only if he also pursued legal studies; so for a period of five years he played at the Josefstadt and at lesser theaters in Zurich, Prague, and elsewhere for part of each year, and for the rest of each year he worked at the University of Vienna. He earned a Doctorate of Laws in 1928, thus the title of Herr Doktor in his case was not (as it and the Italian *dottore* so often are) only conversational obsequiousness to a clean collar. While an undergraduate he had, besides acting, also made some attempts with young friends at small-scale production. Now, at twenty-two, he was engaged by Reinhardt as an assistant director at the Josefstadt.

He distinguished himself there by his intelligence and drive and became known as a man with "brilliant elbows." The *Radfahrer* (bicyclist), as he was also known, had already abandoned his acting career; he was now considered a good judge of play scripts, an efficient administrator, and a valuable constructive critic during rehearsals.

His abilities developed; and in 1931 Reinhardt, becoming busier elsewhere, made him head of the Josefstadt. Preminger's first production, a lavish historical drama about the Austrian painter Makart, was an utter failure. He grasped quickly for a lightweight piece to keep him afloat until he could assemble another major production; that lightweight piece was *Tovarich,* which was a resounding success. More successes followed, many of them adaptations of American and English plays, including *The Front Page, Men in White, The First Legion,* and *Libel.* In 1935 Gilbert Miller, an avid harvester of European fruit, saw the Viennese production of *Libel* and decided that Preminger was the right man to direct his forthcoming Broadway production of that play. Preminger agreed, additionally persuaded by an offer from Joseph Schenck, chief of Twentieth Century-Fox, and by the obviously inevitable advent of Adolf Hitler, the chief twentieth-century fox.

Thus "Praeminger" arrived, a doctor, a Reinhardt protégé, a Viennese success, at a time when an émigré had not only the usual glamour attached by Americans to the theater of Middle Europe but the sympathy evoked, rightfully, by the political situation. *Libel* succeeded well enough. He then went to Hollywood and made his first American film (he had done a little film work in Austria). This first opus was *Under Your Spell* with Lawrence Tibbett. But, although *Libel* was only a good courtroom melodrama and *Under Your Spell* was not a good anything, already a certain myth began to be imposed on Preminger's American career; this fine European artist and latter-day Reinhardt (so the implications swelled) was being forced by horrible world circumstances out of his high natural habitat into the low money-marts of Broadway and Hollywood. The declension was not true, of course; he had never been anything but a successful commercial producer-director, and he never himself said otherwise; but the accent, the three names (he was then Otto Ludwig P.), the complete continental "character," made his truthful utterances seem simply winning modesty; made America, in effect, apologize for its crassness by humbly making him as successful as it could.

What has his career been since then? After the Tibbett film, he made something called *Danger, Love at Work,* then quarreled with Darryl Zanuck about the screenplay of Stevenson's *Kidnapped.* He returned to Broadway and directed a revival of *Outward Bound* with Laurette Taylor, which in time he followed with such well-forgotten items as *Beverly Hills, Cue for Passion,* and *The More the Merrier.* While ploughing these Parnassian slopes, he served for three years as an associate professor of production and direction at Yale. In 1939 he directed *Margin for Error,* Clare Booth Luce's comedy-mystery about the murder of the German consul in New York. The well-known Austrian actor, Rudolf Forster (visible briefly in *The Cardinal*) was engaged for the Nazi. When Forster had unexpectedly to leave America, Preminger assumed the role himself. For more than a decade thereafter, he was irritated by the legend that he had played Nazis for a decade. In fact, he played only three others—in films. But as they were the only roles at all that he played in this country, it is easy to see how the legend arose.

In 1942 he came as close to seriousness as he ever came on Broadway when he directed *In Time to Come,* a moderately interesting play about Woodrow Wilson whose coauthor was John Huston. Soon he returned to Hollywood and Fox and a string of a dozen factory-line pictures. But luck, of an aggrandizing sort, was still with him. *Laura,* the first of that string was more than a big success: to some—to those who, for instance, consider Clifton Webb a polished comedian—it is a masterpiece. Also in the string were *Forever Amber* and a limp version of *Lady Windermere's Fan.* His work thus had sufficient quality, in the loosest "trade" sense, to justify the image—furthered by the pithiness of his public statements—of European cultivation doing its best to survive in Yankee muck.

In 1953 he made his first independent film production, *The Moon Is Blue,* a comedy about defloration, which he had produced in the theater and which now ran into trouble with film censors. It is to Preminger's credit that he fought the censorship action all the way to the Supreme Court, that he won, and that his fight resulted in some liberalization of the Motion Picture Association's code. Equally it is typical of Preminger that his stubborn fight and well-phrased public utterances were in defense of a play that could hardly be more trivial or a more patent money-machine. Again, the coolest of commercial enterprises had, by his intelligent prosecution of it, gained prestige for him.

Since 1953 he has made twelve films, nine of which were his own productions. (One of the contract jobs, *River of No Return,* employed Marilyn Monroe in high boots and high drama.) Up to now it is those independent productions that have fed most fully those who believed that he was a first-rank director battling studio restrictions. His own films have given best display to his directorial ability, which, though it is in my view far below the hyberbole that some *cinéastes* lavish on it, often includes theatrical skill and cinematic imagination. More importantly, in every one of his independent productions he found a way to give it some smack of topicality, iconoclasm, or sensation. *The Man with the Golden Arm* dealt with drug addiction —and got an almost-performance out of Kim Novak, which is to date her trickle of a high-water mark. *Anatomy of a Murder,* besides its frank language, had the endearing Joseph L. Welch as, under another name, Joseph L. Welch. *Advise and Consent* had senators as senators. *Exodus* was the first major American film about Israel (and the first hour of it contains Preminger's best direction).

Then there was the saga of Jean Seberg. For all any one has ever been able to show to the contrary, the world-wide talent hunt for a Joan for the film of Shaw's play was honest. The use of Miss Seberg in the part was a gamble that paid off later for others. She is flaw-lessly photogenic and is capable, when she is well handled, of being herself on screen which, if it is no great achievement, is not nothing either. If she had been launched in her second picture, *Bonjour Tristesse,* instead of in the greatest female role written in English in this century, she might have slipped under the critical wire. *Bonjour Tristesse* is only tedious, but *Saint Joan* is a disaster.

Preminger's use of her in the role, his deafness to Shaw's dialogue, his complete inability to transform the play into a film, indicated a general paralysis of his professional senses when he approached work of quality. With scripts like *Exodus* or *Advise and Consent* or *Anatomy of a Murder,* where news interest or frankness or both seemed to lend weight to what was basically trash, he was at his best. Each of these films allowed him to apply intelligence and skill to shallow material, making it seem better than it was.

That was his forte—until these two latest films. Despite the papal medal that *The Cardinal* won for Preminger, it shocked many who had not perceived the paradox of his career, for it is mere and sheer wide-screen Technicolor movie. Its only Preminger "touch" is the ingenious use of John Huston as an actor. *In Harm's Way* lacks even a touch of the touch, unless one is willing to concede the term to a meretricious flirtation with psychopathology in the Kirk Douglas role. Neither of these films has a veneer of reality like *Anatomy* nor a modicum of well-directed sequences like *Exodus.* They are corn, un-popped and unsalted, from start to finish; and thus they afford the clearest glimpse under the patina of sophistication with which Preminger has overlaid his independent productions: a glimpse be-hind the façade that the public itself has fabricated before this man for thirty years.

There is no new cynicism in these recent films, no adulteration, no decline. His work has always been—as these two films have plainly revealed—that of a commercial showman. Why he has lately omitted the veneer can only be conjectured; it may be back next time. He has just finished a suspense story called *Bunny Lake Is Missing,* with Laurence Olivier in the cast, and since hope is morally obligatory in criticism, one has hopes for this new film, despite the recent ones.

But it can now be seen that the loftier qualities attributed to him have been adduced from matters outside the intrinsics of his work itself—from his frankness about Hollywood stupidity (e.g., "Trends are the cancer of the motion picture business"), from his willingness to battle stars (his parting with Lana Turner on *Anatomy* because she refused to wear the clothes he had chosen, and his substitution of Lee Remick), from his courage in fighting censorship and in hiring whom he pleased (e.g., Dalton Trumbo and Ring Lardner, Jr., when these writers were blacklisted by others). These acts, plus his background, gave him a "character" of consequence. The relative, though superficial, daring of some of his material gave his independent productions a further air of vitality and serious engagement. But they were always—at bottom and in specific gravity—mere money-movies under the trappings. And now that he has made money-movies without the trappings, the surprise strikes only those who have been, in effect, self-deceived.

Reinhardt and von Stroheim are the names that have scented the air around him all during his American career, but he is not those men: he is Henry Hathaway or Henry King or George Cukor with the added glamour of a Viennese background, with steely shrewdness, and with a ruthless sense of publicity—namely, the knowledge that telling a little irreverent truth gets more attention than a lot of conventional sugar. It was a sentimental public alone that considered him a genius in chains; but those chains (and he may have been chuckling at this all along) are tailored to fit—are, in fact, his armor.

England

With a Note on Ireland

Room at the Top (April 13, 1959)

In the plentiful comparisons of the Beat Generation and Britain's Angries, one point has generally been overlooked. So far, only the British group has produced works of more than passing or clinical interest to nonmembers of the set. Prominent among these works is John Braine's vivid novel, *Room at the Top*. It has been blessed with a film incarnation which is, in my view, better than the original.

It is the story of young Joe Lampton, an ex-RAF sergeant, who leaves his stifling Midlands home to take a job in the Town Hall of a larger town and who is determined to make his way. He is good at his work, as accountant, but his chief asset is sexual. He cold-bloodedly sets out to woo the daughter of a local tycoon and eventually wins her. En route to the top, he becomes involved with an older woman, married, who falls in love with him and for whose death he is morally responsible.

From one viewpoint it is, like *An American Tragedy,* a story of class and economic conflict focused under the glass of sexual encounter. From another viewpoint it is a story of the futility of complete reliance on conscious planning in human affairs without making allowance for the mines and time-bombs of the unconscious.

Neil Patterson's screenplay, praised by Braine, has strengthened the story line by rearrangement, excision and development and has—in the case of the rich girl, for one—improved the characterization. This is, in fact, that phenomenon in films: a script that makes its drama out of the development and counterpoint of character. The plot is secondary. Life is propagated on the screen and, as always,

177

that in itself is automatically fascinating. In a play or film, only dramatic insight and skill can propagate life: but once the characters breathe, they are interesting if they simply pursue their ingrained desires, without clever plot twists and surprises. (Witness Turgenev and Chekhov.)

I suppose I must note that the dialogue in this film is much more frank than usual. I do this reluctantly, for fear of false emphasis. The people speak as we feel they should—as they speak in the book or in any serious contemporary novel. It is a disgrace that other films are bowdlerized, not a triumph that this one is lifelike.

The director is Jack Clayton, whose only previous picture was an excessively arty short, *The Bespoke Overcoat*. But Clayton's years as an assistant director have borne remarkable fruit; this work is not a promise, it is an achievement. His use of the camera, his eye for evocative locations, his ear (even the heel clicks in the Town Hall corridors contribute brisk immediacy)—all these are extraordinary and create intensity and texture. Even more extraordinary is the way he has made the very tempo of the film match the stages of the story. For a while the pace is swift, restless, impatient, as Joe arrives and scouts the territory. Then as the relationships form and deepen, the tempo gradually broadens—the way compulsive conversation with a stranger evolves into easy, relaxed conversation with a friend.

All these accomplishments one might expect from a talented film man who has learned his job. The surprise is in what Clayton has achieved with actors. Those who have seen Laurence Harvey may not credit that he gives, as Joe, a performance of subtlety and color, springing from inner resources one would not have suspected in him and, in any event, would not have believed he knew how to use. Equipped with a Midlands accent, Harvey fuses persuasively his feelings of revenge for centuries of peasantry behind him, for personal slights suffered, and the discovery in himself of emotional reaches that make his calculated victory hollow.

Alice, his mistress, has been made French in the film, presumably to accommodate Simone Signoret. The transformation is painless because Alice is an outsider anyway, and because Miss Signoret is so heartbreakingly effective in the role that it is now inconceivable without her. Following her good performance in *Casque d'Or* in 1952, she had declined into screen-star immobility, providing only a handsome face behind which the spectator was invited to imagine emotions.

Here, however, Clayton has got from her a rich, sophisticated performance, saturated with the musk of femininity—a fatalistic sexual pilgrim's progress from attraction to passion to passionate love to death.

When Donald Wolfit last appeared in New York, the critics, in sheer ignorance, called his fine, old-fashioned style "ham." As the tycoon in this film, he demonstrates again the power of a resourceful "big" actor who has in him the electric charge of theatrical presence. Two others are outstanding in an unexceptionable cast: Donald Houston, remembered for his performance in *Under Milk Wood,* who is winning as Joe's friend, and Hermione Baddeley as Alice's friend whose apartment is the lovers' trysting place. The film world needs a law forcing producers to offer first to Miss Baddeley all parts for which Hermione Gingold or Renée Houston might later be considered.

Neither as novel or picture is *Room at the Top* the best example of the Angries' quandary: that of the Redbrick University graduate struggling in a society where he is educated above his class origins and further frustrated in a small country that lacks sufficient opportunities for an increasing number of educated young men. Joe is neither "overeducated" nor democratic. He is an adventurer who yearns for power, not equality, and he has before him the example of his future father-in-law—a Yorkshireman married to a Mayfair type. *Room at the Top* is basically no more contemporary a story than *Tono-Bungay.* But as a drama of human drives and torments told with maturity and penetration, it is a rare event among English-language films.

Look Back in Anger   (September 28, 1959)

An American arriving in London in 1956 found that a "dramatic renaissance" was going on, as evidenced by a spate of critical articles and countless decibels of chat. But when it came down to cases, the renaissance amounted, at that time, to one play: *Look Back in Anger.*

I went to it at once and, as it happened, sat behind a visiting Broadway producer. His bored comment after the second act: "I knew that other broad would go for him." I could not reduce the play quite so blithely to its theatrical obviousnesses, but neither was it possible for an American familiar with Odets, Kingsley, Miller, and others to view Osborne as the new messiah. Experienced English playgoers knew these authors too, of course, but had not lived through the events or inhabited the climate that had produced them.

Like so much that is written by the Angries (and this play is virtually their Pentateuch), it seems to Americans an example of time lag. In a country without a true aristocracy, the upsurge of the working and middle classes took place earlier because, basically, the only barrier between them and the upper classes was money. It takes longer—one war more—if the barrier is inspissated with crusty centuries of inherited social status, tradition, and servility.

We must not infer from this that Osborne and his fellows (though many of them are Socialists) are proles, anxious to overthrow the Establishment in order to rule. Osborne's hero, Jimmy Porter, would be as bored by that prospect as by his present condition—just as J. B. Priestley, the old Labourite, is bored now by the tedium produced by the realization of some of his youthful hopes. The Angries are not in revolt against poverty or exploitation as such; they are, in an age of dying gods and living bombs, in revolt against hopelessness. They are starved for causes, and, equally with indigenous dogmas, the majority of them reject one of the most vital causes on earth, the Communist dogma.

But it is the way they see their dilemma, the ensealed quality of their hopelessness, that produces the basic defects of much of their art. Beneath its slashing, vicious dialogue and its swift sexual excitement, *Look Back in Anger* is in effect one long whine: a complaint by Jimmy because he is stuck in the mid-twentieth century and no one is doing anything to provide him with a credo, to make ambition tenable. Thus, although this play reminds us of earlier American plays, it has neither their propagandistic nor their implied meliorist force.

Still a play doesn't evoke widespread serious response unless it touches contemporary nerves. At a discussion in the theater after the performance I saw, numerous young English men and women stood up and said that the play spoke for them. Recently, a young English author, who has just spent a year here, told me that he dreaded returning home to the provincial university where he teaches, and

most of his reasons were virtually word for word from Osborne. Now
an American Osborne could say practically the same things about an
American provincial town, but our response to the New York production of the play was less intense for the reasons outlined above and
because our young people think (or pose as if thinking) they have
reached Stage Two, have gone past protest to withdrawal. Nevertheless the play found an audience here and evoked reaction. Certainly
there is something in it hot and recognizable.

My own view is that *Look Back in Anger* is a partial statement of
existentialism, put in broad, biting, somewhat sophomoric terms. It is
a recognition of the lonely condition of contemporary Western man
—minus the additional recognition that this condition is a grave opportunity, not a final defeat. This is not to say that Jimmy and Alison
ought to walk out at the end chins high and hearts singing; but it is
most definitely to say that their negativism has a positive base if one
searches it out. To be stripped of the earthly and cosmic certainties of
the past is to be lonely indeed, but it is also to be free of illusions.
More mature writers than Osborne have seen with him that the released prisoner may, quite understandably, long for the haven of the
cell of his fathers, but they have also seen that he has given up snug
imprisonment for demanding opportunity. If there is no longer a
comfy old world, there is room to make another. If there is no God,
there is still man.

As for the future, which concerns Jimmy at least as much as (in
his view) the contemporary tattiness of Merrie England, Osborne is
equally quick to settle for shrill, literate cries rather than to face facts
and possibilities. If you believe in the inevitable atomic annihilation
of the world, suicide is cheerier and also manlier than sitting around
waiting for it, complaining the while. (How disappointing it is going
to be for the Jimmy Porters if there is no H-bomb holocaust by the
end of their lives and they find that they have moped about for
nothing!) Only a fool would take it for granted that, simply because
the results would be so destructive, there will never be an atomic war;
but nobody—I repeat, *nobody*—including Jimmy Porter, really believes that destruction is inevitable. Just look out your window. Or
ask yourself whether you would have spent today as you did if you
really believed it.

But, it can be argued, Jimmy thinks that life would still be a sham even if *e* had never equaled *mc* squared. He takes a walk in this film through a park whose benches are lined with mumbling misshapen old wrecks and uses them as a proof that life is a futile mockery. Aside from the fact that the selection of those old faces is a stacking of the cards, one wants to reply that life has always been a futile mockery, and yet great things have been done. One wants to shout back at him: "Why should *you* have guarantees of security, happiness, and health for a hundred years? Mozart scrabbled for a living and died at thirty-five."

Its incomplete view of both the social and philosophical position of its time is reflected in the play's construction and motivation. Why is Jimmy sentenced to run a sweet-stall? Why could not (for instance) a good trumpeter like him, who loves jazz, play it professionally? Why is the visiting actress compelled to stay with him and his wife? Why does the wife come back apologetically at the end as if she were the wrong-doer? These questions have an added significance in a play like this. With ordinary fare, they would be only technical flaws; with Osborne they signify a snipping and forcing of truth to fit a prearranged thesis. The falsities of much of this play *qua* play are artistic flaws in the very deepest sense. Thy are not merely technical errors, they are a kind of philosophical perjury.

One is finally persuaded that Osborne is looking back in somewhat puny resentment—not in any kind of full-bodied anger. We say at last, "What's so special about Jimmy Porter? Who *wouldn't* like life to be perfect?" But most of us have learned that kicking our wives (or husbands) and flouting conventional "decencies" are the most transitory of satisfactions and the least useful of postponements against the real angers, the inescapable true horrors that men must face, have always faced, and sometimes can survive. This play, considered together with *The Entertainer* and *Epitaph for George Dillon,* convinces me that Osborne is as of now a generally brilliant, theatrically imaginative undergraduate—in danger of becoming a case-hardened distorter.

As to the picture itself, Tony Richardson, who staged the play and makes his film debut here, reveals that he is a quick learner, especially from Orson Welles. The picture moves swiftly, arrestingly, and has many striking graphic effects à la Welles (example: dissolving from the flowers falling on the grave to the falling of the curtain). Richard Burton, though too old for Jimmy, plays him excellently, lending, as any actor of this part must do, all the varied color he can command to a relatively monochrome role. As Helene, Claire Bloom reaffirms that she is one of the two or three young screen actresses whose domain is sheer, flooding emotion; when well directed, as here, she is extremely moving. Mary Ure, repeating her stage role as the wife, is good but perhaps a bit too appropriately milky. Gary Raymond is winning as the pal. The distinguished English director Glen Bryam Shaw makes one of his rare acting appearances as the colonel.

Nigel Kneale's screenplay distills the play fairly well. The new episode of the Hindu peddler in the market seems a rather strained effort to enrage us, but we must be grateful to Kneale for writing in the part of Ma Tanner, who is only mentioned in the original play. He has provided an opportunity for Edith Evans of which she makes the most. Anyone who is interested in acting—as distinguished from self-expression, self-flagellation, or trick accents and make-up—ought to see *The Nun's Story* and this film. Dame Edith, as the ethereal Mother Superior in the first and the earthy old Cockney in the second, tells us quietly but magnificently what art is.

The Entertainer (October 17, 1960)

The Entertainer, John Osborne's second play and (with Nigel Kneale) second film, confirms the opinion of him derived from *Look Back in Anger.* He has theatrical imagination, fierce sympathies, and a gift for trenchant dialogue, but he also has flawed perspective and imperfect artistic honesty. He is that perennial, the promising writer; but he breaks his promises as he makes them.

Although in concept *The Entertainer* is more exciting, it is a slighter work than the first. Archie Rice, a seedy music-hall comic, has a second wife, two grown sons and a daughter, and a father who is a retired music-hall star. Archie is a shrewd, selfish animal who deliberately lives in fantasy—a sort of whistling past the graveyard of dead hopes. His only realities are girls and draught Bass ale. The story takes him through the end of illusion to the finish of his stage career. Finally, Archie's only course is abandonment of the halls and emigration to a drab job in Canada.

The most patent manipulation for the jerking of tears is the use of news about the soldier son. (It all takes place during the Suez crisis in 1956.) First he is reported missing, and that is exploited for a family scene; then he is a prisoner about to be released, then he is reported killed; and each of those stages is milked. Osborne could have stretched it out indefinitely.

Why does the daughter leave her London job to stay with her family? She is not asked. Why does she abandon her useful social work and refuse to marry her fiancé? The author simply needed her on hand for his purposes (and, in the film, leaves her final status quite unclear). The old man's death in the wings and the checks that the supposedly sharp Archie writes before he has money in the bank, these too are transparent devices that spread a layer of old-fashioned hokum over a play that is meant to be fearlessly truthful.

We can have even less faith in Osborne as social critic. As an index to postwar Britain, the Rice family is relatively useless. The same shabby theatrical story would have been true fifty years before and could be true fifty years hence in any society that Osborne desires. Does he think success will come to all performers in a perfect world? Will there be no self-deception and drink and frantic fornication to keep off the shadows? And if this is to take his story literally, it is his fault for not having made his people larger. They represent little more than themselves.

Osborne's inconsistencies go further. After animadverting at length about moldy old Europe and Archie's fantasies, he tries to wring pathos out of Archie's shedding of these for a life founded on fact in a new world. Worst of all is the lack of correlation between the Rice ménage, as symbol, and Britain 1960. Visitors to Britain today may not be charmed by all its improvements but cannot feel that they are in a depressed country. This is already a considerably dated play.

The result is something like a spotty opera in which there are some good scenes but not much over-all validity. By developing the theme of Archie and a girl he means to exploit, the film has more of a spine than the play; but it is still only a series of quarrels. Laurence Olivier, in the title role, does the best impersonation of a song-and-dance man by an actor since Alfred Lunt in *Idiot's Delight;* but otherwise his performance is, for Olivier, somewhat disappointing. He creates a telling self-disgust (the picnic scene with the daughter is particularly good) but he indulges in Hamlet-y gazes too deep for

Archie (the scene in the caravan) and sometimes offers us lip-chewing *vice* acting. The net is a gallery of a studied effects, some of which succeed resoundingly, rather than a seamless, realized performance.

As his wife (admittedly a simpler part) Brenda de Banzie is superb. Her drunk scene is one to which all Studio actors should be taken and held fast by the nape of the neck until they have seen it a dozen times. Joan Plowright, despite her Kewpie-doll voice and face, is appealing as the daughter. Roger Livesey, the father, depicts well a faded petty grandeur.

Eclectic is the word for Tony Richardson's direction, which is to say he has a good memory. (The tilted camera from Duvivier, the sharp cuts to visual shockers from Hitchcock and Welles, etc.) The exterior photography, done at Morecambe, a Lancashire seaside resort, is sufficiently vivid to make one avoid it for life.

A Taste of Honey   (May 14, 1962)

A fascinating outline history of Western civilization could be graphed by a chronology of the stories of outstanding epics, dramas, novels. Surprises would occur; for instance, the idea that, for many centuries, literature was concerned only with adventures of the nobility is occasionally contradicted from Hesiod onward. But since the French and Industrial Revolutions, crowns have virtually been replaced by common men. Out of this a curious corollary has arisen: the poorer the characters, the truer the truth of the work must be.

To this, the mid-twentieth century has made an addition. Not only do poverty and low caste certify truth but moral eccentricity intensifies it. "Who cares about rich people?", a remark I heard apropos of *Tender Is the Night* when the novel first appeared, could today almost be amended to "rich and/or conventional people."

A few years ago a nineteen-year-old Lancashire girl named Shelagh Delaney wrote a successful play called *A Taste of Honey* which deals with a sensitive adolescent working-class girl's discovery of love, her difficulties with her mother, her friendship with an understanding boy, her reconciliation with her mother. Thus described, it might have been written in 1900. But this seventeen-year-old's first amorous experience is with a Negro sailor who leaves her expecting a child; her mother is a quasi-tart; the boy who befriends her is a homosexual. By now the general assumption is that a play and film about such subjects must be more honest and interesting than those about conventional people; and to question this is to betray a retrogressive and probably censorious mind. Works like this, we are assumed to assume, help to illuminate "the human condition" (a phrase that is beginning to replace "integrity" in the jargon of TV circles).

This possibly sardonic preamble backfires on me to some extent when I admit, as I must, that a great deal of *A Taste of Honey* is touching and none of it is boring. Part of this may be due to the humorous quality of its shock content. (The girl, curious about homosexuals, says to her homeless friend: "I'll let you stay if you'll tell me what you do.") Besides, Miss Delaney's dialogue is lively, her sympathies are warm. Basically, however, the film seems a slice of eccentric life that impressed her when she saw it or its components around her in Salford. She was right both in theory and in the event to believe that if it moved her, it could probably be made to move others; but such a conjunction of unpleasantnesses, no matter how wryly handled, is bound to take on a pathological color at second hand. We can think, "Poor unlucky kid;" but it's hard to think, "That's life." I wonder whether it has not become a sentimentality to take for granted that "the human condition" refers primarily to the wretched in estate and in sex life. I do not argue for a return to Victorian canon; but the *assumption* that the truth about poor and/or aberrant people is truer than the truth about commuters seems to me one of the snares of facile liberalism.

Miss Delaney's film cannot even be considered a social document, a report from the Lancashire lower depths. Although I doubt that she is in love with poverty, I think she would resent her work's being viewed as social propaganda. She has grown up in a world where poverty and sexual unconventionality are part of the materials of art, and she has written about these people with no more apparent thesis than if she were writing about Mayfair.

The motion picture, like the play, is essentially a meandering introspective narrative, not a drama. The mother's wedding still seems a marriage of plot convenience, and, instead of concluding, the film fades out. This would be quite acceptable in the vein of poetic realism if we could feel that something had been arrived at between mother and daughter or even that nothing would ever be conclusively arrived at between them. Still the work is more effective on screen than on Broadway. Joan Plowright converted the role of Jo into a veristic vaudeville for herself, in which she shone. Tony Richardson (co-director of that production and director of the picture) has had his chief triumph in the firm by discovering a newcomer named Rita Tushingham and evoking from her a performance that takes the role from the appealing gauche theatrical into the privacy of a child's secrets and binds the whole work closer to its source.

The first glimpse of Miss Tushingham is startling. She is chunky, thick-legged, broad-nosed, wide-mouthed; only her voice and her searching eyes are immediately attractive. But in a few minutes we know that within that substantial trunk is a sassy modern Ariel. Her Jo is scared, self-reliant, thoroughly appealing. Miss Tushingham (and *there's* a name for an actress to conjure with!) is now working on the London stage. I look forward to her next film to see whether there is more to her—or, at least, more of the same. The aging-party-girl mother is a fairly easy part, and Dora Bryan is well up to it. Murray Melvin, who resembles a lonely llama, has the shy affection requisite for the homosexual. But Paul Danquah is entirely inadequate as the Negro sailor, and Robert Stephens, the excellent young actor who played George Dillon in New York, is miscast as the mother's friend. Casting "against type" is refreshing, but there has to be a fundamental affinity that makes the surface disconnection not only unimportant but paradoxically helpful. Stephens, for all his ability, lacks conviction as the spiv; besides, he seems too young to care for the mother.

Richardson's direction is, as usual, decidedly mixed. His use of Miss Tushingham and of Melvin is fine; his miscasting of Stephens and his employment of Danquah are deplorable. His direction of some of the intimate scenes is perceptive; but we are again smacked with shots of tawdry beach resorts as in *The Entertainer* and close-ups of ugly people as in *Look Back in Anger*. His "flight from make-believe" drives him right into the arms of pseudoreality. His camera technique, too, is still insecure. In the beginning occur some grainy, hand-held shots in *Breathless* style—a style inexplicably used and dropped; and he still cannot resist hyperdramatic cuts, from a quiet scene to the loud beginning of the next, with the loudness irrelevant to the new scene. At present he is an English Sidney Lumet.

The Loneliness of the Long Distance Runner   (October 1, 1962)

The social paradox of England has been that the mother of parliaments, of Magna Charta and slave emancipation, has treated its own working class with the ruthlessness of a Russian boyar. This is not a matter of long-past history—Hogarth's or Mayhew's or Arthur Morrison's London. Many thousands of people still living in England have known circumstances that would make a Southern sharecropper's lot seem almost enviable. Reconciliation between the world-leading liberalism at the top and the dirty serfdom at the bottom has been slow in coming; and only in the postwar years have working-class themes become a major part of English art.

The Loneliness of the Long Distance Runner, derived by Alan Sillitoe from his well-known short story, tells of an eighteen-year-old slum boy, Colin, who is sent to a Borstal reformatory for robbery. The governor of the place looks on sports as salvation, and ability as a distance runner is discovered in Colin just when the governor realizes a dream: a track meet with a toffs' public school. Colin is trained for the event, and as he jogs around the countryside, there are flashbacks that illuminate his past. On the day of the meet (which begins with an excellent uneasy scene in the dressing room—the Borstal boys on one side, the posh boys on the other) Colin easily outruns the opposition star, and the governor swells. But a few yards before the finish, Colin stops and, with a bow, allows the other boy to pass him and win; thus deflating the governor. Colin has a very small armory against the Establishment; he has used his chief, if pathetic, weapon.

Tom Courtenay, who plays Colin with the grim secretiveness of a small time-bomb, has the grainy look of a teen-age old man. Michael Redgrave is appropriately hearty and ineffectual as the governor, and Avis Bunnage, Colin's mother, has a fierce-eyed, respectable sluttishness. Compliments to Tony Richardson, the director, must be put negatively: this is his least tricky picture to date. Only occasionally (the newsreel-type shots in the mess hall, the star flashes in the retrospects) do intrusive effects mar the immediacy and concern.

The film makes a point (valid) and strikes an attitude (questionable). The point is basically the same as that of *Saturday Night and Sunday Morning:* the "new" English working man feels almost as frustrated and antagonistic as ever. He has an indoor toilet now, a telly, and sufficient food, but his remoteness from whatever his job is, his sense of being exploited, his feeling that he has little chance for worldly advancement or spiritual connection are virtually as strong as ever.

The film's questionable attitude is the proletarian concept of "them" and "us." Everything about "them" is wrong and everything about "us" is right or excusable. It is the self-pity of diluted Marxism, the assumed martyrdom that made American audiences in the thirties root for a worker-hero no matter how much of a slob he was. Colin is offered a job by his deceased father's plant and says: "Why should I sweat my guts out so that they can have all the profits?" Then of course he has no money, needs some in order to have fun, and steals. Fundamentally the system is blamed for his condition, although his father's superstitious ignorance and his mother's infidelity obviously contributed to it (and if those factors are blamed on the system, then—by logical extension—nobody is responsible for anything, including the bosses, who too are products of their environment). In tune with this, the morning after the robbery the police suspect Colin and badger him. No shred of evidence exists as to why they should pick on him; they are arbitrarily adduced as further symbols of oppressive authority. (Why, incidentally, does the shrewd Colin hide the money in a drain pipe where the first heavy rain washes it out?)

While we see flashes of runaway boy being recaptured and roughly used, the Borstal boys sing Blake's *Jerusalem* at an assembly. This seems weak irony. Penal cruelty is universal—even, it is rumored, in worker-states. We can now see that the failure to build Jerusalem in England's green and pleasant land is at least partly the fault of the Bottom Dogs (as it is elsewhere). It will no longer do, as social critique or emotional rally, merely to boom at the Top.

Expresso Bongo   (April 11, 1960)

If, to believe the old saw, one wields more power by writing a nation's songs than its laws, then Great Britain has been a Yankee province for many years by musical fiat. One of the small things that embarrass an American in Britain (not Coca-Cola or tail-fins) is the fact that the British nowadays seem to have virtually no popular

music of their own. Lest you think this a trifle, imagine how odd it
would sound if every jukebox and radio crooned foreign tunes at us
either with British singers or with native ones imitating British accents.

The reasons for this musical imperialism are fairly clear: prior
American industrialization pushed the mass production of films
and jukeboxes—and tunes—faster than elsewhere and made export
imperative; also, the Negro elements, so important in the "new" popular music, had their best chance to flower here. In any event the
Americanization of popular music abroad, and of contiguous matters
like dancing and show business, now seems almost complete.

Sooner or later we were bound to reap the harvest of this Pax
Tympana. One early fruit is a film called *Expresso Bongo* made from
a successful London musical which was expanded from his own short
story by Wolf Mankowitz. Fast, hard, frantic, the film is American to
the teeth—or, rather, just short of them, for only the accents are
different. The songs, the musical-show world of the story, the characters, are derived from American sources.

It is a sort of *What Makes Limey Run?*—the tale of a penniless
young hustling theatrical agent who discovers a teen-age singer and
ingeniously promotes him to success with a record company and with
the TV program of a fading blonde *chanteuse*. All the characters are
out of Damon Runyon via the Mile End Road and Soho.

In addition the whole method of production is American—a technique recognizable to those familiar with, say, George Abbott and
George S. Kaufman. Every scene is played a shade faster than necessary, including love scenes, as if the speed knob on the phonograph
had been turned ahead slightly, and all the dialogue is written in tight-
packed wisecrackese which *sounds* like life but is really the twentieth-
century American theater's equivalent of blank verse. For it is not
realism but real speech distilled and heightened. No girl in the world
ever spoke like Juliet, and no agent or bandsman ever delivered
himself so unceasingly of swift, apt punch lines as these people do. It
is an American convention, an abstraction, and here it comes back at
us across the sea.

Not to mislead, let me say that the film is, like its hero, very clever,
never boring, almost entirely likable. Val Guest, the director, has
been a diligent student of our one-two punch technique; each scene is
built at a sharp incline to an insistent point—indeed, sometimes

snapped off just before the top of the incline, agreeably leaving the point to your imagination. Meier Tzelniker is comfortably professional as the recording executive, and there is nothing much to complain of except that two songs, left over from the stage version, occur vestigially and incongruously in "straight" scenes.

Still, although it is all slick, to one viewer it is vaguely depressing. I got the feeling that London was already filled with skyscrapers and jive and that one world—indivisible and homogeneous—was well on the way. Midst pleasures and palaces, soon, there will be no place unlike home.

The most extraordinary aspect of the film, however, is the fine performance of Laurence Harvey as the agent, interesting not only in itself but as another step in Harvey's career. That career is exceptionally interesting because until *Room at the Top* he didn't seem to have one. From *Romeo and Juliet* to *The Silent Enemy* he was only an attractive young man with a pleasant if unutilized voice and remarkably well-combed hair. Then, as Joe Lampton, he seemed to crack out of a plaster mold, to breathe, to strike and suffer, to *be*. As Johnny Jackson, the luridly colored cartoon of an agent in *Bongo,* he plays with flawless technique and grasp, attacking at high speed, dropping in tender asides to his girl as he machinates, employing an overdrive of energy and address that elevates the pages of a smartly contrived script into the fantasy world where they belong. Sylvia Sims, his girl friend, plays competently, but she merely gives and takes as any merely competent actress would. Harvey overrides his scenes, charges them with a vitality that lifts them even when others are speaking—not by mugging or egotistical "business" but simply by an intensity of attack and imagination that sets his environment vibrating. (Cagney and Brando have this quality, too.)

What made the change in Harvey? Why did he suddenly evolve from pleasant manikin to actor? One can only guess. Jack Clayton, the director of *Room at the Top,* may have been one factor, and it is neither impertinent nor irrelevant to infer that Harvey's marriage to that shining actress Margaret Leighton brought him benefit of counsel. His theater appearances with the Old Vic doubtless exercised him further. But it may be that to carry a figurative knife and speak with an accent gave him the release he needed. I once knew an actor who was bad only when he appeared without heavy make-up—beards, wigs, false noses. Perhaps the ice was cracked for Harvey by the chance to assume the Midlands accent and the savage realities of Lampton. He is equally but quite differently good in the Cockney-Jewish accent and violent fakeries of *Expresso Bongo*. If he keeps his film diet varied, his acting frank and full and interlards it with stage work to keep his sources clear, we all may have the fun of watching an artist develop.

POSTSCRIPT. As to Great Britain's musical revenge in italicized kind, more chickens have since come home to roost—the Beatles and their kin, whose songs seem derived from American "country music." These young men even adopt heavy American accents in singing that contrast strongly with their accents in speech.

As for Laurence Harvey, his subsequent career makes my hope —justified, I think, at the time—seem forlorn.

The Angry Silence   (December 26, 1960)

Thus easily did Stephen Blackpool fall into the loneliest of lives, the life of solitude among a familiar crowd. . . . By general consent, they even avoided that side of the street on which he habitually walked; and left it, of all the working-men, to him only.

So Dickens wrote in *Hard Times* about a working man "sent to Coventry" by his mates for refusing to join a strike. Something over a hundred years later, when the labor-management balance is quite different, the British have sent us *The Angry Silence,* a well-made and disturbing film about a worker in the same fix.

I'm All Right, Jack in satire and this film in earnest treat of items on the debit side of labor progress in the last hundred years, particularly the last thirty. No one with a grain of selfish practicality, let alone social conscience, can wish for a reversal of that progress. But no one with a view of the ultimate purpose of that progress (surely more than the abolition of poverty) can shut his eyes to the facts on the debit side. This new film is concerned with two of those facts: the bullying of management by workers with lately acquired muscles, and the risk of loss of individual conscience in the worker.

Richard Attenborough plays an English factory-hand who refuses to go out on a wildcat strike called for purposes of maneuver only.

When the strike is over, he is shunned by his fellows, his life is made miserable, his son is tormented. He is so bewildered by all this that he almost regrets the decision he is stuck with. He has not taken any reasoned stand; he has simply been forced into his position through anger at being pushed. Now he finds himself supposed by some to be a hero, exploited on TV and in the press. The boss himself wishes he would quit (although, in the spotlight, he can't fire him). Then an even more arbitrary and sudden strike is called, the same worker refuses to join, and this time is so badly beaten by young toughs that he loses an eye. The film ends with his mates' shock at the malevolence unleashed by their thoughtlessness.

Technically the picture is virtually above reproach. Bryan Forbes, an English actor turned writer (he appears briefly as a reporter), has put his story in pungent, well-characterized dialogue. He and Attenborough have coproduced the film carefully. Guy Green and Anthony Harvey have directed and edited it to bear always on the point. Arthur Ibbetson's photography is a ruthless album of the ugliness of factory and factory workers' life. Attenborough and Pier Angeli (as his Italian wife) give performances that are representative because they are not consciously typical (as "little people" so often are in American films). They are human beings first and therefore can state a case for their group. Bernard Lee, the shop steward, Geoffrey Keen, the works manager, and Laurence Naismith, the managing director, seem never to have done anything but those jobs. And Brian Bedford and Brian Murray, as a pair of no-longer juvenile delinquents, are suitably impenetrable.

The film has one very serious fault: its catalyst. The wildcat strikes are provoked by a mysterious agent who comes to this industrial town from London, not from union headquarters, and manipulates Bernard Lee according to secretly telephoned instructions. The object of the first strike seems to be to pave the way for the second, which disrupts the manufacture of an ICBM. We are left with no possible conclusion other than that the agent is a political *provocateur* out to disrupt British industry, if not defense.

No doubt such agents exist, there and here, but to use activities of a Communist(?) plotter as the basis for a film on the excesses of the labor movement seems to me eccentric and melodramatic. Also, it suggests that labor ills would end with the elimination of foreign agents. I wish that this film had been based on one or more of the

truer problems: feather-bedding, jurisdictional strikes, gangster dom-
ination, for examples. We don't need quasi-thrillers about labor; we
need films that show industrial society examining its progress for
flaws. As it is, this is a work of good texture erected on a flimsy,
almost irrelevant base.

Still it elicits two reflections. First, Dickens would have recognized
many of the details; the Western world still lives in the protracted
shadow of the Industrial Revolution. Second, American film-makers
have not touched this toweringly important subject.

The Trials of Oscar Wilde; Oscar Wilde   (July 25, 1960)

I can't recall an occasion before the current Oscar Wilde films
when two pictures on the same subject were released simultaneously.
Comparison is inevitable and necessary. Since they contend for attention (presumably few people will see both), it might be convenient to
treat the films something like political tickets, to run down the line-
ups and compare them. (F or M will indicate the Peter Finch or
Robert Morley film.)

Stars. Finch, if only because he is physically less fitted for the part
than Morley, has had to exercise his imagination to a much greater
extent than his rival. In the past, Finch's besetting temptation as an
actor has been to let the masculinity of his presence and the velvet of
his voice do most of his work for him: merely to appear and let you
take it on credit that such a fetching fellow could not possibly be a
poor actor. This has resulted in some vacuous performances gar-
nished with sex appeal. Here, however, he has made a strong and
subtle effort to generate character, and if there are not enough touching moments, the fault is also the script writer's. He creates a warm,
mellow, and troubled figure whose witty remarks seem the overflow,
rather than the purpose, of his being. His infatuation with Alfred
Douglas and his forebodings about it are tinged tragically.

Robert Morley is by now a corrupt actor, which is not to say he is
unappealing. I remember his stage performance of Wilde some twenty-
five years ago as having cut close to the nerve, conveying a feeling of
something fine caught in an incongruous but elegant body. By now he
has become a one-man business—R. Morley Inc., Specialist in
Elephantine Urbanity, Elaborate Phrases Humorously Mouthed to

Order. He does it all with impeccable timing and poise, and occasionally he comes close to moving us, but it is too late for him to bother about acting. He has developed a unique and highly successful line of work, and he is entertaining when he sticks to it.

Alfred Douglas. John Fraser (F) is perfect: Grecian, volatile, a minx without mincing. John Neville (M) is rather too venerable for the part and a bit fruity: an actor full of pear-shaped tones and distressingly perfect diction.

Queensbury. Lionel Jeffries (F) is a crabbed, frightening, somehow understandable madman. Edward Chapman (M) is an old-fashioned heavy.

Edward Carson. James Mason (F) gives the prosecutor the appropriate Irish brogue, Ralph Richardson gives him Richardson incision. Not much to choose between them.

Direction. Ken Hughes (F) has, with the exception of the long opening scene, managed to lose the staginess that often dogs Victorian films, courtroom films, and films about playwrights. His picture achieves a good cinematic flow. Gregory Ratoff's direction (M) is deplorable: and so is the lighting.

Screenplay. Here Jo Eisinger (M) has an edge. Ken Hughes (F) has written a less lumpy script, one which—again excepting the first scene—avoids being an anthology of *bon mots* and famous names. Because he uses all three trials, he gives a fuller sense of Wilde's protracted torment. And (partly because of Fraser) his script is much more convincing about the Lord Alfred relationship. But he has skimped a crucial matter which is developed more fully by Eisinger. What convicted Wilde was not his purple-eyed liaison with Douglas but his association with a lot of wretched male prostitutes. It is conceivable that, with the aid of his own eloquence on the subject of "pure" male love, a man of Wilde's eminence might have been acquitted. But when that grubby troop began to parade in from the male brothel, Parnassus blew up and Wilde was finished. Also, Eisinger attempts to explain Wilde's refusal to flee and his almost insanely incredible testimony by having Wilde say that he felt like a character in a play with no will of his own, speaking foreordained words. The matter was, of course, enormously complicated: among other things, I think that Wilde, who for all his bohemianism was an Irish Victorian of strong religious bent, willed his own punishment; but Eisinger at least sketches in an explanation.

On points, then, the Finch film is better, if unsatisfactory. But

neither film faces the real issue. Both pretend that Wilde was martyr-
ized because of a platonic love that was misunderstood by Philistines.
In fact he was pilloried because of acts which, if they had been
heterosexual, would have elicited about equal parts of conventional
shock and envy. What was on trial here, essentially, was a person's
right to be homosexual. It was simply too early in the calendar of
social progress for Wilde to claim that right.

Saturday Night and Sunday Morning   (April 17, 1961)

The new school of British social-realist films now encounters
a second difficulty in this country. The first, which did not prevent a
few of these films from finding an audience, was the time lag; American art discovered the proletariat some thirty years ago. The second
hurdle is simply surfeit.

This is a pity because the latest of these British films, *Saturday
Night and Sunday Morning,* is one of the best of the movement, and it
is the first one that faces certain emotional implications for the
present-day working class. Arthur Seaton, its hero, is not out of
Dreiser or Lawrence or John Braine, surging upward; he is a proletarian, consciously trapped in his class, both exultant in and exasper-
ated by the improvement of his lot over his dad's. Better factory
conditions and full employment and the National Health Service have
given him armor against poverty and the boss's threat of discharge;
but he is shrewd enough to see that these benefits have sapped the
dynamics of the working class, made them relatively resigned, and, in
a sense, put gilded locks on the class barriers. Naturally he is not
against the improvements per se; he is against the implicit attitude, on
the part of both workers and bosses, that now his class ought to be
content. He is bursting with ego, energy, and youthful cleverness.
Unionization and the labor laws have had the Calvinistic effect of
predicting his fate too accurately. He knows what he will be earning
at sixty-five, what he will be eating, where he will be living—even
how many of his teeth will be missing and where he will go to get the
dentures.

The latest economic news from Britain is that things are not *quite*
All Right, Jack, and it is possible to imagine, without flippancy, that

in their heart of hearts young Arthur and his fellows are not entirely dismayed about this. At least it will upset the deadly sameness of their lives. This is not to say that all workers long to be thrilled by the threat of unemployment or that a few years of depression varies the diet happily. But on the emotional level, not the economic or social, some action is better than none to a young buck, and hardship at least provides outlets for anger through protest.

His only outlet is the Saturday night binge at the end of a boring week. "What I want is a good time—all the rest is propaganda." Plenty of beer and girls, and, as much to prove his nerve as anything else, an affair with a pal's wife—which gives him the chance to slip out the back door as the husband comes home.

The friend's wife becomes pregnant, by Arthur, and much of the film deals uneuphemistically with a futile quest for abortion. Even though Arthur has met a girl who attracts him, he offers to marry the wife, but she is wiser than he is. She knows that to accept his offer would be to chain herself to a hulk of resentment. She decides to stay where she is, have the baby, and take the consequences. Arthur also takes his consequences: a beating from the husband's friends, and love for the new girl. He recovers from the former in a week, but the latter, because he loves the new girl sufficiently to marry her, will trap him for life.

Alan Sillitoe has adapted the screenplay from his good but wildly overpraised novel. Generally the screenplay is pungent and fast, with a few superfluous episodes. (The sequence in which the bereaved husband breaks the funeral-parlor window is self-contained and contributes nothing new in characterization.) Its chief virtue is its aura of iron fate, which is a long way above the finger-marked contrivances of John Osborne.

Albert Finney, who plays Arthur and who has previously been seen here only briefly as the soldier-brother in *The Entertainer,* is already one of the most celebrated young actors in England. His face is not an outstandingly good actor's mask; it is not a distinguished or attractive face and, as yet, it lacks mobility and subtlety. But he forces his way ahead, carrying his fairly dead pan before him. There are touches in him of the seething animal vitality of Brando and the compelling abrasiveness of the young Cagney. He has what might be called resident power; his presence *continues* effortlessly while he is on camera, without mugging or distracting from his fellow actors.

Rachel Roberts plays the friend's wife with the sullen yet clear-eyed ferocity of a woman who means to have "a bit of fun" even while she sees the futility of it. Shirley Anne Field, who was touching as the beauty-contest winner in *The Entertainer,* plays the sweetheart with sexual sensibility.

This is the first long film directed by Karel Reisz, a former colleague of Tony Richardson's in the British Free Cinema, who has made a prize-winning documentary and written a book on film editing. It is an extraordinarily able piece of work, free of the exhibitionism that often curses those who come out of the world of theory and cinema club. There is no artiness, no attempt to draw attention to himself. Richardson means us to notice the director and uses every trick he can remember to do it. Reisz is content to reveal his milieu, his people, and his story straightforwardly and sympathetically. Figuratively, he keeps out of the way of the film and lets it work on us. Of course this means, in practice, that he is making all the right moves, not doing nothing. For example, he has selected the right place and light for each scene (the park for the parting with the wife, the football field for the walk with the girl).

By this blunt "presentation" of his characters, while never abandoning the camera's mobility, and by editing which is clean and interesting without trying to jab us every time he cuts to a new sequence, Reisz has achieved the ideals of horizontal motion and vertical texture.

The Kitchen   (October 16, 1961)

The thing that would astonish anyone coming into the service quarters . . . for the first time would be the fearful noise and disorder during the rush hours. . . . You cannot grill a steak two hours before it is wanted. . . . The result is that at mealtimes everyone is doing two men's work, which is impossible without noise and quarreling. . . . It was for this reason that during the rush hours the whole staff raged and cursed like demons.

These lines, from Orwell's description of his experiences in a Paris restaurant (*Down and Out in Paris and London*), also fix the dominant note in *The Kitchen,* which is set in London. The film is an

adaptation of a much-discussed play by a much-discussed young English dramatist, Arnold Wesker. Along with Orwell, Wesker reminds
us forcibly of the little nuggets of hell that lurk just on the edges of
our lives: big kitchens, mines, laundries, to name a few.

The restaurant hell is particularly ironic because the calm dining
room pretends that the hectic kitchen doesn't exist and because there
is something ridiculous in an agony that rises out of fixing chops and
fish and salads. But the hell is made real; Wesker and his director,
James Hill, plunge us headfirst into the texture and insane rhythm of
the place at its peaks of fever.

Such plot as there is in this short film (an hour and a quarter)
concerns an emigré German cook (solidly played by Carl Mohner)
who is in love with a married waitress. When he realizes that she is
not going to get a divorce and when he learns that she has aborted his
child, he goes berserk, chops gas pipes with a cleaver, smashes glasses
until his hands are bloody. Set around him are character vignettes of
Englishmen (several kinds) and an assortment of Europeans.

Like Arthur Miller's *A Memory of Two Mondays,* this short work
is a dramatized memoir of an early job, but additionally Wesker
means his kitchen as a microcosm, and he gives you no chance to
escape his meaning. ("This stinking kitchen is like the world.") But
after he has reproduced kitchen life pungently, he seems to have only
one thing to tell us: that the men and women who work there would
like to be out of it. The thinness of Wesker's comment on his material, the surface facileness of his microcosm, is glaringly mani-
fested in his treatment of the owner, who wanders through, like a
boyar among his serfs, watching, clucking, being mildly kind in self-
defense, but who has in effect only two lines. Whenever anything goes
wrong, he says, "Sabotage." And after the running-amok, he asks the
German what in the world he wants. Doesn't he have food, a job,
good wages? "What is there more?" the boss asks, bewildered. It
seems a bankrupt attempt to portray the bankruptcy of materialist
society.

What are the Socialist Wesker's hopes for the German and his
friends? If the play is an indictment of the callous capitalist world,
what does Wesker think the kitchens of Soviet restaurants are like
at mealtimes? Or, if that is a repugnant question to a democratic
socialist, what then would it be like in Wesker's personal New Jerusalem? If these workers knew that they were not to be cast out into

the alley when they were old, would that make the work any less fiendish during rush hours?

The only logical implication of Wesker's play is not socialist but nihilist, that society itself—which makes restaurants—ought to be abolished. But this, I think, is to credit Wesker with more lucid intentions than he had. His film is a valid but essentially inartistic and, in a serious sense, meaningless picture of a life trap by one who was lucky enough to escape it.

A Kind of Loving   (*Show,* October 1962)

There seems to be a growing belief in Britain that a serious film is one made in an industrial town. The British have taken a somewhat longer time than the rest of the Western world to admit the workingman as a protagonist in art. (Compare the dates of Zola and Lawrence, of Odets and Osborne.) Having discovered him, they are now in danger of getting drunk on drabness, of assuming that a work that contains sunlight and even a moderate luxe is either frivolous or shallow. *A Kind of Loving,* which won the chief award at this year's Berlin International Film Festival, is the latest fruit of this flourishing gray tree of social realism. Like *Look Back in Anger, Room at the Top, Saturday Night and Sunday Morning* and *A Taste of Honey,* it was shot in the industrial North of England, center of the Industrial Revolution and now center of the Angry Artistic Revolution.

Based on a novel by Stan Barstow, a Yorkshire miner's son, and adapted for the screen by Keith Waterhouse, author of the novel *Billy Liar,* and Willis Hall (who helped Waterhouse convert *Billy* to the stage), it is a cautionary tale of courtship and early marriage. The hero, Vic Brown, is a young draftsman struck by the blonde beauty of Ingrid Rothwell, a typist in his factory. After a bus and movie-balcony courtship, they make love one day in her home when her mother is away. Instant pregnancy, that remote possibility so much more certain in fiction than in life, occurs.

A few months later, the pair are married and are living in that house with the mother. Vic's feelings fluctuate between love sharpened by desire and revulsion sharpened by imprisonment. Ingrid, thriving as mater and warder, still worships him. The mother-in-law hates him. An accident causes a miscarriage, and Vic feels trapped for nothing, as it were. Blowup follows binge, and he goes running to his adored married sister for comfort: she makes him face round to his responsibilities. At the end, he and Ingrid are settling into a small flat, free of the devouring mother, and their life has a chance at its share of what the British Weather Bureau calls "sunny intervals."

The film has several extraordinary virtues. The Hall-Waterhouse script refines and heightens Barstow's undistinguished novel, retaining the best of the book and extrapolating some telling moments of its own. (Examples: the scene where Vic's father, a railway worker, introduces him with taciturn pride to a fellow railway worker; the scene where Vic goes into a druggist's for a particularly male purchase, is unexpectedly waited on by a woman, and comes out sheepishly with a bottle of hair pomade.) The frankness of dialogue and of incident is never any more disturbing than our continual rediscovery that sons and daughters are highly sexual beings.

Denys Coop's fine photography makes the most of a palette devoid of sunlight. He transmutes grime and fog into a visual suggestion of the smell of tabloid newsprint.

John Schlesinger, who has directed television and short films and here makes his first full-length feature, shows quickly that he has compassion and perception as well as an eye for composition and for angles which underscore mood. If as yet he lacks the subtlety and unfaltering pace of Karel Reisz (*Saturday Night*), he is much more secure than Tony Richardson (*The Entertainer, A Taste of Honey*), less dependent on the heavy-handed comment of background detail, less reliant on "shock" cuts—that is, a jump from one scene into the startling opening of the next, with the shock irrelevant to what follows. A former actor, he builds his film out of the interplay and rhythm of dialogue, rather than with intrusive editing or hypodermic musical score. The music, by Ron Grainer, is reticent and apt.

Alan Bates, who was "Jesus" in *Whistle Down the Wind* and the sadistic younger brother in the Broadway production of *The Caretaker,* plays Vic with such direct goodheartedness that even his recalcitrance affects us as the sulkiness of a child whom basically we like. His hushed infatuation and his puzzlement at its short life are equally touching.

June Ritchie, who makes her debut as Ingrid, does not quite reach the depth of being helplessly but happily overwhelmed that Shirley

Anne Field conveyed in *Saturday Night;* but her performance is never false. Thora Hird, a well-known "road" star in Britain, plays the mother-in-law with a bourgeois smugness that is perhaps this world's only justification for homicide. Mention must be made too of Bert Palmer, complete with National Health Service teeth, as Vic's affectionate father, and Pat Keen as the sympathetic but severe married sister.

It may come as a surprise, after such a list of virtues, that the film is in my view a disappointment. For the first half-hour or so, I thought it was going to be a successful, honest picture on a subject that is almost always faked: courtship and marriage. It is honest enough, but the pregnancy, the enforced wedding and subsequent difficulties reduce its impact—not because they kill romantic feeling but because we are diverted from familiar universals to familiar plot. The line between truth and triteness is thin; the film crosses over.

A more serious fault is the implication—in locale and in naturalistic devices—that it is making a serious social comment. The secretary of the British Board of Film Censors is pleased with the film because "It says that the anticipation of marital privilege is liable to produce great unhappiness not only for the boy and girl concerned but also for their families, and it also says that a sexual attraction, especially one that is variable, is not alone a basis for a successful marriage." There, if you like, is a statement clothed in itchy blue serge. It is a reasonable statement of the movie's implications from one point of view. It is merely necessary to add that there is a little more to the matter than that. The picture quite clearly states that despite the universal dream of perfect freedom and perfect love, the forms of job and marriage provide an attainable life for many who might otherwise end in anarchic disaster. In short, it proves that Thoreau's "quiet desperation" is often as much a haven as a prison. But all this raises a question as to the necessity of the film's milieu to the proving of its point.

Vic is out of the working class in a "white collar" lower-middle-class job, but the very same story could have happened to an upper-class youth. John Braine's *Room at the Top* needed its industrial-town setting to show the new social mobility. Sillitoe's *Saturday Night* needed its lathe-worker hero to show that the new neon-lighted union-ized worker still feels a Calvinist doom even at higher wage levels. Barstow's book—and this film—has no such imperative. It could have been set in Kensington or a garden suburb; its hero could have been an undergraduate or a junior stockbroker.

The outburst of the Angry Young Men that dates from 1956 was welcome and necessary, but a style that is followed for its own sake becomes a cliché with astonishing speed. It is just as easy to make bad art about poor people as less poor ones—easier, in a way, because extraneous empathy can be used to mask inferior work. *A Kind of Loving* is certainly not a bad film—it has numerous solid merits, but the gravity that it tries to adduce from its milieu is hollow. There is plenty still to be mined for art in British lower-class life; but if British artists assume that this is now the only good source of art or that lesser material can be strengthened with a lower-class setting, the invigorating rebels will soon become the Angry Young Establishment.

Billy Liar   (December 14, 1963)

The three Englishmen principally responsible for *A Kind of Loving* have now produced *Billy Liar*. This is the second metamorphosis of the work, which was originally a novel by Keith Waterhouse; it was dramatized by him and Willis Hall and was presented successfully in London and elsewhere. The material is simple: the fantasies of a twenty-year-old provincial clerk that are his refuge from the frustrations to which circumstances and weakness of character have sentenced him.

One of the strengths of this film is that it really relies on its material. There is minimal plotting, as such. Several things happen to Billy in the course of the story: the two girls to whom he is simultaneously engaged find out about it and throw him over; the girl he really likes leaves for London without him; his grandmother dies; his pipe dream of a big-city job explodes. But the emphasis of director and authors is on organic development, not on contrivances of conflict and climax. The basic purpose is to explore Billy's character, and the motions of the story are merely sufficient to put it on view. This is intelligent risk-taking in a film, and here it is largely successful.

Billy is a clerk in a firm of undertakers, which profession we see from the inside. (Miss Mitford will note that, in smarminess at least, the British Way of Death is not very different from ours.) His problem is that he is normal, in his dreams and even his daydreams: he is abnormal in the way that his daydreams influence his actions. He cannot help lying even when there is no need for it, just to affect in some way the reality that he hates. When a neighbor asks about his father's health, Billy, for no reason, invents an illness and operation. When complications follow, he lies more desperately. Similarly he has pointlessly lied his way into his two betrothals to girls whom he does not want to marry. Then, whenever matters become especially tight, he imagines himself in trooper's uniform with a submachine gun, spattering his tormentors with bullets.

John Schlesinger slips the film easily in and out of the fantasy sequences: the trooper flashes, or Billy's imaginary country, Ambrosia, whose dictator and defender he is. The chief bond between Billy and his beloved is their mutual imaginary country. He also has a few visions about sex, about suffering in prison and writing it up, of the transformation of his middle-class parents into toffs. Additionally, we see Billy play-acting in life, with his fellow clerks or alone in his boss's office where he wallows in mimicries. Moments like these— because they delve into byways of whimsy hard to define but universally true—are the film's best.

In terms of what he has to do, Tom Courtenay, of *The Loneliness of the Long Distance Runner,* is versatile and funny. In terms of what he is, he lacks conviction. One cannot believe that two girls would be fighting over him and that the "free" girl would have chosen him above all the rest. Julie Christie, as this girl, is adequate but is handicapped by the fact that she has been told that she is a striking new personality. We get a great many smiles. Mona Washbourne, Ethel Griffies, Finlay Currie are excellent as various local types. In his first dramatic role, as Billy's father, the well-known BBC figure Wilfred Pickles has appropriate vinegar.

As one expects by now from a Waterhouse-Hall script, the dialogue is lean and swift, the characters generally well understood. The exception to this is Miss Christie's role, which seems rootless and weakly motivated. There is also a weakness in the device of the firm's Christmas calendars: 200 of them that Billy omitted to mail and has kept in his wardrobe at home. (He has pocketed the postage money.) Why are they so difficult to get rid of? And if it is difficult, why does he carry them back to the office itself, a few at a time, to flush them down the toilet? The sequence seems forced. In contrast are numerous subtle and felicitous touches, like the dance band on the midnight train by which Billy and his girl plan to leave for London. The musicians' sleaziness seems to predict the future of the runaways.

Schlesinger and his authors have a weakness for scenes in which a character sits and thinks until he reaches a decision. (Billy does it here in his bedroom.) But this director knows how to get the most out of his settings (cemetery, office, hospital, sooty hills) and how to make scenes flow in and out of rooms, up and down stairs, through streets, like coursing water. In his increasing skill with the film form and with actors, there is the sense of a watchful, responsive talent.

Despite its North Country setting, this is not just one more English social-realist film, telling us of the plight—fixed or altering—of the working class. As is made clear with the shots of council houses under the credits, the concern here is with the new middle class, enlarging in Britain as it has already enlarged here, with the young among them deluded by propaganda of possibilities into believing that all things are possible for them. The facile comparison of Billy with Walter Mitty does not hold. Mitty is a middle-aged householding husband whose fate is molded and made, who knows it and dreams instead of drinking. Billy is still in process of realizing his boundaries, has not yet quite reached them. The mythology of advertising, the Benzedrine of mass communications implant and pump up the dream. (Billy's idea of escape and realization is to become a script writer for a comic.) Industrial democracy ("All Things Are Equally on Sale to All—As Long as You All Keep Buying") *must* make him believe that all things are possible: so that he will buy the magazines, the TV set, the pop record, the new ties. If they will make him look and act and talk like Frank Sinatra, maybe he can have Frank Sinatra's life.

But he will never leave the little humdrum street. First, there is *not* room at the top, not that much. Second, only extraordinary luck or drive (more important than extraordinary abilities) can blast him upward. Some do it; many more do not and can, if they choose, console themselves with fantasies. What is needed, of course, is anger at the professional lies, the false promises of possibilities that, even when realized, are not worth much. The few at the top get their pink Cadillacs by pushing the dope dreams of pink Cadillacs. *Billy Liar* is a good allegory of the striptease that the Bitch Goddess performs, just out of reach, before she sends the wide-eyed watcher back to solitary satisfactions.

Darling (September 4, 1965)

John Schlesinger, the director of *A Kind of Loving* and *Billy Liar,* in which he showed verity, humanity, and increasing cinematic skill, has now made *Darling,* in which the skill is notably heightened —perhaps at some expense to the other qualities. *Darling's* first effect is dazzling; its net effect is something less.

Frederic Raphael wrote the screenplay from an idea by himself, Schlesinger, and Joseph Janni, the producer. It concerns a modern English girl, a model with a model's vague ambition toward acting, who is intended as a contemporary symbol: morally undernourished, conscious and regretful of this, unable to help it. She is supposed to be telling her life story to a magazine (always a thin device—there is plenty in the film that could neither be told nor printed). Married early, she then falls in love with a television writer-interviewer who leaves his wife and children for her, as she leaves her husband. After an abortion which affects her more than she expected, she begins an affair with a sleek PR man merely out of momentary boredom with the writer, who spends all his spare time on a novel. (An apt warning to writers not to take up with easily bored girls.) When the writer finds out, he leaves her. She still loves him but is now cast adrift on an ocean of get-and-take. After various adventures, she marries a rich Italian prince with seven children. Oppressed in her *palazzo* and still in love with the writer, she seizes a chance to fly back to London; sees him; is finally rebuffed.

As the heroine, Julie Christie (who was the "free" girl in *Billy Liar*) makes a strong impression. She has an expressive, unusual face and an attractive voice, but she is not yet a controlled or subtle actress. Her chief effects come from her vivid personality in this tailor-made part. As an actress her colorings tend to be primary; she is happy or sad, frightened or frisky, all convincingly enough, but the gradations between are not yet within her grasp and seem not even to be in her imagination at present. Her performance can be compared with Dirk Bogarde's as the writer. His techniques and the sense of his complete being continue to mature with all the consistency that the film world permits. Here he underplays with a delicacy and tact, a beautiful suggestiveness, that create this man's privacies, unspoken. His glances, pauses, shaded inflections are the result of imagination and empathy at the service of sure craft; and the result is a great deal warmer than that cold description may suggest. It is the best piece of underacting I have seen since Denholm Elliott's performance in *Nothing But the Best,* and uses a much wider range than Elliott's performance. Laurence Harvey, the PR man, glides through his role like a snake through oil. Nothing that can really be called acting is needed, only a nice easeful assortment of mannerisms, which Harvey supplies competently.

Raphael's dialogue is almost always bright, pungent, brisk. The sequence in which the girl and the writer fall in love is written with understanding and *tendresse.* The Capri sequence with a homosexual photographer, in which the girl plays at living with him like a sister, has the reality of a hopeless asexual dream in a life harassed by biology. And as against *La Dolce Vita,* which comparison *Darling* cannot escape, Raphael's symbol of integrity is credible. The old author whom the writer and the girl visit for a TV interview is an appealing, unself-conscious integer of integrity, unlike the juvenile conception of the intellectual in Fellini's film.

But, as in Raphael's screenplay of *Nothing But the Best,* there are heavy and uncomfortable elements. Alan Bates told us early in the other picture that this is a "filthy stinking world;" here the photographer says that life is "a great big steaming mess." Both instances are more glib than grieving. The other film shifted tonal gears gratingly about halfway through; here there are two grating elements. Toward the end the girl suddenly turns out to be Roman Catholic. But the author has not portrayed her as a Catholic, devout or lapsed. To depict the immoral behavior of a girl reared in Catholicism (especially when we are privy to her thoughts) no differently from that of a girl reared in another religion is a serious fault, and it turns her late Catholicism into a plot device to facilitate her Italian marriage. The last episode, in which the writer takes her to bed on her brief London visit, only to spurn her afterwards, is quite incredible. One cannot believe that this man, as he is drawn, could have been so vindictively cruel, indeed could physically have functioned in bed knowing what he planned to say to her. It is the action of a brute or a moral sadist, and since he has been shown to be neither, it seems plot mechanics.

Schlesinger's direction, too, ranges from the succinct to the blatant, from the breathtakingly deft to the clumsy. Much of the film moves with stunning cinematic fluency: the way the girl meets the writer, the swift passage (a walk with a priest under an umbrella) in which her return to religion is noted, a sequence in which she models for the photographer—these are just random samples of the use of film language to tell much with little and to tell it incisively. But there is also a good deal that is like the palm-in-the-face shove of Tony Richardson. As a charity-bazaar speaker in a posh house mentions helping people irrespective of color, we get close-ups of turbaned black boy-servants; as he speaks about the world's famine, we see a stout jeweled lady picking the meat out of dainty sandwiches. As Miss Christie reads (quite badly) John of Gaunt's dying speech about England, we get a mocking close-up of a photograph of Queen Elizabeth. The shock-cut, that desperation tactic, is often used, and twice in its lowest form: the mask. Once we cut to a scary mask which turns out to be a child playing on a lawn; and a party sequence ends with a close-up of a man clapping on a mask, from which we cut away. The last shot pans from a newsstand displaying the "Italian" princess's life story to a toothless woman singing *Santa Lucia* in Piccadilly Circus. It is ugly enough, but what does it signify? Weren't there toothless street singers in more decorous epochs? Outside of the small Cartier-Bresson fillip, what use is it as a final comment?

These egregious effects, markedly derivative, are stuck like rhinestones on the film's smooth fabric, and their flashiness helps to define Schlesinger's abilities. He has unusual intelligence, sympathy, knowledge of acting and film technique; he is also a director without a style, who feels he needs to deck his work in borrowed finery. Again a comparison with *La Dolce Vita:* That picture is much hollower than *Darling* and on second viewing is quite tedious, but there is not a frame in it that could have been made by anyone but Fellini. The sequence of the fake miracle, Ekberg in St. Peter's, the final walk through the woods, essentially vacuous as they are, are visually unique and unified in manner—the world as scanned by one man's vision. The contrary is true of Schlesinger. There is hardly a frame in *Darling* that could not have been made by another director—Reisz, Anderson, Richardson, Godard, or others. One can hope for a style to develop in Schlesinger, but one cannot sanguinely expect it. In his three full-length films to date, with all their virtues, there is small indication of a strong personality.

This film underscores an ironic contradiction. In an age concerned with the existence of morality, with what we can do to be saved, the most difficult matter in art is to delineate immorality convincingly; but positive qualities are still artistically graspable. When Schlesinger takes us through the initial love and first bedding of the pair or on the visit to the old author or on a visit to the girl's sister (excellent loving satire), the film rings true. But the scene in the empty board room when Miss Christie walks on the table, the gambling-hell scenes, the Paris orgy are all strained. They are not glimpses into Sheol, they are just tired movie naughtiness. Decadence remains the hardest quality to depict in art, especially when (as here) it is equated with promiscuity or homosexuality. By now, only what could not be shown in a film might possibly be convincingly decadent, and even then it would not prove that a character was rotten. We know too much of the private lives of many otherwise admirable men and women to believe that some sexual and other practices negate a person's social worth. An age of spiritual starvation, from which this girl knowingly suffers, cannot be dramatized merely by random fornications. After all, there has been plenty of bed-hopping in religiously replete eras.

Because of its adroitness and its sheer entertainment, it is hard to see how *Darling* can be anything other than a large success for Schlesinger. One does not wish him otherwise. But his progress as a film artist now seems to depend on whether he is willing to settle for gleaming surfaces like Bryan Forbes (Schlesinger is unlikely to become a Fellini), or whether he will insist on an inner rationale and validity in his work: whether he builds upward from the most stringent perceptions toward a virtuoso display of them or begins at the top with slickness and adds just enough smart dialogue and facile bitter comment to provide marketable *Weltschmerz*.

This Sporting Life (July 20, 1963)

Lindsay Anderson, the British director and critic, is a pioneer of the "new" film that has arisen in Britain since the Second War. His short documentary *O Dreamland* (1953) seems to have been a seed bed for much that is in the later social-realist films of Tony Richardson and others. In addition, Anderson is noted for his theatrical direction in London; this includes *The Long and the Short and the*

Tall with Peter O'Toole, *Serjeant Musgrave's Dance, Billy Liar* with Albert Finney. He has at last been enabled to make his first feature-length film, *This Sporting Life*.

The screenplay, by David Storey from his own novel, tells of a young miner turned footballer who lodges in a Midlands city with a widow a bit older than himself, who batters his way to heroism on the playing field and batters his way into the reluctant widow's bed. He is not a mere brute but he has brutish power, and he is largely restricted to it as a mode of expression. His hunger for love, for *her* love, heedless of her condition, drives him to shatter her private sanctities and, in time, to shatter her. The stress kills her (a brain hemorrhage) and leaves him a lonely scarred bull charging blindly around the football field. It is the story of an emotional need that is converted to egoism by rejection, that destroys what it prizes by insisting on loving without understanding.

From Anderson one expects a concern to make the film respond to life with immediacy and heat. To a considerable extent this is the case here. From its opening on the field (and it is rugby they play, all brawn and smash—not deft, dancing soccer), we get a sense of sport as microcosm, less a game than raw antagonism, an outlet for energy and hate and frustration that society no longer provides elsewhere. All the football sequences—aided by Denys Coop's photography, Peter Taylor's film editing, and Chris Greenham's sound editing—have the shocking effect of a fist thumping solid meat.

The first three-quarters of the film are in flashback adroitly woven with the present. This technique neatly pins the exposition and development of the story to a present point of interest that is moving forward. The encounters between the man and the widow—and encounters are what they are, not love scenes—are harrowing in their ravage, their desperate embraces, their sense of hopeless schism. The final furious quarrel between the two is as terrible as any between man and woman that I can remember on film. We feel them tearing the flesh off each other as, all the while, they wish that the world could be remade, that time could be turned back to when they were born.

Anderson is helped greatly by his two leading actors and, no doubt, has helped them in return. Richard Harris, an undismissible figure in previous, smaller roles, here has a part that makes the most of his ability to transmute his sheer physical power into eruptive emotion and commanding presence. He seems compounded of the forces of youth: anger, sex, loneliness, arrogance. This first film leading role will, I hope, lead to parts with chances for variety and further subtleties.

Rachel Roberts, who was excellent as Albert Finney's ravening lover in *Saturday Night and Sunday Morning,* is equally but quite differently excellent as the widow. From the start she strikes notes of fierce resignation: glad she is through with the turmoil of love and sex, fearful of the young man, savagely defensive of her isolation. We see the man progressively affecting her, but this is no waking Sleeping Princess; it is sex that is being stirred, little else, and she doesn't like it. The picnic scene, as she watches the man playing with her children, is a small gem of interest grudgingly revived. And—with Harris —her final fight rocks the screen. The range of Miss Roberts' perceptions and powers is now further proved.

Not all the film is so fortunate. Most of the weaknesses in script and execution are too commingled to be separable. The team backer, overplayed by Alan Badel with oily clichés, is introduced with suggestions of villainy, the criminal figure often hovering on the edges of commercialized sport. But no such thing: he turns out simply to be a business man who owns a piece of the team. The vicious and criminal implications are pointless, just trite hang-overs from past sport films. The old man who scouts for the team is drawn at length as a kind of shabby Fate (with a hint of homosexuality) who keeps materializing out of the shadows. Toward the end of the film he disappears, unexplained, unfulfilled. The episode in which Harris takes the widow out for the first time is a gauche scene instead of a scene of gaucherie. In a posh restaurant he puts his feet on a chair, insults other guests, chivvies the waiter—all quite unbelievable in view of the weeks it took him to get the widow to come out with him and his anxiety to please her. The woman walks out in understandable embarrassment; yet when he follows her home, she agrees to go to bed with him—an incredible ending to an incredible episode.

The film's viewpoint wavers. It is almost entirely a "first-person" picture, through the man's eyes, but occasionally it goes to other viewpoints, as when we see the widow sitting on her bed listening to the drunken lodger come upstairs. This weakens the artistic consistency, our feeling of the man pounding at the gates wondering what is really within. And the symbolism of the spider on the wall over her deathbed is so crude as to thrust us right "out" of the film.

The whole last sequence, after the separation of the lovers, is a disintegration, not a conclusion. Time has to be filled out in the structure to give the widow a chance to have her illness and reach death's door. The man goes off to a flophouse, ostensibly because the old team scout once lived there but more likely because the director wanted the visual contrast; then, arbitrarily, without any dramatic point of change, he returns, learns that she is in the hospital, and finds her in time to see her die. Then he mourns in the empty house. These last events, instead of being climactic and agonized, give us a sense of waiting around for "The End." We feel the man waiting for it, too. These are not dramatically conclusive actions, they are simply reverberations of the conclusion (the separation) that has already taken place.

The script's basic thematic flaw is that there is no real interaction between the football story and the love story; they are two quite separate entities. If Harris had never become a football star, it would have had no substantial effect on his relations with the widow. They would have taken a bus to the country instead of his big car, he would have got her a cloth coat instead of a fur coat. It was not his money or celebrity that swayed her (or else their whole story collapses). Conversely, if the widow had never existed, it would not have affected his football career a jot. It was not to impress her that he tried out for the team nor did she have any important relation to his cockiness and trouble there. The title, *This Sporting Life,* hints at a relationship and comment that are missing.

This film shows Anderson's awareness that social realism for its own sake is (and in England has reached) a dead end. He is trying to comprehend people, not to document an environment. But the vehicle he has chosen—the story of the poor lad using sport as a means to climb and being exploited by it as he exploits it—is a familar one. (*Golden Boy* is the best of a score of examples.) And he has not compensated completely for its familiarities. All the elements are not carefully controlled, and the occasional banalities are jarring. But the picture's fine qualities—the torrential man-woman scenes, the football fury, the imaginative use of flashback—are what we would have expected from Anderson and what make us look forward to his next film.

The Guest   (January 25, 1964)

Harold Pinter has been writing plays only since 1957, when he was twenty-seven, and one of the proofs of his validity, of the way his "note" fits into modern harmonics, is the speed with which he has become a fixed and recognizable point of reference. Those who have seen even one Pinter play know what is meant by the "Pinter quality," whether they like it or not. In fact, one proof of his validity is that (like Beckett, like Ionesco) one need not like his plays in order to perceive his artistic reason for being. One can say, with both truth and amusement, that "liking" a work has become a secondary criterion with much modern art. Pinter has quite evidently touched a contemporary nerve, but, more important, he has arisen like an urban Anglo-Jewish genie from a subconscious cavern in our society, simultaneously expressing and creating certain mysteries.

The Guest is the first film made from a play of his—the best-known play, *The Caretaker*. It is a fascinating, funny, eerie film, a work of murky evocations boiling out of grubby naturalistic minutiae. That is, of course, the Pinter method, but in this film we are seeing that method used at its best so far. This is not the usual—or unusual —good film version of a play, in which the problems imposed by the second medium have been "licked." One feels that, at last, the work has been fully revealed. Much of Pinter's writing has been done for radio and television and then reproduced on the stage. His plays show the (largely beneficial) marks of this. *The Caretaker* was written directly for the stage but now flowers in a closer form where the smallest subtleties of expression can buttress his naturalistic mode, where magnified presence can lend greater implications to silences and hints and physical objects, where the skillful placement and shifting of the audiences by camera movement and angle can underscore his intent to draw us into confined areas, literally and figuratively. Even the elimination of conventions like the act-break and the intermission helps; for those conventions have bred pat expectations in us—of the act "curtain," of progressive ascents of plot slopes, which *The Caretaker* does not fulfill nor try to fulfill. On film it becomes a flowing, engulfing, sometimes rightly claustrophobic work: slightly condensed but fully realized.

The events of the story are so simple that they are difficult to describe meaningfully. Aston, a reticent man, lives alone in a top-floor cluttered room of a small abandoned house in a poor London district. He befriends and takes in an old derelict who has been fired from a menial job in a café: in time Aston offers him a job as caretaker of the house. Aston's brother, Mick—a taunting quasi-sadist—harries the derelict when his brother is away, countermanding his orders. Eventually Aston, himself irritated by the cantankerous old man, puts him out. It is obviously thin plot material; such material is usually used by a good writer because he means to concentrate on plumbing depths of character. But virtually everything we know about these three people is revealed fairly early. After the first third or so, almost the only new important character facet is that Aston has been in a mental hospital and has had shock treatment. Nor can I believe in any of the various symbolic programs that have been drawn from the play: Marxist, Freudian, Existential, Christian. Heavy allegorical weather has been made out of the fact that the derelict talks about getting down to Sidcup, a suburb, where his "things" are, including the papers that will prove who he is; and of Aston's frequent references to the shed he plans to build in the garden. Any attempt to define a *schema* in the play is futile, because I do not think it is a planned work in anything like the usual sense.

Pinter's method, I believe—which explains why small incidents or story organisms can serve him—is a kind of automatic writing, filtered through a temperament, a view of the world, and dominant needs and hopes: guided by technical skills and refined by talent. But basically the skills and talent are following a skein through forests of experience and memory. Obviously, in a large sense, that is what always happens in creative writing, but here it occurs in a much narrower sense.

In Greenwich Village in the thirties lived a famous character named Joe Gould, who was setting down *An Oral History of the World*—hundreds of notebooks in which he had for years written everything he heard everywhere. That was pathology. Pinter's work is art but, essentially, it is Joe Gould marvelously distilled. Pinter's plays are *overheard:* snatches of conversations in pubs, on buses, in the streets: with the extra intensity that such sudden snatches have, with the frequent paradoxes of diction (the derelict's language is as formal as it is vernacular and vulgar), with the poignant questions raised by the fragment heard in a doorway as we pass. (What did she mean? Who *are* they? *Why* won't he go to Aunt Minnie's? Our own lives keep hurrying us past before we ever get the answers.) Pinter stitches the fragments together into a fabric full and thick enough to convert wispy pathos into central mystery. Thus his patchwork quilt of conversational tags, knitted both by his subconscious and his compassion, spells out grave questions: Who are we? Today, that is. And why?

It is much more stream of memory than so-called stream of consciousness: Pinter seems not be mining his own life. Once he invents or remembers an initial situation, he then (I believe) lets his characters tell him about themselves. For example, I doubt that he planned Aston's shock treatment from the beginning; it occurred to him, and it seemed to fit and enrich. Always *The Caretaker* is teased with humor, but as Pinter has written, it is "funny up to a point. Beyond that point it ceases to be funny, and it was because of that point that I wrote it."

When we admire him, we are really admiring his ability to look into a crystal ball of the humdrum and see not the future or past, but the fantasy-cum-dread that runs parallel to the present reality. The danger of his style and temperament is repetitiousness. So far, his plays have struck generally similar notes. But he is now only thirty-four. The "Pinter play" has, as I have said, filled an evidently felt need, but that need is now, I should say, well filled. I hope that the Pinter of forty or fifty or seventy will have found other resonances to sound in himself and in society, and perhaps even quite different techniques.

The performances and direction are excellent. The three actors of the original production are, like the play itself, even better in the film: Robert Shaw, Alan Bates, the younger brother, Donald Pleasence, who has the part of his life as the derelict and is, to put in it one pale word, perfect. As for Clive Donner, I hope that in the present craze for flash and filigree in direction, his quiet imagination, unusual perceptions, fine control will not be overlooked.

The Knack   (July 10, 1965)

Richard Lester's film version of *The Knack* is so teemingly imaginative, so fertile in invention, that he forces the viewer to a rare regret: a wish that that director had been a little less inventive, had

balanced the pirouettes of sparkling exuberance with a few more interludes of straightforward storytelling. Lester has burrowed into Ann
Jellicoe's comedy and, with the help of an adroit adaptation by
Charles Wood, has exploded it into a film (no calmer verb will do);
but he has lost some of the compass points of the play.

The comedy, as directed by Mike Nichols in New York, was an
amusing bag of youthful sexy tricks: about intelligent shy Colin who
owns a London house in which self-confident Tolen rents a room.
Tolen has many girls; Colin has virtually none. Another youth named
Tom casually happens into the house as sympathetic observer. Along
comes a girl named Nancy, just arrived in London, who by asking a
question at the window, changes all lives, including her own. Those
who know the play may think that the matter of fidelity to the *Urtext*
is unimportant, but even a creampuff has a recipe, and Lester has lost
some of the comedy's shape. It is on grounds like this that the
cinematically gifted sometimes falter. Lester is splendidly talented,
and he shows it here even more than in *A Hard Day's Night;* but
(unlike the Beatles picture) we end by admiring him more than the
film.

To tick off all the disagreeable points so that we can get to the
praise: There were two moments in the play that gave it impulse
and conclusion, and both are missed here. Nancy put her head in the
window and asked the way to the YWCA; here she wanders into a
junkyard where Colin and Tom have just bought a bed, asks her question, but forgets it as she joins them in the middle of the high jinks. We
lose the feeling that her adventures begin at "ground level" with an
innocent question, then soar away. At the end, Colin's angry flare-up
at Tolen is what settled Nancy's mind; here the flare-up is missing
and the ending lacks resolution. Colin seems to win by default. There
are a few other flaws; some of the quick dialogue is lost, some of the
(deliberately) non-sequitur dialogue goes on too long, some touches
are only silly gags (for example, the water-skiing sequence).

But—and it is the hugest "but" in a long time—what pleasures.
Even before the titles, from the moment the film starts—with Colin's
dream-exaggeration of Tolen's waiting line of teen-age beauties in
Avedonlike light—it is furiously, fancifully zestful. Jabs, stabs,
pranks, irreverences cascade through it. (Her Gracious Majesty,
monks, sex quirks are some of the targets pinked as we hurry along.)
There are parodies of Godard, Truffaut, and Resnais that, for a
change, are funny. There are dozens and dozens of swift visual jokes

that come out of Keaton through Tati with such high spirits that they are not derivations but healthy offspring. (Note a little scherzo with a fence of old doors around a lot where buildings have been demolished.)

A serious achievement of the film—which gives it a dimension far larger than Miss Jellicoe's original—is that it is played against a muttering chorus of oldsters in the street, who comment on the cavortings of the four young people in strings of clichés. For instance, when Colin and Tom are struggling to get over park railings, we get close-ups of a couple of old ladies remarking as one would on performing animals. Most of these choric comments have evidently been "stolen": presumably shot by Lester apropos of subjects that would stir oldsters' ire, then juxtaposed with scenes from his story. Thus the film is made a heartening snap of the fingers at Decorum, Respectability, and Low Spirits, a sort of *L'Allegro* of Shepherd's Bush. The final truthful jab is in the very last sequence as Colin and Nancy stroll down the Embankment: we see that Tolen, the defeated amorist, has joined the croaking chorus.

Rita Tushingham, who played the first Nancy on the London stage, is in the role again and is perfectly all right. But she is reaping a reward that usually accrues to male actors; she gets overpraised because she is not good-looking. Virtues are read into her acting on the assumption that a girl as plain as that *must* be immensely talented in order to be in films at all. She is spirited, convincing, and sometimes has a comfy-slipper, rainy-day sex appeal; but, to me, there is not much more. Michael Crawford is extraordinarily pleasant as Colin, Ray Brooks is almost but not quite credible as the rooster, and Donal Donnelly has a toothy, taking, Irish openheartedness.

Lester has done well with them, but it remains his picture: one that helps to confirm a new generation in film-making. It is a generation born since the advent of the sound-film, people who do not translate ideas into film terms but who think, create, breathe, purely cinematically. Influences and inheritances from the novel, play, painting, which can all be seen as themselves in the work of some of the best directors, have been well digested in Lester's work, have been turned into cinema tissue. He is one of the film's New Men. There are risks in the sheer joy of being a New Man, in skimping (as noted) some of the obligations raised by the job undertaken. But there are also delights in it, and Lester has filled his film with them.

The Playboy of the Western World; The Quare Fellow

(March 30, 1963)

Two pictures from Ireland underscore a little-noted fact: there is, in effect, no Irish film. It is a nation crammed with fascinating histrionism, some of which is on the stage; a nation rich in dramatists. The commonest of truisms is that the great English comic writers are Irish: Sheridan, Goldsmith, Farquhar, Wilde, Shaw. (And Shaw's Mrs. O'Flaherty claimed that Shakespeare was born in Cork.) There are film studios in Ireland used mainly by British and Americans. There are Irish technicians, some Irish directors. Why are there not more and better Irish films—a body of work comparable to what other European countries have produced?

Poverty cannot be the sole reason; no country in postwar Europe was poorer than Italy, which was deep in film production before foreign aid was realized. Neutrality in war, which some assert is a national soporific, cannot be the reason; look at Sweden. Censorship is a more likely reason. It is a standing joke among writers in England that failure to have your book banned in Ireland is an intellectual disgrace. In a Dublin workshop I have seen a huge stained-glass window intended for a League of Nations building years ago, which was prohibited from representing Ireland abroad because one of its many panels contains a bare-breasted woman. Yet censorship has not stifled the Irish Theater, which manages to thrive and survive.

Another reason for the lack of Irish films is suggested by the screen version of Synge's *The Playboy of the Western World*. Of all speakers of English, the Irish are certainly the most word-intoxicated. Synge himself has recorded how he picked up locutions from farmers and tinkers and beggars. In the preface to *The Playboy* he said:

> When I was writing *The Shadow of the Glen* . . . I got more aid than any learning could have given me from a chink in the floor of the old Wicklow house where I was staying, that let me hear what was being said by the servant girls in the kitchen. . . . In a good play every speech should be as fully flavored as a nut or apple, and such speeches cannot be written by anyone who works among people who have shut their lips on poetry. In Ireland, for a few years more, we have a popular imagination that is fiery and magnificent, and tender. . . .

That was written in 1907, and there is small indication that the love of language and gift of phrase are dwindling.

But the film is not primarily a verbal medium. In the theater—outside of its classic mode, at least—one says generally only what one cannot show. In the film one can show even more and thus needs to say even less. The kinetics of the form may run counter to the Irish temperament.

The Playboy, besides illustrating yet again the difficulty of transposing good plays to the screen, highlights this conflict between the Irish national genius and the film form. These characters exist not only in their speeches but in their use of speech as a certification of existence. It is verbal opera, with arias *seriatim.* The dialogue could not be much condensed for the picture because the plot would be meaningless without the fullness of the context, which means the fullness of the language. It would be like cutting to the plot of an opera; and as with opera, it is comfortable on the stage, uncongenial on the screen.

Nothing about the production compensates. Brian Desmond Hurst has directed dully. Even the outdoor scenes seem static. The camera focuses on the slope of a sand dune; then two characters come over the top of the dune and sit in the center of the focus. Simple details are slovenly; inside the tavern we see through the open doorway that the sky has a wrinkle in it. The cast is mediocre, with Niall McGinnis, the best as mad Old Mahon. Siobhan McKenna is considered by some a great actress; to me she is sometimes a satisfactory one. Here she again leaves me unstirred, with her obvious and somewhat labored effects, her heavy unexpressive features. Additionally, Pegeen Mike is supposed to be "a wild-looking but fine girl of about twenty." Miss McKenna looks no more wild than, alas, she looks twenty; she seems the coeval of the Widow Quin, which badly unbalances the drama. In another curious piece of casting Gary Raymond, an English actor, plays Christy and is so worried about his Irish accent, which keeps wearing thin, that he has little ebullience and vigor.

An American, Arthur Dreifuss, wrote the screenplay of Brendan Behan's *The Quare Fellow* and directed it. An Englishman, Anthony Havelock-Allan, produced it. An English actress, Sylvia Syms, has the leading female role. But it was made in Ireland from an Irish original and mostly with Irish actors, so I think it must be called an

Irish picture. I cannot compare it with the play because I left after the first act of the miserable London production. The film sustains interest. It tells of a country youth, just arrived in Dublin to be a prison guard, who has dewy eye-for-an-eye concepts of justice. As he accompanies an older guard and is concerned with the hanging of a murderer, his views change. The story involves him with the condemned man's wife who is lodging nearby. The plotting creaks, but the prison atmosphere is created dismally well, and the result is a passable if unexceptional little sermon against the rope. Walter Macken, the actor who is also well known as a novelist and playwright, is substantial as the older, sadder guard.

As film *The Quare Fellow* is much better than *The Playboy;* the material and the method are much better suited to the form. But it is only a modestly acceptable picture, not remotely comparable with other Irish achievements in drama and literature. Besides, the language is only American-pared Behan.

The Irish film, in any consequential sense, does not yet exist. (Macken's recent *Home Is the Hero,* in which he starred, only confirms this.) What is needed perhaps is a transmutation of the Irish poetic sense from flow of word to flow of vision; the dramatic sense is already there in abundance. If the new medium ever truly touches Irish fancy and anger, the small country may have as disproportionately large an effect on films as it has had on other arts.

France

Back to the Wall; The Lovers; The 400 Blows

(December 7, 1959)

The most interesting film news from France in the last year has heralded the rise of a group of about twenty new film directors, a number of whom are not yet thirty years old. I have now seen three of their films. All of them display remarkable competences, although none of them is a satisfactory picture.

Back to the Wall, directed by Edouard Molinaro, is the most successful of the three and is the most disappointing, because it attempts so little. It is a hard-bitten suspense story about a husband who discovers his wife's intrigue and devises a blackmail scheme to separate her from her lover. There are, of course, unforeseen conclusions. The plot has two holes in it: the wife's reaction to the husband's revelation of what he has done with the lover is incredible; equally so is the husband's lapse that leads to the denouement. (Apologies for all these ambiguities, but there is unwritten law about suspense films.) Molinaro's style owes something to Clouzot in its tight, driving quality and the way it pushes your nose into the pivotal horror. But the picture does not frighten, as Clouzot's pictures do; most of the time it merely makes you go "tsk-tsk" at the husband's devilish ingenuity. However, even without these imperfections, it would be disappointing that a bright young man wanted to make simply one more shallow suspense film.

Gerard Oury and Jeanne Moreau are persuasive as the husband and wife, Philippe Nicaud is unpersuasive as the lover, and Claire

221

Maurier is attractively worldly as a café owner.

The Lovers, directed and written by Louis Malle, is in essence as silly a picture as I have seen in some time, but although it is much less successful on its own terms than is Molinaro's, it is much more welcome. For it is, as it should be, a young man's film, not an aping of slick success. A young provincial wife, bored with a busy husband, toys with the idea of taking a lover. The husband invites the candidate to their house for a weekend. After her car breaks down, the wife is given a lift by a strange young man whom her husband also invites to stay. That night—probably one of the most drawn-out in screen history—begins with animosity between the newcomer and the wife and progresses through courtship to love-making to a morning in which the youth and the wife drive off together to start life anew, leaving her intended lover, her husband, and her child. We are asked to believe—and to sympathize with—the thesis that one satisfactory sexual encounter, presumably her first such, is enough to make the wife spurn her whole past as a wasteful sham and go off with the young man who has brought her the Truth so pleasantly and quickly.

The wisdom of the film is thus somewhat less than profound and indeed is somewhat dated. It belongs to the "I tell you, Sex is beautiful" school of the early part of the century; at the latest, to its thirties' manifestation, when it was believed that to master Van de Velde was to master life. One shudders for the future of the pair, particularly the woman. But the film's unrestrained romantic plunge into the Reality of Sex is at least purely youthful. We cannot help being touched by its naïveté, but we can certainly hear a fervent, whole-souled note.

Malle, a former film critic, has made his picture generally well, with the help of the beautiful photography of Henri Decae. (It contains the best use of a wide screen for intimate scenes that I know; here we are not made to think, as usual, of two disembodied heads lost on a prairie.) Malle's sense of statement is unreliable; he doesn't know when he has made his point and ought to move on. The all-life-in-a-night idea is worn thin; and the climax—the love-making—is detailed to the degree where the viewer either has to leave the theater so that the couple up there can be alone or else giggle to render it make-believe so that he can stay. A sense of proportion and a larger view of human verities will doubtless come to him. Meanwhile it is clear that Louis Malle has a real lyric and technical gift.

Again Jeanne Moreau has the leading feminine role and in a dour-mouthed way acquits herself well. Again the lover is uninterestingly cast.

The 400 Blows was directed by François Truffaut, also a film critic, and is another in the long line of French films about lonely children which includes *Poil de Carotte* and *La Maternelle*. The title, I gather, is a literal translation of a phrase meaning the entire gamut of punishment. Its theme is that of the unwanted child who behaves worse and worse because he knows he is unwanted and who thus eventually "justifies" those who want to be rid of him. It is executed here only passably, particularly in the light of its two predecessors just mentioned. This kind of film succeeds to the degree that we suffer with the child, and I was too aware of devices and derivation to be much moved. Truffaut ends his picture some time before its close and uses a photographic trick to conclude it. The baffled boy's face simply freezes into a still photo; is it a symbol of paralysis or does it predict a news story about a suicide?

Some of the film is technically accomplished, in a slavishly veristic tone. The interiors are lighted in an overhead, silver way that suggests a cross between tabloid technique and silent movies; and most of the street scenes have been photographed with concealed cameras so that the actors are surrounded by the realest of extras. Indeed Truffaut is so interested in photography and photographic naturalism that he has omitted to stir us theatrically. Still, if he does not sacrifice his ability on the altar of trivial facsimile or ingrown "cinemism," Truffaut, who is only twenty-seven, may proceed to good film-making.

The boy, Jean-Pierre Leaud, is well schooled but stolid. Claire Maurier is in this picture, too—convincing as the mother who is torn between affection for her son and a certain regret that he exists. Albert Remy is friendly and blusteringly weak as the father, and Jeanne Moreau (again!) makes one of the briefest of guest star appearances as a woman walking a dog.

That these pictures are variously faulty is less important than that new directors are finding work in French films. (The only Hollywood director under thirty is, I believe, Stanley Kubrick.) Youth is by no means necessarily a directorial virtue, but a film world that gives opportunities to young directors of talent is not only insuring its future, it is also refreshing those who operate in it at present.

POSTSCRIPT. The New Wave and Truffaut himself have gone on so celebratedly that further comment is in order, both on the phenomenon as a whole and *The 400 Blows* in particular. Truffaut's later films emphasize that the subsequently famous Truffaut style is virtually absent from *The 400 Blows*—in fact, there are proportionately more touches of that style in his previous short *Les Mistons*. His first feature now seems more markedly a hybrid in its concept: it fluctuates between the subjective in which we share the boy's secrets (like his adoration of Balzac) and a blunt Zolaesque report (like the crassness in the police station). It is neither hot introspective recreation nor a consistent naturalism whose very clinical coldness is meant to burn. I think it is this wavering of view, rather than an interest in photography, that keeps the film from being deeply stirring—one way or the other—and keeps the boy's performance from fullest effect. Throughout, we know that we are being told succinctly what we ought to feel, rather than actually feeling it.

But that succinctness is now much more apparent and the film seems executed much better than "passably." (Possibly it was disappointment at not being moved as much as the materials promised that led to the first opinion on its technique.) Its incisiveness, its unsentimentality, its sense of urgency and elision are extraordinary in a first full-length work. And although Truffaut is himself and although "New Wave" is an unsatisfactory catch-all term, the technical virtues of his film are relevant to this whole movement.

In 1959 twenty-four French directors made their first feature films; in 1960 there were forty-three more first features. (The "wave" continued into 1961, then began to ebb.) Not all of these films have been shown in America (nor in France); not all of them that we have seen have been interesting, nor have all those that were interesting been followed by more good work from their makers. Still the explosion is fascinating—an outburst of new, full-length work unsurpassed in film history.

One reason for it, I think, is that it took place in Paris, which for a hundred and fifty years has had a tradition of daring its new artists to new art. Further, in Paris there are two institutions that have galvanized and sustained enthusiasm for films: the Cinémathèque Française, the French film archive which, in two film theaters, provides a continuing stream of "revivals"; and the monthly magazine *Cahiers du Cinéma* (of whose editorial board Truffaut is still a member) which supports theoretical and aesthetic positions that are intensely intracinematic—views that are a reaction against values and impulses cognate to those in other arts—and which seeks to develop and exalt purely cinematic standards.

In this atmosphere there arose a generation that—in a somewhat happy sense—had grown up largely in a kind of ignorance. Most of them had been children during the Second World War, had received their higher education (if they had any) after the war, and had begun their careers in the postwar era. The political uncertainties of postwar France, the Vietnamese and Algerian wars, the growth of ideological disillusion almost into an ideology, a conviction of sterility and vacuum in society and in traditional art, produced a group of young people who "escaped" into films with a sensual devotion that made other concepts of escapism seem pallid. They took refuge in films as a haven from the reality around them and as a generator of new, different realities. Cinema became their university, their religion, their cosmos, their small talk. They had no need translate their thoughts into film terms; they knew, and wanted to know, no other way to think.

The advantage of this condition, for those of them who wanted to direct, was that it gave them a daring and a freedom of flight that judiciousness might have discouraged. Their success depended primarily on this reveling in the means of film, in their cinematic ebullience. To them a film, even a quasi-autobiographical work like *The 400 Blows,* was its own reason for being. This was in sharp contrast with, for instance, such an artist as Renoir who *used* the film: for humanistic ends. In proof, what it meant was that when a New Wave film was made interestingly enough, it transcended its (frequent) lack of specific gravity, its possible triteness of subject or shallowness of perception, could even make virtues of its technical lapses and gaucherie.

These new directors—not all of whom were young—got their opportunities because, first, production costs were relatively low and, in some cases, state aid was available, as it was to Truffaut. Initially exciting results spurred both incipient makers and financiers. Young men and women scraped together money in frantic and sometimes funny ways, scrounged for additional backing, improvised and extemporized and scratched to get films started—and finished. The New Wave was at bottom less a wave than an epidemic of faith and of desperation—a desperate hope that film might prove to be an answer to much that was harassing French society and culture. But this hope could not have been taken entirely seriously even by many who allowed themselves the pleasure of luxuriating in it. Ebullience is not enough, and modern life is especially and swiftly abrasive. Such a movement, which might have lasted twenty or thirty years a century ago, ran its course in little more than three.

Still it had launched some extraordinary talents, some of which are discussed hereafter, in an eruption comparable—in initial force at least—to the era of American silent comedy. It could not prosper like that era because many of these Frenchmen were mere enthusiasts— frequently esoteric ones—rather than artists, and their work failed to connect with an audience of either size or weight. But this group, happily ignorant of almost everything except film history, film means, film possibility, film reality, was able to start with a burst that bypassed apprenticeship.

Thus Truffaut's first feature, made when he was only twenty-seven after having directed only two shorts, speaks with confidence from its first frame. He lacked a sure touch in discrimination of materials, in control and balance of tone and thematic development, but patently the camera was the instrument he had been born to use.

Jules and Jim   (May 7, 1962)

Love has its risks; and the risk of loving art as much as the French do is that one can become so interested in invention and refinement of technique, so immersed in the atmosphere of art, that one loses sight of purposes. It is a confusion of the sheer happiness of being in the studio (paint or film) with the reason for being there.

Jules and Jim by François Truffaut is an instance. No viewer can be unmoved by its joy in imagination, by the way Truffaut runs to the film form to experiment and dare, by his pure reveling in the powers and possibilities of the medium. Nor is this to patronize the picture as a mere attempt; there is very much in it that is beautiful.

The story is about a triangle which is at first isosceles and ends up virtually equilateral. Jules and Jim are two young writer friends in

1912 Paris, the former an Austrian, the latter a Frenchman (who insists on the English nickname). Together they explore art, sport, love of women. Jules falls in love with Catherine, a French girl, who eventually marries him. Jim loves her, too, but says nothing, contenting himself with another girl who loves him but whom he declines to marry. The war separates the two men. Afterwards, Jim visits Jules and Catherine and their daughter in the Rhineland and discovers that Jules is unhappy because he is no longer truly Catherine's husband; she has lovers. Still Jules is satisfied as long as she will live with him. Jim and Catherine become lovers (with Jules' knowledge), then she tires of him because he cannot give her a child. Jules and Catherine move to France, near Paris. There is an attempt by Catherine to renew the affair with Jim which ends when she threatens to shoot him. He runs away. Some time later the three meet amiably in a film theater and go to a country restaurant. While Jules watches, she invites Jim for a drive and plunges the car into a lake. Both Catherine and Jim are drowned; cremated; Jules sees the ashes interred and walks away through the cemetery.

The disjointed effect of this synopsis is not unfair to the film. It begins as a lighthearted *vie bohème* comedy of Colette's Paris (with charming music by Georges Delerue). The war intervenes—at too great a length for its importance to the story. Then the triangle resumes with a changed tone: Strindberg's goddess-gutter view of women combined with the Emancipated Neurotic of the twenties. The shift would be interesting if it were a true modulation: time finding the bones beneath the flesh-bloom of youth. But the structure seems haphazard, full of irrelevancies, almost cantankerous. What starts as a rueful-happy Gallic *Design for Living* tilts sideways to become semipathological study—to no perceptible character or thematic point. Besides, in this script by Truffaut and Jean Gruault (from a novel by Henri-Pierre Roché), there is a growing disparity between what is said and what we see. Jules says he puts up with Catherine's behavior because her presence blesses him to whatever degree she remains in his life. Jim worships her on more or less the same ground. But where is this warm beneficent woman? We see a self-indulgent sensualist, self-consciously sensitive, full of whims and impatience, who never really does anything for anybody and who—because she is finally rejected by Jim—kills him and herself in front of her husband. And even this seems pettish caprice; she and Jules were again living together pleasantly and just happened to meet Jim at the movies.

Goethe's *Elective Affinities* is quoted in the film, and there is a hint that a parallel is intended. Although Goethe's novel deals with a quadrangle, it has certain resemblances in story and idea. But can the deaths of Catherine and Jim have been contrived for the same reason as those of Ottilie and Edward? Goethe said: "Either morality triumphs or is defeated. . . . Ottilie and Edward had to perish after they had given free rein to their inclinations. Therein consists the triumph of the moral principle." Can this heavy sentimentality have been Truffaut's goal?

The patchwork effect of the script is reflected in Truffaut's direction, which returns us to the matter of art for art-making's sake. The film is such a fireworks display of cinematic techniques and devices that our first impression is that we are in the hands of a master. Soon, however, we feel that we are only in the hands of an imaginative enthusiast. The film is filled with intense close-ups, lovely lighting effects, swift cuts, investigations of texture. There are freezes and resumptions of movement in mid-scene as the camera is arbitrarily stopped for a moment; there are sequences in which the camera is hand-held for no apparent reason; there are trick fade-ins. (On a black screen the upper right corner of the next shot is seen then it spreads out to fill the screen.) Some of the newsreel shots of the war are distended to fill the wide screen, some are used in their original 35 mm. width.

Shot by shot, almost all of the film is visually exquisite. (For one example, the shot in which the three shutters of the white beach house are thrown open in the brilliant morning sunshine.) But there is no controlling sense of style or of pertinence, only a coltish enjoyment of the camera's potentialities. What is the point of the scene in which Catherine's nightgown catches fire and Jim extinguishes it? Why the long silence when the trio sit down to their first meeting after the war? Why the long song she sings with her lover Albert? Because Truffaut enjoyed these scenes in themselves; that seems to be the only reason. They are all well done but are unrelated to the whole, thus despite their excellence of execution—in fact, because of it—make the film ultimately disappointing.

As Jules, Oskar Werner has a sweet, tousled quality, full of canine patience. As Jim, Henri Serre presents a handsome Gauguinlike face but does little more. It is Jeanne Moreau, as Catherine, who gives not only the pivotal but the best performance: mercurial, egocentric, tyrannical, appealing. Whether she is kidding her own femininity in newsboy's cap and painted mustache or sitting as *hausfrau* in steel-rimmed spectacles and high shoes or embracing a lover, she is supplying a better performance than the part can support. Her Catherine is a character in search of an author.

Truffaut said in a recent interview:

My films are circus shows. . . . After the elephant comes the conjuror; after the conjuror, the bear. I even arrange an interval round about the sixth reel because people may be getting a bit tired. At the seventh reel I take them in hand again and try to end up with the best thing in the show.

When Diaghileff commissioned Cocteau to work for his ballet company, he said, *"Jean, étonne-moi."* This seems to be Truffaut's principal aesthetics. There is a lot less here than meets the eye, but what does meet the eye is frequently astonishing.

POSTSCRIPT. Further acquaintance underscores three of the elements noted above. First (as with *Wild Strawberries*), despite the dissatisfaction that *Jules and Jim* may leave, its execution is one of the brilliant achievements of the postwar film era. If there were even more flaws in it than, in my view, there are, it would still be a treasury of delights: in exhilaration, tenderness, wonderful rhythmic variation, understatement. On an extensive visit to European filmmakers (to be described later), I asked a couple of dozen directors who their own favorite directors were. Few names came up regularly; one, with both the young and old, was Truffaut: for *Jules and Jim*.

Second, it becomes clearer that Catherine always wanted Jim and that she married Jules almost out of pique because of a missed date at a café. One may at least infer this in the cryptography that Truffaut, like other artists, chooses to use along with his art. But this is not to say that she would have been any happier with Jim or faithful to him.

Third, connected with this, it becomes clearer that Catherine is a psychopath, not the goddess that she is considered. The very fact that she would marry on the basis of a missed date—and it was *she* who was an hour late!—is symptomatic enough; but it becomes evident that what at first seems charming caprice or waywardness is mental disorder. Early in the story, when conversation displeases her, she plunges into the Seine. When she goes to the seaside with her friends, she has an impulse to take along a bottle of vitriol. Throughout, the infantile insistence on immediate satisfaction develops until, when Jim is to marry his mistress, she murders him and herself—in front of her harmless husband. The film begins with such happiness and vivacity, we are so much affected by the men's view of Catherine, that it all cloaks the story's fundamental nature: psychopathic regression.

The allusions to Goethe now seem part of Jules's self-devised smoke screen. The film is not concerned with moral principle and is not in any serious way a parallel with *Elective Affinities*. Goethe is part of Jules's own dramatization of his role with Catherine.

The performances of the leading roles become intensified in the qualities described. Henri Serre seems more wooden, Oskar Werner more subtle and endearing, Jeanne Moreau more delicately volatile. The film begins and continues with such a flood of spirited invention that even on the third or fourth viewing, one wonders whether the high level can be sustained. It does in fact falter, in the sequence about the letters exchanged between Jim in Paris and the pair on the Rhine; then picks up a kind of saddened momentum for its closing sequences.

Because of its spirit, because of the un-American innocence-in-sex that pervades it, it has become for some American intellectuals—both men and women—a kind of dream film, a *belle époque* soap opera in which they would like to be involved. Enamored of the idealized, free, "continental" life for which they seem to hanker, they are notably protective of the film and resent any imputation to it of thematic vagary, mere flamboyance, or—especially—the possibility that it is in essence a horror story, not a *chanson triste*. Still, this side of blindness, the stimulation of fantasy is a legitimate function of art; and whatever its shortcomings, *Jules and Jim* is one of the moments when the history of the film suddenly glows.

Shoot the Piano Player   (July 9, 1962)

François Truffaut's *Shoot the Piano Player* was made before *Jules and Jim*; the reception of the latter has apparently prompted the importation of the former. It is welcome, too, although on a smaller scale it has the same proportion of shortcomings to virtues as the other film. Truffaut's public statements contain lots of blithe assertions: "I'm lazy, and when the day for shooting a film arrives, I don't have a finished script . . . I may find myself changing my notions about what I want to do right in the middle of making a film. And on days when I'm feeling merry, I shoot merry scenes, and on my gloomy days I shoot gloomy ones." These utterances would be affectation except that the finished films bear him out. They really do have an air of improvisation, and they burst into blossoms of high jinks or intensity, sometimes quite irrelevant to story and previous mood.

For example, this film opens with a man running down dark streets, fleeing pursuers. He rams into a lamppost and is helped to his feet by a passing stranger. He then walks a couple of blocks with the stranger who chats with him about his wife. They shake hands and part; then the brother visits the hero and the film begins. The street encounter was the kind of intimacy that can occur between strangers, and it has an excursive charm which (as with some moments in *Jules and Jim*) Truffaut simply felt like pursuing, that's all.

The rewards of this free-verse approach are ample if the director can support it with warm invention and cool skill. Truffaut has plenty of both. The disadvantage is that the net effect is patchy and tends to detract from the subject matter. Recently a dinner companion told me that when he was in London in the thirties, he went to a midnight movie and saw a feature film that started with a costume sequence, then had a snatch of a musical, then a chunk of a gangster picture, and so on. He thought he was drowsy and was just not following. Next day he was told that the British quota laws of the time made it mandatory to show a domestic feature at least once a day with every foreign feature. In order to exhibit profitable Hollywood pictures, the English studios would sweep an hour-and-a-half's worth of bits off their own cutting-room floors, paste them together and, to satisfy the law, would run them off at midnight when no one was expected to see them.

Their solution is a *reductio ad absurdum* of the Truffaut method. In the midst of a kidnaping scene, the criminals get into an avuncular discussion about first names with the young victim. When a hood says that if he's lying, he hopes his mother drops dead, an inset shot shows his mother dropping dead. All these touches are funny or moving, but we sometimes wonder whether we've dozed off and missed a transition.

The film is based on an American crime novel, the genre that many French intellectuals glorify, particularly the group around the magazine *Cahiers du Cinéma,* for which Truffaut used to be a critic. It is an imitation Humphrey Bogart vehicle, and the film's paradox is that Truffaut weakens the suspense with his digressive gusto, yet that gusto is the best element in it. The hybrid result is neither a tight crime story nor a sound crime satire like Huston's *Beat the Devil.* But there are fine sequences. The scene in which the hero and the "nice" girl go to bed for the first time compresses a long passionate day into a two-minute poem, beautifully composed.

Charles Aznavour, the pianist-hero, reticent and small, may do for short men what Ezio Pinza did a decade ago for middle-aged men: make them popular sex images. There are three competent young actresses in the film, Marie Du Bois, Nicole Berger, and Michele Mercier, the last of whom seems much too lovely to be a low-priced tart.

The Soft Skin   (November 14, 1964)

François Truffaut's latest picture is a failure. His triangle story is disappointingly trite in every regard and the conclusion is, alas, laughably melodramatic. But it should not be overlooked that, granted the poor script and the casting of the uninteresting Françoise Dorleac as the other girl, there is hardly another director who could have made this film with, so to speak, the camera in the palm of his hand. Three moments show Truffaut in top form: an undressing scene in which some intercutting of close-ups of the man's face increases not only sexuality but pathos; a scene in which, when the girl suddenly appears, he crumples a telegram he has been writing to her and we cut to the crumpled words "I love you" as he looks at her face; and a night scene in which, after she has telephoned agreeing to meet him next day, he walks around his hotel suite with an unchanged face, unconsciously turning on all the lights.

POSTSCRIPT. As noted, Truffaut was born to make films. The still unanswered question is whether that is sufficient for a full career of film-making.

Where the Boys Are; The Love Game   (January 30, 1961)

Where the Boys Are is an American comedy dealing with the annual Easter vacation pilgrimage of thousands of college students to the Florida beaches, where boys go to meet girls and *vice* is very much *versa*. Middle-class morality is here isolated and magnified. The boys want the most with the least obligation; the girls want maximum attention without losing their Most Precious Possession. If the idea sounds revolting, the picture didn't invent it—it was taken from contemporary mythology. The script, which follows the escapades of four girls, is written in jaunty pop dialogue, and the picture is helped by the bloom of two newcomers named Dolores Hart and Paula Prentiss.

Alongside this film let us place a recent French picture called *The Love Game*, directed by Philippe de Broca, who is twenty-six. This is the first imported comedy of the "New Wave" and, to me, is one of the most original works which that rather disappointing wave has so far produced. The American film has at least four plots; the French film can scarcely be said to have one. It deals with a Parisian boy and girl who live behind their curio shop and, to make an attempt at drama, it includes another boy who lives across the street and is a quasi-threat to their happiness. But the object of the picture is merely to convey how these two young people feel at various times: elated, jealous, suddenly depressed, and so on. There is a sequence of some minutes in which they simply cavort about their shop after a bit of good news and which is one of the most charming scenes to appear on film in years. Jean-Pierre Cassel and Geneviève Cluny (who supplied the idea for the film) make you a little jealous not to be their age and (according to your sex) in the slippers of one or the other. At the end these two people, whom we have often seen in bed, are on their way to be married.

Let us avoid facile comparisons with *Where the Boys Are*. For one thing, we are all a bit tired of comparisons between continental worldliness and American puritanism. For another, these comparisons are usually falsely based. Middle-class morality is virtually and virtuously the same everywhere. Anyone who acted on the belief that all American youths behave like those in the MGM film and that all French youths behave like those in *The Love Game* would be in for some pleasant and unpleasant surprises.

The Joker   (September 4, 1961)

Lightness of heart is not the same thing as laughter and is much more difficult to achieve in the theater. Mere technical skill can produce laughter, but gaiety is a mood and the one that looks false most quickly. Which of us has not at some time squirmed while watching merry revelers hoist papier-mâché tankards and declaim "Ha, ha, ha"?

All praise and all gratitude, therefore, to Philippe de Broca, the twenty-seven-year-old Frenchman who is director and coauthor of *The Joker*. In his first film, *The Love Game,* de Broca showed that he was able to capture high spirits without making them seem captive. In his second film he has created a soufflé so light and lovely that it produces two tandem effects: after the first five minutes we fear that it cannot be sustained; and after the first ten minutes we hope that it will never end.

The story concerns young Edouard who lives with his two illegitimate babies, his brother, his sister-in-law, his elderly uncle, and a pretty, submissive maid in a fun-fair house in Paris which makes Steinberg's cartoons seem prosy realism. Brother Guillaume is a photographer, his wife, Pilou, is a quasi-journalist, and the family makes its happy-go-lucky living by posing for historical murder photographs to illustrate Pilou's lurid texts. Edouard occasionally assists, but his chief occupation is to savor living.

The film is built around his love for a beautiful married woman, his eventual attainment of her, his realization that she has no wings, and his refusal to be earth-bound. The ending of the film is so abrupt that it forces you to consider *why* it is abrupt; and thus tells you more about Edouard and the theme.

The facile comparison for the film is with *You Can't Take It with You,* but here it is as if that play had been written not by two clever jokesmiths, but by a sexily irrepressible poet. This film's camera work is airily excellent, every scene is imaginatively articulated. Its unique achievement is its quality of movement, which is choreographic throughout. Indeed, Edouard and his family burst into actual dance at various moments, the way old Yiddish actors used to melt into song in the middle of long speeches, but aside from this the whole film is conceived in terms of dancelike and musical movement, like a Chaplin or Tati film.

De Broca has clearly found "his" actor in Jean-Pierre Cassel, who also played the leading role in *The Love Game*. Cassel, lithe and lyric, endows Edouard with the somehow endearing egocentricity of the intensely effectionate. Geneviève Cluny, who too was in the first film, is takingly and unconventionally logical as Pilou. That character is not to be confused with an actor named Palau who, as the uncle, is a master of courtly idiosyncracy. As the *princesse lointaine* Anouk Aimée is desirable and—later—understandably undesirable.

There is lilting music by Georges Delerue, and there are exceptionally good subtitles by Rose Sokol.

When one considers the complex technicalities of film-making, de Broca's achievement in creating a spontaneous, thistledown quality is all the more admirable. He has taken the *légèreté* that we have all felt part of the time and abstracted it to make a whole world.

The Five Day Lover   (January 1, 1962)

The young French director Philippe de Broca is now dear to many of us for his first two films, especially *The Joker*. *The Five Day Lover* is not equally sound in theme and plot, and its resolution—the familiar credo of the complaisant husband—is the merest excuse to justify what has gone before; but any plot, any excuse is sufficient to justify such vivacity in love and sex, such pleasure in the fact of pleasure.

Again, Jean-Pierre Cassel is de Broca's Harlequin, an actor who rarely smiles and rarely needs to, because out of the fluency of his movement, the tempo of his gait, the relish of his love-making comes all the *brio* that he needs. He tells us about his feelings with nice obliqueness; e.g., awaiting a girl's visit, he straightens his tie in a mirror, scowls at himself, then bursts into a few stamping Spanish steps.

Jean Seberg is the girl and, wearing her hair long, an attractive one. She is like a plant that has prospered by transplanting. For the present, there is no need to hail her talent, but France and French directors have released whatever there is in her of spontaneity, of warmth and fun. Micheline Presle, whose effect as woman and accomplishments as actress are not yet challenged by Miss Seberg, and François Perier, a not quite certain actor, complete the principal quartet.

The title doesn't mean a lover who stays five days; it means a week-day lover, as against a husband whose attentions are available only on weekends. Cassel is an ex-salesman being kept by Miss Presle, a successful couturier. He commences an affair with Miss Seberg, who is married to Perier and is the mother of two. She tells her husband that she is spending her afternoons with her friend Miss Presle who, in turn, doens't know that her lover is deceiving her. If the plot sounds asthmatic, treat it like an opera libretto. Believe it if you choose; its real purpose is to provide a framework for solos and ensembles.

There is no scene in this film, no single shot, that is not planned by de Broca with taste and a sure sense of line. He can hold his own with other directors in the sheerly pictorial. (See the long shot under the great trees at Chantilly.) But in the matter of making each scene reveal itself in *movement* he has few peers and fewer superiors. He is also especially sensitive to the complementary purpose of settings; his décor is his chorus. In *The Joker* the crazy house kept commenting on the characters; here the furnishings of Cassel's flat combine luxury and lubricity in a cozily seductive way.

All three de Broca films have been escape pictures for adults. *The Love Game* and *The Joker* made us realize what we ought to have been doing when we were young. *The Five Day Lover* celebrates the sense of romance that befuddles our lives but to which we must cling if only to make sobriety seem worthwhile by contrast. Breathes there a man with soul so dumpy that he has not wanted at some time to storm into a smart restaurant just after it has closed, with a beautiful girl on his arm, scattering banknotes to headwaiter and staff as he goes, taking a table in the huge empty room, ordering wines and a feast, and summoning violins?

That Man from Rio   (September 19, 1964)

It ought to have been clear by now that Philippe De Broca is one of the most talented of the younger French directors, yet he is the one who is generally least well esteemed. Now he presents *That Man from Rio,* and it is possible that this delightful film will only further seal his neglect.

Why? Because he is orthodox in his methods. He is not a skimmer of Proust, Freud, and Dada like Resnais, a "pure" cinematist like Godard, and idiosyncratic like Truffaut, nor a leech on the breast of existentialism like Malle. So far as technique is concerned, there is not a sequence in any de Broca film that could not have been made before the Second War. In our frantically experimental art world, absence of technical innovation has come to be equated with absence of merit or individuality. We might remember that, for instance, there is no line of Robert Frost that, technically speaking, could not have been written before the turn of the century.

All that can be claimed for de Broca is that he has wit, tenderness, dexterity, a superb eye for composition and color, a prodigious sense of rhythm and of movement, a perfect command of the medium, and—his curse—high spirits. The swift, captivating flights of Truffaut seem very much part of a grim age, a kind of spoof reaction against dark contemporary reality. De Broca has what can be called timeless high spirits—the youth that all men have had for at least some part of their lives. He is miraculously able to abstract and sustain this quality in films.

His new picture plunges further into extremes of physical action than his others: less of the lightfoot escapades of Clair, more of the breakneck dare-deviltry of Harold Lloyd combined with the mock bravura of *Fanfan the Tulip* and the quintessence of all the corny hidden-treasure movies ever made. The insidious virtue of this film is that, although de Broca never means us to take any of the excitement quite seriously, it is nonetheless exciting. Jean-Paul Belmondo is a soldier with a week's leave in Paris who goes to visit his girl and sees her kidnaped, abducted to Rio because she knows the whereabouts of a statue that her anthropologist-father had buried a few years before. Immediately Belmondo hustles his way on to the same jetliner and has a series of adventures in Rio, Brasilia, and the jungle that are a small encyclopedia of action-slapstick, each sequence executed with ballet precision. At the end of the week, before his pass expires, the soldier is back in Paris safely with his girl. The film could have been a bit shorter to advantage; the light-airplane episode, with the ignorant Belmondo at the controls, could have been spared. But the good-humored irrationality with which he starts running after departing automobiles (then we cut to his arrival at his destination, only slightly winded) makes up for any small faults.

Belmondo, who has been making too many films too heedlessly, makes this one just heedlessly enough: sufficient concern to concern us, sufficient disregard to keep it funny; with plenty of the justifiable assumption that he is appealing but without being bumptious about it. Françoise Dorleac has the right cool zaniness for the girl. Jean Servais, the gang chief of *Rififi,* the "good" priest of *He Who Must Die,* is so excellent an actor that he turns a now-I-have-you-in-my-power scene into a valid dramatic moment.

Breathless   (February 13, 1961)

In addition to her function as aesthetic conscience of the Western world, France has always been a pioneer in morality. I don't mean matters like the so-called "French farce," which has as little relevance to French life as to anyone's; I mean, for instance, the fact that *Madame Bovary* was published in the same year as *Little Dorrit* and three years before *The Marble Faun.* The French continue to explore in both areas. Much of the result can be written off as mere excursion, still they *do* it.

The penalty of this virtue is high expectation, which is why the much-discussed New Wave of French films has been disappointing. Although several good films have emerged from it, it has been more a Young Wave than a new one. Now, with the appearance of *Breathless,* we have a film that is new aesthetically and morally.

The director—whose film this is in a way that few American films belong to their directors—is Jean-Luc Godard, who is thirty and who wrote the screenplay from an idea suggested by François Truffaut, director of *The 400 Blows.* This is Godard's first full-length film, and it quickly establishes that he has a style of his own and a point of view. He tells here the story of a restless, dissatisfied young man, and his camera follows the protagonist about like a puppy, wheeling and reversing and crowding up close; switching abruptly (without dis-solves), as abruptly as the young man himself loses interest in one matter and goes on to the next. Style and subject are perfectly matched.

That subject is the anti-hero—not to be described by that favorite cavil word "amoral" but immoral and living in an immoral world. He may have got there because of his revulsion or our exclusion of him, but that is where he now lives by upside-down standards. Already familiar to us through numerous works from Jarry through Céline to Camus, he now appears on the screen: stealing, mugging, murdering —and engaging us. We do not bleed for him as the child of uncongenial parents or as an underprivileged waif. He is not to be cured by any of the cozy comforts of psychoanalysis or social meliorism. The trouble with this young man, although he does not specifically know it, is history. If we understand him, it is because we know that he is contemporary society *in extremis*: that the dissolution of religious foundations and conceivable futures are in him carried to the ultimate, short of suicide.

Yet this film is not a bid for sympathy, it is an assault on those who can be lulled by thinking that the leak is at the other end of the boat and anyway we're only one-quarter under water. The film says, as have many French novels and plays, "If you concentrate on hoping for a revival of the past, we will all drown. We must find another boat that will float in contemporary storms." What the new vessel is, Godard presumably does not know, any more than the rest of us; but (to change metaphors) at least he knows that it is fatal to cling to the bosom of the dead mother just because she is not yet stone cold.

The story is simple: it is one long flight. Michel, a young Parisian drifter, steals a car in Marseilles, kills a policeman who follows him, hides out in Paris with an American girl (pregnant by him) while he tries to collect money owed for past thefts so that he can run off with her to Italy; finally he is betrayed by her and is shot by the police while running away. He continues to run—down the unheeding street —until he dies at the corner.

The style is all. The first two minutes make you think this is going to be a breezy Gallic comedy about crooks. A shapely girl accomplice signals Michel when to snatch the car. Then, as he speeds out alone through the country, he sings, talks to himself, comments on the beautiful weather, finds a pistol in the glove department, plays with it as he drives, going "pop!" at the sun. He is soon cornered by a policeman and the gun does in fact go "pop," but the actual shooting is not much realer to Michel than the pretended one. This playful, almost charming violation of the very bases of civilized behavior is typical of the film.

Although it exists in an anticonventional world and although

Michel's hero is Humphrey Bogart, this is not a hard-boiled film. It is the epic of a romantic outlaw, as egocentric as romantics and outlaws always are, whose life seems the only natural one to him. It is a film of flawless consistency and uncompromised truth. It may not be *our* truth, but that of course is not the primary point.

Jean-Paul Belmondo, a young ex-boxer, makes his film debut as Michel and demonstrates that he is a capable actor: he has imagination, sensibility, and the ability to behave credibly. Also, he is the male equivalent of a *jolie laide*. Jean Seberg, of unblessed memory, is his American girl, and is quite adequate. Godard sensed that her personal quality (not her quality as actress) was exactly right for the part and has helped her to get it into the film.

POSTSCRIPT. In Shaw's *You Never Can Tell* an "advanced" woman returns to England after an absence of many years and is told by a friend that her ideas will no longer shock anyone, that there is only one place where they would still be considered advanced. "The church, perhaps?" she says. "No," her friend replies, "the theater." Films are not much closer to the frontiers of thought than the theater (although they sometimes seem so in America because the best films from abroad contrast so favorably with the best American plays). *Breathless* was the first significant film statement of the philosophic view so memorably put by Camus in *The Stranger* almost twenty years before.

A technical point and a thematic point need to be explicated. In photography and editing, Godard moves here to a new distillation. We often see the beginning and the end of an action, with the middle implied. The photography, much of it done with a hand-held camera, was kept as informal as possible (for one sequence Godard pushed the cameraman in a wheel chair). The by-now celebrated bedroom scene was in fact shot in a small bedroom, with the actors almost having to sidle past the camera. The result of this jump-cutting and informal photography is not factual: it intensifies fact into art. A documentary style could have been attempted by fixing the camera at the far end of the room and zooming in for close-ups. Godard wanted to evoke the essence of body-scented, close, bored, but actually quite affectionate sex—in swift, veristic, uncomfortable statements. It is the kind of effect that imitators fumble by mistaking it for reportage and that Godard himself has almost parodied in later pictures with distention and bemusement.

Thematically, Michel's shooting of the policeman is echoed at the end by the girl's betraying him to the police. The reasons for her action are not explicit. She is fond of him and is bearing his child; on the other hand, he is messing up her life and her very affection for him ties her to his dim fate. These counterfeelings seem to cancel each other into nullity, in which state her betrayal becomes that famous phenomenon of the Absurd, the *acte gratuit*—the action done simply because one does not refrain from doing it. Once I saw a small child at a cocktail party who was permitted by her parents to pass the canapé tray. The tray tipped slightly, the canapés began to slide slowly, and the child watched with complete fascination as they all fell to the floor. It is something of the feeling I got from the betrayal, in subsequent viewings of *Breathless*. The child did her action without moral reference, simply interested to watch it going on. Godard's girl does her action because she has no moral reference strong enough to keep her from the pleasant pain of the act and its consequences.

My Life to Live (October 12, 1963)

Jean-Luc Godard's directorial debut, *Breathless,* was one of the best films of the new French group, trenchant and anarchic. His next two full-length films have not been shown here; all we have seen is the episode he made for *Seven Capital Sins,* which was commonplace. His fourth feature, *My Life to Live,* is empty and pretentious. Much arty apparatus has been employed in it, but it only emphasizes the absence of content.

Godard tells here the story of a contemporary Parisienne, a sales clerk, whose poverty forces her into prostitution and who is eventually murdered in a fight between two gangs of procurers. She is meant to be a victim of blind forces that have nothing against her specifically, that simply run over her as a truck crushes a bug. This sounds like a potentially good film, but Godard has not made it. His picture is only a collection of stylistic devices, without characterization, without credible motivation, without even the pathos of a believable puppet at the mercy of believable mindless evil. The display of devices begins right at the beginning. The first shot is of the backs of the heads of the girl and her ex-husband sitting at a café counter; the shot lasts a good five minutes while they talk.

This technical eccentricity is intended, I suppose, to undermine our possible objections to the vacuousness of the scene and the irritation of the manner; we are to be persuaded that the director who dares to do this *couldn't* make a scene as hollow as this one seems to be. Similar devices follow. In fact, the whole film consists of effects laid on like flat impassive strokes of a broad brush, one next to the other. Many of the scenes move obliquely, and abruptly, and are intrinsically dull: a long conversation with a café philosopher; the writing of a letter, photographed large word by large word; a long excerpt from Dreyer's film *The Passion of Joan of Arc,* which the girl attends and which is meant to be, I think, a booby trap for facile symbolists. As is her name—Nana. (In other words, you prove your cleverness by not taking Joan's martyrdom as a parallel for Nana's; and the Zola reference is to be ignored as too obvious. Such are the games of the chichi.)

The film is divided into twelve episodes, each with Brechtian titles, but neither the titles nor anything else tells us, for example, why, though Nana has a job, she cannot pay her rent and is forced into prostitution or why she is killed by the rival gangs although she is not in the crossfire of their fight. The omissions and intrusions are so dogged that we are meant to be ashamed to ask these questions. *La vie,* we are supposed to know, is *la vie, non?* For me, however, it was not *la vie* but *la vogue:* emptiness modishly dolled up.

Godard's first good film left us wondering whether it was a lucky accident. The most charitable view is that the question is still unanswered. His new picture seems to exist simply for discussion in gassy film journals.

A Woman Is a Woman   (December 5, 1964)

A Woman Is a Woman is like a further initiation rite in a secret society. The cult argues that Jean-Luc Godard is a director to the medium born, with such ease, freedom, daring that he largely ignores the "literary" cinema of story form and revels in the resources of film as such; plays with them in *jeux d'esprit* that, through their own beauty, more than compensate for the absence of conventional elements. This would be quite acceptable if true. What we have here is a torpid and clumsy picture whose spirit and lightness do not compare with what some other directors have given us while telling a cohesive, well-constructed story. If Philippe de Broca had directed this very same material, he could have made it tolerable; de Broca has already handled a comparable film with infinitely more success (*The Love Game*). Godard is a magician who makes elaborate uninspired gestures and then pulls out of the hat precisely nothing.

A young unmarried Parisian couple are living together. She, inevitably, is a stripteaser; thus, we are beyond conventional unconventional morality. She wants a baby and he does not. She threatens to ask someone else to father it, and he angrily agrees. There is some flirting but no fathering. Finally the young man complies. All this is decked with tricks: words printed on the screen like chapter headings, poses, parodies, fancy cutting, all of which are supposed to provide cinematic texture. There are also a lot of annoying "in" jokes. Jean-Paul Belmondo, presumably amusing himself in the secondary part of the nonfather, stands at a bar next to a girl. She turns around; it is Jeanne Moreau. (About as novel as that gag appearance of Crosby in Hope pictures.) He asks her how *Jules and Jim* is going. (Knowing chuckles from the clique.) She replies, "Moderato." (More chuckles, because they know that he and she have made a film called *Moderato Cantabile*.)

What exceeds these objections is a feeling of distaste, founded on a suspicion that Godard is displaying his private life. The girl is played by Anna Karina, who is Mrs. Godard, a commonplace actress and unfascinating personality. The little games and teasings of the twosome seem reproductions of private frolics between Mr. and Mrs. G. that he thought just too cute to keep to themselves. If I am right in this, he was wrong.

Contempt   (January 2, 1965)

Those interested in Brigitte Bardot's behind—in Cinemascope and color—will find ample rewards in *Contempt*. Jean-Luc Godard's film seizes every chance to display Miss Bardot nude and prone to suggestion. The story, adapted from Moravia's *A Ghost at Noon,* deals with a French couple in Rome. He is a screen writer hired to revise a

script of *The Odyssey* for an American producer; the producer wants
the wife; she develops contempt for her husband because she has the
impression that he does not object to her humoring his boss.

The film travels fairly quickly for about the first half-hour. Then
follows a scene in which the husband and wife, moving innumerable
times from bedroom to bathroom to living room, debate whether or
not they should accept the producer's invitation to Capri. I suggest
that this sequence, which seems to run about twenty minutes, can
serve in all film schools as an archetype of arrant egotism and bankrupt imagination in a director. Godard has nothing to say here that
could not have been done in about three minutes. He has deliberately
spun it out, ostensibly to recreate the languor of one kind of marital
quarrel but really (in my view) to draw approval from his clique.
They were basically impressed, I believe, more with the nonchalance
with which he treats an expensive medium than with any intrinsic
achievement. Underneath the arty prattle about his supposed style,
one can hear their unconscious gasps: "That film must cost so-and-so
many thousand of dollars a minute! Any commercial hack would be
concerned to make each minute count for something. But Jean-Luc
doesn't *care!*" The hidden referent here is not aesthetic but budgetary
bravado.

In an early scene there are some striking shots of Greek statuary,
which suggest that a parallel between mythology and the story is to be
attempted. It is not. Jack Palance, who looks like Attila and acts
worse, plays the producer. The one piquant element is the performance of Fritz Lang, as a director. Although the part quickly becomes
the sterotyped mid-European sage that we all came to know in this
country in the post-Hitler years, full of *gedämpfte* wisdom and quotations, Lang nevertheless has some richness of personality.

The Married Woman   (September 11, 1965)

The Married Woman is Jean-Luc Godard's best work to be
seen here since *Breathless*. This means, to begin with, that he had a
more interesting face to photograph (Macha Meril's) than that of
Anna Karina, which has dominated—if not oppressed—too many of
his films. This is not a small matter in a Godard picture because the

fixing and exploration of the photographed face (not acting, as such) is a matter of mystique to him. But more important, he has used his armory of experiment, trick, imaginative innovation for a perceptible and communicated purpose.

We spend twenty-four hours with a young Parisienne. We begin with her and her lover in bed. Then she meets her husband, who has come back from a business trip, and eventually they go to bed. The next afternoon there is another rendezvous with her lover at an air-port hotel. These three amorous episodes are the film's being; the rest is subsidiary. There are interludes of varying interest: a dinner party conversation; a visit to a doctor in which she learns that she is preg-nant (she is not sure of the paternity); overheard conversation in a café (the hallmark of recent French films). There is a lot of the familiar Godard apparatus: the chapter titles on the screen (pointless and affected as ever); the improvised dialogue (passages in which the principal characters, the doctor, a child, seem to be responding to an unheard interviewer); accidents are retained (the moment when Miss Meril slips and falls in the street). There are visual puns. We see a traffic sign reading *Danger;* the camera closes in until it reads *ange.* At the airport the girl passes a sign reading *Passage;* the camera separates it into *Pas sage.*

But with the help of his customary photographer Raoul Coutard, Godard has made the bedroom scenes genuinely sexual and humanly genuine. He calls the picture "fragments of a film made in 1964," and the fragmentary feeling is consistent in the sex episodes. At the end of each quiet brief passage, there is a quick fade-out, then a quick fade-in, as if we were going to a different place or time; but it is the same scene, continuing. This cinema punctuation is deliberately used—or misused—to break these relatively continuous episodes into arcs and shards, to place on us the burden of assembling them in our minds into a kind of collage. The mind responds because the pieces are intriguing; the fragmented effect keeps the scene from degenerating into conventional Gallic bedroom *tristesse,* jars our sensibilities into an apprehension of some depth. The camera concentrates on the girl, so we undertake these experiences largely from her viewpoint; and although there are no scenes of passionate love-making, the net effect is of a solitary person in the midst of the heat and puzzles of sex. There is stream-of-consciousness verbalizing in these scenes; she con-tinually whispers disconnected and irrelevant phrases. This contributes little because the *idea* of the device is all, the *contents* of the device are nil; and it soon becomes wearisome.

This is a general fault of the film. Almost every idea or fragment has initial impact but small content. Godard persists with it, and tedium sets in. The rhythm of the picture is sting and tedium, sting and tedium.

Yet the over-all effect is of a lonely loveliness. The exquisite compositions in the bedroom scenes—sometimes merely two hands reaching for one another on a sheet, sometimes a navel staring at us, sometimes a rounded leg—all are tokens of a quintessential but indescribable reality, set inescapably in an entangling context of verbiage. The words are inevitable and inevitably inadequate; the facts remain. Around this embattled arena of sex moves the girl, lying (and how appropriate it seems) to both men. She tells the lover she has warned the husband she will leave him; she tells the husband she has long since left the lover.

Throughout we get from her a sense of strange and somewhat estranged curiosity. She is trying to find out what relationships mean, whether the word love—which she keeps using, almost as an incantation—is any definition of what she feels or whether it is a mere sop to a heritage of sin-consciousness or perhaps a mere aggrandizement of physical attraction. The whole atmosphere of the film is sexual— backgrounds of bra ads as she walks along the street or flicks magazines, the lubricious talk of a housemaid. And through this sea of sexuality this girl swims and floats—secure because she is attractive, but insecure because she does not understand the extent or meaning of her powers and appetites.

Godard, who had come increasingly to shine his talents on his own circus acts, here reserves them most of the time for his subject; and it is a measure of his success that he makes us ignore moral judgment. The theme is natural history. The girl's behavior seems neither wicked nor French-farce sly; she has, in essence, our sympathy.

Last Year at Marienbad   (*Show,* May 1962)

As I left the theater after seeing *Last Year at Marienbad,* I heard a man say grimly to his wife, "Boy, I sure pity the critics on this one." He had evidently seen none of the tens of thousands of words already published about this film in Europe, where critics enjoyed themselves at sorting out its meanings.

Last Year at Marienbad is a relatively short film—ninety-three minutes—directed by Alain Resnais, who made *Hiroshima, Mon Amour*. He commissioned the original script from Alain Robbe-Grillet and worked closely on it with him. Robbe-Grillet is one of the three or four leading figures among the New Novelists of France, and those who know his two chief works, *Le Voyeur* and *La Jalousie,* have something more than a glimmer of what to expect in this film.

It takes place in a huge baroque palace—actually Nymphenburg in Bavaria—which has been converted into a deluxe hotel. A man (never named—no characters are named) meets a young woman. He tells her that they met last year at Marienbad, or perhaps some similar place, and were lovers. She denies it. Through a complex series of flashbacks, we see various versions of this past encounter as it may or may not have happened. She is accompanied by a man who may or may not be her husband. The putative husband plays an implicative match game with the man all through the film, always beating him. The man insists that the woman leave the "husband" and go away with him, as he says he asked her to a year ago. At the end, the man and the woman probably leave together.

The indefiniteness of the story is part of the film's fabric. Resnais and Robbe-Grillet have disagreed publicly about whether the pair actually did meet the year before, and far from being embarrassed by differing views about their collaboration, as, say, Billy Wilder and I. A. L. Diamond might be, this director and screen writer apparently take their disagreement as a certificate of success. This film, they claim, is like a piece of sculpture that may be approached from many angles—all things to all men.

But the gauzy story is only one note in the work's tonality. Resnais has said that, before shooting *Marienbad,* he drew up a complete chronology of its events on graph paper; while he was shooting, he told actors that the scene in hand followed a certain other scene in time sequence but would not appear there in the final editing.

The plainest point of the film is that it does not intend to tell a chronological story. It tries to isolate and reproduce the emotions of its situations, drawing (as all our minds do constantly) on the past and the possible future, and on a time area where we put elements of past and present into combinations that may never have happened and may never happen but that influence us nonetheless. The film is an attempt to make visible the intangible—the lightning play of mind and memory and impulse.

To describe Resnais's method in detail is as impossible as it would be unhelpful. Much more to the purpose is to observe that he uses a free range of cinematic devices: intercutting, sometimes so brief as to be subliminal; swift series of still shots; quickly successive scenes of a character in the same composition but in different clothes and different lights; repetitions of whole sequences from the same or from different viewpoints (he even repeats one zooming close-up of the woman in more and more intense light to the point of almost white overexposure, presumably to stimulate the increasing intensity of the image in the narrator's mind). The other guests in the hotel sometimes freeze motionless as the protagonists move among them, sometimes behave normally, sometimes are seen to speak but cannot be heard. At one point, we watch a duo of string musicians sawing away while we hear an organ playing. Sometimes the hero recalls on the sound track an episode which is not quite what is happening before us; later, the episode is repeated more or less as he had previously described it.

As in Robbe-Grillet's novels, the film's planes of time dissolve, resolve, and redissolve continually, like prisms in a kaleidoscope. The most realistic detail—a statue's face, a broken glass—by its juxtaposition with other shots takes on an unreal, suggestive quality. Kafka said, "The strings of the lyre of modern poets are endless strips of celluloid." This film is an imagist poem. It is neither a narrative nor a drama but an endeavor to render subjectivity coruscatingly whole on the screen.

About the acting there can be small comment. The actors are usually not asked to be much more than elements in pictorial compositions, required to stand thus and look thus, rarely with emotional progress or transition in any one shot. Giorgio Albertazzi, the man, has a genuinely romantic face; Sacha Pitoeff, the other man, has a mysterious death's-head face. There is really not much more to be said of them. Delphine Seyrig, the young woman, is handsome, but we are sometimes distracted from the emotion her face is supposed to evoke because her attitudes keep reminding us of fashion models'. Thus the chic photographers pose their girls in rich settings, even to

the averted head and the ineffable secret sorrow that seems inseparable from *haute couture*. (Indeed, Miss Seyrig's gowns are by
Chanel.)

Anyone familiar with fantastic, surrealist, or "experimental"
movies will recognize all the cinematic effects described above. Technically, there is little new in the film, as Resnais was the first to
declare. He and Robbe-Grillet have used their method, not as in-
ventors, but as devotees. They feel, as others have felt before them,
that the conventions of art lay a false logic on the mercurial inner life
of man, that plot contrivances are the real obscurantism, that the only
lucidity is to present inner life as it is. I assume that it is to emphasize
this belief that they have placed their unconventional work in a highly
conventional setting: a palace and gardens that are the result of
imposing strict order on nature.

Resnais's film style is much like Robbe-Grillet's prose. The latter
writes in orderly grammatical sentences, not in expressionistic
fragments or rhapsodies; his fracture of tradition comes from the
content and sequence of sentences. So Resnais almost never uses
distortion, or freak shots, or double exposures; virtually every frame
in the film is a clear and lovely photograph. To use an analogy in
painting, Resnais has combined the loneliness of the di Chirico surrealist vista with the exploded time of Picasso's cubism, but with this
simple yet important difference: he has not distorted any of his
elements. It is as if he were willing to accept orderly surfaces because it is the disorder beneath those surfaces that interests him. He
seeks the disorderly true reality under the orderly false reality of the
surface.

The critical search for meaning in this film is, to me, meaningless.
Let us define "meaning," for our purpose, as the belief about an
aspect of life that strikes us as basic or residual in a work of art after
the initial emotions and sensations it arouses have passed. In this
sense, *Last Year at Marienbad* has no fundamental meaning. Mac-
Leish's familiar line tells us that a poem should not mean but be; a
film, Resnais obviously thinks, should not mean but see.

A somber search for meaning is always the curse of an unusual
work like this one. The analysts and aesthetes approach it with
pigeonholes and cross-references at the ready, seemingly more interested in explaining it than in experiencing it. But the authors want
us simply to let the film happen to us, not to ferret for symbolized

theses, not to compare it with plot movies as we watch, any more than in a love affair of our own we would constantly compare it with a movie love affair. In this ostensibly arty film they are trying to remove what they feel are the barriers that art erects between maker and viewer. They disavow significance; they seek only effect. This film, they imply, *is* what it *does to you;* a congress of sensations; no more, perhaps, but no less and no other.

Nevertheless, one analytical question must be raised. Does *Marienbad* open up artistic immediacies to truth or is it simply a case of art anarchy?

Let me qualify my answer at the start by saying that I'm glad that the film exists and I should enjoy seeing more in the same style. But I believe that this kind of film is self-limiting and eventually futile. This is not because of accepted definitions of art. The fallacy in this style is that if it is followed absolutely rigorously, it leads not to art but to madness. No one moment of time *can* be completely stopped; no one encounter or thought *can* be traced in all its permutations and ramifications. Joyce's novel about one ordinary day in the life of one ordinary man is a titan's masterpiece; still, any reader can find gaps in its inclusiveness. Art that tries to set down everything, and to set it down as it occurs, must end like a man trying to pick up too much and dropping what he has. Every honest artist who ever lived has known that he told partial lies, that he had to settle for less than he could see or know in order to tell *something,* and has, therefore, compromised with some kind of abstraction or arrangement.

The Resnais-and-Robbe-Grillet alternative is to reject the contrivances and arrangements of art; but far from being a move of liberation, this is, in fact, the most slavish realism. It tries to reproduce actual inner life instead of distilling it, as even the most Zolaesque naturalism does. The logical end of their method, its ultimate purity, is to see that there is falsity in any attempt to reproduce the truth, no matter how faithful; that for full, uncontaminated emotional truth, each member of the audience must go himself to Nymphenburg and hover in time between present and past, among varying shades of reality. Pressed to perfection, nothing can satisfy this quest for fidelity to life but life itself, of which any art must always be only a delegate. This true-map-of-the-mind style, arising from a hatred of tired formula and fakery, inevitably founders on the faintly sophomoric failure to distinguish between life and art.

Further, the possibilities for extension of self, provided by other styles, are negligible here. A film like *Marienbad* is, in its way, only a "recognition" film, like a domestic comedy in which you watch kids who behave just like your family at home. When all is over, you are not deeply moved; you have spent most of your time checking whether or not the representation of the functions of mind and imagination corresponds with your own experience.

For myself, there is infinitely more reward in the films of (for paramount example) Antonioni, who is equally disgusted with stale formulas but who replaces them with new and appropriate abstractions, with new art, rather than with figurative mental tape recorders. Because he is interested in character (as *Marienbad* is not), he involves us to a degree that disembodied reproduction of inner processes can never reach. Strictly speaking, Antonioni rearranges and distorts certain realities as Resnais tries not to do; but Resnais's efforts lead only to duplication of experience, and Antonioni's freshly seen artistic order results in illumination of experience. After *Marienbad* I knew more about Resnais and Resnais's search for reality; but after *La Notte* and *L'Avventura* I knew more about myself.

Muriel   (November 16, 1963)

Alain Resnais has followed *Hiroshima, Mon Amour* and *Last Year at Marienbad* with *Muriel*. *Hiroshima* is a film that diminishes gravely in retrospect and on further viewing; *Marienbad,* outside of the *brio* of its psychological delving, has not so far to diminish. His new film lacks the extreme methods of the latter but has some of the dramatic oppositions of the former. But Resnais seemingly has run out of any organic new technique, and, stuck with a reasonably logical story, has impasted on it illogical editing, extraneous symbolism, inexplicable inserts, and overlapping sound tracks in order to hold his franchise in the avant-garde.

The story concerns a mature woman (the handsome Delphine Seyrig) who keeps both an antique shop and an irresolute son in Boulogne. She is visited by an old ex-lover who is accompanied by a "niece," complete with quotation marks. The woman's son has a girl friend, but he is haunted by the memory of another girl named Muriel, a victim of the Algerian war in which he served. A counterpoint (touched by possible deceptions of memory) between the son's love, blighted by one war, and the mother's, blighted by an earlier one, might have had some lyrical result; but the affected apparatus of the film makes that impossible and leaves us chiefly with irritation. I gladly relinquish my share in any debate that this film may stir up. Life is too short, and art, as against artiness, too engrossing.

Cleo from 5 to 7   (September 10, 1962)

An advertisement for a correspondence school of authorship begins: "How Do You *Know* You Can't Write?" Well, for that matter, How Do You *Know* You Can't Be a New-Wave Director? Have you tried? Follow these simple steps and be the first in your gang to make an art movie.

1. Get a good cameraman. The worst of these films is interestingly, if not beautifully, photographed.

2. Get a story. This is less important. Your story need not be gripping or valid.

3. Cast the female lead with a photogenic girl, not necessarily an actress. Be guided by the soulful expressions of high-fashion models.

4. Lay it on. "It" is the New Wave repertoire of stunts, camera techniques, and cutting. Examples: Use freakish faces for minor characters (this is candor). Use a little nudeness (this is maturity). Include long walks through a city, preferably Paris; just long, pointless walks—to show that you are as free of plot contrivances as Antonioni. Dwell on such *bizarrerie* as street performers who swallow and regurgitate live frogs or who push hatpins through their biceps (this shows how ugly life is and how you are facing it). Let your microphone record snatches of irrelevant conversations at neighboring café tables (this wraps your story in a naturalistic web). Retain the footage where passers-by stare into the camera (thus you prove that you "stole" your film from the street and that you wear your *rue* with a difference). Do not omit Resnais backward jumps (cutting back to a moment just passed), as this expresses a mystique about time. Have your heroine sing a torch song, Judy Garlanded with

Angst. And if you can work in some silent-film burlesque, à la Malle, you will demonstrate both your superiority to and your respect for early movies.

All these devices, and more, occur in a French picture called *Cleo from 5 to 7,* written and directed by Agnes Varda. The film is worth comment because Miss Varda, who is in her mid-thirties, is one of the few female directors anywhere and because she is said to be one of the ideologists of her school. (A French Film Office booklet says that she *"représente le 'sexe faible' au sein des réalisateurs de la Nouvelle Vague."*) She has made a number of documentaries; this is her first full-length work.

It does not deal, as you may think, with France's much-vaunted marital *cinq à sept.* Miss Varda tells the story of a Parisian *chanteuse,* Cleo, in the two hours before she is to hear the results of a biopsy. It opens with a portentous tarot-card sequence under the titles, in color; the rest of the picture is black-and-white. The two hours are marked by the director's notes at the bottom of the screen ("Cleo 5:03-5:07," "Cleo 5:07-5:11," etc.), so we expect a minute-for-minute two-hour film. However it runs only eighty-six minutes. We see a cross section of a woman's life: her rich lover, her career, her loneliness in the midst of teeming activity, and how this crisis brings her a chance for Real Affection. Toward the end she meets a soldier in the park and their compressed, months-in-a-minute romance burns like a hard, MGM-like flame. He accompanies her to the hospital where she gets good news.

The pat shape of the story, its very cleverness, the shallowness of its emotional exploration, the heroine's self-conscious dramatization, make it merely a flashily dressed-up conventional tear jerker, a sob sister of the works of Fannie Hurst. The avant-garde trappings disguise nothing; it is Irving Berlin orchestrated by Stravinsky.

Cleo is impersonated by Corinne Marchand, a voluptuous pop singer, who responds like a silky circus horse to Miss Varda's *Weltschmerz* whip. Her behavior and the entire film seem almost a parody of the best things done by Truffaut, Godard, Resnais, Chabrol —a sedulous exercise in what can be called Cleo-realism.

Perhaps Miss Varda has been badly served by the timing of her first appearance in this country. Although her work now seems thoroughly imitative, she may have been something of a stylistic innovator. But what is irrefutable is her weak instinct for truth, her defective judgment of this posturing, novelettish tale as a work of resonance, worthy of or redeemable by all the apparatus of current French cinema modes.

Landru   (April 27, 1963)

The story of Landru, the "Bluebeard" who was found guilty of murdering eleven women in the early twenties, has been made into a screenplay by Françoise Sagan which has been directed by Claude Chabrol. The film is occasionally bumpy but completely absorbing. Miss Sagan has said: "Landru killed eleven women, all right." (This was, in fact, never conclusively proved.) "But he was gay and had charm. . . . The French were delighted with him. . . . That is why Chabrol and I decided to make this a tender film, barely touched now and then by corpselike emanations. This will be no horror film."

It is not a conventional horror film, but neither is it gay or, essentially, tender; nor is it overtly satiric like *Monsieur Verdoux,* with which it must be compared. Chabrol uses wide cinematic resources— color and its absence, motion and nonmotion, music both pro and contra mood, slapstick, high comedy and high romance, and gruesomeness—to make an existentialist film about a man facing all of life every day. Miss Sagan's introductory contradictions are only a few of the many. What the film says is that *everything* is true, to some degree, for everybody; no two qualities are mutually exclusive. Goering feeds his canaries from his lips. Landru loves poetry.

There are a few inferior moments in script and direction. The sequence of the fortuneteller's maid is cloudy. The direction of some episodes—the bed scenes, the court scenes, tea with the sisters—is beneath the imaginative best in the film. But, in the main, the story is told exquisitely, with intriguing ellipsis, with moving emphasis. (Chabrol has a nice sense of when to use the close-up.) In 1917 Landru is a Parisian dealer in second-hand furniture with a wife and four children, living in middle-class poverty—overstuffed apartment, clean clothes, and no cash. He hits on the idea of marrying and murdering wealthy women; no reasons for this particular choice are given. We know only that he is attractive to women (his wife is accustomed to his long absences). He inserts a personal ad, draws three likely replies, and is off.

With each of his victims, Landru is courteous, virile, nonmocking even in the eyes of the audience who know that he is lying. He has rented a villa in Gambais. (The fact that he always buys a round-trip ticket and a one-way ticket—from the same clerk—is a hint that he is deliberately planting a clue that will lead to his capture some day.) There, with each woman, an idyll is enacted so romantic that the murder, each time, comes as a surprise. To the sound of opera or waltz, the happy victim is shown in closer and closer close-up, until the film freezes into a still picture, still smiling. Then we cut to smoke pouring from the chimney; then to an elderly English couple in the villa next door complaining about the stink. In the first murder there is also a shot of a meat grinder clamped to the kitchen table.

From each woman Landru gets money in some way and returns with the booty to his patient family who, of course, know nothing. The pace accelerates. After the next victim, the aforementioned maid, there are quick glimpses of some plainer victims, until he meets the German widow of a French soldier. He takes her to the villa and is busily stoking the stove when church bells start ringing and people burst in to announce the armistice. The widow is saved and Landru's murder career is ended. He never attempts it again. The point of this, underscored as it is by inserted newsreel shots of World War I, need not be labored. During his adventures he has acquired a mistress. It is in her flat that the police nab him, tipped off by the victim's sister who recognized him in the street. Landru is absolutely calm; pre-destined, as it were.

He is still calm when he comes to trial three years later, witty, dignified, protesting his innocence. This continues even after he is sentenced. When he is being led out of his cell to the guillotine, his lawyer asks whether he really did kill the women. "That," he says, "will have to remain my little secret."

There is not space to detail all the felicitous directorial touches, only to assure the readers that the film is full of them. Chabrol does not have the same free flight in the film stratosphere that Truffaut has, but he has vision, rhythm, insolence, pathos. There are two other outstanding elements in the film. The settings and costumes by Jacques Saulnier and Maurice Albray are excellent. The mistress' apartment, for example, is in itself a Colette novel. Second, and related, Jean Rabier's color photography is used not only for obvious enrichments but to stress that no one "looks" like a murderer or a victim, no place "looks" like a murder setting. Murder, as well as beauty, occurs.

Charles Denner, the Landru, is short, unhandsome, solid. For the role he is bald and heavily bearded. His iron, relentless voice, combined with his intense manner, makes him potent in his attractions and as a man of secrets. No other role really amounts to much, but Michele Morgan is especially touching as one of the victims.

Few Americans can remember Chaplin's *Monsieur Verdoux* clearly. Based on the same Landru story, it was released here in 1947, but the professional patriots were whooping about Chaplin, the film was picketed and, within the year, was withdrawn, never to be shown here again. I saw it only once and, sixteen years later, cannot rely on memory for qualitative judgments. However, with the help of James Agee's three-part review, some comparisons of story and character are possible.

Chaplin set his film in the Depression, made Verdoux unemployed, gave him a crippled wife and one child whom he adored, made all his victims repellent. *Landru* is counterpointed with the war; he commits his crimes for his wife and family but does not deeply care for them —his wife in return loathes him. Five of his eleven victims are lovely. Verdoux spares a lonely girl because she is a widow and sympathetic to his misanthropy; she becomes the mistress of a munitions manufacturer. Landru spares a girl who might have been a victim because she is spirited; she becomes *his* mistress. Verdoux is a virtuoso part with plenty of flourishes for a great actor, pantomimist, comedian. Landru is a relatively "straight" part for a good, forceful actor.

Both stories, then, are set in contexts of disruption—war and depression—when hope is dear and life is cheap, when traditional virtues, not necessarily false, are derided. Chaplin made Verdoux a loving husband and father, made the victims repulsive, so that he could at least bring the audience *with* him through the murder attempts (he commits only one killing in the film), so that he could shock them with this behavior in a "family" man but hold them for his lesson that murder-for-money is the logical extension of business. He spares the lonely girl and treats her paternally to reinforce his essential innocence; her fate confirms that the world cannot be cheated.

Chaplin's film, which was generally hated, was called noncon-

formist, Swiftian. *Landru* is absolutely conformist—he does not protest about life that forces him to this; he accepts it as his inescapable
rotten fate, as against his neighbor's differently rotten one. The film is
not in general tone satiric, and although its shape and style have
imagination, the content of most scenes is realistic. *Verdoux* is the
work of a mind nourished in nineteenth-century idealism, angry with
the world's enmity toward love and life. *Landru* is the work of contemporary nonidealistic minds, inquisitive rather than hopeful,
insistent on the rights of love but aware that it never appears unac-
companied by various uglinesses. Their protagonist makes not the
slightest bid for sympathy. He does what he has decided to do, not as
Sartrean gratuitous acts but as acts which represent the best of his
ability to cope with life as he feels forced to face it. Others can repair
shoes or construct buildings; he can murder. Some of his victims
happen to be beautiful and winning, but Landru knows that this
makes his crimes neither more nor less monstrous.

He is never afraid, never repentant, never explanatory. Verdoux
gives the world a statement in the courtroom and his cell. Landru
simply asserts his innocence.

Verdoux is a rebellion against the falsities of the past: the hypoc-
risies of religion, war, materialist morality. *Landru* is an acceptance
of the present, very hard beneath its lovely surfaces and "tenderness."
It leaves us wishing we understood why he protested his innocence if
he committed these crimes without fear and with a rationale; but even
that question—posed in such a provocative and well-wrought framework—helps to make the film memorable.

POSTSCRIPT. Since the above was written, there has been a chance to
see *Monsieur Verdoux* again and, unfortunately, to be disappointed
in it. It is a film that has been sanctified by suppression. It corrobo-
rates what Chaplin implies in his autobiography: that he was never
entirely comfortable in films once the advent of sound destroyed the
pantomime tramp (whom he managed to preserve through *Modern
Times*). In *Monsieur Verdoux* as in *The Great Dictator* (q.v.), he
attempted to play a quite different character but had to fall back on
the tramp to help him; so we get Verdoux, in the midst of the grim
parable of his life, wooing a widow ridiculously, falling backward out
of a window, and so on. Such instances are funny in themselves, but
they are patent proofs of Chaplin's insecurity in the role of Verdoux

as such. The practice converts the serious elements in the picture into lumps of gravity. The film does not dramatize its theme as *Landru* does; it tells a semiburlesque story with occasional genuflections to tragedy. (In addition, some of the supporting cast—like the forlorn girl—are staggeringly bad.)

I do not suggest that Chabrol, Denner, or Miss Sagan remotely approaches the Chaplin stratosphere of genius, which is certainly, if sporadically, apparent in *Monsieur Verdoux*. But in my view *Landru* —miserably underestimated in this country—is a more cohesive, cogent, and pertinent dramatization of the Landru story than Chaplin's film.

Testament of Orpheus   (May 14, 1962)

Jean Cocteau has made his valedictory film, *Testament of Orpheus,* a sort of sequel to his *Orpheus* (1950), which contains some of the same characters along with some friends of his, including Picasso. It is a fantasy in which he (in person) enacts his search for beauty and states his aesthetics. What an extraordinary man he is, ranging from authentic poetry to successful chi-chi, a laureate both of Oxford University and of *Vogue*. His last film is considerably tedious because it seems so thoroughly passé; Beauty with a capital B went out with Oscar Wilde, and the poet as self-conscious hero is deservedly suspect. But every time you're ready to dismiss it all as gifted affectation, he does or says something genuinely imaginative and enlightening. He once wrote that, when he was a child, his family had a neighbor whose carriage was washed weekly with champagne. In view of such a childhood, one can only congratulate Cocteau on achieving as much with his many talents as he has done.

Sundays and Cybele   (December 15, 1962)

A twelve-year-old girl named Patricia Gozzi gives a performance of unusual depth and range in *Sundays and Cybele,* a film about an amnesiac man. He is a young ex-pilot who lost his memory in a plane crash and now lives with his ex-nurse in a French town. He becomes friendly with the child, who has been abandoned by her father at the local orphanage, and he takes her for walks every Sunday. In the course of their Sundays together the child and the man regain confidence in life and in themselves; but word of their friendship gets around, his motives are misinterpreted, and it ends unhappily.

This slender story, although it is stretched and padded, might have had considerable poignancy. But the pair's walks around lakes and through woods are done with some self-consciousness about their lyric quality and with insufficient originality and invention. Once the tone of these scenes has been established, we know what the scenes "stand for" and simply wait for them to finish. This is partly the fault of Serge Bourguignon (whose first feature film this is), but it is equally the fault of Hardy Kruger, who plays the man. I have always thought Kruger something of a lump, but here he reaches new depths of doltish impassivity. When his mistress tells him how madly she loves him, I had the feeling that they had photographed her rehearsals with a stand-in.

Bourguignon also shows a weakness for shooting scenes through shutters and keyholes and in rear-view mirrors of moving cars, all for no intrinsic reason. But the performance he evoked from young Miss Gozzi and the style of some of the picture show that he has ability. If he can rid himself of his weakness for trickery and, in future films, can justify each scene as poetic or passionate or whatever instead of merely hanging a figurative label on it, he may become a genuinely good director.

Pickpocket   (June 8, 1963)

The French director, Robert Bresson, has a large reputation although he has made only seven films in twenty-nine years. It is a shameful fact that only two of them have been shown publicly in this country: *Diary of a Country Priest* and *A Man Escapes*. Now *Pickpocket* (1959), his most highly regarded work, is brought here— another service of the New Yorker Theater. It deals with a young Parisian who gives up his studies to become a professional thief. We

see him pick his first pockets, join a gang, and become really professional. The film is distinguished from ordinary crime pictures by its
stoic manner, its quasi-Dostoevskian relationship between a detective
and the criminal, and by the vaguely Nietzschean rationale of the
hero. He believes himself an exceptional man who needs not live by
slaves' morality.

For me, the film falls far short of its praise elsewhere. Technically,
Bresson much too often opens a scene with a shot of the setting
into which the characters walk or holds the camera on the setting
after the characters leave; it makes for recurrent stasis. He repeats
shots—like the hero climbing the stairs—for no discernible reason.
As for the script, the girl who falls in love with the thief is a Gallic
platitude. (Including her exceptional beauty. Doesn't a French young
man ever encounter a merely good-looking girl?) Her feeling for him
is a cabaret parody of silent Left Bank passion. But the chief fault is
that the hero is a vacancy, not a character. Martin La Salle, who
plays the part, has a bony, sensitive face, but no deader pan has
crossed the screen since Buster Keaton. The besetting fallacy of
modern French films and novels is the belief that nullity equals
malaise and/or profundity.

Still, *Pickpocket* is made in a muted, concise style that bespeaks
intelligent guidance. If it is never really stirring or involving, it is
never pretentious or boring, and its very taciturnity gives it some
haunting effect.

Trial of Joan of Arc   (February 13, 1965)

Of the making of works of art about Joan of Arc, there is
presumably no end, and understandably so. She is a figure who
presents new facets of interest to every generation. The books about
her pass ascertainable number. The composers who have treated her
include such different ones as Tchaikovsky, Verdi, Honegger. (The
first time I ever heard Tebaldi was in Verdi's *Giovanna D'Arco*—
which includes a love scene between Joan and King Charles!) The
plays run from Shakespeare's political cartoon in the First Part of
Henry VI through Schiller up to the peak of Bernard Shaw's *Saint
Joan,* then on and down on the other side (Frank Harris, etc.).

The film world began early with the subject. The imaginative pioneer Georges Méliès made a *Jeanne d'Arc* in 1900. Cecil B. De-Mille made *Joan the Woman* in 1917, with Geraldine Farrar, a war-time recruiting-poster film to show that all Anglo-Saxons owed a debt of honor to France in atonement for Joan's martyrdom. More re-cently, Ingrid Bergman brought Maxwell Anderson's *Joan of Lorraine* to the screen, alas, and Otto Preminger tortured Shaw even more than he tortured Jean Seberg. The outstanding film version has been Carl Dreyer's silent *The Passion of Joan of Arc* (1928), in which, incidentally, Antonin Artaud appears.

I had thought Dreyer's version austere until I saw Robert Bresson's latest film, *Trial of Joan of Arc*. It challenges the Dreyer work both by concentrating, like Dreyer, on the trial and by attempting a cinematic treatment that is even more severe. Outside of the fact that Dreyer worked largely with close-ups and that Bresson uses mostly medium shots—from the waist up—the new film pampers the eye much less. There is none of Dreyer's figure composition against white walls, none of his small-scale Eisenstein feeling with soldiers. With a few exceptions, and they are very consciously interludes, the bulk of the film consists of shot and reverse-shot—flip-flop—between Joan and her interrogators.

One's immediate question on learning of the existence of this film is: "Why—after Dreyer?" After seeing it, the only answer that I can supply is that Dreyer's film was silent and this one uses the lines that exist or can logically be derived from the records of the trial. For those whose French is up to it, there may be simple majesty in the dialogue; otherwise it does not seem to have been worth the effort. If, like me, one depends on subtitles, one is principally aware of their inadequacy and of the work's imprisonment within its scheme. The fact that this is one film that might be helped by excellent dubbing is, for me, an argument against it as film.

Florence Carrez and Jean-Claude Fourneau play Joan and Cauchon in the film's key, by doing almost nothing. The picture is one more offering at the altar of Bresson's cinematic ideals: extreme distillation, economy, astringency. "Less Is More" has never been believed by anyone more devoutly than by this man; and in his previous films he has shown this devotion increasingly. But it reminds me of the old joke about the man who tried to live on less and less food, decreasing the amount daily, and when he finally got it down to nothing, he died. One cannot argue with Bresson's purity of intention or of execution. But, as in other matters, is purity enough? Very little in this film is moving except the rather easy emotion of Joan's incineration. The picture runs only a bit over an hour and hardly has time to be tedious; but I would rather have been moved by Joan's passion or even by such mundane matters as cinematic composition and sweep than have been aware, almost exclusively, of the director's purity.

The Devil and the Ten Commandments   (October 19, 1963)

Julien Duvivier is, in all senses, an old pro. He has made about fifty pictures in about forty years and, no more than most human beings could do, has not consistently made masterpieces. He has, in fact, made some quite poor pictures in recent years; but in the thirties he made *Poil de Carotte,* one of the loveliest of films about children, *Un Carnet de Bal, The Golem* with Harry Baur, *La Fin du Jour,* a film with Victor Francen and Louis Jouvet about an old actors' home, which is a treasury of good performances. If we are tempted to say that Duvivier has not lived up to his promise, we must remember that he never really made a firm one. In 1949 Paul Rotha wrote:

There is no question that Duvivier is an accomplished director . . . but the intermittent promise that he would develop a characteristic style of his own has not materialized. Perhaps this is because, while his work is expressive, he seems to have very little that he earnestly desires to express. . . . Every Duvivier film contains moments of craftsmanship so admirable that one wants to take him seriously, but how can one be serious about the body of his work as a whole?

The comment is still fair and is borne out by Duvivier's latest picture, a collection of episodes called *The Devil and the Ten Commandments.* Only seven commandments are dealt with, and none profoundly, but all save one are treated in perfectly skillful, highly entertaining style. The vignette of the stripper married to the concierge, which I thought weak, comes early and leaves early; all the others have revue-sketch point, either amusing or touching. Duvivier, who

FRANCE 263

has had a hand in all the scripts, understands that an episodic film must imply such a point in each section and must keep its word.

Plots with twists should not be untwisted in advance. Let us note only that the little melodrama with Charles Aznavour is well sustained; the episode in which Alain Delon learns the identity of his parents is a neat heartstring-tugger; and the religious parable in which Fernandel plays God (no less) is excellently turned. If the finish is foreseeable, the wait for it is amply filled with Fernandel's straightforward, unembarrassed portrayal and with a dram-of-despair performance by Germaine Kerjean as a dying old farmwoman.

On the light side, Michel Simon has a salty holiday as a blasphemous handyman in a convent; there is a slick *pas de quatre* among two married couples with Françoise Arnoul, Micheline Presle, Claude Dauphin, and, oddly, Mel Ferrer; and the finale is a Clairlike farce about thievery with Jean-Claude Brialy and Louis de Funes.

Doubtless I have been well primed for this picture by the recent spate of omnibus films by different directors, full of damp New Wavelets and flavorless Italian ices, usually inconclusive or dull, mere vacuous self-expression. Duvivier, as Rotha noted, has had very little that was burning inside him to get out. He makes films to make money, and to make money he has to entertain. One produces at least as many poor films that way as from motives of art, but when Duvivier succeeds, he entertains well. How pleasant it is, once in a while, to be in the hands of a man who is the twentieth-century, widescreen equivalent of a skillful strolling player.

Les Abysses (December 12, 1964)

The French film *Les Abysses* has drawn exceptionally high praise from Sartre, de Beauvoir, Breton, and other eminent French writers. It recounts relatively factually the case that inspired Genet's nonfactual play *The Maids*. In 1933 two young sisters named Papin were maids in the employ of a wine grower in the Bordeaux region. The house, once prosperous, had become shabby. The man and his wife and his married daughter had gone off on a trip. Left alone, the maids ran riot in the house, wrecking things, panicky because they knew the place was going to be sold and they were frightened about

their fate. The family returned unexpectedly, but the rioting continued. Prospective buyers arrived, which drove the maids even more
frantic. In a paroxysm of fear-hate-joy they murdered Madame and
the daughter.

The first point to consider is the film's execution, which in every
aspect is excellent. The portrayals of the two sisters—by two sisters,
Francine and Colette Berge—flicker like flames, are interlocked in
fierce symbiotic tension. Paul Bonifas, the master, is a pouter pigeon,
irrationally blinded by self-concerns, Pascale de Boysson, the daughter, creates a well-meaning, sensitive ninny. The screenplay by Jean
Vauthier is stripped to athletic litheness and (to judge by subtitles) is
written with electric, funny savagery.

Controlling all the above, and doubtless in some measure responsible for it, is the direction of Nico Papatakis. This is his first film. He
is forty-six, of Greek-Ethiopian parentage, and lives in Paris where he
is the founder-manager of a cabaret theater, for which he has directed many plays. He has made the film immediately arresting and
consistently gripping. All the elements are extraordinarily fine: camera composition and movement, editing, and, especially, the performances. Papatakis has a keen ear for voice and tempo, has a
subtle sense of relationships, a gift for macabre humor. Everything in
the film conveys the director's intelligence and discrimination. As for
its odd rhythm, Sartre's description cannot be improved on: "sharply
cut, broken, bouncing, frozen."

But as to the stature, the philosophical implications (if any), of
the film, one can disagree with the statements of both Papatakis
and Sartre, which in turn disagree with one another. We have here an
account of two psychotic girls; there can be small doubt of the
psychoses from the outset. They are neither metaphors of an author
(as in Genet's play) nor rational beings. They are carefully drawn
pathological cases, full of monstrous fears, gloatings, glees, aggres-
sions. They create havoc, destroy furniture and furnishings, waste
great casks of wine in the cellar. And when all this is discovered by
the owner and family, it is tolerated by them! By the owner and wife
because they owe the maids three years' salary and cannot discharge
them, by the daughter because she has a Lesbian fixation on the
younger maid. But, in the relatively realistic context of the film, those
acceptances for those reasons are equally crazy. For instance, the
wasted wine amounted to more than the money owed; the soup

spewed in the daughter's face by the maid (to name only one outrage) would, rationally, have affected sexual attraction. To measure *The Maids* by logic would mean deafness to tonality; but the tonality of this film makes objections in logic inevitable.

Thus one is forced to disagree with Papatakis's statement: "In a sense, the guilt lay not with the two servants alone—nor even the masters who oppressed them. But in a philosophical sense the fault is with all who contribute toward the *laissez-faire* attitude that allows such conditions to persist around us, without interference." This— not the first time a good artist has misrepresented his own work— seems completely inappropriate. The film is not a document of social injustice or indifference. Two demented girls work for people who are almost as demented as they are. There is no touch of Zola's *Earth,* of people brutalized by social conditions. Who in that household was rational enough to be guilty of *laissez-faire?*

At the end of the film there is a note that, at the subsequent murder trial, one sister was given a death sentence, the other thirty years, but that the court asked with heavy sagacity, "Who is truly guilty?" My answer would be: the court. All of them, maids and surviving father, ought to have been committed to a mental hospital.

Sartre strikes a quite different note in his enthusiasm. He says nothing of "conditions" or indifference. "The cinema has given us its foremost tragedy. Its theme: Evil. . . . [The sisters] incarnate naked violence—hatred—and the desire to kill. It is not a question of curing them of evil—they *are* evil! . . . two wretches who, in the manner of timeless tragedy, must carry out the sentence meant for them, their fate and their destiny—inevitably to place themselves forever outside the Law." But they are outside the law to begin with, any civilized law, as insane persons. And it is not in the least in the manner of timeless tragedy for psychotics to be protagonists. Further, it makes nonsense of morality to call psychosis Evil. Surely Evil implies power of choice or at least knowledge of one's nature. These two girls have neither power to choose nor even any power to take knowing perverse pride in their inability to choose.

One cannot stretch to supply an invisible framework for the film by placing it in the society we know and saying that the theme is evil because society's greed and incomprehension drove the girls mad. There is no hint of this, and even if there were, then what drove the family to their equally unbalanced toleration of the maids' behavior?

To say that the world is responsible for *all* of them is further to demolish the director's statement that the film dramatizes indifference (it leaves no one to represent indifference) and also Sartre's statement of tragedy (it makes them all witless protagonists).

Because of the nature of the story and its tangential association with Genet, one last point must be examined: its relation to the Artaudian theater of cruelty. I find this relation tenuous. The Artaudian theme is the catharsis of repressed sado-masochisms by theatrical events, mythic rituals that explode unacknowledged real forces into unreality, thus purging society toward a healthier community. In its balletic synthesis *Les Abysses* moves toward an Artaudian mode; in execution it is a superreal work. But it releases no repressed violence, as Artaud would have intended. All we can feel is compassion for sickness, impatience to get a doctor. It is not a ritual drama, an altar offering to dark gods, but a clinical casebook written with considerable poetry. A film by Papatakis, with the Berge sisters, of Genet's *The Maids* would have been a much more fitting match of methods and matter. This present film is, in a lesser way, like Gielgud forsaking *Hamlet* to read us Saxo Grammaticus.

Chronicle of a Summer   (May 15, 1965)

Dan Talbot of the New Yorker Theater in Manhattan continues his estimable work of importing neglected, noteworthy foreign films. One of them, much discussed but unfortunately disappointing, is *Chronicle of a Summer,* a "straight" documentary, made in the method called *cinéma-vérité,* a method developed since the improvement of the hand-held camera and portable sound recorder. These improvements afford more flexibility, and they offer more possibilities for impromptu, spontaneous shooting.

No sooner had these mechanical improvements been achieved than lead-brained sociological types—particularly in France—came clomping into cinema, shouting that at last it was free of studio arrangement, fictive device, at last it could show Life. What (to begin with) this indicates of their understanding of art is too pitiful to be belabored here. But what has resulted from most of their efforts is ludicrous. Some cinema verists, notably Americans, have put the theory to highly interesting tests. But what has been accomplished by Jean Rouch and Edgar Morin, the makers of and participants in *Chronicle?* Liberated from the bonds of studio arrangements, dollies, mike booms, they have taken some shots of people walking in the street; principally they have filmed and recorded interviews at dinner tables, in living rooms, on stairs. It is all about as "liberated" cinematically as the film clips on your nightly TV newscast.

The object of this exercise was to discover how people were feeling in the summer of 1960 in Paris. The answer: real bad. Most of them, students, workers, intellectuals, are as shruggingly *triste* as any revue caricature of café existentialism. There is a particularly distressing section when Morin, who is interviewing and whom we quickly come to loathe, presses a patently neurotic Italian girl to tell us more and more of her troubles. I didn't want *cinéma-vérité* for her, I wanted an ambulance to the nearest analyst. As if the general jawing were not bad enough, the film concludes with the subjects of the interviews watching the films of their interviews and then discussing them. I suppose they then watched the film of their discussion and discussed *that.*

The simple point that men like Rouch and Morin cannot or will not understand, quite apart from the truth of art, is that to dispense with studios and make-up and script and obvious artifices is no guarantee at all of unalloyed objectivity. This film is still a work of selection and reveals much about the selectors. It reveals that, for their subjects, Rouch and Morin selected victims of *Angst.* It also reveals that, under and because of the duo's portentous gab in the film, they are stupid.

Life Upside Down   (September 11, 1965)

Life Upside Down, a first film written and directed by a young Frenchman named Alain Jessua, is a work executed without flaw. From first moment to last, it is made with the delicate rigor of a good sonnet. It travels directly but with no sense of rush; it selects its metaphor and symbol without fumble or flashiness. It *understands* what it is about. It is spellbinding, and, insidiously, it almost makes us chuckle with the near-appeal of its central terror.

This is a poem of schizophrenia. It depicts how a young Frenchman passes from seeming normality to complete withdrawal. It does
this with clinical fidelity (as far as I know) but with more than
clinical intent. Its purpose is entirely subjective: to show how a man
of some seriousness and intelligence feels as he moves into that mental state—as contrasted with how he looks to the world. There is no
violence, nothing even remotely disgusting, yet it is a film of the
deepest horror because it shows—finely and with seductive unreason
—how the man's mind converts his growing affliction into euphoria
and philosophic triumph.

The story is enacted while he recounts it on a tape recorder. He
lives with a pretty, affectionate model—so domestically that it is a
surprise when he proposes marriage; we have assumed that they are
married. His real-estate job is dull. Truth—of his life, of the teeming
life around him—seems always just out of reach. Although he is very
fond of his girl, he is no longer passionate about her. All, in other
words, seems normal enough.

Then they go to a movie theater (to see her brief appearance in
one of the commercials shown in European movie houses) and afterward they join some friends in a café. In the midst of conversation he
suddenly excuses himself. We think he is going to telephone or relieve
himself. Instead he just walks across the room and starts to play a pin-
ball machine. And, as he tells us on the sound track, this sudden
withdrawal is his first experience of a feeling of well-being, a feeling
that recurs for him—and which, of course, we see as "attacks." He
runs to his illness (which he never thinks of in that term) like a
religious zealot to his faith. That is the pathos and the fascination.

His odd behavior at his wedding costs him his job, and his wife
thinks he is busily looking for a new one when he is just wandering
around Paris, experimenting with ways to render people and objects
invisible: simply by staring at them. The camera renders this excellently, showing how the intensity of staring at an immensely magnified object makes it disappear from the "attention" of our vision.
Then he disappears for three days, without knowing it; he comes
home as if he had been out for a walk. Since he seems well, his wife
concludes that he has found another girl. She attempts suicide and
finally leaves him because she thinks he is no longer interested in
her.

This is true, obviously, but not in the way she thinks. Left alone, he pushes the furniture out of the bedroom and sits on the floor cross-legged, staring at the wall, conquering the "objectness" of objects. When he tells a doctor of his discoveries, the doctor asks him to visit a friend who is collecting such stories—a mental hospital, of course. At the end, the young man sits cross-legged on the floor of the white, white sanitarium room—still and happy—interrupted only by the meals brought to him, he thinks, by his wife cleverly disguised as a nurse.

Charles Denner, who was excellent in the title role of *Landru,* plays the young man with an overwhelming conviction of quiet, mysterious, rapt, saintlike joy—as he sinks further and further away. Anna Gaylor, the girl, provides the right note of warmhearted bewilderment. The photography by Jacques Robin, which converts the pedicuring of one huge toenail into a massive statement of gross materiality, also renders the growing whiteness in the film into antiseptic unreality.

When I first saw *Life Upside Down* a year ago (in Venice), I thought it only a splendid case history, and thus a bit gratuitous. A second viewing, after a year, greatly enriches the pathological verity and transforms it into a slow lyric of departure, which throws oblique sardonic glints on the question of reality. When he is describing his triumph, the young man refers to what I suppose is Pascal's famous line: "All the unhappiness of men arises from one single fact, that they cannot stay quietly in their own chamber." This film revolves this statement in three lights: that of the philosopher's purity, the guru's spiritual exaltation, the immurement of the mentally sick. There is no question as to which of these lights finally holds the young man, but the teasing attendance of the others is the film's particular beauty. Alain Jessua's first work is a gem.

Sweden

Wild Strawberries   (April 27, 1959)

Ingmar Bergman, the Swedish director who writes his own scripts, is one of the most interesting and irritating film artists alive. There is no one making full-length pictures today (as distinct from experimental shorts) who is more aware of the poetic potentialities of the film. Yet of the four Bergman pictures I have seen, one is dreadful, one pretentious, one moderately good, and the latest, *Wild Strawberries,* teeters on the edge of complete realization.

(With foreign pictures, sequence of American release is not necessarily sequence of creation, nor do we always see all of a man's work. We get films as and if they filter through import channels.)

Even the inferior picture, *Three Strange Loves,* was distinguished by an investigation of emotional relationships far below the surface of most movies. His pretentious film, *The Seventh Seal,* was, to me, symbolically opaque and allegorically illogical; yet obviously it is the work of a man to whom the camera is a lyric instrument, who has large imagination and superb techniques.

Smiles of a Summer Night was a wry, rueful sex comedy, a Victorian period piece. A friend of mine said it would have been a fine picture if a Frenchman had made it, and indeed it is worried by an un-Gallic laboring of points and an obvious load of philosophical baggage. Yet here again is a film by a man with a sympathy for arresting themes, with an eye for the possibilities of the human face, with a power to make the very form of his film serve his theme.

Wild Strawberries deals with a seventy-six-year-old doctor on the day he is to receive an honorary degree. He wakes from a dream of

270

his own death, and drives from Stockholm to the university town of Lund with his daughter-in-law. She is to rejoin the doctor's son who teaches at the university and from whom she has been estranged by his coldness. On the way she tells the old man that his son has inherited his coldness from him. They visit a house where his family used to summer when he was young and where he picked wild strawberries with a girl he loved and lost; he visits his mother, ninety-six, who is encased in the egotism of the ancient; he picks up several hitchhikers who represent various elements in modern life. At the end of the day, after the ceremony, he goes to bed in his son's house, honored and sadder.

There is much in this film that is extraordinarily beautiful. The dream sequence at the beginning is a blend of Caligari and Kafka. The old man's reminiscences of his youth at the country place are done with a warm sense of family fun that makes one yearn to have been part of it. Bergman's touch in establishing period feeling is swift and sure—we see a young man seated in a tree reading a book, dressed in white trousers, white shirt, tie, and straw boater, and we know at once where we are. He has a gift for eccentric characterizations, like the neurotic couple to whom the doctor gives a lift and who shortly cram the interior of the car with their almost palpable unhappiness. And his basic concept—a day's ride, a life's journey—is a sound one.

Yet despite the jewels he has strung on this thread, the picture does not satisfy: precisely because they are separate jewels, not architectural blocks in a structure. The film is a series of events which do not relate or accrete strongly enough. For example, the opening dream—in itself haunting—is full of symbols which we feel are being established for later use. But only one of them—the watch without hands—is fulfilled later; the others are just vivid images that seem to have occurred to Bergman.

Without growth, the picture does not fulfill a fundamental requirement of drama: the protagonist is unchanged at the end. We are *told* he is different, he utters a few lines to that effect, but they seem appended, not a convincing development. At best, the immense symbolic apparatus of the picture has produced a very small result. This criticism is not academic; it is arrived at by the viewer's solar plexus which is knotted with impatience at the sight of all these good materials left unfused.

Bergman has had extensive theatrical training and experience and has recently been appointed director of the Royal Dramatic Theatre in Stockholm—at forty-one the youngest in its history. It is possible that, in contrast to the theater, he looks on the film as a free form, an opportunity for rhapsody and for that psychic exploration dear to the Scandinavian spirit and difficult on the stage. In fine imaginative surges, he tries to pry with his camera between close-knit life and death, between eternity and now. His films have an air of quest, of probing, of beating at great doors that he wants to open for himself and us.

Heaven and we know that this ambition is rare and valuable in films. But if my theory is right and Bergman does view the film as a medium liberated from theatrical disciplines, he will, I think, continue to make pictures studded with beautiful episodes which an audience conditioned to form and resolution must attempt to finish for him. His scripts have a certain resemblance to the plays of the late Ugo Betti; they paddle around on great, timeless, heartaching seas. We can be grateful for the glimpses thus afforded but, although we do not expect final answers from mere fellow men, we are left dissatisfied by the errant voyagings.

This notice would be unfinished without mention of the excellent performance in the leading role by Victor Sjöström, who as Seastrom directed in Hollywood from 1923 to 1931 and has since been acting in Sweden. Some old actors' faces have an odd childlike purity; it radiates from Sjöström. Of his many moving scenes one moment stands out particularly. In a dream sequence, his parents, as they were when he was a child, are sitting on a rock while Father fishes. They see him, as he was then, and wave to him. We see the old man as he is now, and, with all the sadness of time past and passing, his eyes fill at the sight of them. It is lovely.

POSTSCRIPT. Although several subsequent viewings clarify the use of more of the symbolism, they do not alter much of the criticism above. Nevertheless they put the picture in a higher place. With increased familiarity, its texture seems increasingly exquisite, its technique more magical, the articulation of the dream scenes more tartly imaginative. Also, Victor Sjöström has died since the above was written, and, for me, that extrinsic fact colors the film; it has become that admirable man's valedictory.

Still the picture is unsatisfying, mainly because of its virtues. They raise expectations—in themselves and in the large issues they touch —that are not fulfilled. *Wild Strawberries* deals superbly with some familiar contrasts: of past and present, of the differing blindnesses and egotisms of youth and age, men and women, of the sound of the passage of time on even the happiest days. Bergman handles these matters without sentimentality and with unfailing effect, but finally one feels that the apparatus of potentially profound drama has been confined to a plateau of pathos.

The Magician   (October 12, 1959)

It is now clear that we must resign ourselves to the present state of Ingmar Bergman's virtues. He is too fond of his defects to overcome them, if indeed to recognize them. The Swedish director is now established as a Divine Amateur: enormously gifted, often technically dazzling, essentially undisciplined. Well, it is a familiar role in art. John Barrymore in acting, Thomas Wolfe in writing, astonished and moved us, and we waste the benefit of their virtues by dwelling overmuch on the difference between them and the best artists. That difference is not, necessarily, a matter of integrity. On the contrary, it is an exaggerated devotion to self; the difference, in fact, is the degree of egotism.

In *The Magician,* Bergman's merits, if not quite as pronounced as in *Wild Strawberries,* are still extremely impressive, his defects just as strongly marked. It is the story of a mysterious mesmerist in Sweden a hundred years ago who arrives with his troupe in a small town, is brought to a rich man's house by the police chief and ordered to give a performance. Overnight a drunken old actor dies. It is revealed that the mesmerist is a charlatan, his "male" assistant is really his wife.

The list of questions that could be posed about the inconsistencies and inconclusions in this film is too long to be detailed. But here are two major ones: When the mesmerist is tempted by his hostess, why does he beat himself like a Dostoevskian saint being swayed from his holy course if, as we learn later, he is only a cheap vaudevillian groveling for tips? And, if he *is* a fake, why is his grandmother shown to have genuine witchlike powers?

The only real answer to these and similar questions is that Bergman felt like doing these things at the time, regardless of what preceded or followed them in the film. We must face the fact that his pictures are always going to annoy and captivate us; because, although scene by scene we are generally fascinated, we are all conditioned by a culture in which form is relevant to content. Either this makes us Bergman's inferiors because we are still enslaved and he is not, or else it makes Bergman a flawed artist. No doubt archaically, I cling to the latter belief.

The drunken old actor in this story says that he has trudged so long looking for truth in the dark without success, but now he has found that the truth lies in the search itself. Bergman, like the actor, agonizes toward truth but does not know—and it is clear now that he probably never will—that there is an aesthetic in that forward motion that can keep it from staggering.

But let us, as noted above, settle for his virtues. He can invest a film quickly and surely with poetry and mystery, for he is a man of serious mind and serious imagination. Numerous sequences are masterly, like the one in the attic, where the rationalist is almost frightened out of his reason. Some of his mannerisms are now recognizable (for instance, deleting the sound as the horses pull the wagon through the shadowy forest in order to heighten the eerie effect), but at least they are not prosaic mannerisms. The film to him is interesting only as a freehand way of asking immense questions, whether in drama or comedy. At his best he can be compared with that other Scandinavian teaser who, wonderful at times, never truly becomes supreme: Isak Dinesen.

Two other points about Bergman are important. He is one of the relatively few film directors who can be criticized in quite this vein because he writes his own scripts. The film that you see is the one he conceived, not the one he was engaged to execute, and much of the texture comes from the fact that the conceiver and (broadly speaking) the executant are the same. It is like the happy, almost lucky feeling one gets when a good poet is also a good reader of his poems (Dylan Thomas).

The second point is that, like few other current directors, he has assembled a stock company of actors and technicians who respond to him and, as such a company should, evidently think him the greatest man alive. Gunnar Fischer, his photographer, Oscar Rosander, his film editor, and Erik Nordgren, his composer, are now like extra senses of Bergman's. Among the actors are the gaunt Max von Sydow, the coolly beautiful Ingrid Thulin, the enchanting Bibi Andersson, the incisive Gunnar Björnstrand. Their reappearances in differing roles of differing importance in Bergman's films provide more than a sense of theatrical ensemble: at a deeper level, the creation of so many characters by so few actors gives us a sense of the Promethean range of human nature.

I hope strongly that no qualifications in the above will deter any reader from seeing this film. To miss Bergman is to miss a unique and valuable experience in contemporary art. But, for me, Beerbohm's remarks about Yeats are apropos. "I often had the pleasure of meeting Yeats, and I liked him," he says and describes him as

. . . remarkable, mystic and intense. . . . But . . . I felt always rather uncomfortable, as though I had submitted myself to a mesmerist who somehow didn't mesmerize me.

Bergman's films affect me more than Yeats did Beerbohm, but, like Sir Max, I am not quite mesmerized and wish that the mesmerist, admirable in so many ways, had been more successful.

POSTSCRIPT. There are those who think that *The Magician* is a disguised autobiographical comment: the mesmerist is Bergman and the hocus-pocus is his means to evoke the mystery and terror of life even though he knows the means are tricks and that he is only a traveling player. If so, all to the good. This vulgarly truthful view of art is possible only to an artist, not to the arty who are shocked at the suggestion that there is artifice, sometimes fakery, in art. But even in this view, much of the film's action is still inexplicable (such as the mesmerist's beating himself when alone) and some of it is padded (such as the maid's flirtation with the coachman). The allegory view simply alters the locus of criticisms, it does not answer them.

A Lesson in Love   (April 25, 1960)

The store of early Ingmar Bergman films has not yet been exhausted. Last fall we were shown *Three Strange Loves* and *Brink of Life*—the former a murky little investigation of various kinds of sexuality, the latter a surprisingly conventional "cross-section" film of

sensual hate as the maid. The two murderers, Axel Düberg and Tor Isedal, are credibly cruel, therefore frightening. Bergman has helped Ove Porath, as their younger brother, to give a moving little performance.

As might be expected, the sense of medieval life is excellently maintained. For a split second or two, you can find a portion of your mind asking: "How in the world could a camera have been present?" The scenes of violence are superbly done. (An interesting comparison might be made between the rape-murder here and the bathtub murder in *Psycho*. Bergman horrifies us at the act; Hitchcock horrifies us at himself—his cynically adroit exploitation of the act.)

But the bulk of the picture is a religious-moral charade. It is like looking at a series of scenes of a large medieval tapestry, each well composed, each representing a station on the way to the point of the parable, all of it (except for the visceral moments of sex and blood) rarified and abstract. We are left with the sense that a lesson has been spelled out—in huge, cloudy symbols of a high romance with God.

Intrinsically, too, there are faults. The frog which the maid encloses in a loaf of bread is either too obvious a symbol of the persistence of hate or too obscure a symbol of persistent paganism to be effective. The maid's encounter with the bridge-keeper seems irrelevant. The silence of the maid about the daughter's fate is unexplained. If she feared what the father would do to her, why did she return? If she returned, why didn't she speak? The vengeance scene is so long that it verges on the ridiculous. The father and mother enter the murderers' chamber, fasten locks, take bags from one man's arms, slam a knife into a table, yet the sleepers never stir. Then the father wakes them and has to kill them separately. Theatrically and otherwise, it is an irrational scene.

Still the film is valuable because of its concerns. In the introduction to his recently published screenplays, Bergman, the son of a Lutheran minister, says, "My father and mother were certainly of vital importance not only in themselves but because they created a world for me to revolt against." Subsequently he says, "Regardless of my own beliefs and my own doubts, which are unimportant in this connection, it is my opinion that art lost its basic creative drive the moment it was separated from worship." Apropos of the rebuilding of Chartres Cathedral and a figurative contemporary parallel, he says, "Regardless of whether I believe or not, whether I am a Christian or not, I would play my part in the collective building of the cathedral." These quotations support a view of Bergman as a Protestant's Protestant, rebelling that he may love, attempting (particularly in this new film) to shear away modern preoccupation with good deeds in the hope that he may find again the pure strength of Luther's "justification by faith"—salvation by belief alone. He is a kind of cinema Kierkegaard, who sees everyone trying to make life easier and has set out to do what he can to make it harder.

The hazard, which he has by no means escaped, is that his films have become essentially arenas of spiritual wrestling for the author through his characters, rather than disciplined artistic experiences whose prime purpose is emotional involvement of the audience. Even for the most serious viewer, the final result—in this new film as in others—must be called a failure in relation to the totality of its existence as art work; but it is a failure that serious film-goers will not want to miss.

Secrets of Women   (August 7, 1961)

Secrets of Women is a nine-year-old Ingmar Bergman film in which he uses one of his favorite photographers (Gunnar Fischer, who later did *Wild Strawberries* and *The Magician*) and several of his company of players whose faces, if not names, are becoming happily familiar to us. The film consists of three stories, told by three wives, of turning points in their married lives, and in them are sketched ideas that Bergman later developed in *A Lesson in Love, Smiles of a Summer Night,* and *Brink of Life.*

The first episode deals with a young wife who has a brief, disappointing affair with a childhood sweetheart and whose husband's pseudosuicide attempt, when he learns of this, may help to renovate their marriage. The second tells of a Swedish girl's garret love affair in Paris with a young Swedish artist, his return to enter the family business, and her refusal (at first) to marry him when, learning that she is pregnant, he is afflicted with remorse. Both of these episodes are unfocused and unsatisfactory. The first hints at a neurosis in the wife which no Sacha Guitry ending could cure; the second omits the very turning point which it is supposed to dramatize—the reconciliation between the young pair. But the first has some subtle interplay between the lover and the wife, and the second is adroitly told. Bergman characterizes the girl without words. When she grabs a glass of water on her night table, she gulps it and drenches herself. When she drops the glass next to the bed and breaks it, she steps out next to it with bare feet. When she runs water in the basin, she carelessly allows it to flood over. All this is done *en passant,* without italics, and before the sequence is ninety seconds old, we know a good deal about the girl.

In the third episode, especially well played by Gunnar Björnstrand and Eva Dahlbeck, method and matter are matched and the result is delightful. A self-satisfied but not humorless tycoon and his loving but neglected wife are stranded overnight in a stalled elevator, and, in the course of the night, provide themselves with an anatomy of their marriage. Promises are made in the suspended island which, of course, are broken when the castaways return. A cultural anthropologist might note that this is one more work on a theme that seems to have started with Ibsen. The theme states that women are wise and all-seeing, that men are merely clever children, and that, for their egos' sakes, their wives allow them to think they are dominant and deep.

It is interesting that almost all the works in this vein have been written by men. Pause, ladies, and consider: who is kidding whom?

The Devil's Eye   (September 25, 1961)

The Museum of Modern Art in New York has just issued a sad little brochure called *The Cinema of Orson Welles,* sad because it ought to be called *The Maimed and Nonexistent Cinema of Orson Welles.* In twenty years Welles has been permitted to film only seven of his projects, only one of which (*Citizen Kane*) was released in the form approved by him.

Compare this with the "cinema" of Ingmar Bergman. In sixteen years he has directed twenty-two films, and it can be assumed that he had control of the final versions of most of them—perhaps all. The difference is not in talent; Bergman has not yet made a film as consistently good as *Kane.* The difference is a socioeconomic one between Sweden and the US. Bergman has written that, during the filming of *The Virgin Spring* in a northern province, he and the cast and crew stopped work to watch some cranes fly over, then ran to the top of a hill to see them better. "And suddenly I thought: this is what it means to make a movie in Sweden. This is what can happen, this is how we work together with our old equipment and little money . . . how we can suddenly drop everything for the love of four cranes floating above the treetops."

A particular beauty of this situation—being an artist with a cosmos to roam in instead of spending your life in a basically hostile world looking for jobs—is that it gives the director a healthy chance to vary and to frisk. Bergman's latest film, *The Devil's Eye,* he calls a *rondo capriccioso,* and when I saw the words, I thought, "What luxury."

He has evidently had a good time making this film but has not completely avoided the pitfall in such cases of having a better time than his audience. Any criticism of a Bergman film begins, of course, with the fact that it is far above the general run and deserves a cultivated person's attention. However, *The Devil's Eye*—of all his films since 1955—seems the one least worth Bergman's time, even as a caprice.

The title comes from an Irish proverb which, I suspect, was invented by Bergman: "A woman's chastity is a sty in the Devil's eye." We begin in Hell where a rotund Devil in modern dress has a sty caused by a Swedish vicar's virtuous daughter. He chooses Don Juan, of all his guests, to return to earth and rectify the matter before her marriage. The Don is being subjected to exquisite punishment; he is continually visited by beautiful ladies whom he once had conquered, and who, just as they acquiesce again, vanish. Satan agrees to shorten Juan's punishment if he will sully the vicar's daughter.

Juan fails. But he falls in love (quite understandably, since she is played by Bibi Andersson) with the girl, and his torment is intensified by unrequited love. However, the term is reduced because Satan's sty is cured: as a result of Juan's visit, the girl tells her husband a little lie on their wedding night.

To tackle the Don Juan theme is to invite comparison with some impressive predecessors. In their light, *The Devil's Eye* fails, despite the fact that Bergman rings some wry changes on the story: as when Juan, incognito, tells the adventures of Don Giovanni to the marveling vicar and his family.

Bergman is one of the film world's most seductive directors for the eye, but he has also always relied substantially on dialogue. In fact he has written most of his screenplays himself. This film is a high comedy, which by definition lives principally through dialogue, and unlike *Smiles of a Summer Night,* the compass is relatively small, thus focusing the work inward on its dialogue still more acutely. The subtitles are good, but I have the feeling that even Swedes may feel that this film is excessively verbal.

Bergman uses all his magical repertoire to compensate for this; and the photography (by Gunnar Fischer) has the peculiar Bergmanesque quality of sharp outline and soft shadow. But the level of sheer entertainment in the film is not consistently high, and the total contribution to art work on the subject of Juan is small. Let us say that it is one of the Bergman films that are worth only one viewing.

Jarl Kulle is not my idea of history's champion amorist, but he can suggest dignity and depth. Sture Lagerwall (Pablo) has a tight-skinned, seamed, striking face which he uses to advantage. And Miss Andersson is one of those girls whom all the males in the audience want to marry.

Through a Glass Darkly (March 26, 1962)

Gray, ranging from the pearliest shade to the edge of black, is the tonality of Ingmar Bergman's *Through a Glass Darkly.* A bare, ruined choir of an island in the Baltic, a few stone cottages, a few trees, an old hulk of a fishing boat, marsh and naked field. The light and the milieu are cleansed to the point of abstraction, like simplistic modern architecture.

On this small island is the summer home of a novelist, whom we see with his adolescent son, his married daughter, and her doctor-husband. The daughter has recently been released from a mental hospital where she was treated for schizophrenia. In the course of the film's twenty-four hours, she discovers that her father and her husband know her case is hopeless; we see her disintegrate in a series of violent attacks. During one fit, she seizes her brother, who, she knows, is in the throes of adolescent libido, and commits incest. At the end of the film, accompanied by her husband, she is en route by helicopter-ambulance to a hospital, presumably permanently. The father and son, left together, have their first moment of full communion.

These are the only four people we see. The helicopter pilot is only a knock on the door. Bergman thinks of the film as a "chamber" piece.

The trouble with this quartet is that its themes are undefined and its resolution unconnected with them. The father is an egotist, more interested in his writing than in his family, to whom even the daughter's illness holds horrible promise as material for his art. But the results of his egotism are not explicitly dramatized. The son does not seem an especially deprived child; his unhappiness is not much more than that of any sensitive adolescent, adored or otherwise. Although the daughter must be affected by the father's central coldness, we cannot believe it is the cause of her trouble. In daily discourse he is affectionate enough; besides, she is enfolded in the perfect love of her husband. Are we to understand that the father's egocentricity is the dynamics of the situation (as it was in *Wild Strawberries*)? Then why does the film concentrate on the daughter's anguish and hallucination and make the father's story quite secondary? In fact, the father is going through a hell of his own, deriving from a middle-age crisis in morale, and it would be perfectly just to accuse the others of lack of sympathy on *their* part.

In the last scene, where the boy is left shattered and baseless, he asks his father whether there is any reality in life. The father's answer is love—either the giving or receiving of it, its loyalty or treachery, but love as the one foundation of reality. This has a faintly Chayefskian ring until we realize that, as the title indicates, the answer derives from St. Paul's trio of graces. *The New English Bible* renders the "greatest of these" not as Charity but as Love, and if we read it as more closely connected with *caritas* than *amor,* it may indeed be the foundation of reality. But we are still left wondering how the father arrived at that belief through the progress of the film or, if it was always with him, what use it was to him if it had so little application in his life.

Unlike some other postwar directors who have turned their backs on traditional dramatic structure, Bergman gives us the feeling that he seeks a relatively traditional structure and in some measure fumbles it. This new film is a Strindbergian study in mental torment and noncommunication at close range, but without the unity and cumulation it leads us to expect. The result is a collection of gripping scenes, always carrying an underlying sense of breast-to-breast confrontation with Jacob's angel, but no clear contest, no decision.

It is almost superfluous to note that the film is beautifully made: visually exquisite, ingeniously knit. Harriet Andersson's performance of the deranged girl is stark, beleaguered, violatile; she seems at the end virtually to exude an odor of unhealth and agony. Gunnar Björnstrand, her father, adds to the glacial element of the son in *Wild Strawberries* a malaise that gives the novelist greater richness and makes the cold elements themselves more affecting. Max von Sydow shows further versatility as the patient husband. Even in the way he runs, he delineates character—as unlike the Knight in *The Seventh Seal* as are the two centuries. Lars Passgard, the son, is adequate.

After all, however, it is the visual and emotional tonality we remember, not the theme. For the eye and for the spirit, it is a study in varying shades of gray.

Winter Light   (May 11, 1963)

Ingmar Bergman's *Winter Light* is relatively short (eighty minutes), but then none of his films is long. Most of them run ninety minutes or so. Like *Through a Glass Darkly,* the new one is a "chamber" work; i.e., he uses relatively few actors and settings. The time span of the story is shorter than in the last film. There is no score; the only music occurs in church services.

It takes place on one wintry Sunday in a country clergyman's life, between matins and vespers. The subject is another aspect of the subject of the last film, a crisis in faith. The pastor, a widower, is having an affair with a spinster schoolteacher who loves him and wants to marry him but whom he does not love. One of his parishioners, a fisherman with three children and a pregnant wife, is in a state of depression, deepened by the immanence in the world of nuclear-bomb threats. Brought by his wife, the fisherman talks to the pastor after morning service. The pastor's own spiritual bankruptcy is glaringly revealed in their talk. After the fisherman leaves, there is an agonized dialogue between the pastor and the teacher; then word comes that the fisherman has killed himself. There is a visit to the death scene (by a stream); another tormented exchange between the teacher and the pastor in her schoolroom; a visit to the new widow to tell her the bad news; then on to another church at twilight, where the pastor slips back almost desperately into clerical routine.

The theme again is how, what, whether to believe. The protagonist is again middle-aged (played by the same Gunnar Björnstrand who was the novelist in the last film. There is even a reference to the "spider God" which reminds us of the appearance of the insect during the daughter's hallucination in that film). Bereavement of his beloved wife, abrasion by the teacher's attentions, bewilderment by his incompetence in faith have put the pastor in a state of crisis. And the crisis is all the worse because it is a continuing one; nothing changes. His confession of spiritual vacancy does not alter his priesthood; he continues. Bergman seems to be saying that life was once lived in expectation of answers, now it is lived in continuity of questions. Crisis no longer leads to resolution.

For him the special agony is the tearing of the bond between God and man. Unlike Antonioni, whose work also concentrates on this matter, he does not believe that man invented God and must now be manly enough to admit it and destroy him. Bergman is concerned to find a way of living with—at the very least—the memory of God.

His films grow more spare. Economy of means in art is almost always a virtue, but in these last two pictures the spareness seems connected with a feeling that the script has been filmed, rather than that it is a film per se. The distinction is between a story that has been worked out on paper, then illustrated on film; and a story that has merely been planned on paper for fulfillment on film. Bergman is such a master director that he can make these works *seem* like films. In *Through a Glass Darkly* the sheer pictures were exquisite and moving; in this film, effects like the bravura of the letter scene are telling. (Alone, the pastor starts to read a letter from the teacher. We cut to a close-up of her face and, almost without a break, the camera holds on her for several minutes while she simply speaks the long letter for us.)

But here, as in the last film, the basic conception, the very compactness, have an unintended result. It would be no surprise to read that it had been adapted from a short story or a novella; its atmosphere and ambition are literary. The definition of "cinematic" is not, of course, absolute, and it is men like Bergman who have the responsibility to keep redefining it. But *Winter Light* reduces, in essence, to listening for verbal revelations, for explorations of self in words. This is doubly disadvantageous in a subtitled film (or a dubbed one), but it cannot be prime cinema even for Swedes. The crucial matters have not been much externalized, do not depend much on anything we can *see,* in encounter of person and person, person and place, even (as in *Wild Strawberries*) place and place. There seems no organic reason why it had to be a film.

There is another weakness along with this, possibly underlying it. First, let us note that we never doubt the existence of his people. From the start, even though the first minutes are a communion service, he manages to convey personalities and individuals. But after we have noted the reality of the pastor and the teacher, the quiet, freezing helplessness of the fisherman, the film depends on the penetration in us of the pastor's doubt. Beneath the intelligence of the film's execution, the spiritual problem seems merely stated, merely recognizable. We understand well enough. "Oh yes, *that* trouble." But it has not been vitalized and freshened to hurt us as it ought to. The tangential matters of the teacher's hopeless love and the fisherman's despair, which are supposed to reflect on the central problem, are more interesting in themselves. (Here, too, why does the suicide affect the pastor and the teacher so slightly? The pastor's emptiness was the last barren place the fisherman touched, and he knows it, but he looks down calmly at the fisherman's body. And why the teacher's coolness about it? If Bergman means their apathy to be meaningful, the meaning is not drawn.)

Björnstrand, Ingrid Thulin as the teacher, Max von Sydow as the fisherman, could not be bettered. They give human gravity to an almost abstract exercise in God-famished theology. I hope that in his next picture Bergman will use them and others of his "company" and his wonderful fluency in a work that does more than restate a familiar problem as a problem: that *dramatizes* it, even if it is familiar, and gives it life and insistence as film.

The Silence   (February 22, 1964)

A foreign director said to me after seeing Ingmar Bergman's last film, *Winter Light,* "It's a rich director's picture." He explained that, in his view, its economy of cast and settings, its brevity, were less the result of artistic refinement than of laziness-cum-arrogance bred of success. I thought his remark more funny than true and still do; but Bergman's latest, *The Silence,* gives it another meaning. Bergman—in his current phase at least—is exemplifying the saw about specialists: men who know more and more about less and less. He may not be a "rich" director, but in spite of the passion in this film he is a more aloof one than he was. He is anatomizing narrower and narrower circles of material; and the emphasis is on the dissection rather than on the revelation.

Two sisters are traveling through Europe toward their home in Sweden. Ester is unmarried, Anna is married and is accompanied by her eleven-year-old son. Ester suffers a violent attack of an unnamed but obviously grave illness. They must stay overnight in the capital of a fictitious country (where a fictitious language is spoken). In a deluxe hotel, Ester takes to her bed; Anna leaves her son with Ester and goes out. After witnessing some violent love-making in the balcony of a theater, Anna picks up a waiter (as she reports later to Ester) and goes to an empty church with him. She returns to the hotel and washes herself in view of the avidly watching Ester, who clearly has a sexual interest in her sister (which, as we have seen, she pacifies with onanism). Then Anna goes to another room in the hotel with the waiter, senses that Ester is outside the door, makes her come in to observe, forces their love-hate polarity to flare. Meanwhile, the boy has wandered about the hotel, has encountered a vaudeville troupe of dwarfs who have entertained him, has visited the old waiter in charge of their floor. Next morning Anna departs with her son, leaving the sister to follow later.

The film is patently a symbolic work about alienation. But its symbolism is its defect; it breaks down into a series of discernible metaphors, rather than aggregating them into an organic and effective work. We are constantly aware that there is a code to be read and we spend our time reading it. Some of the metaphors of alienation:

1. The three travelers in a city where they understand nothing.
2. The gulf between the sisters who love-hate each other.
3. The dwarfs who are cut off from the normal world and have to make their own community.
4. Anna and the waiter making fierce love though they cannot converse.
5. The country itself, presumably cut off from the world by the

military rule of which we see plentiful signs.

6. Ester, a translator by profession, trying to plumb foreign words.

7. The old waiter unable to communicate the story of his life to the boy even with photos—which the boy hides.

8. Ester's parting letter for her nephew, containing some of this country's words (especially "heart" and "hand"), a hope for communication in later life.

9. Contradictorily, Ester preferring onanism and Lesbianism because she cannot stand the idea of being fertilized—dying, she denounces the propagation of life.

I have doubtless missed other symbols. But that the film is a rebus, with clues to be hunted in it, indicates its limitations. It almost seems to have been contrived as an exercise for that school that looks on criticism as cryptography. Doubtless much can be made, for example, of the fact that the film begins and ends with close-ups of the boy, but it will have to be made by someone else, as will the explanation of why this well-loved, well-bred, intelligent boy pees in the corridor of this posh hotel.

Buzz has attended this film since its Swedish premiere because of its sexual frankness, which indeed it has—in three scenes, particularly. A friend who saw it in Sweden described those scenes to me, and, by his description, they have been slightly condensed for America. But the irony is that the film suffers nothing by this condensation; we are quite clear about what is happening and about its steamy quality. So I am still stuck with my old observation: foe of censorship that I presume to be, I have not yet seen explicit sexual details in any film that were necessary to it. Whatever was cut out of *The Silence* has not hurt it.

In no aspect of execution is this film below the high standard that Bergman has set for himself. Stroke after stroke is laid on swiftly, freshly. We know we are on a train at the beginning, not by the usual, tired, establishing long-shot but because the boy's head is seen against the unmistakable velour of a train seat and we hear the groan of the wheels. Bergman so easily creates such an atmosphere of import that, in fact, its excellence only emphasizes the vacuousness of the piece. His casting is, as always, impeccable. Hakan Jahnberg fills the role of the old waiter with kindliness. Jorgen Lindstrom, the boy, has a sweet mouselike face that counterpoises the women's faces well. As Ester,

Ingrid Thulin, the teacher in *Winter Light,* is faultless. As Anna, Gunnel Lindblom again smolders powerfully.

Any purportedly complete judgment of Bergman as director is bound to be faulty, because we know nothing of his theatrical work, which is the major part of his career. But film is the field in which he creates the whole work, and it has become for him the field where he works on psychological-philosophical matters that trouble him. If we had seen two or three seasons of his stage productions, the direction of this film might have additional resonances for us; but that would not expand the film's content. *The Silence* is, we are told, the third of a trilogy. Increasingly, in *Through a Glass Darkly, Winter Light,* and this film, he has used his means more economically and has affected us less, has made us feel we are seeing passages from private journals. The sketches are well done, the material is promising; but the art—in terms of the fulfillment in our response—has not been made. This film is Bergman musing, and we have intruded.

All These Women   (October 31, 1964)

Ingmar Bergman is merciless to his admirers, who get their severest trial so far in *All These Women.* My own admiration for him is shaken but persistent. This new comedy is intended as a double-barreled spoof: on himself and on critics. A master cellist is in his gorgeous summer villa surrounded by women: a wife, a sponsor, a maid, a mistress, a student. To the villa comes a critic who also composes, intent on writing a biography of the master. We never see the cellist; we see a great deal of the critic and the ladies. There are many attempted jokes about the master's venery and veneration; there are various adventures of the critic in seeking admission to the presence. One route leads through a boudoir.

All is in flashback; we open with the master's funeral and recount the last four days of his life. There are subtitles, tinny phonograph music; there are pratfalls, transvestism, comic tangos, custard pies, fireworks, explosions—all the mechanics of physical comedy. (There are also some unamusing broad jokes, particularly one about how the master teaches the ladies the cello.) But it is all apparatus. There is no wit in the film's conception, no humor in its execution. We seem to be expected to admire it because in it we see a Great Man unbending, acknowledging human frailties. As for the satire of the critic, surely Bergman has more to accuse critics of than venality and the egotism of frustration.

Jarl Kulle, the critic, who repeatedly pulls a long quill from his sleeve to scribble minutiae, cannot be entirely blamed for his tiresome performance; clearly he is obeying orders. So, alas, are Bibi Andersson, Harriet Andersson, Eva Dahlbeck, and other gifted persons. It is a reminder of how helpless good actors are against poor material and unwinged direction.

This is Bergman's first color film, and it is disappointing even on that score. He has set it *circa* 1920 and has, seemingly, wanted to suggest a confectionery feeling: as if the characters were different flavors of ice cream, photographed in almost horizontal light that seems filtered through meringue. But once the bonbon feeling is established, it is not used. The color, too, shows no particular resource of comic invention.

Little in any of Bergman's films indicates that he can make us laugh. His best comedy, *Smiles of a Summer Night,* is more barbed than funny. *All These Women* is intended to be hilarious; but the gift of splitting sides is not in him.

His recent films almost seem designed to test our faith in him. Either they have had paste-diamond brilliance (*The Devil's Eye*) or have been deficient in effective drama (*Winter Light*) or portentously vague (*Through a Glass Darkly*) or anesthetically cryptic (*The Silence*). No one who has seen these films could doubt that they were made by an artist of extraordinary ability; but any one of them is unsatisfactory. Bergman maintains his position as one of the world's eminent directors by the talent evidenced in his recent works rather than by the works themselves.

Italy

The Roof (May 11, 1959)

The directing-writing partnership of Vittorio De Sica and
Cesare Zavattini has produced some memorable films—*Shoeshine,
Bicycle Thief, Miracle in Milan* and *Umberto D.* Together with the
best of Rossellini, these are the flower of postwar Italian neorealism,
which, after the horror of war and in disgust with the factions that
caused it, wanted to make blunt statements about the contemporary
world. But to me there were always latent fallacies in neorealism and
they have overwhelmed the latest S-Z film, *The Roof.*

Zavattini has said that he dislikes conventional screen stories because they impose dead formulas on living social facts and create
"metaphorical" situations. "If I use living, real characters with which
to sound reality, people in whose life I can directly participate, my
emotion becomes more effective, morally stronger, more useful." The
logical outcome of these beliefs is to use nonactors, which is what this
team has done.

How fine it sounds. How vigorous to sweep away the tinsel with
which the merchants have burdened film. But analysis shows, I believe, not only the sterility of the theory but also that the virtues of
the S-Z films derive from the very elements they abhor: metaphor and
contrivance.

Was the script of *Bicycle Thief* improvised as the events of the
day's shooting dictated? Or was it carefully prepared by Zavattini
(from a novel, incidentally)—arranged and pruned for clarity and
growth? Were the nonactors simply turned loose before the camera,
or were they carefully coached, wheedled, flagellated by a brilliant

291

actor-director? The choice propounded by the neorealists is between "living, real characters" and the arts of acting and writing, but the choice is spurious. De Sica and Zavattini have not, despite their theory, given up the latter for the former because the two are not mutually exclusive.

But in *The Roof* they have tried again, more obstinately than ever, to make that false choice, and they have forced the issue so far as to produce their first dull film. They strove to make this film as much like life as possible. Therefore its hour and a half contains moments of pathos and humor and excitement together with long stretches that are not particularly interesting. Just like your life and mine.

The story was developed from a sketch that Zavattini wrote in 1952 for an episodic documentary about Italy (never filmed) and deals with the search of a young couple for a house in overcrowded Rome. Finally, with the help of friends, they build a tiny one-room house overnight. Italian law provides that, no matter where a house stands, people cannot be evicted from it if it has a roof and a front door that closes. The problem is to finish, to get the roof and the door on before dawn and the police come. The idea is appealing. If Zavattini had been more concerned with character development and story texture than with avoidance of "metaphor," if De Sica had invested one-quarter of the rehearsal time to appropriate professionals that he gave to eliciting versimilitude from nonactors, this might have been a moving film.

De Sica's preference for nonactors (they cannot even be called amateurs) is well known. In speaking of Ingmar Bergman recently, I suggested that this theater director looks on films as a free form, a chance for rhapsody. De Sica—even more experienced in the theater —also sees the film as a contrast to the theater, not as a free form but as a medium for nonacting, for *being*. But the postulate quickly wears thin because he cannot let his nonactors *be,* he has to try to make them act. Sometimes (and this is a tribute to his enormous talent) he succeeds fairly well, as in *Bicycle Thief;* but how often in *Umberto D.* I wished he had started with a good actor in the title role.

De Sica's revolt is, presumably, against both the star image—the famous actor who is so familiar that the audience has difficulty in believing that he is poor or Elizabethan or jilted—and against the very techniques of acting themselves, as being too visible on the screen. We all know multiple dreadful examples to substantiate these dislikes; but they do not prove that the extreme opposite is either true or a solution.

The seduction of the camera lies in making us think that because it can state a thing forcefully, it necessarily states it meaningfully. We have all seen salon photographs of dewdrops on petals, of brick walls and sand dunes that seem to have been made simply because it was possible to make them. But the camera speaks so emphatically that it is only after the initial impact of the utterance that we realize that little has been said.

The neorealist film-maker, drunk on photography, looks at an actor playing a bumbling youth on the stage and thinks: "With my camera I can record the real bumblings of a real youth. *Ipso facto,* how much better." Because it is possible, it is therefore an improvement. It would be wasting the advantages of film to bring that actor out of the theater before the camera because the film allows us to use the bumbling youth himself.

Some directors have shown that this procedure can have startling, often beautiful results. The combined efforts of *artists* behind the camera sometimes can secure enough good photographs of nonartists to be woven into a good film. But this is the exception; the dogged dedication of artists to nonart eventually produces banality in story and vacuity in performance.

The outstanding pictures of De Sica and Zavattini represent a triumph of their art over their denial of it. Let them leave real people and the photographic mentality to *Life* and the newsreels. Without blinking one jot of reality but with developed, conscious screenplays and competent actors, they could make films that would truly crystallize the spirit of their age. Their present obsession seems to me like that of the neorealist playwright in Pinero's *Trelawny of the Wells* (1898) who thought the theater would at last come into its own if it discarded painted drops and wings and used real doors and real doorknobs.

Two Women   (May 22, 1961)

Two Women was directed by Vittorio De Sica (whose name, despite his shortcomings, is an incandescent one to me) and stars Sophia Loren. The screenplay, made from Alberto Moravia's novel, was written by De Sica's long-time collaborator, Cesare Zavattini, whom some consider the best screen writer alive. Every moment of the film is the product of talent, experience, and empathy. Its flaws— and it has some—are imperfections in a serious and moving work.

The story concerns a young Roman widow who closes her shop in 1943 and goes back to her native province with her thirteen-year-old daughter in order to escape the convulsions of war as the Allies advance on Rome. It happened that I lunched with Moravia while he was writing this book, and although he said of it only that he was writing "a different kind of war novel," he mentioned that, under the Badoglio government, he had been forced to hide out on a mountain top near Rome. For nine months, he said, he had lived in a pigsty. Obviously this period provided a basis for this novel.

The Italian title, *La Ciociara* (The Woman of Ciociaria), expresses the sense of the work better. The Ciociaria is a district in the mountains southeast of Rome. An important element in the story is the feeling of return—the woman's shearing off the urban veneer in time of trouble and becoming again a *Ciociara*. One of the many memorable touches is the scene where she and her daughter get off the train impatiently when it is delayed en route. She shows the city-bred girl how to make a pad of her kerchief, put it on her head, and balance her suitcase on it; then they kick off their shoes and walk together down the road.

Cesira and her daughter Rosetta are taken in by farmers who are already sheltering some refugees from nearby towns. One of them is a young teacher, Michele (Jean-Paul Belmondo), who dotes on the child and falls in love with Cesira. But she is too preoccupied with caring for her child and herself to respond properly. We follow her fortunes on this hill top for some months as she scrounges, forages, struggles, and lives. At last the Germans retreat past their hill, and a party of them force Michele—at pistol point—to come along as their guide.

In the wake of the advancing Allies, Cesira and Rosetta start back to Rome on foot. Then, in a bombed-out church, they meet the war they have been trying to avoid. In a blood-freezing scene, full of soft chuckles and the padding of feet, mother and daughter are cornered and raped by a number of Moroccan soldiers.

The final episode is weak because time has obviously been compressed; events that ought to take days or weeks occur overnight. Rosetta is so shattered by what has happened that she feels virtue is pointless and sleeps with a truck driver for a pair of stockings. Her mother's remonstrations have no effect on the almost catatonic girl. Then comes the news of Michele's murder by the Germans. The child's love for the dead man cracks the ice, and she bursts into tears, back once more among the living. So Michele, by his death, has done a last service for the two of them. The film ends with mother and daughter weeping in each other's arms. The picture recedes, growing smaller in the center of the screen, until it is a photograph in an album, a split second out of anguished human history.

Because of this compression toward the end, the film lacks a certain feeling of "arrival," but the feeling of the journey is well articulated. The placement of the film in physical and moral locale is unerring. De Sica and Zavattini, like Moravia, were not interested in heroes but in people, some of whom are sometimes heroic. Michele is the one anti-Fascist in the film and, until he goes consciously to his death, he is only a talker. Cesira and the other women giggle over the sexual attractiveness of Mussolini, which seems to have been as much a factor in his political success as was that of *der schöner Adi* with German women. The Moroccans who commit the rapes were brought along by the French with full knowledge of their uncontrollability because they were fantastically brave soldiers.

The quintessence to which this film distills is the necessity for survival. It is the marrow of the peasant bone. Ideals, says this film, are not intangible essences, they exist only in people; so, first, the people themselves must continue to exist. That is not the whole truth nor the popular truth in a country like ours, which has been geographically divorced from both world conflicts, but it is nonetheless true.

Physically, Sophia Loren is not as suited for the part as, say, Anna Magnani might have been. But her beauty does not prevent her from giving a full-blooded performance, earthy and female, brimming with laughter and sex and devotion and selfishness. I hope—in vain, I know—that Miss Loren will never again make films outside Italy. On her own ground (like her heroine), and especially with the help of De Sica, she is splendid.

Those who have seen *Breathless* may think Jean-Paul Belmondo's bitter performance of the immoralist is the measure of his abilities. As the affectionate, impassioned Michele, he shows that his range is wide and his sensibilities are far-reaching. Eleanora Brown, as Rosetta, and Raf Vallone, as a very male Roman, are good.

As for De Sica, his essentially theatrical style flavors the film wonderfully. Antonioni is exploring the emotional possibilities of film techniques themselves. Bergman, who spends most of his time in the theater, turns to films as a by-product of his theatrical work, as Picasso turns to sculpture. Fellini is closer to De Sica than either of these; still Fellini is as interested in dramatizing with the camera as with actors. De Sica, alone among first-rate directors, is also a first-rate actor, and seems to feel that the film is not where he alters style but where he benefits by what he knows of the stage and of acting. For all his past use of nonprofessionals, the actor seems to him less a component of the film than its reason for being. He is perhaps the outstanding example of the wedding of theatrical and cinematic mastery. *Two Women* is quick with theatrical vitality.

Yesterday, Today, and Tomorrow   (March 14, 1964)

Yesterday, Today, and Tomorrow is a puzzling title because it all takes place today. This Italian film has three episodes, all entertaining and one (the first) exceptionally so, each of which has Sophia Loren and Marcello Mastroianni in its leading roles. The first story, in Naples, was written by the renowned Neapolitan playwright-actor Eduardo De Filippo. Miss Loren, the pregnant wife of an unemployed workman, supports him and their first child by selling black-market cigarettes. When the police come for her, she discovers that the law protects her from arrest during pregnancy and for six months after. She thereupon counts on her husband to keep her out of jail for years to come. He complies as long as he can, but a day arrives when he fails.

The second episode, adapted from a Moravia story by Vittorio De Sica's long-time collaborator Cesare Zavattini, is a brief bit of *dolce* Milanese *vita,* in which Miss Loren, panoplied by Dior and conveyed by Rolls-Royce, suggests an affair to a modish Mastroianni. The story profits by its brevity and by the contrasts on both sides of it.

The third, Zavattini's own script, tells of a Roman *poule de luxe* in a penthouse apartment overlooking the Piazza Navona, adjacent to a penthouse occupied by an old couple with a grandson who is a seminarian. Unintentionally the girl temporarily deflects the youth from his devotions. But the chief interest in the piece is the interplay between her and Mastroianni as a Bolognese merchant who visits her on his business trips to Rome, a man of comically intense, self-relished ardor. When he thinks that they are snuggled in for a weekend, he declares that he will never move from her bed ever again. "Mushrooms can grow on me!" he shouts.

All three of these stories are fairy tales of Italy, as the so-called Ealing comedies are of England: fabrications woven out of popular mythology and wish. For examples: all Neapolitans are mutually helpful and have hearts of gold; their prisons are spotlessly clean and are quiet pleasant places all round; the slum wife, who has seven children, never changes in shape, gains a wrinkle, or loses a tooth. But, as romances, these stories are enjoyable.

Miss Loren's Neapolitan is her *Gold of Naples* pizza-seller all over again, hearty, shrewd, and, in several senses, free-swinging. As the Milanese she has appropriate bored *tristesse*. Her *Romana* is a somewhat sloppy sentimentalist about everything but her job. But it is Mastroianni who contributes the gems. His bedraggled Neapolitan husband, his frenetic Bolognese caprioles are delightful. Those with a smattering of Italian can relish the varying accents of the two leading players in the three cities.

De Sica directed, and lest his contribution be dismissed as negligible because there is little cinematic virtuosity as such, let us remember his knowledge of acting and that it would be blind to separate what we enjoy in these performances from the benefits of his influence.

Marriage Italian Style   (January 9, 1965)

According to Vittorio De Sica, there are, in directing, two De Sicas: the one who made *Shoeshine, Umberto D., Bicycle Thief;* the one who made such films as *Yesterday, Today, and Tomorrow* and his latest, *Marriage Italian Style*. The former are his own work whose purpose, in his phrase, is "to follow the solitude of humanity"; the latter are entertainments, based on stereotypes about Italy and Italians.

I talked with De Sica last summer in Rome just after he had

finished *Marriage Italian Style* and, later, attended one of the music-recording sessions with him. (As the orchestra throbbed a neo-Mascagni passage, he turned to me, tapped his bosom with two fingers, and said augustly, "Vairy rich. Vairy Neapolitan.") He was happy at least to have made a film even in altered form, from the well-known play *Filomena Marturano* by the beloved Neapolitan dramatist-actor Eduardo De Filippo, but he was unhappy about the title put on it to capitalize on the success of the *Divorce* film. "A terrible title. Distributors always have bad taste."

The story begins when a middle-aged man's middle-aged mistress is suddenly stricken, seemingly dying. He is engaged to a young girl, but at the priest's request he marries the mistress on her presumed deathbed. Flashbacks tell us how they met during the war in a brothel, how she fell in love with him, how he got her an apartment, how at last she moved into his house and took over the management of his businesses. We return to the present, and the dying woman of course does not die. (For one thing, stars don't disappear that soon.) She has tricked him into marriage to protect herself. He takes countermeasures, including annulment. She presents him with three surprises, of varying ages. Quarrels, separation, reconciliation.

It is all old-fashioned theatrical nonsense; it is all excellent fun. First, because Marcello Mastroianni is the master and Sophia Loren the mistress. Second, because De Sica keeps it appropriately fast-moving or appropriately tender. Third, because he casts his films, even in the smallest bits, to the film's great advantage (like the gnomish dressmaker who follows Miss Loren excitedly in only one scene). Fourthly, because, despite the rather grainy Eastmancolor, his evocations of Naples are "vairy rich." And last, because this trumpery story is played against a backdrop of fact. Example: during a scene in which Mastroianni calls for the tart shortly after the war, there is an orator in the background exhorting a group of women and children to rally to the royalist cause.

De Sica complains that he can no longer get money to make his "own" pictures, that he is permitted to make only commercial films, but claims that they are "commercial films by an artist." Doubtless he would prefer his own films, but doubtless, in proof, he also enjoys making these pictures. Through the joints of their large artifices seep numerous small truths, just as in the midst of wildly improbable opera, individual arias can have credibility and beauty. *The Umbrel-*

las of Cherbourg is a recent example of a film that falsifies even its stereotypes. De Sica's film, too, deals in stereotypes but, by regard for them and by art in their use, makes them entertaining. The picture is false in shape, but not in what the shape contains.

Part of its truth is achieved by national self-satire, a mode in which Italian films are beginning to lead the world. Luigi Comencini (*Everybody Go Home*), Mario Monicelli (*The Big Deal*), Dino Risi (*Love and Larceny*) have all done good work in this vein, none better than De Sica. When the mistress is brought home sick, a servant is called to go for a doctor, and the servant is so distressed that he himself almost has hysterics first. This and many other examples are so satirically true that they give a kind of substance to the plotty proceedings. De Sica and Company seem to be nudging us all along, saying, "We are Italians playing it up *Italianissimo,* but with bits of verity at the compass points so that we all don't get lost."

About Mastroianni, one can only say again that there is no finer actor of his generation on the screen. Miss Loren is, as always, at her best under De Sica's direction. I asked him why this was so. He said, articulating his English in a careful, rather majestic way, "She has confidence in me. She is a *filodrammatica* [an amateur actress]; with beauty, with talent, but she needs to be handled. She does not read the script first. I read it beforehand to her. That way I, too, get the 'sense'—not of the meaning, of the ballet. Acting is music for me."

None of this is betrayal of Miss Loren for she has often publicly acknowledged her debts to De Sica. This latest result of their collaboration is again effective, if slight. One can certainly wish that she and Mastroianni and De Sica would tackle material of more substance; but let us be grateful for large favors.

L'Avventura   (April 10, 1961)

At last. Michelangelo Antonioni is an Italian director who has just made his seventh film and who is so highly esteemed abroad that there has already been an Antonioni Festival in London. For the eleven years of his career no Antonioni film has been released here. Now at last comes *L'Avventura,* which is the sixth of his works.

The first ten minutes make it clear that this is the work of a discerning, troubled, uniquely gifted artist who speaks to us through the refined center of his art. We may even "like" this film, but those first ten minutes indicate that liking is not the primary point. We "like" Maurice Chevalier, but do we "like" *Wozzeck* or *No Exit?* If so, all the better, but we know from the start that it is irrelevant to their effective being.

This is not to say that *L'Avventura* is an unpleasant or uninteresting experience: simply that it does not come out of the wings like a chorus girl with a grin on her face to make a hit fast.

The setting is contemporary Italy. Anna, a wealthy Roman girl, is having an affair with Sandro, a fortyish architect. They go off on a yachting weekend—together with Claudia, a close friend of Anna's—as guests of a dissolute princess. The party lands on a small island north of Sicily to bathe, and Anna, who has been moody and depressed, disappears. The island is searched without success; Claudia and Sandro stay overnight with a shepherd while the others go for the police.

And now the focus shifts. As in *Madame Bovary* (for example), we see that the prominent figure of the opening has been used merely to take us to the heart of the situation and, having delivered us, recedes. We never see Anna again. Sandro has increasingly to force himself to look distraught and to search; Claudia is increasingly disturbed because her genuine anxiety for her friend is being elbowed by her latent desire for Sandro and her subconscious realization that now she can have him. Before they have left the island—less than twenty-four hours later—Sandro has kissed her and has made her realize that she is glad of Anna's disappearance.

However, motions must still be gone through. They all go to Sicily following a sketchy clue that Anna may have fled with some fishermen, and Sandro, accompanied by Claudia, spends some days in more and more desultory search. During the search Sandro and Claudia become lovers, and criss-cross the path of the pleasure-seeking princess and her party as they make their way to the south of Sicily. The film ends in a palatial hotel in Taormina; Sandro has already been unfaithful to Claudia and she has already forgiven him. Or rather she accepts what they must accept in order not to spend all of life in tears, fights, futile beating against the facts of their natures and the moral temper of their time. They settle for what they are.

Over this slow, divagating search for the lost girl, which is really

Claudia's discovery of herself, Antonioni hovers with his camera: peering, following, lingering to savor a place after the people have left it. He is more interested in personality, mood, and the physical world than in drama; and it is this—if we apply conventional standards— that at times makes his picture seem to have lost its way. But Antonioni is trying to exploit the unique powers of the film as distinct from the theater. Many superb film directors (like De Sica) are oriented theatrically; Antonioni is not. He attempts to get from film the same utility of the medium itself as a novelist whose point is not a story but mood and character and for whom the texture of the prose is as relevant as what he says in the prose.

By purely theatrical standards, this film could easily be condensed by any skilled cutter—the search on the island, the visit to the deserted town, the kisses of Sandro and Claudia in the field. But when it is all over, you see that this condensation would sharpen the pace at the expense of the purpose. Antonioni wants the discoveries of this pair to occur in something more like real time than theatrical time. Obviously it is not real time or we would all have to bring along sandwiches and blankets; but a difference of ten seconds in a scene is a tremendous step toward veristic reproduction rather than theatrical abstraction.

The story is Antonioni's. The theme is upper-middle-class morality —not low enough to be corseted by suburban respectability, not high enough to be subject to *noblesse oblige*. These are Chekhov's people in Italy today; and, like Chekhov's people, we see them overripening before they drop. It is no accident that much of this film takes its indolent way across Sicily (Danilo Dolci's Sicily!—with disease and rooted poverty screaming just off-stage). It is an important part of the design that Sandro is disgusted with his professional success, which has betrayed his youthful plans. In profligate harmony with Sandro's resolve to get as much mundane compensation as he can, there are the princess and her *ami,* who wearily puts his hand in her bodice to flatter himself and her; and the frantic wife of a jaded husband hungrily devouring a nineteen-year-old admirer.

It is part of this design that makes Sandro spill ink on a young artist's sketch, deliberately hurting this reminder of his own youth in order to provoke a fight, then hurrying back to the hotel to make love with Claudia in order to substitute a little of the present for the lost past.

I wish that a few loose threads had been omitted (the mysterious boat we never see, the hint that the smugglers know where Anna is). And I wish I could expand on more of the fine touches like the blaring sound truck whose popular song carries us and the immanence of contemporary vulgarity into Claudia's bedroom; and do more than note the beautiful melancholy of Lea Massari (Anna), the sense of life in a sexual ambience conveyed by Monica Vitti (Claudia), the attractive but slightly shallow resignation of Gabrielle Ferzetti (Sandro).

In this film Antonioni stands quite apart from the Italian neorealists. He does not try to show life "as it is" but as he sees it. In the sense that his films are intensely personal in viewpoint and style and poetic rather than naturalistic, he is more comparable to Bergman than to his fellow Italians. But there is a great difference. The fountainhead of Bergman's films is mysticism: is the God-man relation still viable? Antonioni seems to have answered that question in the negative; thinks men have to learn self-reliance or crumble; is hoping for the possibility of hope.

La Notte   (February 26, 1962)

Michelangelo Antonioni's La Notte is so perfectly congruent with our concerns, so piercingly honest, that it is close to a personal experience. Such an acutely subjective reaction is not always the purpose of art, but it is his purpose and he has achieved it.

The story is spare. In Milan live Giovanni and Lidia, a novelist and his wife, childless, in their thirties, married some years, affectionate with each other but no longer in love. The film covers about eighteen hours in their lives: a visit to a dying friend in a hospital; a publication-day party for Giovanni's new book (which he fears may be his last); a long lonely walk by Lidia through the city; their visit to a night club where they see an erotic balancing act; an all-night party at a millionaire's villa where each of them meets someone who— temporarily, at least—attracts him. At dawn they cross the huge lawn together, the tired dance band still playing. Behind some trees they sit. She reads to him a tender love letter, addressed to her. He asks her who wrote it. "You did," she replies. Stung with anguish for his lost

love, he seizes her. At first she denies him, saying she doesn't love
him any more. He persists and she gradually acquiesces. The film
ends with the couple making love on the grass. Whether they will be
able to remake their love is undecided.

The film has no plot. It is a series of events given their dynamics by
the depth of character of the two people passing through them: a man
and a woman, once in love, who still live with and like each other but
who have floated apart out of fingertip's reach. Seen through their
eyes, vibrated through their nervous systems, the incidents in the
film—sometimes unremarkable in themselves—take on the propor-
tions of a pilgrimage. This is because their relationship is not sexual
ennui or a stage in marital intrigue; it is the result of their being
perceptive people in a world inimical to confidence, therefore inimical
to lasting love. With no sense of strain whatever, this pair step forward as protagonists of the age's love tragedy: the lack of a whole,
oriented self to give in love.

I must make it clear that this is not just one more European film
about "the moral collapse of our time"—the label that every lurid
French or Italian film carries to justify its luridness. *La Notte* is
certainly concerned with the theme of Yeats' *Second Coming;* the
best *do* lack all conviction, while the worst *are* full of passionate intensity. (See the millionaire host.) The film exists in an ambience that
is post-Hitler, post-Stalin, post-Bomb, in a society caught between
the far-reaching but iron-lined avenues of Marxism and, on the other
hand, a creeping corpulence fed extensively by military preparations
to deter Marxism.

But Antonioni is no glib, self-scratching Jeremiah. He is not
merely past outmoded hope, he is past despair. He looks at this new
environment as his home and, having decided not to die, lives. His
characters are in their habitat and know it; they face the task of
imagining a viable future. As for their marriage, we see them discovering the geography of the island on which they are cast, recognizing
that other lovers are at best excursions that will only take them to
other islands, that in the fact of mutual compassion there is justification for compassion, that they can stay together because they are
somewhat consecrated by knowledge of each other's weaknesses and
by the time they have passed together. The film finishes without
rosiness but with the cleanliness of scouring candor, a sense that the
worst is known.

"I know what to write," says Giovanni, "but I don't know how to write it." Like every artist in history, he sees more than he is capable of expressing, but, unlike them, he has no relevant framework within which to strive. He no longer knows how to speak or the point in speaking. "A writer is an anachronism," he says, "doing something that can't be done yet by machines." The horrible moment for him comes when his industrialist-host offers to take him out of his anachronism with a job as corporation historian and publicity director; an offer made with all the lubricity of the materialist ego that knows how to reinforce itself with the quasi-idealistic. The horror of the offer is that Giovanni realizes its aptness. The job would at least fill a gap in him, even though he knows it would be one long, plump suicide. But the real purification by this horror comes near the end when he tells Lidia of the offer and she says, "Why not?" When she who knows him and has admired him can say that, it is rock bottom for him. Her bland acceptance is the shock that may reawaken him and connect him with a revised world.

As for Lidia, the death of their friend Tommaso is the end of her last link with selfless love. Tommaso, who was never physically her lover, worshiped her, and almost convinced her (she says) that she was intelligent. Giovanni spoke to her only of himself "and I loved it;" but now all that is left of Giovanni for her is an ego that doubts itself. The loss of Tommaso's love—the only one without ego—is like losing parents a second time. She is reconciled to loneliness, even to her husband's quest for illusions of refreshment in other women, both because she is no longer jealous and because she wishes him well. But at the end, if she is not convinced that he is again capable of his former love, she at least knows that he realizes this and is ashamed of it, instead of accepting it; and in that shame is a possible seed.

Marcello Mastroianni, as Giovanni, gives a performance of utter comprehension and delicacy that *begins* by being true and then goes on to harrow us. Jeanne Moreau, who plays Lidia, has seemed to me until now a film actress in the least complimentary sense, a woman whose performances were for the most part albums of varyingly interesting photographs. Under Antonioni's hand, what was semblance has become vitalized. "The director," he says, "must know how to demand," and he has demanded well of her. She moves through this film like a sad suite of airs. Her face, elegiac and passionate, seems to brood over this film, even when she is absent.

Monica Vitti, brunette in this film, has a less complex role as the millionaire's daughter, but gives it waywardness without coyness and sex with sensibility. Bernhard Wicki (the director of *The Bridge*) endows his brief appearance as Tommaso with the clarity of the dying and the pride of a man who has faced his limitations—all this so sharply that the later news of his death makes us feel a loss.

As for Antonioni himself: I have now seen *La Notte* three times and I speak carefully when I say that I think he is making a new art form. In this film, even more strikingly than in *L'Avventura,* he is forging a new language apposite to a changed world. For a society theistically based and teleologically organized, the concepts of drama that derived substantially from Aristotle have sufficed for centuries. The film was born to that inheritance and, out of it, still produces fine works (although with a perceptibly increasing tinge of nostalgia). Antonioni has seen the dwindling force of this inheritance and is finding means to supplement it. He is achieving what many contemporary artists in his and other fields are seeking and not often with his success: renewal of his art rather than repetition.

Jackson Pollock, Hans Hofmann, and their kin are exponents of dissatisfaction rather than recreation. The antinovelists, in their frustration with the limits of the conventional novel, ask readers to share their professional problems rather than to be affected as readers. Brecht jostled the traditional drama healthily, but his theater is didactic, aimed toward a different godhead—a temporal one that now seems sterile to many. The so-called Theater of the Absurd faces reality rigorously and poetically, but a theater of images and no characters is limited to disembodied effects—and each author seems to have one reiterated effect. Who needs to see another play by Beckett or Ionesco or Pinter? In films, too, the avant-garde—Cocteau and many others—have tried to find new methods; but they, too, have so concentrated on the attempt that they have neglected to communicate much content. A more conventional artist, Ingmar Bergman feels present spiritual hungers as keenly as anyone, but his films so far, for all their superb qualities, exemplify Mulligan's line to Dedalus: "You have the cursed jesuit strain in you, only it's injected the wrong way."

Antonioni, however, seems to be making the miracle: finding a way to speak to us about ourselves today without crankily throwing away all that went before and without being bound by it. He is reshaping the idea of the content of film drama, discarding ancient and less ancient concepts, redirecting traditional audience expectations toward immersion in character rather than conflict of character. He is reshaping time itself in his films, taking it out of its customary synoptic form, wringing intensity out of its distention, daring to ask us to "live through" experiences with less distillation, deriving his drama from the very texture of such experiences and their juxtaposition, rather than from formal clash and climax and resolution. Fundamentally, he gives us characters whose drama consists in facing life minute after minute rather than in moving through organized plots with articulated obstacles; who have no well-marked cosmos to use as a tennis player uses a court; who live and die without the implication of a divine eye that sees their virtues (whether men do or not) and cherishes them.

John Grierson once said that when a director dies, he becomes a photographer; but Antonioni gets emotional utility—in a film about *people*—out of surfaces and compositions. He uses photography for enrichment, not for salon gasps: for example, the scene where Lidia goes for a ride in the rain with a man and the downpour seems to put the car in danger of dissolution.

The sequence that best represents Antonioni's style is the one in which Lidia slips away from the publisher's party and wanders through the streets. Conditioned as we are, we *expect* something; we think she is off to meet a lover, or to kill herself, or to get involved in an accident. But nothing happens; and everything happens. She strolls past a bus conductor eating a sandwich and is fascinated by his existence and his appetite in the same universe with her; she passes two men laughing uproariously at a joke and she smiles, too, although she has not heard it, anxious to join them, to be one of the human race; she encounters a crying child and kneels briefly and unsuccessfully to comfort it; she tears a flake of rust off a corroding wall; she sees two young men punching each other ferociously, watches horrified, then screams for them to stop. (The victor thinks she must be attracted to him and starts to pursue her, and so Antonioni touches another old tribal nerve.) Then in the suburbs she watches some boys shooting off rockets. She finds she is in a neighborhood that she and Giovanni used to visit years before. She telephones him and he drives out to pick her up.

By drama-school definition, it is not a cumulative dramatic se-

ITALY 307

quence. It is a miniature recapitulation, deftly done, of the possibilities of life: a child and an old woman, a man eating and a man punching, sunlight on a fountain and a greasy lewd stallkeeper. Antonioni holds it all together with something like the surface tension of liquids and, by not commenting, comments. It is essentially as drastic a revolution as abstract expressionist painting or Beckett's litanylike dialogue, but Antonioni has not estranged us in order to speak to us about loneliness; he has not sacrificed the link of recognition to make new images; he has not had to use absurdity to convey the absurd.

Of every directorial technique he is an easy master. I specify only two. His use of sound: the low-pitched conversation in the hospital is interrupted by the passage of a helicopter like a pause in music so that the hushed key will not become tedious. His symbolism (which is unobtrusive): the mushroom cloud of smoke that envelops the boy who fires the rocket, and the fact that Giovanni meets Lidia after her walk in front of a long-abandoned church.

For me, Antonioni has made in *La Notte* and in *L'Avventura* the most subtly truthful theatrical works about the relation of the sexes since Joyce's *Exiles*. But he has done more. In *La Notte* has has used a vitiated marriage as a metaphor of the crisis of faith in our age, the faith within which profoundest love and pettiest whim have always been contained. He has used his camera as a hound of non-heaven ranging through the streets of Milan to find the beauty in necessity, the assurance in knowing that one can live without assurances. This film leaves us less deceived; thus with the truth in us less encumbered.

Eclipse; Il Grido   (December 29, 1962)

"There's no need to know each other to love," the heroine of *Eclipse* responds to her lover's question; then adds pensively, "Perhaps there's no need to love." If these statements are not specifically the theme of Michelangelo Antonioni's film, at least they outline the domain in which it lives. *Eclipse* is the third part of what he considers a trilogy, with *L'Avventura* and *La Notte:* three varying inquiries about the nature and possibility of love in our time, inquiries as to

whether love—which, as we understand it, is after all a relatively
recent invention—is in a crisis similar to those of religion and social
organization.

Vittoria is a modern girl in modern Rome, and we must appreciate,
to begin with, that this is different from being modern in New York
or Cleveland. In a city where automobiles use a bridge that was built
in 50 B.C., change is not integral in the mode of life. The calendar
and the clock either bereave you or liberate you, depending on your
viewpoint, but you are always conscious of difference from the past.
Vittoria, clad in chic dresses, moves against apartment walls covered
with the latest art, in a district of Rome so new that the air seems to
quiver with atonal chords. She and this district seem "unplaced;"
when she goes down into the heart of old Rome, she seems Italian.

Here is all that happens in the film: Vittoria leaves a man named
Riccardo with whom she has had a long affair, having ceased to love
him. One day she goes to the Borsa, the Roman stock exchange
(which is built on the ruins of an ancient temple!), to see her mother.
The mother, a widow, has substituted money-drive for sex and is daily
in the Borsa to tend her holdings. Vittoria meets Piero, her mother's
young broker. In the course of a few days the pair are mutually
attracted, fall in love, begin an affair. At the end they are happy
with each other, but both are haunted by a presentiment that their
love—that love itself—cannot last.

With this slender story, Antonioni evokes a city, an era, a psyche.
His now-celebrated eye for texture and composition is, if anything,
clearer. His sense of rhythm is acute. And what has become his
hallmark—a feeling of purity, of absolute control and dedication—is
manifest from first to last. In *Eclipse* he intensifies certain of his
colors; some contrasts are stronger than those he has used before.
The opening and closing scenes are long passages of silence; and in
the body of the film there are passages of manic frenzy.

The opening sequence, about three minutes, is in Riccardo's apartment at daybreak. He and Vittoria, exhausted by a night of pleading,
refusal, quarreling, have nothing left to say; the fan whirs in the air
heavy with argument. She needs to gather her strength even to speak
the final good-bye. The closing sequence is a series of shots of Vittoria's neighborhood, as afternoon wanes into twilight—about seven
minutes without dialogue and without any of the principals.

This closing sequence has already caused much discussion.
It has been called by some the ultimate bankruptcy of Anto-

nioni's style. By others it has been seen as his statement that man must come to terms with his new environment before he can love. Others have seen it as a symbolic message conveyed by shots of a nurse wheeling a child, a jet plane's vapor trail, the headlines about atomic war and peace in the newspapers carried by home-coming working people. I offer no alternative "key" because I don't view the sequence as a cryptogram. To me it is simply a sounding board against which the story, now ended, resonates for a while, as a pedal may hold the closing notes of a piano piece. The drama, as such, is finished, but Antonioni doesn't want the film to finish yet, he wants us to linger in the specifics of the film's world and to let the story echo. It is quite simple and quite daring, and it is not a trick. It is an action in art by a self-confident artist.

The contrast with the above—the frenzy—is in the Borsa scenes, a wild arena that churns with continuous rush and clamor, but the men in it are inwardly calm, precise, predatory. The residual effect is something like that of opera: people standing next to each other scream at each other because that is the norm of the place. Antonioni makes it difficult for you to believe (which is his point, of course) that these scenes occur on the same planet as the film's opening and closing scenes. The Borsa sequences are the hyperbole of the frenzy that underlies all our lives. (Their noise is teased by an interruption —a minute's silence for a deceased member, which is obscenely funny because in the silence we can hear the brokers' brains turning over.)

Vittoria's parting with her first lover, the meeting and involvement with his successor, are shown with remorseless and rewarding truth. Antonioni is so sure of his truth that only a few (film) minutes after Piero and Vittoria skirmish into bed, he has them do a burlesque of the encounter—on a later day—already able to laugh at their first aggressive, naturally antagonistic intercourse. Less successful for me was a sequence in which Vittoria visits the apartment of a Kenya-born Englishwoman, inspects Kenyan photographs, then blacks up and does a parody native dance. It is well-enough done, but it is peripheral; its implications—about the clarity of primitive life— might have been taken for granted.

On the whole, however, the picture provides a stream of small stabs, shocks, gratifications. An airplane flight to Verona, which is an interlude of joyous unattachment between the two affairs; the episode in which Vittoria follows a fat, flat-footed man who has just lost a fortune on the market, picks up a scrap of paper on which he has idly doodled at a café table, and finds that he has been drawing flowers; the sequence of the courteous drunk who bows from the street to Vittoria in her window, then steals Piero's car and ends up dead in a lake—all these have a Chekhovian touch: non-extraordinary events, poignant enough in life, made more poignant not by heightening but simply by being extracted from life and juxtaposed in art.

Yet, although *Eclipse* is as consistently interesting as the other two films in the trilogy, it is not nearly as moving. I think this is because Vittoria is more a symbol than a person—almost a pageant figure, the Spirit of the Modern Girl. Her uncertainties and frustrations seem selected to represent a social group, rather than to create *her*. A large part of the reason for this—the sense that she is a compilation of recognizable problems rather than a person in her own right—is that we get from Vittoria no feeling of individual motion. We have no idea of the possibilities from which uncertainties have kept her. She is not even a bona fide floater. All we know about her nonsex life is that she does translations. (Does this pay her considerable rent and clothes bill?) The architect in *L'Avventura,* the novelist in *La Notte* were men whose possibly fruitful and happy lives, we could see, were harrowed up and thwarted. We are asked to feel much the same about Vittoria but without the same basis. I am not saying that she ought to be a frustrated artist or intellectual. But if we could sense that there was *something* she wanted in life to which contemporary malaise was an impediment—even if it was only to be a happy floater—it would deepen her shadows, make her a woman. Her context and presentation are so beautiful that we must be interested in her, but the sadness of the earlier films—of an *individual's* condition—is missing.

Monica Vitti does her best with the role, which is a great deal. She has *sagesse,* humor, sensitivity. But she lacks the materials she was given previously: the fascinated revulsion of the girl in *L'Avventura* watching herself fall into the arms of the lover of a friend so lately presumed dead; the precocious maturity of the rich girl in *La Notte* who sees herself being used as an emotional refuge by an older couple. Here she has little character.

Piero is inevitably more vivid because he is enormously active in a job he enjoys, and is not coarsened by it. He resembles the hero of Walker Percy's novel *The Moviegoer*—also a stockbroker—who says:

Money is a good counterpoise to beauty. Beauty, the quest of beauty alone, is a whoredom. Ten years ago I pursued beauty and gave no thought to money. I listened to the lovely tunes of Mahler and felt a sickness in my very soul. Now I pursue money and on the whole feel better.

This effect, of deliberately choosing to live in worldliness without surrendering to it, is emphasized by the casting of Alain Delon as Piero. His gray-eyed poetic face shouting buy and sell orders across the Borsa pit is an epitome of the necessary paradoxes of our time.

Il Grido (*The Outcry*), made in 1957, Antonioni's last film before the trilogy, was released here recently and offers substantial comparisons. The story of an itinerant mechanic who wanders through the Po Valley with his small daughter after his woman leaves him, it is a meaty but relatively unrefined film. There is little in it of what we would now call Antonioni's style. (Chiefly a scene where the child wanders through a group of asylum inmates who have been taken out for a walk.) But two points about it are closely related to his subsequent work. First, it begins with a woman leaving a man, as do all the films in the trilogy. In *L'Avventura* and *Eclipse* the parting is literal; in *La Notte* the wife has figuratively left her husband. Second, it is a chronicle of a human being looking for a *modus vivendi* in a hostile world. In *Il Grido* the story, emotionally impelled, gathers social-political weight and includes some dollops of propaganda. (The old man teaching the child the *Internationale,* the peasants' demonstration against the air base.) In the trilogy Antonioni has moved inward; one may infer that he no longer sees solutions in dogma of any kind.

With this inward movement his style has flowered, has left poster-like demonstration for poetic scrutiny. He now has such mastery of the vocabulary of film that he can violate rules to his purpose. For example, there are no dissolves in *Eclipse,* yet there is no choppiness of transition; the miraculously keen editing makes time his servant. One feels in his work, as one does rarely in any art, that he has said exactly what he wants to say exactly as he wants to say it.

But if there is not a flabby or false moment in *Eclipse,* it has none of the overpowering emotional quality of the previous two films. And, undeniably, it has some visual effects reminiscent of those films—like the heads seen against stark white walls. Whether these repetitions are design or limitation it is not yet possible to say. In a real sense we won't know all about *Eclipse* until we see Antonioni's future work. Meanwhile, although I cannot claim the enthusiasm for this picture that I have for its two predecessors, it is a happiness to know that, in the muddled, half-strangulated world of film, a powerful and pure artist continues to work.

(May 11, 1963)

Richard S. Fuller of Philadelphia writes that *Eclipse,* as now being shown in New York and Philadelphia, has been cut since I viewed it. A call to the distributor brought the ready reply that this was true: three minutes have been taken out (half of it from the end) because "people were bored." The immediate reaction is outrage, yet on what ground does one stand in this outrage? Cutting of films after review is commonplace, especially in subsequent runs after the first-run. But the valid criterion is not that it is done after the review but after the artist has finished with it, even if this is done before review. And that would apply not only to films but to books, which are often cut when translated, operas which are cut and transposed, and plays. (Does Kenneth Tynan's enthusiastic review of Frisch's *Andorra,* as he saw it in Berlin, apply to the play as adapted for Broadway?) I deplore the *Eclipse* cuts with all vigor, but I know that anyone's protest about these practices in general is useless. Nor can I think of any satisfactory labeling plan to warn the public. Ground rules would have to cover cuts by distributors, cuts by censors, additions made by producers after directors have finished, and several other variations. We simply have to console ourselves with the fact that, in the realm of performing arts, the film—as against theater, opera, ballet—is much the securest against tampering, and, I suppose, be reluctantly grateful for that.

(May 18, 1963)

Another letter about the cutting of *Eclipse,* this time from Detroit. William C. Stone writes that, when he saw it, the film ended with the last parting of the lovers; all of the concluding seven minutes were deleted. I have already noted how barbarous I think this crowd-pleasing cutting is. (Does it really please crowds? Will hordes of people like the cut version who would not have liked the original?) I still cannot see that the lines are clearly drawn, in this nebulous area, for a Great Crusade. But since the tampering is done hopefully to please ticket buyers, they ought to complain. If any film you see does not correspond to the version you have read about, here or elsewhere, I hope you will at least protest to the theater manager. Perhaps you will even want to write to the distributor. (For *Eclipse* this is Times Film Corp., 144 West 57 Street, New York 19, New York.) Ethically and artistically, if not legally, you have been defrauded.

Le Amiche   (March 23, 1963)

Le Amiche (*The Girl Friends*) is earlier Antonioni, made in 1955 before *Il Grido* and the trilogy. Its intricate story is woven around the residence in Turin of a young *couturière* from Rome: her arrival to manage an expensive fashion salon, her meetings with women, her acquisition of a lover, and, because of an emotional outburst, her return to Rome. The worlds are those of the upper middle class and of art (like the trilogy), and some of the sequences are superb. There is an expedition to the beach that prefigures *La Dolce Vita,* and with subtlety and ellipsis, expresses as much as Fellini's orgies. All of the picture is intelligent and interesting, but it slants on a literary bias. It seems more a filmed novel than a film. It is expertly done and would be a small jewel for a lesser man, but it lacks most of what Antonioni has since learned to do by film means alone. It has his subject matter and some of his complexities of spirit but not much of his subsequent style.

Red Desert   (February 20, 1965)

With Michelangelo Antonioni's *Red Desert,* the art of the film advances. This masterly creator has, in all his films shown here, opened new possibilities. Now, with his first use of color and with other elements, he further enlarges our vision of what a film can be and do.

The story chiefly concerns Giuliana, the young wife of Ugo, an electronics engineer in Ravenna. They have a boy of four or five. Corrado, another engineer, visits Ugo to recruit skilled workers for a job in South America. Ugo tells him that Giuliana has recently been in an auto accident, was not badly hurt, but is still suffering from shock. (In fact, as we learn, it was a suicide attempt, and the "shock" is her explanation to Ugo of her state of mind.) During Corrado's stay in Ravenna, he visits a shop that Giuliana is going to open, to occupy herself; asks her to accompany him when he drives out to interview a worker; goes on a party in a seaside shack with her and Ugo and friends. All through this, Giuliana is living on her nerve-ends, trying desperately to become "normal," to become *something*. Ugo has to leave for some days on business, and during this time their little boy has a short episode of fancied paralysis. When this passes, Giuliana's disquiet does not pass. She goes out, more or less purposefully to Corrado's hotel. They make love. Later, after they part, she wanders aboard a ship, encounters a Turkish sailor, has a brief, pathetic, disconnected conversation with him, neither one understanding the other. In the last scene she is walking with her little son outside Ugo's factory. The boy asks her why the smoke from a certain chimney is yellow. She says it is a warning that it is poisonous. Doesn't it kill birds? he asks. By now, she says, the birds know all about it and don't fly through it. They walk out of the film, and it ends.

The story is both dry and full, austere and intense. It is a series of incidents with sufficient but minimal connection, not cumulative drama of well-made scenes; yet each of these terse incidents is more than a skin-and-bones gesture (à la Bresson), it is implicative and revealing. Antonioni has always been interested in symbology. His method here is not—as it has been—first, to try to move us in new ways and, second, to have the symbols beneath the emotion resonate within us: it is to hold us, to fascinate us into reading the hieroglyphics he has unearthed, dating from the mid-twentieth century. The figures on these tablets suffer, embrace, reject, but their actions weave a second symbolic language that is the primary meaning and effect.

Or, in another figure, the story is not placed in the usual dramatic topography of valleys and mountains. It takes place entirely on the heights of character and action; thus the gradations, as in any view above the clouds, are only the relatively slight ones among peaks. Though these gradations are thus more subtle than if one were looking up from far below, they are nevertheless there. But a film that begins and continues at this high altitude makes assumptions between you and itself—about the valleys of character detail and the slopes of plot cumulation. Admittedly the atmosphere of the heights is perhaps a bit chilly, but it stings and clarifies.

The setting of the new industrial town and Giuliana's neurotic state help to illuminate each other. The Ravenna we see is a manufacturing seaport. (All through the film, ships pass in the background.) But by his vistas of factories, inside and out, of new dwellings, of radar installations, even of slag heaps, Antonioni is not making any trite charge of ugliness in the modern world. He is searching out the new life in it, the means of living in it. He has jarred Giuliana into a state of shock to make her hypersensitive—like a clairvoyant of change, of a means to accept life as it is and as it is going to be. In his press conference at the 1964 Venice Festival (where *Red Desert* won the Golden Lion) Antonioni said: "The story was born when I went to Ravenna, which I had not seen for some time. The film was born on the spot and the color was born with it—the industrial ambience of the film." In an interview (with Jean-Luc Godard) in the November 1964 *Cahiers du Cinéma,* he says further:

My intention . . . was to express the beauty of this world where even the factories can be very beautiful. . . . The line, the curves of the factories and their chimneys are perhaps more beautiful than a line of trees, of which the eye has already seen too much. It is a rich world, lively, useful. For me, I try to say that the sort of neuroticism which one sees in *Red Desert* is entirely a question of adaptability. There are some people who adapt themselves and others who have not yet been able to do so, for they are too tied to structures or rhythms of life which are now bypassed. This is the case with Giuliana. . . . If I had chosen a normally adaptable woman, there would not have been any drama.

This can be expanded to say, also, that if he had made the film in black and white, the urgency and immediacy of the neuroticism would have been lessened. The color serves several ends. First, quite simply, it is the best use of color I have ever seen in a film, exquisite in itself. It would be a quite wrong emphasis, but one could say that the film is worth seeing for its color alone. (And also that there is a buried history of modern painting in it, from the Impressionists through Mondrian to Hopper and Wyeth.) Second, the color underscores the color in the new world, a usually disregarded facet. The age of plastic and mold-injection and die-stamp is an age of heightened colors. Third, he has used color subjectively. Antonioni has said that he had an entire marsh painted a certain shade of gray because that is the way Giuliana and Corrado felt when they looked at it. A small room of the seaside shack, where a lot of sexual teasing and talk goes on, is painted a shade of red, off which, so to speak, the talk can rebound. "It is necessary to intervene in a color film," he says, "to take away the usual reality and replace it with the reality of the moment." Yet this subjectivism is gently handled, is complementary, is never carried to musical-comedy lengths. Fourth, color makes the environment a character in the drama. I know of no film in which a greater tension exists between the movement of the story and the places through which it moves.

As the film begins, we hear electronic music; then, over it a woman's voice vocalizing. It is an apt overture. These juxtaposed elements separate, and we hear the *vocalise* again later, in an interpolated idyl. Giuliana is the exponent and victim of these two themes. She is very much herself, a woman in crisis, but she also has something of the abstracted quality of a masque figure. (Those who have noted that Antonioni builds his films around female characters may also note that he has Monica Vitti to build them around. It is one of those happy occurrences in the performing arts when the advent of the right executant evokes the best work of a creator.) A recurrent method used to open a sequence is a shot of a background in slightly blurred, diffused focus in which Miss Vitti then appears, very close, in sharp focus. Thus the world is made the scenery of her stage, both in the sense of the author's use and the sense of Giuliana's own neurotic egocentricity. I would concede, however, that both senses are given a bit too much play; something less of Giuliana's gazing out of windows or backing herself into corners would have heightened the impact of both.

The film is susceptible of considerable textural and thematic analysis. Here I can deal with only two moments. The first is a small skillful device. In the opening scene, outside the strike-bound factory,

Giuliana, suddenly ravenously hungry, buys a sandwich from a worker
who has already taken a bite out of it. Her insistence on buying a
sandwich already "begun" is a small arresting gesture, unextravagant,
just odd enough to make us wonder about her at once. The episode of
the child's paralysis, which turns out to be spurious, is a painful
mirror-image of the mother's troubled state. Psychiatrists know that
young children apprehend and reflect neurosis in their parents; when
a child is disturbed, the physician often asks that the parents (at least
the mother) be treated. Suddenly one morning this little boy cannot
walk or stand. During this siege, while waiting for the doctor's diag-
nosis, the mother distracts her son with a story, which we see as she
tells it: about a young girl and a lovely, deserted pink beach (the
closest we come to a literal substantiation of the film's title). This girl
swims in the transparent water in the bright sun, sees birds and
rabbits, is alone and happy. One morning she spies a sailing ship,
unlike any other that passes by. She swims out to it and finds that,
mysteriously, it is unmanned. It turns about and sails away. She
swims back to the beach and hears a woman singing (the *vocalise* we
heard under the titles of the film). She cannot find the woman. "One
mystery is all right, two is too much," says Giuliana. "But who was
singing?" asks the boy. Giuliana replies, "Everything. Everyone."
The story is finished; and when she returns to his room, a little later,
she finds the boy unconcernedly walking about.

The obvious contrast of the idyllic spot with the factory milieu is
certainly not the prime point of the episode. (Anyway, whenever
Antonioni approaches an obvious point, he always redeems it with
fresh vision.) The episode is a qualified adieu to that girl's world of
sailing ships and wilderness and untrammeled freedom: qualified, not
because there is the slightest doubt that such a world is almost gone
but because it is sheer romanticism to think that such a world was
free of mystery, of unanswerable questions. Giuliana says of the ship,
"The girl was used to the strangeness of men and she was not surprised." The strangeness of men was and will be—in the natural
world, in the machine-monitored world. Thus Giuliana is telling *herself* the story, with that perception of her trouble that neurotics often
have rationally as they try to make their way toward health emotionally. In her mind, her best mind, she knows that it is rankly sentimental to think of our times as deterioration.

A personal example: When I walk through the New York neigh-

borhood where I lived as a child and which is now a forbidding
canyon of glass-and-steel apartment houses twenty stories high, I am
tempted to sigh, until I think that in 2065 men will walk through
these streets, then lined with fifty-story buildings, and will yearn for
the bygone "human" days of twenty-story buildings.

It is worth noting, for argument, that the Italian press is to some
extent anti-Antonioni. Some of their critics seem to resent the fact
that he is Italian: as if he does not fit their conception of the Italian
character, which is not much different from the travel-poster stereo-
type. After the Venice premiere a Milanese paper predictably referred
to *Red Desert* as *"ancora una volta il 'michelangiolesco' giochetto"*
—once more the "michelangelesque" little game. (By contrast, and
again predictably, some of the French press went to the other extreme
and immediately hailed it as an imperishable masterpiece. The film
has been a success in Paris.) But if there is anything that this film is
not, it is "once more" of anything. The same artist left the same
highly personal imprint on it, but it is different both in style and
subject from his trilogy.

In style there is small trace in it of the distention of time that was
germane to the trilogy, immersion in the extended moment. The handling of scenes is much more theatrically elliptical, and the editing,
with rare exceptions, is pared. There are no marked lingerings on
scenes, as if the pedal were being held down after the chord was
released—a device often, and effectively, used in the trilogy.

As for subject matter, the trilogy was concerned with differing
aspects of love as the medium of hope in our world. This film is
stripped to naked essence—hope or nonhope unadorned: the prospect of human life in the midst of whirling changes. We live, as we
know, in the age of the swiftest transition in history, and all indications are that the speed of change will increase: in everything from
household appliances to concepts in philosophy, the whole architecture of thought. Antonioni seems to be saying, without effervescent
cheeriness, that what was valuable can be preserved or can be transmuted to a new viability: that the future may contain new, at present
inconceivable, values.

His film reaches no grand resolution. The affair with Corrado does
not "cure" Giuliana. Her isolated dialogue with the Turkish sailor is
not a "come-to-realize" scene. There is no guarantee that she is on

the Road to Happiness. But she has finally accepted what has been no secret from her all along: that "what happens to you is your life"; and the very story that she herself tells her son evidences that she has within her a treasury of truth on which she may some day have courage to draw.

There are only three important characters. As Ugo, Carlo Chionetti has the right face and voice; not much more is asked of him. Miss Vitti is, as noted, the perfect Giuliana. She is asked to carry the film and she succeeds. Her vocabulary of uncertainty, in speech and gesture, is rooted in the certainty of her distress, her shame at her distress, her shameless display of it, her anger at the strength of others.

The principal and, to me, only serious flaw in the film is the casting of Richard Harris as Corrado. What he does is suitable enough; he has affecting ease and unexpected gentleness. But (this is a persistent Antonioni habit) what point was there in using a non-Italian who had to be dubbed? (At times rather perceptibly.) In Venice, when Antonioni was asked why he used Harris, he replied wryly that he chose Harris because he was thirty. "In Italy we have many actors of forty, like Gassman and Mastroianni, but we don't have any of thirty." I took this small joke as an oblique statement of regret. I hope I was right and that the practice can be discontinued.

I have now seen *Red Desert* three times, and each succeeding time it has not only seemed lovelier in color, it has had an increased sense of motion forward: in thematic penetration and artistic refinement. But pre-eminent in this sense of forward motion is a conviction that, as in his other recent films, Antonioni is not only making art of a high order, he is finding ways to help keep art itself alive. In these days of chance music, action painting and pop art, aesthetic idiocy in prose and poem, monolithic monomania in architecture, in these days when good artists question by act and statement the necessity for art, Antonioni continues to keep the film fresh and relevant: fresh without inane novelty, relevant without facile nostalgic reference. He has often been accused of being literary; if that is an indictment, he has perhaps been guilty, but here he is more purely cinematic than ever. There are few living directors who can be compared with him in level of achievement; there is none who is his peer in shaping the film form itself to the needs of contemporary men.

La Dolce Vita   (May 1, 1961)

A young idealist comes up from the provinces and is corrupted by the depraved city. This perennial theme now reappears in
La Dolce Vita, surely the most loudly heralded foreign film ever to be
seen here. With many virtues, this Federico Fellini work suffers un-
fairly from advance blather; and suffers fairly by comparison with
Antonioni's *L'Avventura,* which deals with some of the same matters.

Corruption, or at least skill in rascality, is well under way when we
first meet Marcello, a young Roman journalist. The film opens with a
gag of his—and a stinging visual effect. A helicopter flies over the
city with a life-size figure of Christ dangling below it; he and a photographer follow in another helicopter recording the effect on people
below, including a crowd in St. Peter's Square. . . .

And we are off on a three-hour account of Marcello's money-sex
jungle. The episodes include: making love with a rich girl in a prostitute's room; pursuing a pneumatic movie star although his devout
mistress has just attempted suicide; exploiting a false vision of the
Madonna invented by two children; an intellectual's party where
Marcello glimpses the life he wishes he shared; taking his visiting
father to a night club and providing him with a girl; an all-night rout
at an aristocrat's huge villa; the shock occasioned by the intellectual's
murder of his children and suicide; and a final orgy in which Marcello
feverishly tries to find ways to amuse his companions.

All of the film's 106 speaking parts are impeccably acted by a cast
which includes Anouk Aimée, the rich nymphomaniac, Yvonne
Furneau, the mistress, and Magali Noel, the night-club girl. Even
Anita Ekberg, as the movie star, is satisfactory. As the journalist,
Marcello Mastroianni, an actor of force and beauty, gets the chance
to display all his talents except his comic ones. Alain Cuny strikes a
credibly grave note as Steiner, the intellectual, and Annibale Ninchi,
the father, contributes a small gem. In fact, the father's episode—his
increasing hilarity and his sudden quiet self-disgust—is the most satisfactory in the film.

Fellini, justly celebrated for *La Strada, Cabiria,* and *I Vitelloni,*
is a director incapable of committing a stale or careless shot to film.
His vision is lively and his command is firm, whether with an intimate
scene (the vitriolic quarrel with the mistress) or a mob scene (the

fake miracle). He makes his actors search for truth and doesn't let them attitudinize en route. He puts his films together with a subtle rhythm and a sense of contrast which, if occasionally startling, usually justifies itself.

Yet about halfway through this film I found myself thinking: "What next? We've had exhibits A, B, C of decadence. How many more?" For Marcello's story is not the point of the picture, it is only the strand on which these exhibits are hung—self-contained episodes which are samples of Marcello's environment. There is no dramatic cumulation. He is no more corrupt at the end than at the beginning; he is only more successful—and is now shorn of the wispy hope of being like Steiner, which was just something to mull about when drunk, like the old reporter's novel.

Fellini has set out to move us with the depravity of contemporary life and has chosen what seems to me a poor method: cataloguing sins. Very soon we ask: "Is *that* all?" We feel a little like the old priest in the story who is bored not only by the same old sins in the confessional but by the necessity to appear shocked so as not to offend the sinner.

There is something inevitably wide-eyed and sophomoric in an attempt to prove decadence by showing us the pair in the prostitute's bed, or Marcello riding piggy-back on a drunken girl, or by having a "respectable" woman do a striptease. (If we could collect five dollars from every suburban New Year's Eve party at which there has been a striptease, we could finance Fellini's next picture.) Anyway, Fellini has loaded the dice by concentrating on the life of the Via Veneto, which has about as much relation to Rome as it does to us: a collection of international floaters of three sexes, remittance men and girls, film actors on their way up or down or through, and attenuated aristocrats. It is an ineffectual Sodom, made more remote by its orgies. I cannot remember a film orgy, from von Stroheim to the present, which didn't seem to recede as it progressed. Such episodes are apparently inherently uninvolving of the audience.

There is a recognizable desperation in all this, for the most difficult thing to render in art today is evil. What is evil in our lives? What will really shock a civilized human being today? Fornications in various combinations and places? Venality? Not likely. "What is sin?" Kafka asked. "We know the word and the practice, but the sense and knowledge of sin have been lost."

That seems a cardinal truth of our time. One perceives it in, for example, William Styron's generally undervalued novel *Set This House on Fire,* which tried to embrace an understanding of fundamental evil and in which the author had to spend much of his time searching for meaningful large examples. It is easy to find small examples: misleading advertising, broken promises to children. But after Buchenwald, who sees Dostoevskian evil in odd matings? After Hiroshima, what signifies a striptease? After Freud, can self-assault evoke anything but pity?

This is very far from saying that life is now all anarchy and amorality. The evanescence of evil does not, theology to the contrary, necessarily mean the evanescence of good; it may in a torturous way mean an increase in good, or at least in compassion, to fill the gap. To hold up a lot of "wicked" pictures, as Fellini does, can do no more now than elicit that compassion. At worst, it reminds us that Fellini's Rome has not changed much since Nero's (if anything, it's improved) and that, like the poor, the shallow ye have always with you.

Antonioni's method in *L'Avventura* is quite different and much more effective. It is not survey, but penetration, not to collect samples but to explore a few people; and it is a scheme always posed against abandonments and possibilities. But what has Marcello abandoned? Parties where ladies recite poetry and sing folk songs instead of stripping and shimmying. Steiner's spiritual bankruptcy is the only tragic subject in the film and it is insufficiently realized. Bereft of a cosmos, of anything more than book-club idealism (which Marcello fortunately never has the chance to explode for himself), Fellini's drama becomes increasingly glib the more he slogs away at it. The execution is excellent; the concept is superficial.

8½   (July 13, 1963)

Like most autobiographical works Federico Fellini's scintillating *8½* reveals more than its author intended. Begin with the title. It derives from the fact that, up to now, Fellini has made six full-length films and has contributed three "half" segments to anthology films. Before we step into the theater, the title tells us that he is clever, and that he sees the film as part of his personal history. It also tells us that he found himself stuck for a title.

The story is about a director stuck for a story, an artist in a creative slump, in the familiar *nel mezzo del cammin* crisis. The director is at a luxurious spa hotel trying to straighten out the script for his next job. With him is his writer, a fair sample of intellectual *manqué* who clings to much European film-making as both a suppliant and a hair shirt. The director is joined by his married mistress who stays at a neighboring hotel. His producer arrives with entourage. His wife arrives and is not deceived about the mistress. One of the best moments is his lying about the mistress to his wife with the face of truth and the wife's knowledge of this and her disgust—principally that he can sound so truthful when he lies; and—one step beyond this—*his* knowledge of *her* knowledge. His mind accommodates this with a perception of the gulf between moral myth and moral fact, then it flies off into a harem-scene fantasy. The film is thickly laced with fantasy—with recollection, projection, wish fulfillment, and a dream girl who reappears throughout. The director, harassed by his producer to come to a decision after months of vacillation about script and casting, is paralyzed by apathy and ennui. At last he decides to abandon the film. Then, in further fantasy, he faces all the facts of his past and present, accepts them, and decides to make a film out of the very elements we have been witnessing.

In terms of execution I cannot remember a more brilliant film. In image, visual ingenuity, subtlety of pace, sardonic humor, it is stunning. We see a wizard at the height of his wizardry, and it has something of the effect, given in contemporary reports, of Liszt playing Liszt. The film opens in a silent dream as the director suffocates in a traffic-jammed car while impassive faces in other cars watch or don't watch. He floats up through the sun roof into the sky, and in a perspective like that of Dali's *Crucifixion,* we look down past his legs along a kite rope attached to them, held by a man on a beach. He crashes—and wakes in his hotel bed.

The telling imaginative touches keep tumbling out one after another. In a dream his dead mother suddenly kisses him passionately on the mouth; when she pulls her head away, it is his wife. When his writer quotes one too many pearls of wisdom, the director wearily lifts a finger in command, two bravoes suddenly appear, slip a black hood over the writer's head, and hang him on the spot. When certain nonsense syllables remind him of his childhood, we go back to his family's house—as spacious and safe as it seemed to him then—when he and his cousins were treading grapes in a tun, then were washed and carried off to bed in clean sheets in their nurses' arms. There is no point in a catalogue; the effects are many and marvelous. The dreams do not fade out and in, they are part of the fabric. It takes a moment to decide whether what is happening is dream or not, and the confusion is probably part of the design.

But when we ask what the theme of the film really is, what the director learns from his crisis about his crisis, what the resolution really means, the answers are less satisfactory. He says at the end, as he watches the dramatis personae of his life dancing around a circus ring, that he has learned to live with his past. There is little indication up to now that he was not living with it; the resolution seems a somewhat hollow convenience to end the film pleasantly. (It could easily be argued that his fantasy suicide near the end ought to be the true end and is the logical conclusion: that the resolved, happy ending in reality is itself a fantasy.) The genuine *raison d'être* of the picture is in the opportunities it provides for Fellini. The reason that certain operas exist is that certain singers existed who could sing them. The prime reason for this film is that Fellini is a prodigious film virtuoso.

What *8½* reveals that is perhaps more than Fellini intended is this: it is not about creative crisis, encountered and survived; it reveals a continuing movement in his work that was first clear in *La Dolce Vita*. Up to then, there had been a generally consistent welding of method and meaning, as in *I Vitelloni* (which I still like best). In *Dolce Vita* there is a strong sense of theme used as opportunity rather than as concern. This sense was strengthened in his section of *Boccaccio '70*. It flowers in *8½*. I offer this observation in appraisal, not derogation. Virtuosity has an aesthetic value of its own, whether it is coloratura singing or fantastic pirouettes or *trompe-l'oeil* painting, and when it is as overwhelming as Fellini's virtuosity, one can be moved by it very nearly as much as by art that "says" something. In fact I don't think that *8½* "says" very much, but it is breathtaking to watch. One doesn't come away from it as from, say, the best Bergman or Renoir—with a continuing, lasting experience; one has to think back to it and remember the effect. But that is easy, for the experience is unforgettable.

Star billing ought to go to the director of photography, Gianni di Venanzo, and the editor, Leo Catozzo, who have wrought assorted miracles. Playing the director, Marcello Mastroianni invests the role with presence and portent. *Divorce—Italian Style* clarified to many what was apparent years ago to some: that he is a skillful comedian. Here he interweaves that skill with his ability to touch the commonplaces of life with dark poetry. Sandra Milo makes a serious-silly pneumatic mistress, Anouk Aimée convinces as the wife, and the rest of the large company confirm another of Fellini's gifts: his ability to cast even the smallest parts perfectly.

Variety Lights (May 15, 1965)

Variety Lights is Federico Fellini's first film which he co-directed with Alberto Lattuada in 1950. It is an undistinguished backstage story of a poor Italian touring troupe of vaudevillians, but the soggy story is well told. Fellini has said that he collaborated so closely with Lattuada that their individual contributions cannot be assayed; nevertheless, there are numerous elements that suggest qualities in later Fellini films. The troupe's expedition to a lawyer's home for dinner and dancing—walking through the woods at night—is reminiscent of *La Dolce Vita* as, obviously, is a piggy-back sequence at a party. The backstage atmosphere is like *Cabiria* and *La Strada*, the small town ennui is like *I Vitelloni*. There are some familiar faces in the troupe: Giulietta Masina, Peppino de Filippo (later the prudish Dr. Antonio in *Boccaccio '70*). It would be purely retrospective foresight to claim that one can predict the virtuosity of Fellini from this film, but there are felicities of execution all through it—whether Lattuada or Fellini—that lift it out of the ordinary.

Juliet of the Spirits (November 13, 1965)

Movies have now gone past the phase of prose narrative and are coming nearer and nearer to poetry. I am trying to free my work from certain constrictions—a story with a beginning, a development, an ending. It should be more like a poem, with metre and cadence.

Thus Federico Fellini, in a recent *New Yorker* article by Lillian Ross, speaking about *Juliet of the Spirits*. What he describes is not a new impulse in film-making; it has been felt by (among others)

such varied directors as Vigo, Ozu, and Godard. *8½* showed—
however unsuccessfully—that this theory was beginning to affect
Fellini. Now, with *Juliet,* which is much less satisfying, the question
arises as to whether the theory is plan or rationalization: whether
Fellini is making films as he really chooses, out of a possibility of
choices, or whether, like so many artists, like his own last previous
hero, he is hard up for material but wants to keep working.

The story is, as he says, the least of it. The wife of a prosperous
businessman, living in Fregene, a seaside town near Rome, suspects
that her husband is having an affair. She employs a detective agency,
and the suspicion is confirmed. She goes to the rival's house to confront her, but the dramatic moment is spoiled: the rival is not at
home and speaks to her only on the telephone, nonchalantly. Her
husband, unembarrassed by her discovery, tells her that she is exag-
gerating his friendship with the other woman, then leaves on what he
says is a business trip and what she knows is something else. At the
end she faces, not desolately but candidly, her life, her position, her
enlarged yet more securely confined self.

Thus it is not by plot but by texture that this picture asks to
succeed. Near the beginning, some friends bring a medium to Juliet's
house, who summons a woman's spirit to speak to her. (It is a
wedding-anniversary party.) This symbolizes the opening of Juliet's
senses to a more complex world than the one of husband, children,
and canalized friendships to which she had been limited. In the course
of the film she becomes closer and more confidential with a friend
(Valentina Cortese) who is a social and sexual floater; she consults
another medium whose atmosphere and message are purely sexual;
she allows herself to visit a beautiful and beautifully kept demimon-
daine (Sandra Milo) who lives on the estate next door. These experiences, and others, are meant to make her explore her past in analysis
and fantasy, are meant to explain her present, her impotence and
powers, the geography of her femininity.

The parallels with *8½* are obviously intended to be obvious. This
film is its female counterpart—*Hers* to hang next to *His.* The age of
the two protagonists is about the same—the moment of realization
that all is not to be realized. There are mediums here as against the
mind reader in *8½,* the female boudoir fantasy as against the male
harem fantasy, the counterparts of childhood memory. (Here a
school play and a libertine grandfather instead of a comforting

mother and a fat whore.) But the effect of these elements is not nearly as striking as in *8½*, and because they develop small pathos or mystery, we become conscious of them as attempts at brilliance.

8½ was, in my view, a work of little profundity, but it had vivid, interesting characters—particularly the three leading ones; it had a crux of considerable moment; and its cinematic effervescences bubbled, relevantly and amusingly irrelevantly, out of the protogonist's prepossessions and concerns. But Juliet is pallid as written and, to make it worse, the person of Giulietta Masina (who is Mrs. Fellini) contributes much less to this character and portrayal than Marcello Mastroianni supplied in the other film. Her fantasies and fantastic adventures seem unrelated to her—they seem neither to spring from her nor to affect her or us as they are meant to: she just plods modestly through. There is this rather dull, reticent, little woman, and then there are these varyingly interesting, unconventional cinematic shenanigans. The picture is schizoid, and because of its schism, even its ebulliences have less glitter than they might have had.

Let us not ask Fellini for the formal drama he says he never intended. Still a poem of character must proceed from a character capable of poetry, in a situation likely to evoke it. Juliet is so near vapidity that her possibilities for anger, frustration, illumination are limited. A wife—particularly an Italian bourgeois wife—may not have problems as susceptible of graphic illustration as a film director's, but these are very small thorns indeed on which a very bony little bird is asked to impale its bosom. The resultant lyric is not greatly affecting. One feels that more could have been made of these same materials. She is the Plain One in a family of beauties, including her mother, thus is a kind of refugee in the citadel of wifedom. But we never feel any genuine anguish when the citadel is shaken (she knows it will not be destroyed); we do not move with her through any felt progress to a new view of marriage or herself or even of her very plainness as protection. There is only a quite extrinsic sense that, with a much slighter base, Fellini is trying to erect the same coruscating structure as before.

But no film made by Fellini can be visually commonplace, particularly when the hyperbolic clothes are by his long-time collaborator Piero Gherardi and when the cinematographer is Gianni di Venanzo, one of the best alive. The dream and recollection scenes are deftly composed and edited. The tiny obscenities (like the two small girls doing the twist) are slipped in as jokes that are jokes on themselves. The theatrical *bizarrerie,* the subliminal references, the volatile rhythms produce the unique, unmistakable Fellini style. There are the dependable Fellini hallmarks: a walk through the woods by a party of widely spaced persons (as in *Variety Lights* and *La Dolce Vita*) and fun with clerical costumes (the nuns in *The Temptation of Dr. Antonio,* the nuns here). Yet even visually this film disappoints. It is Fellini's first full-length color film and the color, if we consider the director, is unremarkable. When I visited him on a *Juliet* location last year in Rome, he said he was "very uncomfortable" about the color. "In a black and white film, the audience collaborates. They see a tree, they *supply* the green, they see the sky, they *supply* the blue. In Technicolor, there *is* the green, blue, and so on. It destroys the collaboration between the audience and the film. How to replace it? How to provide another kind of mystery, of suggestiveness, to replace it?" His apprehensions seem to me well founded, his solutions unsatisfactory. Indeed there seem to be no solutions; the use of color is, for the most part, self-conscious, nervous, *un*used. Generally it seems added, not integral, and much of it is either blatant or old-fashioned. Blatancy: into the neutral tones of the opening scene, a bright red hat is splashed. Old fashion: the spangled drapes in the mistress' house are from a thirties musical. The obligation to have ideas about color seems to have forced Fellini even closer to the surface of his materials, visual and textural, than otherwise might have been the case. (The argument, put forth by some, that he was deliberately using "pop" color, seems more loyal than accurate.) In black and white he might have been able to concentrate, to *play,* more effectively.

For that last element is his chief strength. As I have noted before, the years have decreased the depth of his work, have increased the exuberant dazzle of his cinematic style (except, so far, in use of color). Surely his best course is to make a virtue of this condition, really to exploit it. What distinguishes him from other directors of his eminence is humor. Bergman has proved his short supply of it in his comedies. Antonioni rarely even attempts it. Kurosawa has humorous touches but they are almost always grim, not high-spirited. Fellini alone looks on the world's woes, human travail, with a mischievous eye. Comedy is by no means automatically synonymous with shallowness, but if all that Fellini is now capable of is delightful frippery, then let him delight us. Perhaps, in discontent with the limitations and irrelevance of formal drama, it is this that he is moving toward, rather than what he calls poetry. *8½* was a cascade of bitter, funny, scintillating if not deeply probing jokes on himself: for the silliness of his situation, of his century, of the plight of art, for the silliness of ever having been born. But *Juliet* is not nearly impudent, incisive, mischievous enough. It is almost as if he were inhibited, as if he did not feel the freedom to make the same cynical fun about a woman, about a wife, about a woman's life, as he did about himself.

White Nights; Rocco and His Brothers   (July 3, 1961)

Three of Luchino Visconti's films have now been shown here: *Bellissima* a few years ago, *White Nights* and *Rocco and His Brothers* within the last month. None of them supports his reputation.

White Nights, made from Dostoevsky's long story, is a deliberate departure from the neorealism of which Visconti was a pioneer. It is very much a "studio" film, with atmospheric sets and lighting. The story is transposed to contemporary Italy, padded with jitterbug sequences and a stereotyped prostitute episode, and completely misses Dostoevsky's point: viz., this unfulfilled romance is the only time in his life when this young man will come out of his shell. The film's handsome youth, whom other girls eye, will clearly recover and compensate. As the girl, Maria Schell laughs and cries, sometimes simultaneously; as the young man, Marcello Mastroianni proves yet again that he is as good an actor for his age as any in the world.

Rocco and His Brothers has been acclaimed abroad as a realistic masterpiece. To me it is distended, sententious, ostentatiously frank, fundamentally trite, and thematically unsuccessful. Its theme is the corruption of simple folk by modern city life—a Calabrian widow and her five sons (one of them a child) who come to Milan. But how does the city corrupt them? At the end one brother is a successful boxer, another is joyously married, a third blissfully betrothed and the Alfa Romeo employee he wants to be, and the child is loved by all. Only one brother, Simone, has gone bad, and he brought his egotistical sneakiness with him from the happy homeland.

This is the year of rape scenes. *Two Women* and *The Virgin Spring* contained rape scenes which were harrowing because they were intrinsic to their stories. But the one in *Rocco* is just Visconti showing off, proving how unflinching he is. Simone finds out that Rocco is seeing an ex-girl of his. With a gang of bravoes he surprises the pair, and while Rocco is forced to watch, Simone rapes the girl. It is disgusting because it is false; we feel that Simone would never have done it. He might have beaten up his brother and assaulted the girl, but the combination of the two is Visconti, not Simone. The fight that follows, with its sudden revelation of saintliness in Rocco, is another attempt to give depth to a shallow vessel.

In fact, barring the rape scene and the one in which Simone submits to a homosexual for money, this is a ponderous foreign version of those slum family epics that poured out of Hollywood in the thirties. One recognizes the parts for Cagney, Eddie Norris, Beryl Mercer, Frankie Darro, Ann Dvorak, and Joan Blondell. It even reuses the prize ring as the poor boy's escape hatch from poverty, except that Warner Brothers would not have cast Alain Delon with Greek profile and stringy frame, in the champ's role as Visconti, the realist, has done.

The film talks tragedy where none exists, is full of labored symbolism (the girl opening her arms to receive the knife), and is laden with tastelessly directed acting. The scene near the end where Rocco and Simone lie across a bed weeping and Mama comes in to collapse at their feet in hysterics is pure provincial-theater *prosciutto*. Nevertheless Paolo Stoppa, a fight manager, Suzy Delair, a susceptible middle-aged woman, and Annie Girardot, the tart bandied between the brothers, give good performances.

We are promised other Visconti films. Perhaps they will go further to explain his reputation.

The Leopard   (September 14, 1963)

Luchino Visconti is a director with a large embrace out of which almost everything manages to escape. His previous films that I have seen reveal serious intent, some intellect, some visual ingenuity. They do not reveal a grasp of the essential fine tension between screen and audience: how the film must control the audience, always moving it along at its own speed while the audience tries to race ahead and must always fail to *get* ahead if it is to be satisfied. Visconti's films miss this tension—he plunks down his designs and demands attention for them. So we become bored or wrongly amused and eventually irritated.

The Leopard is the best Visconti that I have seen. The film aims at the same goal as that of Lampedusa's novel: to depict, through the creation of character, a turning point in history. Visconti has not taken the novel as license for a mere spectacular movie. With small detail and large vista he has tried to make the Sicily of 1860. His street battle in Palermo is not only dramatic, clear, and credible, but because it is done with small numbers (Garibaldi landed with a thousand) it dramatizes for us how often the course of history has been shifted by relative handfuls.

All through this almost three-hour film there are images that tell us how times and time have changed. Young Tancredi departs for the wars as for a sporting event, sweeping out onto the palazzo terrace to bid adieu to his aunt and cousins, then down the broad stairs, past the gardeners, to a gig held by a waiting groom. When the Prince's family are traveling to their country home, the wayside picnic is introduced by the opening of a tablecloth as big as many modern living rooms, and while the family eat and drink, the coachmen walk the horses in a circle, cooling them. At the Ponteleone ball, which is the lengthy coda of the film, crinolined girls jump up and down excitedly on a huge bed in the clerestory lighting of Ingres and David and Degas. (The color photography by Giuseppe Rotunno, the art direction, sets, and costumes by Mario Garbuglia, Giorgio Pes, and Piero Tosi are magnificent.)

But in this vein of what might be called texture-making, Visconti never knows when to stop. When the Prince contemplates himself in a mirror or studies a Greuze or in any of a dozen other examples, Visconti's fallible sense of timing betrays him. Also he inserts what in literature would be called set pieces: e.g., the slow camera traversal of the dust-stained Salina family in their Donnafugata pew, a mobile mural artfully composed but of no dramatic relevance. We know the family well by this time, and we know they have just done a journey. Visconti simply could not resist a clever idea that he hoped would win him applause.

It would have been more helpful to us if he had spent more effort on keeping the story lucid. For instance, we have to deduce what

Donnafugata is and why the family goes there. The film has been cut by half an hour for American import, but surely all the cuts couldn't have been wrongly chosen. Part of the trouble must have been in the making of the picture.

Most of the acting is quite bad. Alain Delon, the Tancredi, has some verve in the early part, and Claudia Cardinale at least conveys Sicilian sensuality. But Paolo Stoppa, as the parvenu mayor, and Serge Reggiani, as the town organist, overact stupidly. Burt Lancaster is the Prince, and my fellow alumnus of DeWitt Clinton High School in the Bronx is badly miscast as the scion of an ancient aristocratic line. The strain on the others, who often must speak of his noble bearing and manner, must have been considerable and may help to explain their own bad performances. The film, like the novel, stands or falls with the character of the Prince. The novel stands; the film falls.

A few months ago in the *New York Times,* Bosley Crowther, in one of his periodic praises of dubbing, attacked the "purists" who oppose it. (Does this make him an impurist?) He said that the then-forthcoming dubbed version of this picture would be "a crucial test . . . of the whole issue of making the language in films fit the understanding of audiences." In his subsequent review he delivered his own verdict. In fact, he not only objected to some of the dubbing into English, he even objected to the voice and delivery of the one American in the cast! (Lancaster.) The dubbing *is* disastrous and is particularly annoying when one recognizes the voices of the dubbers while watching the faces of other actors.

Still, although *The Leopard* is ill-made, incohesive, tedious, it has some evocations of Sicilian landscapes and historical essences that are beautiful.

La Terra Trema   (October 23, 1965)

One of the best postwar Italian films is at last available in this country in its original version. Luchino Visconti made *La Terra Trema* (*The Earth Trembles*) in 1948. This two-and-three-quarter-hour picture has been seen in many countries in various versions; in Italy itself, it was shown with a dubbed sound track—pure Italian as against the original Sicilian. Now we can see it as Visconti made it, for which we must—once more—be grateful to Dan Talbot, the manager of the New Yorker Theater in Manhattan who has initiated its general American distribution.

Visconti planned a three-part work of which this was to be only the first part, to be subtitled *Episode of the Sea*. The trilogy was never completed, although cheery analogists may claim that *Rocco and His Brothers*—a greatly inferior and much more widely seen work—is the second part. *La Terra Trema* is set in the Sicilian fishing village of Acitrezza, and its cast is composed entirely of natives. Its theme is man's fight to live in the face of the cruelty of nature and of his fellow man; thus it will sound old-fashioned to the modern sensibility, as indeed it is—innocent of any of the additional colors we now see in the proletarian thesis. But the subject is so genuinely embraced and so lovingly executed that the film's virtues are not mere compensation for simplicity of idea, they make that simplicity welcome.

We follow the fortunes of a family of poor fishermen: Toni, who is the oldest son, his brothers and sisters, his lately widowed mother, his grandfather. Every evening the males, including the old man and the smallest boy, go to sea with a fleet of fishing boats that have lamps on their prows to attract the fish. (Once I traveled to Italy by sea, and after eleven days on the January Atlantic, the first sign of land was the lamp of such a boat, in the early dawn off Palermo. As the large cozy liner sailed by, the fishermen stood in their freezing open boat and waved and shouted welcomes.) Their boat does not belong to the family; they work for the wholesalers, who control prices. Toni is the first to rebel against this exploitative system. He mortgages the house to buy a boat, and the venture begins happily. Then (the tragic flaw, I suppose) he stubbornly insists on sailing out in bad weather. The boat is badly damaged, past the family's ability to repair it. They lose their home; Toni sinks in despondency and enforced idleness. At last the wholesalers complete their vengeance by rehiring him and his brothers. Concurrent with this quite predictable story are the accounts of his fiancée who snubs him when he fails, his next oldest brother who leaves home to seek work (a painful wrench in that society), and his younger sister who succumbs to the local police chief. There is also a quiet romance between his older sister and a mason, done with reticent peasant dignity.

A story that was either more novel or more complex would have worked against Visconti's purpose: to let the lives of these people flow past, to let the characters create themselves. Before long they are individualized at the same time that they become parts of a community in a routine. We soon turn up their street with them and into their house with the pleasant semi-tedium of familiarity. Visconti's style is neorealism at its best; he has unobtrusively induced these people to give a "new" (reconstructed) reality to the facts of life as they know them. There are moments throughout that seem a little slow, but our forbearance with them rewards us with the purpose of this tempo: the recreation of a rhythm of slow, oceanic swells.

Visconti's honesty is the chief beauty of the film. Unlike so much of his work since then, there is no patent exploitation of grim materials, no attempt at dazzling virtuoso direction. There is nothing here but sheer concern, effectively expressed in self-effacing art. A more cynical writer-director could have shown Toni succeeding in his venture and eventually becoming a wholesaler himself; a more sentimental one could have shown Toni, after his failure, resolving to fight the exploiters unto death. (For his failure to do this last, Visconti was called a defeatist by many Italian leftists.) Both of these alternatives might have had some truth in them but Visconti was after a larger truth: not one individual's struggle but the essentially changeless continuum of the fight for existence.

He also resisted any temptation to make lovely pictures (a worrisome flaw in Flaherty's comparable *Man of Aran*). The opportunities were plentiful, but Visconti knew that the fleet of boats putting out to sea is not pretty to the fishermen, and the anxious women scanning the horizon for a missing boat do not feel nobly statuesque.

To see *La Terra Trema* so belatedly, out of sequence in the chronology of Italian film, is to have an explanatory light cast on much that has happened since. For instance, it is now possible to be even fonder of De Seta's *Bandits of Orgosolo,* which deals with Sardinian shepherds or Olmi's two films abut factory workers in Milan and Sicily. They honor Visconti by having learned well from him. On the other hand, it casts a sadder light on Visconti himself, for in his subsequent work he has often interposed himself between the audience and his subjects.

Everybody Go Home!   (December 15, 1962)

Those who remember the hearty Italian films *Bread, Love, and Dreams* and its sequel (known here as *Frisky*) may have wondered what their director, Luigi Comencini, has done since then. Part of the answer is *Everybody Go Home!*, another exceptional film and, like those two, intensely Italian. That is, love and pitiless understanding of Italians fill it: impatience with their stupidities, amusement at their humor, pride in their wit, sorrow at their sufferings, embarrassment at their cowardice, compassion for their heroism. To be Italian, Comencini implies, is to keep an eye out for other Italians, both in admiration and caution.

His film, of which he is coauthor, tells of young lieutenant in 1943 when Badoglio's government surrenders. He has been fighting the Allies and now finds himself attacked by Germans and hard-core Italian Fascists; eventually he joins the partisans to fight the new enemies. As the Italian soldiers light out for home after the surrender, the lieutenant tries to retreat with dignity, then finds himself running; at last he is compelled—by the very Italianness that so often saved his skin—to stand and fight. His odyssey is a compendium of the ridiculous and horrible conditions of the time—a kind of male, military counterpart of Sophia Loren's role in *Two Women*.

The part is played flawlessly by Alberto Sordi: with enough lubricity to let us know that the character is being satirized but not so much that he and his director assume righteous superiority. The difference in honesties between this character and Sordi's somewhat similar part in *The Best of Enemies* is a small lesson in the difference between art and art derivatives for mass consumption. A strange piece of casting is the use of Martin Balsam, an American, as a veteran sergeant. Balsam mimes it well and mouths the lines that someone else dubbed; but why? Where, for example, was Folco Lulli?

Comencini resembles De Sica in that he is not highly "filmic." He is not interested in cinematic style, like Antonioni, nor even in cinematic effects, like Fellini. His chief talent consists in making his camera unnoticed: in telling his story straightforwardly and fluently. There is something pleasantly old-fashioned about this film. Like many good pictures of the thirties, it resembles a leisurely novel; it seems to ramble like a stream investigating every contour of the shore. (Even the photography is as unsubtle as in many good films of the thirties; all skies—even on sunny days—are grayish white.) Comencini appears simply to be saying, "Sit down for a while and let me tell you about some Italians"; but beneath this seeming casualness, he is making every moment count, is giving every scene its point. The result is startlingly candid, wry and affecting.

The Sound of Trumpets   (August 17, 1963)

For a couple of years there has been talk in film journals about an Italian picture called *Il Posto* (*The Job*), the first fiction film by a young documentary director named Ermanno Olmi. The praise, plus its festival prizes, was enough to make one wary, but the news is good. It arrives with a brassy ironic retitle—*The Sound of Trumpets*—and proves to be a delicate, piercing work with a quality that is precious in films: it is personal. We feel that it was made by a man, and not by a syndicate.

A youth, scarcely twenty, comes from a suburb to Milan for a job with an immense corporation and takes the obligatory exam along with other candidates including a girl. He is shy, sober, awkward; she is somewhat more assured because she is pretty and a girl. They pass, are sent for physical exams, then are assigned jobs in different building of the enormous concrete establishment. They meet only rarely. He is an assistant porter at a hall desk. He attends a company New Year's Eve party. A clerk dies in one of the offices. The boy is moved to a rear desk in the office and will work his way up, through the years, to a front desk. Ahead of him, as the film ends, are his life and his death.

In theme there is little new here. The protest against dehumanization has been a steady—and ineffective—note in the Western world ever since Marx sounded the warning against alienation. In films, René Clair and Chaplin repeated it; and there are hints in this picture of the flat, millstone-ground, everyday horror that one finds in the plays of Georg Kaiser and Ernst Toller. Even the poetically synoptic digressions that illustrate some of the older clerks' lives are not blindingly original. The picture's triumph—small but firm—is that it surpasses the demand for mere novelty. It is so strongly felt, so directly built on those strong feelings, that we do not care that we have seen other treatments of the subject, in films and elsewhere. Who wouldn't like to read a good new ode to a skylark? All that matters is the concern and artistry of Olmi's protest.

That is one of the film's most chilling aspects: the protest is Olmi's, not his characters'. The boy and the girl accept the state of things completely: the herd treatment, the company-policy politeness like an airline hostess's smile, the snuggling into a life-long cubbyhole. It is Olmi who is sad and angry. He sees that the "Detroit" syndrome is especially poignant in Italy, not because Italy has a long tradition of personal freedom (it hasn't) but because it has a long tradition of personality. The company party is the thin rinsing of what was once a full wine barrel. The last sound in the film is not of trumpets; it is the *slickety-whirr, slickety-whirr* of the mimeograph machine.

The Fiancés (February 15, 1964)

Filmgoers are not often aware of how much they owe film importers. It can hardly be questioned that the best films of the postwar years have come from abroad, and many of the better ones have not made money in this country. It is due to the importers' taste and initiative that we have seen these pictures. They are of course businessmen, not philanthropists; they have—all of them—imported inferior pictures and obvious trash. Also, it would be easy to list fifty foreign films of the last ten years that were interestingly reviewed abroad and have never been shown here at all. But, after all these stipulations, the debt remains, and, proportionately, to no firm more than Janus Films.

Janus brought the first Antonioni to this country, and most of Bergman; they imported the early Fellini (*White Sheikh* and *I Vitelloni*), the second part of Eisenstein's *Ivan,* Truffaut's *Jules and Jim,* the fascinating Pinter film *The Guest* and, in spite of the financial failure (so far) of Ermanno Olmi's first film *The Sound of Trumpets,* have just presented his second, *The Fiancés.* Lesser works are certainly on their list, but here, in my view, are some solid reasons for gratitude.

The Sound of Trumpets was a lyric but reticent work about a youth disappearing into the maw of a giant Milanese corporation, pathetically happy to be swallowed. Its derivations, in viewpoint and film technique, were clear; but just as clear were the immediacy of the theme to the author and its evolution through his temperament and gifts. The self-confidence to hold fast to familiar material was amply justified by the personal and poignant use he made of it.

His second picture shows an enrichment of style and furthers his theme. His story is a familiar one in Italian life. When I mentioned the title to a friend who has lived in Italy, he guessed the subject immediately. A betrothed Milanese couple, certainly in their late twenties, are unable to marry for lack of money. He is a skilled welder, and his company assigns him to a new plant in Sicily. He must accept the job because it is a rare opportunity, even though it means separation for a couple of years. The girl is desolate because she fears it means the end between them. He assures her that this will not be true.

Most of the film—which could hardly be simpler—is taken up with the facts and feelings of their separation. We go with the man to Sicily—which, to a Northerner, is almost a foreign country. It is a company town, and though nothing is bad there, everything is cheerless: the antiseptic company hotel where he first stays, the bus to the plant, the *pensione* where later he has a plyboard cubicle. In his busy but lonely routine the man fights quietly and without conscious heroism to maintain his person: as he does his work, plays boyish pranks with other grown men in the hotel, walks on Sundays through the hot flat countryside, sits on a curb, strolls (like the lonely dog we see) into a church. Through all this, his sustenance is the girl, in her letters and in his thoughts. One Sunday he goes to the expense of telephoning her, to reassure himself and her. Then he goes for a walk and is caught in a summer storm. He shelters himself in a doorway alone but, we feel, alive. And the film ends: suddenly but complete.

Summaries of Olmi's films may make them sound a bit sketchy and arty, but they are in fact strong, warm, and *continuous*. His perception of reality is intense but he treats it with a fertile imagination not satisfied with documentation, and he uses the techniques of neorealism more tellingly than anyone since the first postwar De Sica and Rossellini films. His casting is acute. Carlo Cabrini, the man, has a stolid but sweet face, capable of the self-concern that is assurance to a woman that she is getting a man, not a sop, yet without the egotism that derogates her. The woman, Anna Canzi, has a face that ranges in expression from the long-nosed headachy opening shots where she looks like a girl with perennial indigestion to the bloom of her natural Italian beauty. She is, of course, both persons.

Olmi has, in the best sense, put them at their ease and has eased their essences on to film. As for his skill, I suggest that the opening of *The Fiancés* can stand as a high example of sophisticated and subtle direction that results in exhilarating clarity. It begins in a dance hall, reminiscent of the cold New Year's Eve party in his first picture. The camera moves from one group to another, then seems to decide to tell us the story of this particular pair. We see at once that there is some strain between them. As she takes a giant pill and refuses to dance and he finds another partner, flashbacks reveal, with elliptical finesse, their relationship and their trouble. There is also a taut short sequence in which, because he is leaving, the man puts his old father in a home. Olmi is admirably sure about what to leave out. These first seven or eight minutes are—not to disparage the rest of the film—a little miracle of construction.

As we might expect, he makes the most pictorially of the salt flats and windmills and drab houses of this district of Sicily. His personal style soars again in the way he handles the exchange of letters between the lovers. The first letter that the man receives, he reads in silence, with no cliché sound track of the girl's voice. With other letters, we go in his imagination to dream scenes where he sees her speaking the words of the letters and to recreations of things she describes, all touched with delicacy, all conveying a sense that the director himself is on the verge of tears. On the verge, only. It is that quiet suggestion—maintained exquisitely throughout—that makes his film exceptionally affecting.

In this second film Olmi seems less concerned with the enmity of the machine age for the human spirit, more with the way humanity tries to persist through it. (Much is made of the slowness of the "natural" Sicilians' adjustment to industrial life. When the plant was opened, the Sicilian workers—used to farming—stayed home on rainy days. When a Sicilian girl comes for a job interview, her entire family accompanies her.) Olmi is presumably saying that the concrete runnels exist and these men must traverse them; but from the supervisors to the workmen, there is some consciousness of this fact, which was not true of the first film. The betrothal protracted by poverty, the couple separated by conventions of the era, is not a twentieth century invention. (See Manzoni.) It was possible to endure difficulties before, it may still be possible. Olmi seems to be telling us that the grim industrial plant is being sanctified, if not softened, by the spirit of the men who pass through it.

To end with my beginning, I believe that those who see Olmi's films will be as grateful as I am to Janus for continuing to bring them to us. I hope that there will soon be more of his work to continue with. He moves through film like a bird through the air.

The Organizer; Bandits of Orgosolo   (May 16, 1964)

According to *Variety*, film attendance has dropped off since the war (because of television) in many countries. In Great Britain, for example, the total number of tickets sold in 1964 was about one-quarter of those sold in 1946. But in Italy (despite television) the total in 1962 was about 70 per cent more than in 1946. And, unlike most countries outside the US, half of the twenty box-office champions in Italy last year were domestic films.

There is a temptation to speculate on the possible reasons: the improved Italian economy, the release of suppressed Italian talent after Fascism and war, the opportunities in the film form that the novel and the theater do not afford. These suggestions, and others, contain some truth, but obviously they do not account completely for the Italian anomaly. Economies in other countries have improved; other countries have talents that were otherwise engaged before and during the war; such countries with substantial literary-theatrical cultures as Norway, Austria, Spain have negligible film activity. The full explanation is not readily apparent. Further, Italian producers, directors, writers are fretting because they are bursting with projects and even this healthy state of business affairs cannot accommodate all that might be done.

Two more examples of Italian activity have arrived, one recently made film, one that took a few years in transit. *The Organizer,* with Marcello Mastroianni, is very interesting and very odd. Its oddness is in its air of anachronism. Here is a story of exploited factory workers in Turin at the turn of the century and the beginnings of their fight for better working conditions. Mastroianni is an ex-professor, sent by (presumably) the Socialists to help them organize their strike and give form to their struggle. There is a gallery of vignettes among the workers: the big burly one, the young randy one, the grieved old man with a daughter on the streets, the teen-age youth who is the head of a bereaved family. There is a group of owners and managers who are, to a man, oily and cruel. But I hardly need describe it. Anyone who has seen a dozen Soviet films of the thirties, dealing with Czarist Russia, could write a synopsis of this plot, including its immediately tragic conclusion, its promise of ultimate victory.

The question occurs at once: What prompted Mario Monicelli, its gifted director and coauthor of the script, to make this picture just now? There is black truth (indeed, far from its blackest) in this account of *fin-de-siècle* Italian labor oppression. My question is not about accuracy but opportuneness: why Monicelli wanted to make it at this moment and how he could recapture the glow of idealism, of Labor on the March, that infuses the picture. Are there no Jimmy Hoffas or Dave Becks in Italy? (Certainly, on the other side, there is at least one Olivetti, humanitarian if paternalistic.) This film goes back to a day when ideas, not facts, were more black and white; thus it has a rue that may not have been intended, a nostalgia that arises whenever any social movement has flourished so far as to become proprietary and plump. The Italian worker is hardly in paradise today, but he has come a long way from the riots, the mass shootings by police and army at the turn of the century. Perhaps the picture is intended as a chastener to the present-day labor leader, a "visitation to whet thy almost blunted purpose"?

Whatever its reason for existence, it has several intrinsic virtues. First, Mastroianni's performance. With Toshiro Mifune and a few others, he is among those film stars who are also fine actors. Like Mifune, he displays versatility without depending on it; that is, he does not put on a different face, assume eccentric characteristics, and expect to be bemedaled merely for that, merely because a handsome sex star has consented to appear unpretty. He seeks internals and relevances, whatever the external form. When he tumbles off the freight train into this picture, he is a dirty, ragged, happy man, pursued by the police and having the time of his life, conscious that he looks ridiculous (the man, not the actor) but rich in sureties. The character grows: in iron, in guile, in the egotism required of zealots, in foible. It is a vivid portrait—unsmeared with third-class Moscow Art actorishness. There is also a scene which will comfort those who mourn that sustained acting is inconceivable in films. The speech in which Mastroianni rallies the wavering crowd to continue the strike is theatrical oratory at a high level, impossible without a sense of line, without adequate voice and fire.

The other actors, especially Folco Lulli as the gruff giant, Gabriella Giorgelli as his daughter, Renato Salvatori as the buck, are satisfyingly good. This is a Franco-Italian production and therefore contains some French actors (Annie Girardot, Bernard Blier, François Perier) who are also, we know, good but are here egregiously dubbed in Italian. (The process sometimes occurs in reverse—Italians in French films—with no happier results.) One could understand a French producer's insistence on having a big French star in a film to insure an investment at home, but what financial good does it do him to have, for instance, the estimable Blier in the cast? It would be a better film with an equally good Italian actor in Blier's role.

Monicelli's direction is inventive, controlled, understanding, particularly praiseworthy in its handling of that ancient cinematic bother —the time lapse. In fact his direction is so good, in an old-fashioned unobtrusive way, that (like Duvivier's in *The Devil and the Ten Commandments*) it will probably go generally unremarked.

Advance word has been ample about the too-long-delayed *Bandits of Orgosolo*, the first fiction film feature by the documentary director Vittorio De Seta. (Not De Sica.) He made a documentary about the shepherds of Orgosolo, an impoverished mountain village in Sardinia, and was so struck by their character and environment that he decided to explore them further in a neorealistic fiction film made with local people. He spent more than a year among these taciturn men and came away with a picture that fixes a life, a place, a social condition.

Michele, a shepherd of about thirty, tends his flock with his twelve-year-old brother. (The roles are played by two shepherd brothers.) By accident Michele becomes an innocent fugitive from the police. The story tells of his and his young brother's effort to save their small flock as they flee the *carabinieri*, hustling the sheep across mountains, hiding them in hollows, but finally losing them. He sends his brother down to live with relatives and accepts the role that fate and the police have forced on him: outlaw.

The pitfalls of sentimentality both in texture and story are nicely avoided. De Seta is so concerned with his materials that the beauty of the picture, while hardly accidental, is almost incidental. Michele's destiny is so clear from the moment he gets in trouble that there is no attempt at irony; the story simply provides the rails on which the film runs. De Seta lacks Ermanno Olmi's breathtaking deftness and power of distillation; his film has little of the high lucidity of art *qua* art that is in *The Sound of Trumpets* and *The Fiancés*. But he too grows strongly and promisingly out of documentary schooling. His resources are sufficient so that he can afford sympathy without being boring or patronizing, and his film, in its chronicle of a fight to survive, has a base as rock-hard as its terrain.

Other Europeans

West Germany, Spain, Poland, Yugoslavia, Russia

Rosemary   (January 25, 1960)

What does it feel like to be a (West) German? An outsider can hazard some guesses. Whether you are sixteen or sixty, you are anti-Nazi, and although you never heard of Auschwitz during the war, you have seen *The Diary of Anne Frank* and you are sorry now about the camps. In the main you are probably glad of Hitler's defeat, though not of Germany's, and happy to live again in a republic. After all, hasn't it proved more practical? Industry booms, and a German general is high in NATO. There are some anti-Semitic flurries, and you may possibly join the march of protest against them; for why should you want the current prosperous democratic status—or foreign aid—disrupted? You are proud of your country's astounding recovery and cannot entirely suppress some small belief in that innate German superiority which you must publicly disavow. What other country could have had such a decade as your 1945-55?

Indeed you have done so well that you can afford self-satire. That is, perhaps, the real "German miracle."

In films seen here this satire has been weakly expressed in the rather toothless *Aren't We Wonderful?*, which dealt principally with the Hitler era, and now much more sharply in *Rosemary,* a postwar story. The latter is based on a successful German novel which in turn was based on the life of a Frankfurt call girl. The novelist, Erich Kuby, is coauthor of the screenplay, and the film has had, reportedly, the biggest success in Europe of any postwar picture.

Rosemary Nitribitt was, in fact, a girl of the streets who became a lady of the boudoir through the interest of several Frankfurt business executives. She was murdered in 1957 and, to no one's intense surprise, her murderer has not yet been caught. Kuby's bitter little novel about her has been transcribed for the screen with some alteration (the *provocateur* is made a Frenchman!) but with its mordant view relatively unclouded.

The story is simple. Rosemary is attractive and available. She is paid by an industrial group to put a tape recorder in her apartment to get secrets from rival industrialists, related with the boyish candor of the tired businessman in bed. She tries to play one group against the other and dooms herself.

The slim plot is somewhat overloaded in the film with apparatus: a chorus of two panders, former pals of Rosemary's who comment on events with Threepenny-Operatic songs; overused motifs like the swishing of a hotel revolving door; and various directorial touches reminiscent of German films of the twenties. The script also drags in a young religious idealist (who tries to redeem Rosemary) and a mysterious stranger, unseen and unexplained, on whom the murder can be pinned.

In the title role Nadja Tiller, a more feminine Hildegard Neff, is authentic and has one particularly touching scene near the end with her first rich protector. She has fallen in love with him and pleads with him to marry her. She conveys well a sense of the hopelessness of this idea combined with the knowledge that only this can save her from strangulation in the web she herself has woven. Carl Raddatz is effective as the quiet man whom she loves, who would like not to be revolted by her; Gert Froebe (the rich man of *He Who Must Die*) contributes his solid wurstlike presence as a tycoon who goes, as customer and confessor, to Rosemary.

But the prime matter in the film is its orbit: adipose success, parades of Mercedes sedans (used almost as characters), luxurious new houses and offices and country clubs. World War I produced a German decadence in poverty; this film depicts the decadence of quick new wealth, of a country climbing, not out of defeat, but because of it. Morgenthau and the war are mentioned to be forgotten; this is a portrait of a victory derived straight from catastrophe.

The stylized and the realistic do not marry well in the film, but its effect is disturbing and tenacious. Basically I think it is disturbing, hardly because the use of call girls by businessmen is news, but because Germans are in a position to applaud—as they have in large numbers—this cynical comment on their regained *richesse*. There is a certain smugness in the very caricature: "What a people we are, to have reached the point where we are capable both of these actions and of satirizing them!"

Additionally, underneath the German democratic umbrella, festooned with items like Krupp's $1800 compensation to each slave laborer, there seems to be in Germany a private satisfaction with the inevitable—a feeling that, because of contemporary East-West conditions and attitudes, Germany had to be forgiven and helped. The postwar West could not afford two enemies and was forced to pardon the gentle folk of 1870–1914–1939. *Rosemary* gives us a look at the forgiven ones looking at themselves: not with the savagery of Brecht and Weill but with the sad shrug of big men taking time to deplore the little cruelties attendant on progress.

The Rest Is Silence; The Threepenny Opera
(September 19, 1960)

André Gide says somewhere that Hamlet's troubles arose from the fact that he attended a German university. Now, *pace* Gide, Helmut Käutner gives us a film derived from Hamlet which takes place in Germany and in which the hero has attended an American university. In *The Rest Is Silence,* which he wrote and directed, Käutner has used many of the character relationships of the play and some character qualities to tell a story about contemporary Germany—a story he tells with intelligence and bitter purpose.

John Claudius, a young Americanized German whose Krupp-Thyssen father had sent him to America as a child, now teaches philosophy at Harvard. He visits Germany at his mother's request to sign some papers relating to the family business. His father was killed fifteen years before in an air raid, and his uncle has married his mother. John suspects foul play, and with the aid of a friend (an English secret service man), he investigates the death. Also resident in the large Claudius house are the old family doctor, named Pohl, his mentally delicate daughter, Fee, and his son who is an ex-Nazi. The story ends with Fee deranged but with John's father's murder proved and avenged.

The summary may make the picture sound like a Mask and Wig Club parody, but it is saved from burlesque because Käutner has not been content to mimic outward form, he has borne down intensely on the use of the form. The result is a provocative film which exploits the atmosphere of quick new wealth amidst the bomb rubble, of swift reversal of economic and political fortunes in this recently barbaric country that is rejoining the society of relatively civilized nations and doesn't quite know what to do about its immediate past.

If one may cite a joke apropos the most staggering tragedy in history, the present West German moral situation is something like the scene in a show called *Jumbo* in which Jimmy Durante, who worked for a circus, was stealing an elephant from another circus, leading it away on a rope. A policeman stopped him and asked: "Where are you going with that elephant?" Jimmy replied: "What elephant?"

"What Nazis?" asks present-day Germany. To judge by their most recent films, the Germans are a group of people—just folks—who were invaded by a group of Martians called Nazis who, fortunately, have since disappeared. Oh, of course some Germans were affected by them, but they are easy to discern because they are all nasty. In this film John sees newsreel shots of his father and his uncle kow-towing to Hitler. He knows at once that his (wretched) uncle was doing it by choice and that his (admirable) father must have been under duress.

Käutner and other German film directors are seeking to make moral statements about their country, and one must be impressed by the poignancy of their concern. Yet of those pictures I have seen, none has faced the primary fact: the majority of Germans and Austrians did not merely submit to Nazism, they embraced it and were able either to support its cruelties or to ignore them.

Thus the ultimate weakness of this picture's comment is that it has no base. Its anti-Nazi view is stated by a character who was nice and safe in America during the crucial days, and its only admitted ex-Nazi (the Laertes character) is made to seem only a young hothead now cooled. As yet we have had no film that attempts to portray the whole historical, economic, psychological impulse toward Nazism, that deals with the state of mind of those millions of Germans who must regard themselves as "decent" human beings and yet remember clearly what they were once happily part of.

As to performances in this film, Hardy Kruger is adequate as John, Adelheid Seeck is striking as his mother, Rudolf Forster is pleasant as Pohl, and Ingrid Andree as Fee is affecting in a part that could easily have been affected. Peter Van Eyck is precisely right as the uncle; he has the real and rare Claudius quality: power plus corruption plus sex appeal. As director, Helmut Käutner has a few mannerisms that he overuses, but he has a good sense of the camera as the journeyer through a story.

That same Rudolf Forster who is the Polonius character above is now on view as Mack the Knife in G. W. Pabst's film of *The Three-penny Opera* made thirty years ago. Thomas Brandon, the American distributor, went to enormous trouble to assemble a complete print after the negative and all prints in Germany had been destroyed by the Nazis, and we must be grateful to him for reconstructing a film of some historical value. But of little more. One is almost tempted to review the critics rather than the film, for the revival has provided a perfect instance of the sententious nonsense that can get written about a picture if only it is (a) old enough and (b) foreign. Influenced perhaps by Pabst's reputation and the dramatic circumstances of the picture's suppression and salvage, various voices have declared that a masterpiece has been restored to us. To this simple barefoot viewer, it was a choppy, stilted, murky picture, done in watered-down Caligaresque sets, full of prolonged hypnotic and hypnotized glances and shabby Keystone comedy. Lotte Lenya is welcome in the part that was written for her, but the picture is generally atrociously acted. Few reviewers have mentioned that many (most?) of the songs in that marvelous score have been omitted from the picture.

The Bridge   (May 15, 1961)

"Hitler" has become a word in common use again. Two or three years ago we had come to mention it as infrequently as we now mention Mussolini; but Shirer's book (begun five years before) appeared in the year of Eichmann's capture, and now, depending on your age, you remember or learn what the Hitlerian era accomplished.

Also aptly comes a new fiction film from Germany—the best post-war German picture that I know. *The Bridge* was directed by Bern-hard Wicki, a Swiss-born former actor who has worked under the talented Helmut Käutner. The screenplay is by Michael Mansfield and Karl-Wilhelm Vivier and is in every way superior to its source, Manfred Gregor's novel of the same name.

The plot framework makes one apprehensive. In the very last days of World War II a group of seven German high-school friends are hastily impressed into the army. The boys are assigned to guard a bridge leading into their own home town. Unknown to them, a kindly superior has posted them there to keep them out of futile combat; they are to be withdrawn and the bridge is to be demolished. But the corporal who knows this is killed, and the bridge is defended against US tanks, almost to the last child.

It seems a contrived skeleton ready for the pudgy flesh of TV or a tear-jerker movie. In proof there is scarcely a false moment in it. Because it is played to character truth, because the camera's record is unadorned with soppy comment, because the cast is concerned with inner realities and lets the pathos fall where it may, the contrivances become the paradoxes of chaos.

With a deftness reminiscent of Duvivier, Wicki introduces and realizes his large cast, creating relationships and the life of the town swiftly. (The crisp sound track is notably acute, especially through these early sequences.) We are not oppressed, as is frequently the case with "cross-sections," by the sense of placards being hung around the necks of the group: the Proud One, the Sensitive One, the Poor One, and so on. They simply seem to *be* these boys, each with interests, shocks, humors of his own, each anxious to get into the army. They are in service just one day (they have had some school training in arms) when they hold the bridge with bazookas and ma-chine guns against tanks and toughened soldiers.

Wicki is as merciless as the facts demand. When a boy plunks a shell into a tank, his pals exult as if he had scored a football goal, while men inside are being roasted. Later, the survivors weep in fright as they cling to the triggers of their machine guns, but the bullets in the belly of the GI whom they shoot hurt just as much as if they had been fired by veterans. In its lucid, impartial insistence and insight, the film achieves the status of art.

Well, the senselessness is plain enough. The question is, whose fault was it? Like many postwar German films, this one takes place in the latter days of Hitler when Nazism was wearing thin and only Germanism was left; but it is clear from such books as Hans Kohn's *The Mind of Germany* that the country had been busy for a hundred years cultivating the soil for Hitler. In Germany patriotism was not the last refuge of scoundrels, it was the first alcohol of the intellectuals—a heady brew of blood-and-steel Nordic romanticism. These boys in their outsize uniforms—from the Junker's heir to the washerwoman's pathetic son—are dream figures at the end of a century-old drunken delusion.

Viridiana   (April 9, 1962)

In this country Luis Buñuel is the most famous unknown director alive, for though much has been written about him, little of his work has been seen here. A Spaniard who spent years of exile in Mexico, he returned to Spain a few years ago to make a film which, once it was shown to the Cannes Festival and had won the Grand Prize, was banned in Spain. Buñuel is again in Mexico.

This Spanish film, *Viridiana,* now released here, is both a good introduction to Buñuel and a characteristic progression for those who know some of his earlier work. The eponymous heroine is a novice in a convent who visits her uncle-by-marriage before she takes her final vows. He is a rich eccentric who is struck by her resemblance to her dead aunt, drugs her (with the aid of a maidservant) in order to seduce her, but is unable to go through with it. Remorseful, he commits suicide. The girl remains to help run his estate and is soon joined by his natural son. The son devotes himself to modernizing the farm; Viridiana devotes herself to housing beggars, leading them (she thinks) toward godliness. One day the beggars are left alone, they break into the main house and run riot. When Viridiana returns, she is almost raped by one of them. The beggars are driven out. The son's practical approach prevails. The maidservant has become the son's mistress, and the film ends with Viridiana, by implication, joining the harem.

As baroque parable, the film is quite legible. The spiritual cannot cut its ties to the physical. (Even though she escapes assault by her uncle, his consequent suicide keeps her from returning to the convent.) God *is* mocked—by men who are essentially animals. The only help for the animal is not metaphysical but worldly action, and even in that context sentimentality is possible. (The practical son buys a dog from a teamster to free it from abuse; immediately another teamster passes with a similarly mistreated dog.)

Cruelty and ugliness, two Buñuel hallmarks, are stamped all over the film. Each of the beggars is somehow scored: toothless or white-eyed or dwarfed or syphilitic. The riot contains rutting behind a sofa and a profane version of da Vinci's *Last Supper*. The neurotic uncle fondles his dead wife's corset and shoes and veil; later, one of the filthy beggars finds these things and puts them on.

Bearing down always on the film is a ruthless disgust, a view of man as more self-deceiving than evil, a belief that all he needs to do is reduce his delusory aspirations and settle for what he is and has, and his life will be sane and healthy. Take short views; trust instincts; and trust that others will do only the same.

The basic "who do we think we're kidding?" attitude is more superficially sardonic than pessimistic. Pudding smeared on a drunken beggar's face, a phonograph blaring the Hallelujah Chorus during the revel, a shot of a cat leaping on a mouse when the son grabs the maid, all seem facile ironic symbols. What keeps the film from being a bore in spite of its philosophic shallowness—in fact, what makes it fascinating—is Buñuel's melodramatically graphic camera, which continually goads us, and his rhythmic sense which, for example, builds the orgy like a bolero. He is a master technician with the outlook of a collegiate idealist who has just discovered venality and lust.

It seems to me significant that Buñuel began his film career in the twenties by collaborating with Salvador Dali. There are few better technicians among painters than Dali, few with an eye for more melodramatically striking compositions, and few who are more slick and unrewarding. One risk of art that deals in shock—to show the viewer the ugliness made by his way of life—is that it is easy to fall in love with the shock process as such. The ugliness in *Viridiana* is less an illumination of the ugliness we make than the logical extension of the career of a man who began (in *Un Chien Andalou*) by slitting a girl's eyeball with a razor.

The Criminal Life of Archibaldo de la Cruz   (December 1, 1962)

Luis Buñuel's *The Criminal Life of Archibaldo de la Cruz* begins like one of his conventional unconventional films, with blood, razors, and sexuality all commingled. Surprisingly, it turns out to be a comic view of these matters, although it never really makes you laugh. Because of childhood experience, a wealthy young Mexican associates desire with killing and tries to murder several beautiful women. In each case either he is beaten to the punch by someone else who kills the girl or an interruption saves the proposed victim. The film has little of the remarkable textures that Buñuel has often achieved; its composition—pictorially and rhythmically—is commonplace. But its narrative is lively and it has the added interest—for those who know other works of this talented sadist—of self-satire.

Diary of a Chambermaid   (April 3, 1965)

Diary of a Chambermaid, Octave Mirbeau's novel, filmed twice by Jean Renoir, has been filmed yet again, this time by Luis Buñuel, with Jeanne Moreau as Celestine. It has been updated to the 1930's and put in a context of the French fascist movement, in an attempt to give social reverberations to the hot goings-on in the country house. Miss Moreau, extraordinary though she is, has now been called on too often to supply characterization omitted by the writer, to provide a worldly aura for a picture by her bland acceptance of the *outré*. Not every film can be given profundity simply by Miss Moreau's taking off her clothes.

Buñuel, the swami of sadism, has now reached the point of self-parody. Here he has an old man who is a shoe fetishist (compare the wedding-dress man in *Viridiana*); here a wild pig chases a rabbit through the woods just as a brute is about to rape and murder a child (compare the cat and mouse in *Viridiana*). Of course there is a knife; I can't remember a Buñuel film without one, from *Un Chien Andalou* to the present. Here the knife is used lingeringly on a goose's neck. Buñuel remains, for me, a highly resourceful technician and a highly neurotic adolescent.

Not on Your Life! (May 1, 1965)

"At present the Spanish film is politically false, socially false, intellectually insignificant, aesthetically null, and industrially rickety." This statement was issued in 1955 by a congress in Salamanca, and in this country we have had small reason to doubt it. We know of an active film school in Madrid, we know of (and have seen) much production in Spain by Americans and British, but we know few Spanish films, and few of the few have been interesting. Therefore *Not on Your Life!,* though finally unsuccessful, is a pleasant surprise.

It is a black comedy: about a young hearse-driver in Madrid, who has trouble getting girls because of his occupation, and the daughter of a public executioner who has trouble finding a husband because of her father's occupation. They marry, eventually, and in order to secure the apartment in the new housing project to which the executioner's job has entitled him, the son-in-law—much against his will—has to take up that job when the old man retires. Much purportedly comic play is made of the young man's reluctance, of the pressure brought on him because his baby needs its new, pleasant home. He hopes against hope that his first victim will be pardoned; in fact, he is somewhat in the condemned man's position, appealing to the priest, waiting for news of reprive. The best scene in the film—simply and scathingly staged—is in a huge bare room in the prison with a small door in the far wall. The condemned man, somewhat resolved, walks toward the door with attendants and witnesses. Following him is the new executioner, weak-kneed and struggling, supported and propelled by two guards who have to summon the priest's help.

There are other sharp-edged scenes, notably the wedding. We know that our pair are to marry. The next scene begins as the organ plays and we see the brightly lit church and many handsome guests. But it is not our couple. The rich pair finish and leave; then as the sacristan and altar boys scurry around removing decorations, our couple are ushered in quickly, to have their ceremony performed by a lesser priest. They have to step over the carpet that is being rolled up the aisle. Their priest has to squint and tilt his missal as, during the ceremony, all but one of the candles is extinguished.

This scene and other gibes—at the civil service and officialdom at various levels—make it seem much more like an Italian film than one made in Franco Spain. And to allow it to be exported! It is true that Buñuel made *Viridiana* in Spain, but as soon as it won a festival prize, it was disowned. *Not on Your Life!* won a prize several years ago at Venice, yet here it is. A whole flock of swallows do not make a Franco summer; let us merely say that it is good to have renewed evidence that the stubborn, beautifully insolent Spanish character survives.

Nino Manfredi, the Italian actor who is a kind of younger, more handsome Ugo Tognazzi, is the hero—presumably and not badly dubbed in Spanish. Emma Penella is the meaty Spanish heroine. (The girl's name is Carmen, the man's is José!) But the outstanding performance—paradoxically easy to overlook and underpraise—is that of the executioner by José Isbert, a lovely old actor, warm and unostentatiously skillful. In effect he kept reminding me of the late Edmund Gwenn. Then I remembered that this director, Luis Garcia Berlanga, had made *Calabuch* some years ago with Gwenn, and perhaps he cast this part with the closest equivalent he could find in Spain.

Berlanga, now forty-four, is one of the two best-known Spanish directors. (The other is J. A. Bardem. Buñuel has been forced to spend so much of his time abroad that he is not much more a Spanish director than Hitchcock is an English one.) Berlanga is noted for comedy and satire, and in this film, which he also wrote, he shows a cruel eye and a deft hand. Most of it is built and moved cleanly: with point and pace. The trouble is that it is difficult to laugh even when four-fifths of the texture is funny because the supporting element—the other fifth—is the garrote. After a while we tell ourselves—possibly in compensation-cum-admiration—that Berlanga is not really trying to make us laugh, even satirically: that the blackness of the black humor is a mask for a nonsatiric statement of natural history: observation of a society that easily accommodates horror, in which a baby is born and sheltered on the profits of garroting and in which an old executioner waxes just as mellow and lovable with the years as any village priest or blacksmith. André Cayatte's *We Are All Murderers* is a violent outburst against man's inhumanity to man. Berlanga's film, in sum, sees capital punishment as only one more human stupidity. Cayatte wants the guillotine abolished. Berlanga, we feel, would doubtless like the garrote abolished but, if it happens, relies on men to supply another phenomenon to fill the stupidity vacuum.

Kanal; Ashes and Diamonds   (June 12, 1961)

Andrzej Wajda is one of the young Polish directors who are responsible for the feeling abroad that the postwar Polish film has had an impressive renascence. None of Wajda's films had, until recently, been shown publicly here, so last summer in London I hurried to see *A Generation,* the first of his trilogy about the Second War and its effect on Polish youth. I found it disappointing: a merely acceptable film about the political awakening of a young factory worker during the Nazi occupation, which was commonplace in story and characterization and which in style seemed a pastiche of various Soviet and French directors.

Now the two other parts of the trilogy have arrived here, and they do not lift the disappointment. *Kanal* (which means "sewer" in Polish) is a film of the Warsaw uprising in 1944 and of an attempt by some trapped Polish fighters to escape the Germans by traveling through the sewers of the city. The sense of trudging for hours hip-deep in slime is so well conveyed that even your olfactory nerve is suggestively stimulated. But the characters are those of any "resistance" picture, with a touch of the Lost Patrol thrown in, and when a voluptuous long-haired blonde of easy virtue rejoins the group just in time to wade out with the young hero, we become well aware that we are in Movieland. The incidents, choice of shots and emphasis are not only trite but egregiously artificial for this subject. It is only that subject—the factual basis of the film—that holds us at all. While we dismiss Wajda's transparent contrivances, we cannot forget that Polish patriots were murdered by Germans in the autumn of 1944 as Soviet forces sat across the Vistula and waited.

Ashes and Diamonds is about internal political faction at the end of the war and has the highest surface gloss of the trilogy. It tells of one day in the life of a young anti-Communist Pole, hired to liquidate a Communist labor leader, who kills the wrong man and then stays overnight in a provincial hotel to kill the right one. The film combines the worst of two widely different artistic styles. On the one hand it is full of unsubtle character actors in unsubtle character parts (the pompous young secretary, the drunken old editor), all contributing tiresome little cameos in pseudo-Moscow-Art-Theater tradition. On the other hand the hero, complete with dark glasses, is out of the lowest stratum of diluted American realism: taciturn, sexy, soulful though brutal, a rebel without a Dean. As in all cheap "serious" American fiction, he is in bed with a girl a few hours after they meet, and both of them find it a poetic experience, with much tristful staring into the dark.

The youth kills his man as fireworks go off symbolically in the sky. His own death at the end is stupidly contrived and is protracted so long that I thought he was going to stumble on into another film where he would make his first entrance wounded.

It should be noted that the picture is carefully neutral in politics. Virtues and defects are fairly doled out both to Communists and their opponents.

The slang term "small-town genius" seems appropriate to Wajda. He has seen a lot of films, is honorably ambitious, and is not untalented; but he lacks taste and originality. At a guess, he is a one-eyed man in a kingdom where most, for one reason or another, are now blind. He needs a more demanding audience close to home.

Joan of the Angels?   (May 21, 1962)

Martians must laugh when they hear us talk of the "world" of art, particularly of those arts that involve language. They look down and see a lot of parishes, each one knowing something of a few neighbors, little of others, and nothing of some, each nonetheless uttering universal pronouncements. This condition has been true of literature for centuries; in half a century it has become equally true of films. A sharp example is Poland, which according to all reports has at present an extraordinarily active and interesting film industry. The Polish State Film School was established in 1949 to train directors, actors, technicians—even critics! Eight production units were formed and are fed by the school. Since 1954 the Poles have been making annually about twenty-five feature films and over one hundred shorts. To my knowledge, only three of the features have had general release here, and a few others have been shown at film societies.

As it happens, I had strong dissents about the three features; and the Polish short I saw at Cinema 16, dealing with the reveries of an aged washroom attendant, was more arty than art. But there are serious talents working seriously in Poland, and the idiocy of the distribution gap between countries is underscored once more by the release of Jerzy Kawalerowicz' *Joan of the Angels?*

Kawalerowicz, called the dean of Polish directors, has drawn his film from the same sources as those of Huxley's *Devils of Loudun* and has changed the locale to Poland. Again a priest is sent by his bishop to perform the rites of exorcism in a convent of nuns who are possessed by devils, but the film compresses and dramatizes the facts. In fact, the priest never met the abbess who, at her devils' behest, accused him of sinning with her; and because he could not confess to a sin he had not committed, his legs were broken slowly, then he was strapped to an iron seat in the Loudun marketplace and was incinerated. In the film he does meet the abbess several times, sees the devils' work in her, is moved to love by her anguish and by the power of her devils, eventually kisses her (through bars), and feels the devils leave her and enter him. To keep them within himself and to prevent them from returning to her body, thus to insure her purgation, the distraught priest commits murder, rendering himself damned.

Attendant to this story is a subplot about one of the possessed nuns who is persuaded to leave the convent and spend the night with a squire before a promised marriage, who is abandoned and returns wretchedly to the convent. The outraged faithful and the ostentatiously fair-minded, disregarding such antecedent works as Maeterlinck's *Sister Beatrice* and John Davidson's *Ballad of a Nun,* may protest that this motion picture is blasphemous or, at best, an attempt by a Marxist state to deride the Church. As for blasphemy the Loudun episode is a matter of fact; as for derision, Kawalerowicz' version relieves the Church of its harsh inquisitional role in the true story. This director and screen writer has tried, I think, to understand love, compassion, and hell within the boundaries of dogma and the strictures of an existent society. (His film can even be read as a comment on the confines of dogma in contemporary Poland.) At any rate, it is entirely free of that slick modern superiority which takes a fast look at a phenomenon like this and says that all those nuns needed was a bit of you-know-what. Kawalerowicz realizes, as Freud saw and flip Freudians do not see, that sexual satisfaction is the beginning, not the end, of understanding; and that sexual problems must be solved within the framework of the society in which they occur. Asmodeus could be driven from Mother Joan's body only by compassion and sacrifice. If the priest had slept with her, it might— temporarily, anyway—have exorcised Asmodeus, but it would have left the recovered abbess a shattered woman. It would be like telling a twentieth-century man with a hyperdeveloped Oedipal drive that the way to cure it is to obey it.

With sympathy then toward the human beings thus tormented, with regard for the ethics of their society, and with concern to examine the conflict between life and dogma as epitomized in this incident, Kawalerowicz has made a film whose every detail reflects strikingly the austerity of its period. The picture is almost literally photographed in black and white without gradations. The white habits of the nuns, the spare wintry countryside, the long bare refectory table and benches in a great stone hall, these help to create the atmosphere of a mortified community living in fear of hellfire, in which the nearby inn is an oasis of sin; a world that considers itself a mere corridor to Judgment. Bergman and Dreyer are the obvious comparisons. Visually, *Joan* does not use the subtleties of *The Seventh Seal* or *Day of Wrath;* it is not a film of suggestive shadows but of knife-edge light and dark. In content, it has less of the earlier works' implied editorial comment; it exists *within* its story.

The performances are uniformly good, but some reservations must be noted. I dare say there is no reason why an abbess should not be as beautiful as Lucynna Winnicka (who is Mrs. Kawalerowicz), but she does seem rather young for the office. Mieczyslaw Voit is moving as the priest but is asked to double as a rabbi whom the priest visits. The result is neither a virtuoso acting display nor material of consequence; the film would be better off without this gratuitous scene. Lastly, numerous shots are held two, three, four seconds too long.

Also, let us hope that the distributor's silly "provocative" question mark will be dropped from the title and that he will revert to the original title, *Mother Joan of the Angels.*

But I want to end positively. This is a film of feeling, insight, and historical texture, fascinating to the eye. It is not easy to forget the strange profane ballet of the white-robed nuns whirling in ecstasy.

Knife in the Water   (November 2, 1963)

The great temptation in the film world these days, internationally speaking, is overoptimism about its prospects. The optimism is fed by the appearance of such young men as Ermanno Olmi, whose first film was *The Sound of Trumpets,* and Roman Polanski, a thirty-year-old Pole, whose first film is *Knife in the Water.* Some optimism, at least, seems absolutely unavoidable.

Polanski, who has been an actor on stage and screen since he was fourteen, is a graduate of the State Film School at Lodz, which is becoming the most celebrated school in the world. Poland's prewar film stature was slight, but there was enough activity to provide sound technical instruction for a new generation. This was grafted on to the rich theatrical tradition of Poland, was sparked by the impulsion of the country's wartime suffering, and accounts for the rise of the Lodz school and the Polish film generally.

After completion of his five-year course at the school, after a "senior thesis" film and several other shorts that attracted wide attention, after an apprenticeship to the late Andrzej Munk (tragically dead in a car accident in 1961 at forty), Polanski has made a first feature with the virtuoso *élan* that one might expect of a gifted, bright young man; but it also has insights and subtleties that are at least a decade early in him.

The picture has only three actors; we don't see another soul. A man about forty and his young wife are driving on a Sunday morning to a lake where they have a sailboat on which they plan to spend the night. Suddenly a young hitchhiker darts into the road and forces the speeding car to screech to a halt. The husband, already irritated by a quarrel with his wife, angrily gives the hiker a lift as far as the lake. Out of self-doubt, not because of anything overt, he quickly suspects a chemical reaction by the wife to the youth. He wants to dominate the youth in her eyes so, after some fencing on the dock, he invites the young man along. We feel that this is a suicidal move which he can't help making, like the boy on the bicycle heading for the tree. A cumulative structure is evolved that finally brings about the husband's cuckolding without his knowledge. Yet he has—one step removed—cuckolded himself.

The film would greatly benefit from about ten minutes' condensation (quite a lot in screen terms). Among others, a scene in which the boy founders at the tiller while the couple are swimming and another with a pick-up-sticks game, during a fight broadcast, are stretched. Polanski is not immune to the art-film disease: infatuation with the sound of one's own camera whir. (I note, too—no doubt with decadent Western patronization—that the husband's extraordinary material success is marked by a wrist watch, a small car, Prince Albert tobacco, a sailboat that subtitles call a yacht.) But the film is generally incisive, affecting, memorable. First, Polanski has kept it mobile without any strain from the cramped quarters and small cast. This is no Hitchcock *Lifeboat* stunt; the restrictions are generative. Second, the film is visually rich; compositions are not merely striking, they are relevant; light is used in complements; shots like the rainstorm seen low across the surface of the water knit us into the drama with intrinsic cinema means. Third, the drama itself.

What Polanski has done is to build a small Sartrean system of tensions and countertensions rooted in character. The chief view is the husband's—an early-middle-aged man who knows better than any wife could tell him what his fakeries are, although he can never admit them; who realizes that his sexual appetite is slowly being replaced by sexual appreciations and anxieties; who in his revealed self tries to substitute richness of experience for richness of promise, in his display of maturities is not only tacitly appealing for compassion but is angrily warning the younger ones that youth is fleeting. Beyond Polanski's technical abilities, his perceptions here are precocious. Interestingly, too, his film is not "Polish" in any sense that we can recognize (admitting that we see far too few Polish films to judge fairly). Its derivations are French-Italian, its material is universal. Further, it is an anomalous film to come out of a state-owned socialist cinema industry.

Leon Niemczyk, the husband, gives a performance of strength imposed fearfully on doubt. Zygmunt Malanowicz has the right face and manner for the young man, challenge without cockiness. Jolanta Umecka is not called on for much in the way of acting but manages to be both well rounded and reticent in the briefest of bikinis.

The Ninth Circle   (August 7, 1961)

According to Donald Richie's article in the summer issue of *Film Quarterly,* the Yugoslavian film industry is in strange imbalance. They produce about a thousand shorts but only about fifteen feature films a year. One of their recent features to reach us—and the first

Yugoslav film I have seen—is *The Ninth Circle,* a story of Nazi-occupied Zagreb. Richie states that Yugoslav shorts have developed their own styles and virtues and that Yugoslav feature-film makers could learn from them. Without having seen the shorts, one can agree that they need to learn from someone.

It is curious that a people who suffered so greatly should make such a synthetic, implausible picture about that suffering. Crudity one could forgive; without patronization, one might even expect it—the Yugoslavian film effort has never raised much expectation in the world. But to romanticize what must be scarred deep in the national soul, in a film photographed in the very streets where things like this happened, argues a kind of artistic bankruptcy, not naïveté. People who want to tell the truth may direct or act or edit badly, but to cram a tragic experience into a pastry-chef's mold requires either cynical, proficient commercialism (of which the film contains no corroborative evidence) or short-sighted dishonesty.

A Jewish girl is stranded when her parents are herded off to a camp, and to protect her, an "Aryan" youth marries her at the request of his parents, who are close friends of the girl's parents. It is a nominal marriage. (This must have happened often in Fortress Europa.) The boy is resentful because he likes another girl, but in time—after he sees how the Jewish girl suffers and how sweet she is—he falls in love with his wife. (This, too, presumably happened in some cases, but already life is beginning to imitate art.) At length the girl is imprisoned by the local Quislings. Our hero sets out to find her, and after a search which would have been difficult for a squad of detectives, let alone one youth, he comes fortuitously upon a clue that leads him to a camp where his wife is in the "Ninth Circle," the innermost area where young women are kept for the amusement of the staff. How he gets to her, manages to steal her from the group, makes love to her in hiding before they attempt to cross the barbed-wire fence, and how they die together on the wire gazing into each other's eyes—all this forms a finale that may impress those who are seeing not their first Yugoslav film but the first film of their lives.

POSTSCRIPT. A visit to Yugoslavia a few years later showed me several more interesting feature films, more competently produced, better acted, and quite honest, if melodramatic—all of them, as it happened, concerned with the Second World War, which continues to figure prominently in Yugoslavian film-making. But though all these pictures were better than *The Ninth Circle,* the short films I saw— particularly the animated ones—still were superior to them.

Ballad of a Soldier   (January 9, 1961)

What has happened to Soviet films? From about 1920 to World War II, the Soviet Union, with its films, gave the lie to those who said that good art could not flourish under Communism. Spurred perhaps by Lenin's early recognition of the importance of this medium to the Revolution, in crude propagandistic form at first, but with astonishingly rapid refinement, the Soviet film rose to international pre-eminence. Hardly a year went by without at least one Soviet film of enduring merit; and the three great Russian directors of the era— Eisenstein, Pudovkin, and Dovzhenko—have something of the same relationship to the world of film as the nineteenth-century titans of the Russian novel have to literature.

Production was surprisingly large during the war, and the main effort was, understandably, again propagandist. But since the war, the Soviet films seen here, excepting the two parts of Eisenstein's *Ivan,* have been shallow works, with almost none of the breadth and energy and vision of the prewar films, disclosing no new director of more than derivative competence, distinguished only by that warm immediacy in acting which Russian actors seem to acquire in the cradle.

The Cranes Are Flying, to name the most discussed and belaureled of the postwar lot, was a puritanical sin-suffer-and-repent story of a wayward wife, studded with such hokey directorial touches as bomb explosions and flashes (in place of Jehovah's thunder and lightning) during her seduction. Now, also garlanded with prizes, comes *Ballad of a Soldier,* which is an innocuous magazine story about a teen-age front-line soldier, granted a few days' leave for extraordinary heroism, and his idyllic, innocent encounter in a boxcar with an equally young girl. The whole is framed with ponderous statements about the son of the village who went forth to die for the motherland, but these cannot give depth to what is essentially an Audie Murphy-Debbie Reynolds script done with black bread and borsht instead of hot dogs and Cokes. Vladimir Ivashov is perhaps more varied than Murphy would be, Shanna Prokhorenko is not as good an actress as Miss Reynolds. Grigori Chukhrai's direction is merely adequate. (Chukhrai, in his recent American visit, stated that he wants to do only pictures that really say something about life. To judge by this work, he would be quite happy at 20th Century-Fox.)

One must deduce that the festivals which crowned this film were impoverished and/or their judges are victims of that snobbism which makes superficiality in a foreign tongue and setting seem profound.

The question remains: what has happened to Soviet films? Here is one answer—in Jay Leyda's valuable history of the Russian and Soviet film, *Kino,* published by Macmillan:

Now . . . outside the Soviet Union as well as at Mosfilm and Lenfilm, the least discussable problem is the contradictions in the medium itself, an art and an industry. The sad, blank chapters in the careers of Stroheim and Flaherty have some motifs in common with the silences of Eisenstein and Dovzhenko. . . . It seems clear that the larger the "plant," the more convenient the equipment, the more organized the distribution apparatus—the greater the danger of the film growing less individual, more uniform, and less worth anybody's effort. Throughout Soviet film history, the films were finest when they had the individuality that any industrial administration, by its nature and purpose, was bound to distrust.

Mr. Leyda concludes hopefully: "A consciousness of this danger is a great step forward."

But we have had as yet no evidence of that step forward. *Ballad of a Soldier* is a self-satisfied little chuckle by a nation indulging in sentimental retrospect about a terrible war, now that it is part of history. There is no point in belaboring this slight picture, but it is part of a flow of films seen here that argue a certain mental adiposity in the Soviet Ministry of Cinema. (This is the determinant; for the hottest-flaming genius who ever lived couldn't make a film in Russia without their approval.) No "step forward" has yet reached these shores.

More than one social-political commentator has noted current parallels in the silhouettes of the USSR and the USA—two huge nonhomogeneous societies, not long out of the frontier era, trying to outdo each other industrially and scientifically; both claiming idealistic impulse, but both rooted in materialist standards because of their competition as much as for any other reason; one calling itself atheist and the other theist with, probably, about equal reality in both labels. Now, in many respects, Soviet films have become like American ones: smooth and hollow, repetitive, designed not to disturb and arouse but to soothe the largest audience possible. The American films are superior technically, the Soviet films better acted; neither group is marked by imagination or creative excitement.

Fate of a Man   (August 7, 1961)

Fate of a Man, a Soviet film, was produced and directed by its leading actor, Sergei Bondarchuk. Based on a Sholokov story, it tells in flashback of a soldier whose wife and children were killed by German bombs, who then is captured and becomes a slave laborer, and who after the war adopts a homeless child with whom he is now wandering the roads, seeking to build a new life. The basic elements are probably true and not uncommon, but the whole is so soaked in self-pity and so daubed with hokum that it estranges us instead of communicating. The overhead shot of the lines filing into the gas chambers is too symmetrical and choreographic; the scene in which the hero saves his life by amazing the camp commandant with his power to consume vodka is too much like a fake-Irish comedy. The unvarying stalwartness of the Russian prisoners and the hero's miraculous escape are other distortions in a picture that holds a faulty mirror up to nature.

The Russians have as much right as anyone else to make their *Guns of Navarone* films, but they ought to make them with a clear romancer's conscience, without pretense that they are uttering pronouncements about a people's wartime agony and the "fate of a man." There is a wide space between the two stools, and this film falls ponderously into it.

The Lady with the Dog   (December 1, 1962)

The Lady with the Dog, based on Chekhov's short story, is the best Russian film I have seen since the second part of Eisenstein's

Ivan. It was adapted and directed by Josef Heifitz, codirector of (among many others) the unforgettable *Baltic Deputy,* and was exceptionally well photographed by Andrei Moskvin who worked on *Ivan* and on Donskoi's *Gorky* trilogy.

Chekhov's exquisite story concerns Dimitri Gurov, a Moscow banker in early middle age, married to an unattractive wife, who goes alone to Yalta on vacation and there meets a young provincial wife. Like him, Anna is unhappily married and is vacationing alone; unlike him, she is inexperienced and unworldly. They have an affair, during which she weeps a good deal, berating herself. This, of course, quickly bores him, although he courteously hides it. Back in Moscow he soon sinks again into his deadening routine of office, club, cheerless home, expecting to forget Anna as he has forgotten many others. But retroactively her innocence and pathos work on him and, parted from her, he falls in love with her after the event. He seeks her out in her town, and they begin a long, sporadic relationship, seeing each other every year or two for a short while when she can persuade her husband to let her visit Moscow. Gurov sees that he has two lives: the hidden one that contains everything that is worthwhile and important about him; and the surface life that contains everything he despises.

And judging others by himself, he did not believe the things he saw, and assumed that everybody else also had his real vital life passing under a veil of mystery as under the cover of night. Every man's intimate existence is kept mysterious, and perhaps, in part, because of that, civilized people are so nervously anxious that a personal secret should be respected.

Heifitz has succeeded in achieving the Chekhovian essence: a paradoxically increasing dramatic tension about a slackening social tension. One of the more difficult jobs in art is to convey tedium without becoming tedious. The secret is to convince us that the hero is as sensitive as we are and that, in his situation, we too should be bored. Thus we suffer with him, not because of him. Heifitz never lets the malaise go too far. He establishes it swiftly (the opening shot is an empty vodka bottle floating among the rocks near the beach) and *uses* it instead of lolling in it.

High among the film's subtleties is its depiction of class strata. Without any heavy party-line underscoring, it tells us—with its snow-covered coachmen waiting in the freezing night, its waiters hopping to the tantrums of the mighty—of Gurov's world, where extreme power and indifference to the lowest class can have the effect (as in the Deep South) of secretly creating self-hate in a man of feeling.

Alexei Batalov, the handsome and capable actor who was in the overrated *Cranes Are Flying,* plays Gurov. Iya Savvina, the Anna, has a three-note twittery voice that is at first dismaying; as the film progresses, we see that Heifitz took a chance on her and won. He wants her to affect us the way she affected Gurov, her very limitations eventually becoming her chief attractions. An actress of range might have done the part better in some ways but would have run the risk of subconsciously suggesting too much competence and awareness.

Two small reservations. Some of the transitions are choppy. As in many good European films of the thirties, we get the impression of being served a series of large, finely modulated sections, not quite as well knit together as they might be. And the closing moments are somewhat abrupt, too final. They do not quite catch the mood of Chekhov's last lines: "To both of them it was clear that the end was still very far off, and their hardest and most difficult period was only just beginning."

Some Asians

India and Japan

Pather Panchali (September 29, 1958)

Pather Panchali, a film from India directed by Satyajit Ray, comes to us bearing five festival awards. Like many pictures from unusual sources, it has been overpraised merely because it exists. However, although it could use condensation by about a fifth and although its story is simple almost to the point of banality, it is rewarding if taken as a dramatized documentary. Its record of the life of a poor Brahmin family in a Bengal village is generally engrossing and well photographed. It is fascinating to note how in the most commonplace daily actions—gesturing, walking, carrying a jug— these people move beautifully, how in the poorest home the bowls and platters, the windings of the ragged shawls, have some beauty. This is not dainty aestheticism but an ingrained part of their ethos: a belief in more than one kind of reality, trebly moving in view of their daily fight against starvation.

Aparajito (February 23, 1959)

Aparajito is the second part of a trilogy by the young Indian director, Satyajit Ray. The first part was *Pather Panchali,* and the third part is being completed now. All three films come from the novel called *Pather Panchali* by B. Banerji, but the first two films—and probably the third too—can be seen independently. My companion at *Aparajito* had not seen its precursor and was not handicapped by this.

However, to one who has seen Part One, two things are now evident. The first film now seems better than it did because the second was made; and the director, Mr. Ray, is in process of creating a national film epic unlike anything—in size and soul—since the Soviet *Maxim* trilogy of 1938-40. Further, as a record of a people's life, in its daily travail and its largest aspects, it bears comparison with Flaherty's *Nanook* and *Moana*.

For this viewer, the value of the first film was mostly along these lines, as a cultural record. The play had less interest than the by-play, the characters were not much more than acceptable types. And the story was so freighted with catastrophe that one began to balk. It is a doubtless regrettable human frailty that when excessive woe descends on one house, the spectator's sympathy palls. He suspects either that compassion is wasted on people so helpless or that the gods, if not the screen writers, have a slight addiction to soap opera.

This question does not arise with *Aparajito* which, in addition to its documentary interest, has much greater interest as a drama than the first picture. Here sorrow, when it strikes, involves us; here, too, the story moves out of a mere struggle for existence into deeper issues that evoke more than pathos; and this gives the characters a light that shines retrospectively on the first picture. For example, I cannot now think of the mother in *Pather Panchali* only as a woman whom trouble has made a scold against her will. The tenderness and complexity of her character as revealed in the second film add dimension to her in the first.

At the end of the first part, a Hindu lay priest and his wife move with their young son from their native village to the holy city of Benares after the death of their daughter and the destruction of their house by a storm, in hope of making a fresh start. It is now 1920, and the second film finds them established in a few rooms not far from the ghat on the Ganges where the father bathes daily and reads scripture aloud for the coppers that are tossed into his bowl. He soon gets sick, insists on making his daily oblations, and dies. The widow gets a job cooking for a rich family and moves to the country with them and her son, Apu. He asks to be allowed to attend school, and there he progresses marvelously. Eventually the headmaster helps him to get a scholarship at the university in Calcutta. His mother is glad, but even more she is frightened; she would prefer him to remain with her and to train for the family vocation of priesthood. But Apu, although he does not mock the past, is on fire with the future. He goes up to the teeming city, gets a part-time job at a print shop to help support himself, and plunges into the university like a rake into debauchery. His visits to his mother become more and more widely spaced. After a postponement of a visit, he arrives to find that she has died. His uncle asks him now to remain and be a priest, but Apu knows the moment and the hour; he will not even remain for the funeral rites. He says he will perform them in Calcutta, and he leaves again for the university.

"Thus equipped with poverty, pride and intelligence the Young Man from the Provinces stands outside life and seeks to enter." So Lionel Trilling has described this classic protagonist who appears and reappears in fiction. As his Bengali embodiment, Smaran Ghosal is shy, courageous, and cruel with the necessary egotism of youth. As his mother, Karuna Banerji is altogether lovely: devoted to and afraid of her son, resigned to his gradual estrangement, and aware—with powers far outside her limited intellect—that changes are coming not only in him but in her universe.

Ray, the director and adapter, is carrying this project forward with the dedication of a man determined to preserve truth about his people for the people themselves and for the world: who means (to paraphrase Dedalus) to forge in the smithy of his art the uncreated conscience of his race. It is this dedication that is giving the work its increasingly heroic quality.

Clearly, too, Ray is learning a great deal about film-making as he progresses. The boggling of transitions, the stickiness of the obviously arty shot, these are absent from this second film. There is still a bit of difficulty with Ray's sense of timing; a few scenes are brushed off too quickly, a few dwelled on too long. But ideals of timing vary from culture to culture, and whether Ray is adhering to the standards of his country or has not yet quite mastered timing as practiced by the Western artists from whom he has learned so much else, it is impossible to say.

Some scenes—like the inconclusive episode of the Brahmin looking for a wife, like Apu's visit to the temple of the privileged monkeys—are novelistic material, discursive in a film. But on the whole, in script and in action, Ray has made the picture move, laying the lives of a few simple people so bare that he has distilled history. We know, when Apu hoists his suitcase to his shoulder and flops his big feet down the path toward the railroad station, that he is on his way to change the motion of the planets. We await the final film, *The*

World of Apu, in the expectation that it will help illuminate the shift of the future from West to East.

The World of Apu   (June 6, 1960)

Satyajit Ray has now completed his film trilogy whose first two parts were *Pather Panchali* and *Aparajito.* The third film, *The World of Apu,* is a considerable departure in tone from the preceding two.

Without a knowledge of the novel on which the whole work is based, it is impossible to say whether this departure is the novelist's or Ray's.* But the break is sharp. *Pather Panchali* was the chronicle of a poor Bengali couple and their children; in the second film we watched the son of the family progress through school days to college, and the picture closed with his leaving the village (and a traditional life) behind.

Both these films, despite their technical and other shortcomings, were remarkable for their revelations about Indian life, their gentle, unsophisticated poetry, and especially for the sense—unrestrained yet inescapable—that this was a national epic. It was, in that regard, a classical work: the characters were all individuals; still, they were telling us a story larger than their own.

The World of Apu is, by that standard, a highly romantic work; its range is narrower—one man's life. It tells of Apu's marriage (in peculiar circumstances), of his falling in love with his wife subsequently, of her death in childbirth, of his *Wanderjahre* in search of soul's peace, and his reconciliation with his son. It has some of the defects of the previous films and many of the virtues; but it has none of the quality of a national epic. Apu is now Apu, nothing more. His story is effective insofar as it strikes personal responses, but the story of India or of today's Bengali is not being told through him.

This necessarily diminishes the film, but it need not have diminished it quite so much if the romantic story had maintained more of a grip in its own terms. The circumstances of the marriage we can accept as a part of Indian life—though how unusual I can't say. (He is a guest at a wedding. Just before the ceremony the bridegroom is

* *Indian Film* by Barnouw and Krishnaswamy (1963) states that the first two films were based on the novel *Pather Panchali* by Bibhuti Banerji but that the story of *The World of Apu* was largely invented by Ray.

discovered to be insane. Apu is implored to replace the groom even though he doesn't know the girl; if not, by custom, she will never be able to marry.) But the sorrows of this Bengali Werther, his wanderings after her death with a staff and sprouting beard, his failure to recover from an emotional wound in the best self-dramatizing style, with much striding across fields into the sunset—these things are divisive between us and the work.

So it cannot be said that the trilogy is sustained satisfactorily to its conclusion. Yet the fact that the last film turns sentimental should not make us lose perspective of the whole. Ray has accomplished a work which, although notably uneven, puts him among foremost contemporary directors by reason of a general purity of vision, devotion, and sheer will to use the film for large pertinences.

Two Daughters (May 18, 1963)

Satyajit Ray is dedicated to putting the nature and truth of his country on film. This gives his work a rooted, authentic quality that most films lack. The attendant risk is the touch of the illustrated lecture on folkways. Two Daughters demonstrates both the quality and the risk.

The picture is composed of two separate stories, based on works by Rabindranath Tagore. The Postmaster deals with a civil servant assigned to a remote village in a thick, steamy forest. There his only diversion is music with the villagers in the evening and there he is attended by a maid-servant, an orphaned girl of ten, to whom he is exotically wonderful because he comes from Calcutta and magically learned because he is literate and knows English. Plagued by malaria and bored by the place, the postmaster requests a transfer. Only when he leaves does he realize how much the child adores him and that he has broken a unilateral pact of affection.

The Conclusion is about a college graduate who comes back to his village to find that his mother has picked a bride for him, an appropriate but unappealing girl. He is attracted to a tomboy who, in her hoydenish way, likes him. He marries her, but, terrified by her loss of freedom, she flees the bridal chamber on the wedding night. The bridegroom, disheartened but wise, goes back to Calcutta to law school. His patience *in absentia* finally calms her; when he returns she becomes his wife in fact as well as name.

Both these episodes are made with love of their subjects, settings, and source (Tagore). And—which is not always the case—the presence of love does not mean the absence of skill. Although neither is a marvel of technique and neither is visually impressive as the trilogy, they disclose to us their worlds. When the departing postmaster walks down the rain-puddled road between thick walls of trees past the squatting village madman, we are given, in a few moments, a distillation of centuries of one kind of Indian life. When the law student appears for his wedding with a tattooed face, the paradoxes of his country are epitomized. Rewards of this kind adorn both episodes, but the basic element is missing: they are insufficiently interesting dramatically.

The story of the worshipful slavey and the commonplace master was antique before James M. Barrie used it. The mother whose educated son won't marry the nice girl she has chosen is simply Molly Goldberg abroad; the tomboy is the young Katharine Hepburn *et al.* on the Ganges. It may be argued that this proves that the stories deal with universals; but a universal treated without depth—even without novelty—is trite, in India or Indiana. In the second episode, which is much the longer, considerable tedium sets in while we wait for the predictable to happen.

In his trilogy, particularly in *Aparajito,* Ray dealt with familiar subjects in a large epic manner. He used nothing as superficial as mere surprise; this national statement of a universal theme involved us because the motions of all human life were involved. In these episodes the small scope and the neat structure change our focus from expectation of the epic to the entertaining. On this level the film moves into a different area of comparison, and it falters. Its enrichments of place and custom are peripheral rather than intrinsic, as they were in his earlier work.

The Music Room   (November 2, 1963)

Satyajit Ray's new film, *The Music Room,* is the story of an Indian aristocrat of declining wealth, addicted to the dance and song of his land, who spends his dwindling fortune on large parties at which the best artists perform in his shabby, huge manison. His wife and adolescent son are killed in an accident. He shuts up the house and lives like a hermit until he learns that a parvenu has engaged a great singer for a feast. The aristocrat reopens his house and spends his last borrowed money on this artist and a party, then is killed in a fall from his favorite horse.

It is a deeply felt, extremely tedious film. On the one hand its Western derivations are patent (the Greek-revival mansion no more than the Chekhovian theme). On the other hand its chief indigenous element, the Indian music, is simply uncongenial and tiresome to our ears. No doubt these are excellent musical performances for those who understand them, but they make us start counting the bulbs in the theater chandelier.

Ray's earlier *Devi,* which dealt with an older man's devotion to dying religion, and *The Music Room* must have much import for Indians but have less for export. We all want to encourage the distribution of foreign films in this country, a matter now severely restricted; but pretense and affectation will not help. Once the minimal "travelogue" value of films like these two is drawn, they become remote: "beautiful" in the deadliest culture-vulture sense.

POSTSCRIPT. The reception of Ray's work is divided—not, as with some outstanding directors, between a serious and a popular public because there is no popular public for Ray, but among the serious public. There is a group that considers him a pre-eminent humanist poet. Another group—mostly of the advance guard—thinks him a well-meaning clumsy ethnographer, dependent on antique film concepts and making what one of them has called UNESCO cinema. If I could, I should like to belong to the first group, but, for reasons stated above, I cannot. On the other hand, the second opinion represents a film conspectus that often accepts flamboyance for art. For me, Ray is a man so close to his materials, so instinct with honesty about them, that he is sometimes blinded to the triteness in his selection of symbol, pattern, metaphor. That is a criticism. It is not a criticism but simply a fact—probably of my cultural ignorance—that much of his material, in music, gesture, ritual reference does not affect this Westerner. He is devoted to singing his country and has sometimes done so with both sweetness and heroic line; but he has by no means consistently solved the continuing problem of how to be true to his parochial materials and immediate to the world. It is not a failure of fidelity or love but of art.

Ikiru   (March 7, 1960)

Ivan Ilych's life had been most simple and most ordinary and therefore most terrible.
                                    —*The Death of Ivan Ilych* by Leo Tolstoy

Tolstoy's entire novella might well be reprinted here for, in a sense, it is the best possible comment on the Japanese film under discussion. The picture is *Ikiru* (*To Live*), and the themes of the two works are the same: the realization of the approach of death; the bewilderment and anger at the course of your past life; the shame of fear; the knowledge that the world has already discarded you, that you merely make others uncomfortable; the inescapable holiness of your last days because you are already in touch with great secrets or the absence of them; and the revelation that only dying is death, that once a man dies, death is finished and all that remains is the man's life—as it was—now unalterable and complete.

The picture begins, slashingly simply, with an X ray; a narrator tells us that this is the stomach of the hero who will die in some months of gastric cancer. Then we see the man Watanabe sitting at his paper-laden desk in the city hall, unaware of his fate, a minor middle-aged bureaucrat in a hive of jealous underlings. He sits there endlessly stamping approval on endless papers and forms, and at once we want to shout: "For God's sake, get out. You've wasted enough time. Get out and draw a few free breaths before it's too late."

We go with him to the hospital where, in spite of doctors' euphemisms, he perceives the truth. We see the initial paralyzing shock, and through quick, beautifully economical flashbacks, done with the understatement of Japanese painting, we see his past life, widowhood, loving care for his son. Then Watanabe arouses from his shock to do something; to use his last months somehow. The first impulse is the frantic one. He withdraws half his savings and, with the aid of a bohemian whom he meets, he tries to go on a spree. But he can't eat the food, the liquor sickens him, the trollops don't really answer his needs.

Then he encounters a bright, vital girl who used to be a clerk in his section and, only for the sake of her company, begins to spend time with her; but she is soon bored with him because all he does is sit and look at her. When she threatens to stop seeing him he becomes panicky and tells her of his sickness, why he needs her, that just once before he dies he wants to touch life warmly, fully, and that he wants her—the seeming well-spring of it—to teach him how.

But she, in splendid ignorance, replies that she doesn't understand him; she simply loves living and enjoys her new job—in a toy factory —because the toys give pleasure to thousands she will never see. The naïveté and obviousness of this reply do not prevent it from answering his question. He moves into a third phase. He returns to the office and takes up a petition of some mothers who have long pleaded to have a swampy lot in their slum neighborhood converted into a playground. Against massive bureaucratic resistance, Watanabe sets out to further their cause.

Here, alas, the film goes into an unduly long coda. When the doomed man begins his mission, we jump ahead to a wake held for him after his death. Various speeches are made at his funeral feast, there are numerous flashbacks filling us in on what happened between the last time we saw him alive and this occasion: how he fought the delays of his office to realize his small ambition. This section is much too fully explored. If the wake had shown us the Deputy Mayor patronizing the dead man but claiming credit for the playground and had then shown us the policeman bringing in the dead man's hat (he died in the playground alone at night), that would have been sufficient. The last scene could have been that of the man sitting alone in a playground swing in the midnight snow, dying happily—if it is ever unobscene to couple those two words.

This is a film rooted in the most universal of truths, the one that cuts across all cultural barriers, all concepts of love, success, God: the fact of mortality. It confronts that fact with honesty and a touching eagerness. Takashi Shimura, who (under the same director) was the woodcutter in *Rashomon* and the leader in *The Seven Samurai,* is magnificent as Watanabe: an actor who creates fiercely the indignity and helplessness and groveling fear of the man newly sentenced, along with the ravening hunger for sensual pleasure, then for spiritual refreshment, then for a crumb of achievement to be his immortality.

Excepting the slack editorial hand toward the end, it would be hard to overpraise Akira Kurosawa's direction. He clearly has all the resources of film technique at his command, and, confident of his knowledge, is not constrained to display them. Fancy montages, whirling effects, bizarre angles are not for him. It is his purpose to make life seem to occur and, like a true artist, he does this by showing less than would occur in life. He selects his elements perfectly, never lets the emotional scenes stray past sentiment to sentimentality, and with unmelodramatic juxtaposition weaves the elements in his story, letting the rhythm as well as the content flick away at our sensibilities with gentle, telling strokes.

As for the wake, which seems discursive, since the ceremonial itself is more meaningful to a Japanese than it could be to us, the irony of its treatment here is bound to be somewhat ineffectual. The purely human elements in the film are placeless; ritual, both in life and art, is parochial.

The only film comparable to this that I can remember is De Sica's *Umberto D.,* which too treats of the failing of the light, but *Ikiru* is, for me, more powerful. (Incidentally, it is a strong refutation of one aspect of neorealism which *Umberto D.* represents. Kurosawa's fine cast, especially Shimura, are more credible and affecting than any carefully coached group of "real" people could possibly be.) Moreover, it is not an exercise in gloom. Because it faces and penetrates and diminishes true horror, the film achieves a measure of Tolstoy's effect: it shrives and strengthens.

Throne of Blood (November 27, 1961)

The brilliant Japanese director, Akira Kurosawa, made an adaptation of *Macbeth* in 1957 which he set in sixteenth-century Japan. It reaches us now under the title *Throne of Blood,* and it underscores a fairly obvious difference between Kurosawa and us: he is Japanese. There is much cheery talk about the international language of art, but film-goers know that there are qualities in films from radically different cultures that will not translate. They are not verbal matters, they are what might be called mother's-milk matters; you have to grow up on them—attitudes, conventions, special tastes.

(A small personal illustration: at a party I was talking to a distinguished Asian director who kept looking idly out the window. I thought I was boring him and soon withdrew. Later my host said, "Please go across and talk to X. He says he was enjoying his conversation with you." Subsequently I saw a film by X in which the hero received some wonderful news with a grunt and a look out the window; and I realized that neither subtitling nor dubbing can bridge all gaps.)

The chief drawback of this film for us is that is reflects *Macbeth* in an exotically distorting mirror. Many in Kurosawa's Japanese audience know the original play, of course, but most of the styles and attitudes of the film are mother's-milk matters to them and presumably affect them as Anouilh's *Antigone* affects us: as a pertinent new restatement of an old story. But, to pursue the parallel, this film to us is something like what Anouilh's play might have been to ancient Athenians. It tells us considerable about the people who made it, but the more it does that, the more it distracts us and emphasizes its remoteness.

"Macbeth" is played by Toshiro Mifune (the bandit of *Rashomon*) with a tigerish vigor that is often impressive but does not convey what we expect of the part—a large man progressively shriveled by listening to voices that convert his ambitions into his ethos. "Lady Macbeth" with her eyebrows painted out and two black smudges high on her forehead, who kneels on a mat and bedevils her husband obliquely with cast-down eyes, can do nothing for us but further widen a schism.

Even in Japan there were some qualities that went unappreciated. According to the invaluable book by Anderson and Richie, *The Japanese Film,* the Noh elements in the witch scenes and elsewhere meant little except to Noh specialists.

Kurosawa is known there as the "least Japanese" of directors and that may be the paradoxical reason why so many of his films are affecting to us. Any Kurosawa film is welcome, including the other adaptations he has made, but we have to hope that they will be more accessible.

Meanwhile, his *Throne of Blood* provides an abstract display of some of his talents, with a few individually powerful scenes like the murder of the murderer of "Banquo." Every moment of the film is seen with an exquisite eye, yet Kurosawa avoids the peculiarly Japanese snare of filming beautiful portraits and landscapes—he makes moving pictures. His pearl-gray, wind-swept medieval Japan is chilly and eerie, and his fortresses of thick wood look stronger than steel. He uses his sound track evocatively: the horses' hoofs, the creak of armor, the padding of soldiers' feet. But the film's inherent contradiction is that it continually reminds us of *Macbeth* and thus of its wide difference from it; it becomes a moderately interesting curiosity rather than an artistic experience.

The Hidden Fortress; The Lower Depths   (March 19, 1962)

Two more films by Akira Kurosawa have been released here, and they are figurative mirror images of each other. *The Hidden Fortress* is cinematically fine but thin in content; *The Lower Depths* is more substantial but clumsy on the screen.

The former is built on the old "journey" idea. In this case a defeated but proud general in medieval Japan has to escort his incognito princess and her remaining store of gold through enemy territory to safety. The version shown here was considerably condensed and could easily be expanded, one can see, simply by including more hazards and adventures. Kurosawa uses action like hues on a brush, shaded or enriched; he establishes characters swiftly; he has a sure eye for pictures that are lovely in themselves yet always advance the story. Though fundamentally there is little more in this film than thrills of the chase-picture level, there are plenty of them, and they are accomplished with a skill and taste that give fights and hair's-breadth escapes an extra dimension. The result is sheer pleasure.

This picture may have been made as a divertissement after works like *The Lower Depths*. The latter is, for a film director, nothing but a problem and, as this greatly gifted man shows, an insoluble one. It takes place in one room and just outside it; it has long stretches of dialogue that must prove static to many who understand the language, let alone to those who follow it through subtitles. Not all of Kurosawa's felicity with actors and with editing can make it live.

He has moved the Gorky play to Japan a hundred years ago but otherwise has not changed it much. Unlike his *Macbeth,* it is not a Japanese variation of the original idea with altered story and *personae,* it is merely a geographical transposition.

In any event, Gorky's play is pretty much dead wood now—a

parade of miseries remote from our own and no longer revealing about others, filled with half-timbered symbolic characters each of whom comes forward for a brief scene at regular intervals. It may once have been shattering naturalism, although it must always have suffered from what Tolstoy called its "psychological inventions;" but after sixty years its documentary elements are dated, and little else in the play, except an occasional passage like the Baron's last speech about the course of his life is still affecting. Additionally, Kurosawa repeats the interpretation of Luka, the holy pilgrim, that Gorky always deplored. Luka is shown yet again as the bearer of the secret of inner peace and eternal life, but Gorky intended him as a cruel, selfish egotist deluding the wretched with false hope. (Satine was Gorky's hero.)

The cast is excellent. Kurosawa's camera pokes dexterously among the embers of the play but can raise little heat or fire; and because we know it is a transposed work, it lacks even the superficial informational interest of a Japanese work of the period. I shall remember it chiefly for Toshiro Mifune's performance as the amorous young thief. I had just seen him as the haughty general in *The Hidden Fortress* and remembered his bandit in *Rashomon,* his *Macbeth,* his false samurai in *The Seven Samurai.* In these two new films this magnificent young man shows further reaches of his art; implicitly chides those who think his teeth-baring performance in *Rashomon* was Mifune and not the bandit; and confirms that he is a powerful, versatile, and magnetic actor.

Yojimbo (September 17, 1962)

In 1860 Japan had just begun its staggeringly swift transition from backward feudal isolation to the world power that was able to defeat Russia with a modern navy in 1905. Prodded by Commodore Perry's visits, the wheels had begun to turn, bearing away the tyrannical shogun, and the traditional hierarchies. Many of the samurai, the professional warriors attached to feudal lords, found themselves unemployed and homeless. Such a samurai is the hero of *Yojimbo* by Akira Kurosawa, one of the world's master directors.

A small town is torn by a bloody feud between two gamblers, each

of whom has a gang of killers financed by a merchant. Quite by
chance, a samurai arrives in this town, with nothing to his name but
his sword and his skill with it; and he decides to capitalize on the feud
by hiring out to one or the other gambler as a *yojimbo* (bodyguard).
He is entirely disinterested—he slices up a few thugs merely to prove
his prowess and send up his price. At the beginning he seems only
the most efficient killer of the lot. As the film progresses and the
gambling factions plot and counterplot, the samurai seems more and
more admirable: by no means an ADA humanitarian but a man of
courage and judgment who has absolutely no mercy for those with
defective honor.

Like Kurosawa's *The Seven Samurai* and *The Hidden Fortress,*
Yojimbo can be compared with a good western. (There is a rumor
that Hollywood is to remake it as such.) It is a well-built, muscular
story—a fine action show. But it is something more: the account of
an anachronistic man, beginning to sense this fact and to face inevitable retreat. That is the core of his venal grimness; he knows that not
only his future but his past—his background and tradition—is
doomed.

Still, what ranks it above most of the better westerns is not its
script but its execution. *Shane* and *The Gunfighter* had Alan Ladd
and Gregory Peck in their leading roles. This has Toshiro Mifune.
Mifune's versatility (the true sort, a range of imagination and resource, not trick voices and make-ups) continues to impress. Admittedly, for those who have never seen Mifune before, his performance
here may seem no more (but no less) remarkable than a strong
"personality" performance by Spencer Tracy. However, against the
background of Mifune's other work, it is not only highly enjoyable
but a bit awesome.

Others noteworthy in the good cast are Eijiro Tono, the gruff
innkeeper who resents the samurai's intrusion but is the first to recognize his worth, and Ikio Sawamura, the constable whose appearances recur like a comic woodwind theme . . . which is a reminder
that the score by Masaru Sato makes good commentary and support.

Kurosawa's technical mastery, freshness of vision, and dramatic
instinct are of the first order. The intensity of his style is built largely
on minimal cutting, and insistence on staying *with* the shot until he is
forced to change or it is obligatorily interrupted by another; he often

follows a character in close-up who takes us to another in close-up. He has also developed effective ways of having actors enter a film shot without letting them seem like stage entrances. Note the moment at the beginning when Mifune is strolling jauntily toward us (the camera trucking ahead of him) and a quarreling father and son run unexpectedly across the road to surprise him and us. Simultaneous planes of action give Kurosawa's scenes depth and interplay (the feet of the tortured innkeeper swinging large in the foreground, the guards squatting just behind him, the constable in the middle distance turning to discover the samurai in the background). He composes good pictures (Mifune and Tono seated, facing away from each other as they converse), yet the pictures never delay the film, they augment it. He uses light and air subtly (the gray, wind-whipped square in which the two gangs line up). He punctuates with vivid images (the edge of the cloak slipping into the chest as Mifune hides, the whirling leaf suddenly pinned by a dagger).

Kurosawa has made twenty-one films, only nine of which have been shown here, and some of those nine were barely glimpsed. The other twelve are possibly of uneven quality, but it seems profligate to be thus wasteful (as far as this country is concerned) of a superior artist's work.

Donald Richie, who is expert in Japanese films, wrote recently that *Yojimbo* is a "hilarious lampoon of empty heroics." To a nonexpert, the hilarity is not apparent. Some of the samurai's killings are done so quickly and against such odds that they produce a giggle, but the giggle rises less from incredibility than credibility, a conviction of the reality of this man and his outsize qualities, a kind of inverted wide-eyed wonder. In the August 13, 1962, *New Republic,* Robert Jay Lifton wrote of the "dry" and "wet" standards of modern Japanese youth, dryness being what we would call "cool" and wetness what we would call "square" or "corny." This samurai is dry with a dryness that would unnerve Frank Sinatra. What is dryer than astounding heroism for no other reason than money?

Sanjuro   (May 25, 1963)

Akira Kurosawa's *Sanjuro* is a further adventure of its title-role hero, the penniless wandering samurai of *Yojimbo,* again played

by Toshiro Mifune. In execution the film cannot be faulted. It seems
to me flawlessly directed, excellently acted by, among others, Mifune
and Tatsuya Nakadai, the pistoleer of the earlier film who appears
here as another archenemy of the samurai. The final silent confrontation of the two, which is snapped by slashing violence, is drama at its
source. But the content of the film is so slight as to be transparent. It
has even less texture than its predecessor, is even more sheerly an
action film: good guys, bad guys and the "lone gun"—a seeming bad
guy with a heart of gold. One wonders how the people who could
make a film so superbly could be content to make one so shallow.

The Bad Sleep Well   (January 26, 1963)

The laws of visual perspective apply to artistic judgment, too,
unless we are careful; an artist's latest work looms largest. We tend to
rank him by it or at least to use it as proof or disproof of what has
gone before. If it is not good, and we have disliked the man, we take
it gleefully as confirmation. If we have liked the man, we are not only
disappointed but embarrassed and may become vindictive because of
our embarrassment. Hollywood puts it more bluntly: "You're as
good as your last picture."

The last picture by Akira Kurosawa, *The Bad Sleep Well,* is not
good. It is so remote in every way from the mainstream of his work
that, except for the opening sequence and the presence of some of his
"stock company," there is no internal reason to believe that Kurosawa did it. It could have been made by any experienced, tamely
imaginative director of films or television. We have now to remember
that lapses can—and often do—occur with good artists, not just in
decline at the end of their lives but smack in mid-career. (Bergman's
The Devil's Eye is another recent, though less drastic, example.) All
it means is that to be a good artist is not, necessarily, to be a god.
Mistakes are possible for him in choice of subject and method; and
once the error is initiated, tenacity in clinging to it as it grows is
almost as prevalent among good artists as bad.

Patience and fortitude, the counsel that Mayor La Guardia used to
give his radio audience, applies to us. Kurosawa doesn't need that
advice. The maker of *Rashomon, Ikiru, Yojimbo,* among others, has
little to worry about in the long run.

His new film deals with bribery at the big-money corporation level in contemporary Japan. A young man, whose father was forced to commit suicide in a corporate scandal, has changed his name, slithered into the company, become secretary to the chief, married his daughter, and begins to extract revenge (a suggestion of *Hamlet*). This he does by using another man, supposedly dead, to haunt the guilty and by means of tape recorders, kidnapings, and an assortment of devices that would have discomfited the Warner Brothers in their B-stung days. Only the first sequence, a wedding in Western dress at a stuffy wedding hall (which could be in Baltimore or the Bronx), has Kurosawa's flavor. The police make an arrest in the foyer, and panic spreads quietly among the seated dinner guests.

But, after that, hyperdramatic tedium.

The picture's one reward is in seeing Toshiro Mifune young, handsome, and sprucely double-breasted. Those who have watched him as a tigerish medieval bandit, a staunch old general, a frenzied Nipponese Macbeth, a deft nineteenth-century thief, or, lately, as a solitary and pragmatic samurai, will at least enjoy marveling at this leonine actor's magnificent range.

High and Low   (November 23, 1963)

I would give a good deal to know something of Akira Kurosawa's mind. *High and Low,* which runs two hours and twenty-three minutes, never for a moment flags in interest and is flawlessly executed; but I have no satisfactory idea why, at this stage of his career, he wanted to make it.

The script is adapted from a mystery novel by an American manufacturer of mystery novels named Ed McBain. Truffaut has recently used a similar American original. The point is clearer in his case. Truffaut wanted to make a semisatiric, semireverential French rhapsody on American "toughness" (*Shoot the Piano Player*). Kurosawa presumably thought that the most elemental of plots, the man hunt, would give him a chance to use the clean lovely lines of his storytelling ability in straight, unwavering perspectives. In terms of technique, that is the film's almost sensual reward for him. But there is nothing deeper. It is just the story of a kidnaping, with some of the light psychological and social trim now in vogue in detective novels. We see how the police finally find the kidnaper. That is all. *Yojimbo* and *Sanjuro,* Kurosawa's recent pictures about an itinerant samurai, were little more than excellent Japanese "westerns," but they did tell us something about the effects of immense social change in Japan a century ago. *High and Low* begins, drives on, ends. No more; no resonance of any kind, if we disregard the jacket-blurb guff about Good and Evil on every mystery story. I would like to know why—apart from the pleasure of making it—Kurosawa wanted to make it.

To say all this is not, I hope, to discourage the reader from seeing the film. Very much the reverse. Two hours and twenty-three minutes of fine entertainment are not a commonplace achievement. Also, from the opening frame (literally) to the last, Kurosawa never makes the smallest misstep nor permits it in anyone else. Every camera angle, every composition, every set, every performance, is—as far as I can see—brilliantly right. Thus, in addition to its chase thrills, the film is full of visual pleasures: his peculiar, paradoxical spare richness that grows out of interwoven movement, unforced yet forceful grouping, and a persistently *following* camera, rather than out of laid-on sumptuousness in detail or color. The very motion of this motion picture is gratifying.

The story, set in Yokohama, is about a rich shoe-company executive (Toshiro Mifune) who has mortgaged himself to the teeth to buy stock for a power fight within his company. Just as he is about to dispatch an aide with the check, a telephone call comes (the one pat stroke in the script). A man has kidnaped the executive's son and wants, as ransom, exactly the sum he has raised for the stock purchase. Mifune, of course, agrees to pay; then his son runs into the room. The kidnaper (who soon realizes this) has taken the chauffeur's son by mistake. Therefore Mifune's choice—between financial ruin and realization of his ambition at the cost of a child's life—becomes, to him, debatable. He finally decides to pay the ransom and alter his business destiny. The child is returned, and the rest of the film is taken up with fascinating detective work.

Although this is not one of Mifune's most demanding roles, it further substantiates his power and versatility. Tatsuya Nakadai, the young actor who played his archrival in both samurai films, is appealing as a police inspector. Tsutomu Yamazaki gives the young doctor-criminal a diluted but recognizable Raskolnikov touch, the intellectual-murderer. So prodigal are the Japanese that Takashi Shimura, the hero of the memorable *Ikiru,* plays a small part with hardly a line.

There are two scenes in this picture, despite its limitations, that I do not expect to forget. The first is a visit to a "dope den" (as the subtitles call it), done like an elongated misty nightmare. The second is the final scene: when Mifune and Yamazaki confront each other in prison. The youth is condemned to death (he has murdered three people in his adventures) and has asked the other man to visit him so that he can prove he is not afraid. The youth is *not* afraid; but he can't stop trembling, and this at last drives him frantic. He leaps at the wire netting that separates him from the visitor, then is dragged out by wardens. We watch over Mifune's shoulder. An iron shutter comes down in front of him, cutting him off the prisoners' room. Mifune continues to sit motionless. The End.

POSTSCRIPT. Some other Kurosawa films that have been seen here briefly are *Stray Dog* (1949), a crime-detection story that is a fore-runner of *High and Low;* his version of Dostoevsky's *The Idiot* (1951), so atypical in style that it is hard to believe that it was made between *Rashomon* and *Ikiru;* and *I Live in Fear* (1955), about an old Japanese man who wants to migrate with his family to escape the next atomic war—the patriarch is played with flawless conviction by the young Toshiro Mifune. With other Japanese directors and with Ray, Kurosawa shares a liability to remoteness in Western eyes—in his case, not in style or subject matter but in some details of gesture and reaction. Yet he is less affected by cultural distance than most. (As I have noted, in Japan he is known as the "Western" director.) Even when his subjects seem slight for his abilities, there runs through most of his work a conviction of mastery that is itself excit-ing. It is not cinematic magic like later Fellini nor *Angst* made visible like Bergman; there is a fierceness in his style, steely-fingered and sure. The many beauties for the eye seem the by-product—inevitable but still a by-product—of a burning, ironic view. What flames in many of his films, contemporary and costume, is hatred. In *Ikiru* it is hatred of death, but in most of them it is hatred of dishonor. Like most ironists and most intelligent users of melodrama, he is an Ideal-ist in deliberately thin disguise.

The Island   (July 30, 1962)

The Island is a Japanese film with a family as its hero—a farmer, his wife, and two small sons who scrabble for a living on the small hilly island that is their home. Their principal ethic is to eat, their family motto is "We Survive."

The unsentimental basis of this film, which it depicts unsentimentally, is the rich texture of love that grows in exigency. As Richard Hoggart and Danilo Dolci record, as observation attests, the children of the poor are jewels rather than burdens, and a man and wife are close because of mutual reactions to years of immanent perils. Each knows always what must be done and what the other will do—until tumor takes the mother and hernia takes the father, until the children marry away. Particularly in cultures where poverty is a tradition bequeathed through the generations, particularly outside cities, the poor are a grim, knit, self-protective society among whom the rest of us move like another race. (See Turgenev's *Sportsman's Sketches*.)

The Island fixes it all: the odd security of knowing exactly their position—on the bottom and ceaselessly struggling; the beauty of their interdependence. The film comes as near as possible to being merely a chronicle. Until the sudden illness and death of the older son, nothing happens except the routine of their life: work, meals, the older boy's school, the traditional holidays. The film's triumph—and its point—is that, before ten minutes are up, we are all members of the family, sharing their perspective, one with their concerns.

The couple's chief daily chore is lugging water for themselves and their crop. They must row a long distance to shore, trudge inland to a stream, carry yokes of buckets to the boat, row back to their island, labor up a steep path to their sloping field where they carefully dole out cupfuls on their bean plants. This chore, by its ineluctability, acquires a ritual quality, and its hard rhythm is the pulse of the film. When the wife spills a bucket accidentally, we expect that the husband will hit her for the sacrilege, and we know that she expects it. After the death of her son, she overturns a bucket in futile protest against the pain and loss, and we know that this time the husband will merely watch the outburst, during which she pulls up plants until her frenzy is spent; then he will turn back to his work. He and she both understand that there is nothing he can say to her; all he can do is to keep the pattern going.

At the start of a film like this, one tenses nervously in anticipation of picturesque shots of peasants against the sky. In fact, there is a little of that, as there is a bit too much of the water-lugging; but these are trifling excesses. Kaneto Shindo, the writer and director, has had a vision of inner meaning, not of *National Geographic* illustrations.

Shindo, who entered films in 1934 and worked for many years as a script writer until he became a director in 1951, has made this picture without a line of dialogue. (There is a lot of music, however—which sounds like French café songs and is inappropriate.) The absence of speech and the subject matter suggest neorealism, but, on the contrary, his film deals a much-needed blow to the fallacies of that school. His principals are artists, not "people." The wife is played by Nobuko Otawa, a well-known actress who is also a writer and lecturer on acting. She and Taiji Tonoyama, the husband, are members of Shindo's "stock company." To note that there is never a moment of doubt in the picture that these two have spent their whole lives on this island is a tribute not only to their art, but to their thorough understanding. This is more than a *Man-of-Aran* combat with the elements. It is a fully realized little epic of the family as the last and the first barrier against chaos: a way of life that needs no rationale, that is its own purpose.

To see how their world meshes—the difficulties met and shared without comment, the children running (*always* running) to do their own appointed tasks—is to perceive the strength in order. Each of the four is a pillar of their common, small universe. It is impossible to imagine these children growing up lost or bewildered; and it is no bourgeois beatification to say the film lays bare the secret of this impoverished family: they are happy.

Woman in the Dunes   (November 14, 1964)

A new Japanese director, Hiroshi Teshigahara, makes an impressive debut in this country with *Woman in the Dunes*. It is the story of an ultracontemporary office worker who goes to a lonely beach on his vacation to pursue his hobby of insect-collecting. He stumbles on an isolated, impoverished fishing village which has built its houses in deep pits in the dunes to protect them from the weather. He stays overnight as the guest of a woman in such a house. In the morning the ladder is not thrown down for him to leave; the village is short of manpower and he is kept a working prisoner. He is to help shovel sand into buckets, which are drawn up, to keep houses from being slowly buried. He is also presumably to beget children with the woman. He is thus press-ganged into the survival and continuity of the struggling village. His evolution in the pit house is, in story and symbol, the material of the film.

The script was adapted by Kobo Abé from his recently published novel of the same name. The film is much more effective than the book, simply because Teshigahara is a better artist than Abé. All through the novel we are conscious of the plot device: a trick situation set up to demonstrate points, like a laboratory experiment. The film shifts our attention from device to drama because the two chief characters and the environment are not only much more convincingly created here but more poetically employed. Even allowing for the fact that it is easier to take a picture of a sand dune than to describe it, Abé's prose (at least in the English provided) does not equal Teshigahara's eye, and the novelist's structural sense—of sentence, paragraph, chapter—is inferior to the director's visual structures, his feeling for rhythm and montage. One of his potent devices is a counterpoint of extreme close-up—almost of pores—to convey the closeness of the pair and the inescapable grittiness of the sand.

Eiji Okada (the man in *Hiroshima Mon Amour*) and Kyoko Kishida are good as the couple. The music by Toru Takemitsu is spare and pungent. Hiroshi Segawa's photography is a somber delight.

A number of themes are implied, a chief one being the concept of freedom. Without leaden explication it becomes clear that the man's life in this submerged house is not *essentially* less free than his previous life; only the adjectives have changed. (Apparent constriction instead of hidden constriction.) The erotic scenes are powerful, and in a relatively discreet way. There is much reason to hope for more fine films from Teshigahara after this fine debut.

PART III

EVENTS

Events

Political and Cinematic

Operation Abolition   (March 27, 1961)

The much-discussed *Operation Abolition* is a forty-five-minute film about the demonstrations against the House Un-American Activities Committee session in San Francisco last May. The purpose of the film is to "prove" that the picketing by college students and the disturbances in the City Hall were brought about by the machinations of known Communists, some of whom were subpoenaed by the Committee. "Operation Abolition" is, supposedly, the name that Communists have given to their program to demolish the Committee; these student protests are alleged to have been part of that program. The picture is now being seen in colleges, clubs, industrial plants and churches throughout the country.

As a piece of film-making, it is not noteworthy. On the other hand, if I were in the propaganda business, I would want to make films just like it. It consists entirely of grainy, jerky newsreel and TV-film clips, interspersed with three addresses to the audience by members of the Committee. Thus you have actuality certified by Congressional authority.

Its very crudity is an asset. When Leni Riefenstahl was making propaganda films for the Nazis, the results were often aesthetically commanding; some of them are still shown at film clubs for certain intrinsic cinematic values. But many of the people for whom this film is intended might be as suspicious of a "pretty" film as they are of fancy foods or foreign accents. No subtle dissolves here, no montages or clever musical score. This film has an air of honest fact, laid on the line without any artistic fuss-and-feathers. This is the way to do it in our country.

391

The recipe is simple. Select film clips which can be juxtaposed to suggest certain sequences and facts whether or not they really were the sequences and facts. Put a spoken commentary behind them which "interprets" them for you and which suggests more than you are actually seeing. (For example, show students being ejected by police; have the commentator report that some students threw shoes at the police and one student seized a policeman's stick and clubbed him. The viewer sees the former and thinks he has also seen the latter.) Then get three Congressmen to make speeches in front of a window through which the US Capitol is visible. That these are three members of the Committee against which the demonstrations were held only adds a note of seeming fairness: because these gentlemen do not berate the students—they are regretful for them as Communist dupes. True, Congressmen Scherer says the students have been "toying with treason" by objecting to the Committee, but the legislators speak of them more in avuncular sorrow than in patriotic anger.

I was lucky to see this film at a showing sponsored by the National Council of the Churches of Christ, which last month passed a resolution expressing "deep concern" about the effects of the film. Before the showing there was a brief talk by Mr. Dean Kelley, Director of the Council's Department of Religious Liberty. Any reasonably well-informed person would snicker (as the audience did) at the easily recognizable platitudes and distortions of the Congressmen, but only an extraordinarily well-informed person could recognize the distortions in the film itself without such a preamble as Mr. Kelley provided. Making clear that the Council is not trying to suppress the film but only wants to insure that it is shown with an explanatory preamble, Mr. Kelley cited inaccuracies, omissions, and questions of which the film states only one side.

There is no point in giving more than a few random samples. The film implies, by juxtaposition, that Harry Bridges was involved in the disorders; in fact, order had been restored before he appeared. The film omits to report that the Students for Civil Liberties explicitly refused to join the Communists who were making trouble inside the committee room. The film's commentator says that the room seated 400 persons and that the Committee issued only 100 passes to its friends; he neglects to mention that each pass admitted three or more persons. We see a sixty-one-year-old policeman who suffered a heart attack in the disturbance; we do not hear about a student who warned the police he had a bad back, was nevertheless dragged down the steps, and had to have an operation. The whole background of the student demonstration is omitted—including the fact that the Committee had canceled its projected Californian visit the previous year after issuing a number of injurious subpoenas, thus giving the subpoenaed persons no chance to clear themselves.

A final note on the film itself. The print I saw carried no production credits of any kind. However, a folder from the Missionary Film Service, Inc., of Seattle offers to supply this film free of charge along with a film strip called *Communism on the Map*. I have seen a report on this film strip by three University of Washington graduate students which says that it describes the US as infiltrated with Communism to the point that in Congress "Communists are so powerful that they can actually bring about the passage or defeat of laws." (Evidently the Committee has a job to do in its backyard.) It also describes the US as being encircled by Communism abroad.

One wonders why the freedom-fighters who are willing to make *Operation Abolition* available to the public without charge are unwilling to have their names associated with it.

Why does all this matter? Here is a fourth-rate documentary, artistically speaking, devoted to a (largely) student demonstration which had no discernible political effect and was not the occasion of any really serious violence. Why was it worth a film? And why are a leading religious association and numerous educators objecting to it?

To me there are two main reasons for its importance. I remember that when I read about the San Francisco disturbances, I thought of what an English journalist had once said to me about European demonstrations: that if controversial meetings were held on Sundays and holidays, they would cause no riots because the demonstrators were all students who used the meetings simply as a chance to cut classes. It was a joke, perhaps feeble; but I had felt a twinge of shame that the joke was inapplicable to the inert American student body of five or six years ago. San Francisco changed that. Here at last was a nationally visible protest against the vicious inanity of a committee which, if history tells us true, is itself un-American in principle. And this protest was made by youth. Political ferment—as distinct from political decision—must come from the young. If the people with the most years ahead of them don't care enough about their government to march, meet, petition, and write in support or in opposition, the country is sick. The young must think their elders are doing unsatisfactorily or how can there be progress? It is the young who are, or ought to be, the least bound to status quo. Kirsanov, a character in Turgenev's *Fathers and Sons,* thinking of young men, says: "I feel there is something behind them we have not got, some superiority over us. . . . Is it youth? No: not only youth. Doesn't their superiority consist in there being fewer traces of the slave owner in them than in us?"

No one senses all this better than the anonymous makers of this film. They acted quickly after this first strong political movement in years by college students; and they are supplying this film around the country to persuade young people and their advisers that protest against authority is, itself, implicitly treasonous.

The second major point is unintentional: what this film shows us—yet again—about the kind of men who paid for it, made it, and address us in it. *They* are not deceived. They know exactly what they are doing, and why. They are not hobbled by ethical considerations; they are pragmatists. Their only ethic is, in irreducible irony, exactly that of their chief enemies, the Communists. The utterances of Francis Walter and Gordon Scherer come from the same brutally cynical, shrewd, utilitarian mold as those of a Khrushchev; only a few of the nouns are changed.

Thus this film is not about misled juvenile prankishness. It is, in reality, a move to control the source of the future. And indirectly it tells humanists, again, that to live is to fight, and not to be discouraged because they can never win finally and completely. Anyway, absolute victory is as much a delusion as any other absolute. This film doesn't signify that the fight and life are getting either better or worse; it simply reminds us that the two are inseparable.

(February 12, 1962)

On January 2, the House Un-American Activities Committee issued a further defense of its film, *Operation Abolition,* admitting only one mistake, since corrected, about Harry Bridges. The American Civil Liberties Union of Northern California has now issued a version of the film called *Operation Correction,* with subtitles applied to show how the time sequences were continually juggled, with revisions inserted in the sound track to reveal deliberate distortion. The ACLU film proves that the men originally responsible for this film and still defensive of it are liars. Is there no Congressional equivalent of Senator Flanders to move for a vote of censure?

Point of Order   (January 25, 1964)

Daniel Talbot and Emile De Antonio have had one of those ideas so obvious that no one thought of it before them; they have acquired the television kinescopes of the lengthy Army-McCarthy hearings in 1954 and have edited them into a ninety-seven-minute film. The condensation is relentlessly gripping; no more "anti-McCarthy" than McCarthy himself was in those hearings; and a frightening reminder that these events occurred on this very planet less than ten years ago. McCarthy's power was created by a mass medium, the press; he sold more papers because bad news always sells best and he fed the hate-hungry. He was destroyed by another mass medium, television, the same way that other hollow heroes of the medium are destroyed: overexposure. I would not myself read any grand democratic assurances into his downfall—that sooner or later the truth triumphs, and so on. I think he was simply on camera long enough to be plentifully and egotistically stupid (the attack on Welch's young assistant, the cropped photo, the phony letter supposedly from J. Edgar Hoover). If the hearings had been shorter so that he could not have become camera-drunk and overconfident, he might have prevailed.

In any event *Point of Order* is a chilling, extremely valuable précis which makes clear enough why he rose, why he fell. (He did not, by the way, crumble under Welch's "at long last" speech; it was the after-effects on the public that undid him, not the moving assault itself.)

My own favorite moments: McCarthy chuckling salaciously and touching his brow in thanks when someone off-camera suggests that he may be the next President; Roy Cohn, unluckily seated some distance from McCarthy at the moment, flicking his eyes to heaven in despair as the Senator starts his attack on Welch's assistant.

After the Ball Was Over   (October 5, 1963)

New York has just had its first film festival, thus following be-
latedly in the steps of such metropolises as San Francisco, Bergamo,
Cork. There were no prizes. Two concurrent series were shown at
Lincoln Center (21 features, 32 shorts) and the Museum of Modern
Art (11 features). The former contained as-yet unreleased new films,
the latter relatively recent films that have never been publicly shown.
The press was asked not to review the films but to comment on the
festival as a whole. My notes follow.

1. Festivals are always imperfect, rationally indefensible, exciting.
This one was a sort of international harvest celebration, and the
feeling in going to it for a concentrated ten days was quite different
from random film-going. Much of the large audience attended many
of the films and seemed to get an understandable pleasure out of the
quasi-ritual act.

But it was madness to run to two series concurrently. I tried for
three days to see the total of three films shown every day in both
places and can recommend it only to those in quest of brain tumor. I
had to drop the Museum series. I was able to see 17 of the Center's
21 films, with attendant shorts, and these remarks are concerned only
with them. Surely New York can support two series *seriatim* so that
we are not forced to choose between them.

2. Three of the features—by Olmi, Polanski, and Losey—were of
exceptional interest and will be discussed here in detail when they
open publicly. The common denominator among most of the others
—particularly the "arty" ones—was tediousness. The persisting sin
of serious film-makers, even some with talent, is reluctance to stop: a
shot, a scene, a film. When the maker has no theatrical sense and his
cinematic sense consists of lingering over very little, of trying to wring
out meanings (usually symbolic) through insistence on trivia, the
result is physically excruciating. I wriggled through many of these
films. And I willingly risk a charge of Philistinism in supposing that
they have been declined by importers because they are boring, not
because they are too good.

Then, while I wriggled, I looked around and saw miles and miles
of people sitting rapt. There is already a strong mystique of acceptance in the hard-core "art" audience. Along with a welcome growth

of interest in serious films, there has grown a belief that anything "noncommercial" is at least worth attention. The film world shares what I would call the anti-Hanslick syndrome. In the nineteenth century, the Viennese music critic Hanslick, like other critics of other arts, made judgmental howlers about some new works. The twentieth century, keenly aware of these conservative errors, is trying to atone for them by embracing every crankishness as creative, every incompetence as liberation from tradition.

3. Yet the audience, as noted, was extraordinary. It was more than the usual milling herd, plodding to theaters on or off Broadway in the endless "hit" parade. They generated the keenest sense of intrinsic interest that I have felt (outside of music and ballet audiences) since the proletarian plays of the thirties, the feeling that they were there because nothing could have kept them away. Much can be forgiven because of this—even their cliquish laughter at the two feature comedies (one American, one French) which seemed to me to be nonexistent without carefully primed viewers.

4. The audience reaction underscored a sense that the film, in this country, is possibly the one art form that is *wanted*. The public needs no cosseting, no National Film Week, like National Library or Music Week. In other arts—fiction and music, for instance—more good work is being produced than there is audience for. The reverse is true in films: there is more eager audience than good work.

5. The shorts varied widely in quality. Of those I saw, cartoons by the Czechs Bedrich and Brdecka, the Italian Bozetto, the Englishman Dunning, the American Vanderbeek, had charm. None of the "live" shorts was memorable except two by the American collaborators Robert Drew and Ricky Leacock, which were both fascinating and objectionable.

I shall not review these two films, I shall only discuss their basic device. They were prepared for television and run about an hour each. The first, *Crisis*, took us into Robert Kennedy's home and office, President Kennedy's office, Governor Wallace's office, while these gentlemen and their associates planned strategy and counterstrategy in relation to the enrollment of two Negro students at the University of Alabama in June 1963. The second, *The Chair*, which dealt with the last-ditch fight for commutation of Paul Crump's death sentence in Chicago, took us into the death house, his lawyer's office, (including two outbursts of weeping by the lawyer), conferences between the weeper and Louis Nizer, who was called in to help, the official hearing of the appeal. No one could be bored at being privy to these occasions, but that in itself is no justification for the films. What dignity, what scope for free discussion are left an Attorney-General and a President, if a camera and microphone are present when they discuss plans? Is a lawyer's work for a client, once considered their affair alone, to be made a *frisson*-fest for movie theaters when a life is at stake?

The line between what the public is and is not entitled to know is an extremely fine one, but it seems to me that these instances are nowhere near it. Albert and David Maysles have made a "cinéma-vérité" film called *Showman,* about the distributor Joseph Levine (not included in the festival), which I enjoyed very much. If Levine was willing to have it made, the only relevant question had been answered. But to make shows of government conference and of legal process seems to me reprehensible. And "shows" is what they are; all the participants knew the equipment was present and they were, to some extent, performing.

The process is symptomatic of a general corruption of the very idea of privacy, a hunger for sensation that is both fed and teased by the mass media. These two films—not apart from but *because* of the importance of their subjects—are vulgarity distilled. Messrs. J. and R. Kennedy, Wallace, Nizer, and the other persons who permitted the making of these pictures deserve the censure of all of us.

6. A festival program, like an anthology, can never entirely please anyone. These films were chosen by Richard Roud, an American-born critic functioning in England. The difficulties of his job are easy to see, but we can also see, through his program notes, that he thought some of the program's lowest points were as good as its best. Those notes gave a faint aroma of silly *cinéaste* effusion to the whole festival, particularly when Mr. Roud effervesced about two of the films (no names please!) whose inclusion seemed completely unjustifiable.

7. *Incidental intelligence:* (a) The festival allowed us to hear the eff word in a film for the first time—in a short that was made, appropriately, by and with William Burroughs. (b) Lincoln Center, site of this serious film festival, is diagonally across the street from the funeral parlor where Valentino's body lay in state in 1926 and caused a near-riot.

The News from Karlovy Vary   (August 8, 1964)

In Karlovy Vary, the Czechoslovakian spa (formerly Carls-
bad) which in July held its fourteenth international film festival, contradictions thrive. A hotel with a plaque noting that Marx once stayed
there has, high on its façade, a small copy of the Statue of Liberty.
Nuns with wide coifs sweep past the *Musée de Charles Marx.* (Its
name is given in four languages.) A few blocks from Lenin Place is
Rooseveltova.

The contradictions extended to the two-week festival, of which I
attended the last three days. The most-discussed film, which I missed,
was a Czech "western" called *Lemonade Joe*—to be seen in the US.
Another Czech film, *The Accused,* which won the Grand Prize, is
said to be highly critical of the regime. (At a belated screening—
without a translator—what I saw made me eager for a subtitled
version.) Another Czech entry, *The Hop Pickers,* despite its title out
of Robert Benchley, was a pleasant wide-screen color musical, dealing with one of the brigades of boy-and-girl students who pick hops
for two weeks during the season and live in segregated dormitories.
Ladislav Rychman, the director whose third film and first musical this
is and who told me that he is "now ready for a nervous hospital," has
obviously been a diligent student of Minelli, Donen, and Robbins; but
it is meant as a compliment to say that the result looks as if it had
been made by all three on a budget reduced by five-sixths.

The contradictions, however, did not extend far enough. Some
films contained no surprises. *Lost Women,* the Argentine entry, was
like a 1933 Kay Francis-Warren William confessional of vice in the
big city. *Current,* by the young Hungarian Istvan Gaal, which won the
"first film" prize, was an ambitious, intelligent, but desperately imitative work—more an account of Gaal's experience up to now of film-
going than of life. A Bulgarian film called *The Chain* dealt with a
doomed political prisoner under the Fascists and how his unsuccessful escape attempt confirms his sense of brotherhood. Bulgaria perhaps does not know a long line of similar works from Galsworthy's
Escape to *The Defiant Ones.* Among the French entries was a natural-
history color film dealing with (ah, those French) the sex life of cells,
insects, fish, mammals—excellently photographed but, like many
such works, a ninety-minute feature with the makings of a twenty-

minute short. *The Best Man,* one of the two American entries (with *America America*), was warmly received, partly because of the attractive presence in Karlovy Vary of Henry Fonda. (The appeal of American subjects and objects is clearly strong. A constant crowd clustered around the large Chrysler in the courtyard of the main hotel.) But, additionally, the breeziness and dispatch of *The Best Man,* which won a special prize, were refreshing compared with some of the pictures from eastern countries.

This is not to say that any of those films was technically poor. All of them that I saw in and out of competition, had high technical standards and competent acting. But one sometimes had the feeling that they were lengthy expositions of doggedly worthy sentiments or aesthetic propositions set forth for critical discussion.

Such discussion was indeed a principal feature of the festival. Every morning an international symposium was held. I, happily, attended only the last. Like so many experiences in life, it only confirmed preconceptions. First, the critics from the Soviet bloc are not one polysyllable behind the West in their ability to spout terms whose thickness does not enrich their meaning. Second, almost all participants labored away at debate to reach the elemental. (The result of one lengthy exchange was the conclusion that the artist must be true to himself.) Third, film, of all art forms, seems to have a belief in collateral or peripheral discussion—not primarily as criticism but as proof of vitality, indeed almost as the purpose of the art. It is the youngest of the art forms and perhaps it hopes to hasten maturity through colloquy. The French director Edouardo Molinaro, after hearing much talk of "problems" (a favorite term), suggested reticently that a director's chief problem is survival: how to live and get a chance to make films.

In this hothouse atmosphere, judgmental language inevitably tends to overgrow. A certain Buñuel picture "is, of course, not one of his very greatest films." A Soviet critic, discussing *America America,* conceded that it was made by a very great master before he went on to fault it. Even in the least useful literary discussions, laurels are more carefully doled. But one aspect of this film symposium applies equally to many other critics: the attitude toward creators. The general tone was that of the child psychologist toward children. "The sweet dear has made this fascinating thing, but of course he doesn't really understand it. He must now just let loose of it and hand it up to intellectual me, who will clarify it for him." Of course the critic knows that he has no job without the creator, but then the child psychologist knows the same about the child.

Each guest was provided with a transistor radio, equipped with stethoscope earpieces, so that he could tune in on German, French, Russian, or English translations of talk or film dialogue. (An Indian delegate thoughtfully reminded us that this was like the UN and that indeed this congress was like a little UN. But, he added with wit appropriate to him, perhaps this UN would prove more effective.) At the end of the festival I felt a kinship with the Czech lady who had been speaking in my ear for three days, commenting by inflection and sometimes directly. ("I am trying to make sense of these remarks, but it is difficult.") Her slightly jaded voice, charming accent, and general quickness of mind made her a close if invisible friend.

This was my first film festival abroad, and if it lacked the bikinis of Cannes, it could not help but be interesting, particularly in this lovely Franz Josef town. But it confirmed that the prime purpose of a festival is as a trade fair (many deals are made for rights in various countries) or as an oblique patriotic occasion, with an icing of artistic purpose. Some of the guests I met move from one festival to another; there are more than forty, including those for documentaries, shorts, and experimental films. The festival buff develops skills: first, at getting himself invited board-free, then at developing a sense about which of the simultaneous screenings to attend and which of the official receptions; and whether private parties are going on. It is a knack, as well as a means of self-preservation.

For myself, apart from some of the films I saw, nothing was more rewarding than an incident at the final ball. In the crowd I looked enviously at a man with a glass of that wonderful Pilsner beer, which was not being served generally. He took my arm and led me into the huge kitchens of the Hotel Moskva where, seated around a large wooden table, were some leading figures of the Czech film industry, most of whom spoke English. My hour with them provided much insight into Czech and other Eastern European production, as well as superb Bohemian meatballs with horseradish and mustard and stein after stein of that unbeatable beer.

Film Thoughts from Abroad   (October 24, 1964)

I have just spent three months in eight countries, on a Ford Foundation grant, to see film-making and films. I visited two festivals, three schools, dozens of gentlemen and ladies involved in the making, distribution, exhibition of films. Herewith some selections from a crowded notebook.

London

Anthony Asquith is probably the most U film director in the world, the son of a Prime Minister, so well-bred that his very casualness is reticent. Shooting a scene in *The Yellow Rolls-Royce* with a bit player who is obviously inept but whom they have to keep because he is in previous scenes, Asquith says: *"Frightfully* good. Now *would* you mind trying it again and just halting before you speak? Thanks so much. . . . That was lovely, but is it a nuisance to try it a bit faster? *Do* you mind?"

Caste distinctions in the cast. A sign in the studio restaurant reads: "We regret that crowd artistes cannot be served during the tea break but must take their tea from the tea trolley."

The British Film Institute is the first of several similar institutions encountered on the trip. Despite the good offices of such places as the Modern Museum's Film Library (New York) and Eastman House (Rochester), there are no American counterparts in scope. The BFI and its foreign fellows are characterized by: enormous archives (including newsreels) thoroughly catalogued; equivalent still collections; large libraries of books and periodicals; numerous publications of their own including books, brochures, monthly and quarterly journals; educational and information services; film rental service; intensive series of film showings. (The Cinémathèque Française in Paris shows three different films a day six days a week at two theaters.) The wry joke one frequently hears abroad is that although America virtually started the film, it is other countries that are preserving American film history. It is shocking to discover how many films have already completely disappeared or have become extremely scarce.

The British contradiction is that, of all the countries with good institutes, Britain is the only one without a large state-interested film school.

As Britain is to America, so the rest of the world is to Britain. The jealousy that Americans feel about the good British films of the last seven or eight years is mirrored in the jealousy that the British feel for recent continental films. Serious London critics seem depressed about local prospects, opportunities, new directorial talent.

Stockholm

Harry Schein, the president of the Swedish Film Institute, a lithe energetic man of forty, a retired chemical engineer and quondam film critic, has devised a plan—put into effect last year by the government—that has already revolutionized Swedish film and will be adopted next year by Denmark. Because of television, entertainment taxes, and other factors, Swedish production had declined from about thirty features a year to twelve. On May Day, 1962, Ingrid Thulin (Mrs. Schein) delivered a provocative public address criticizing the Social Democratic Government for its neglect of artists. Schein then published a book called *Can We Afford Culture?* Parley and programs followed for all the arts. (Next year twenty-five authors will have guaranteed incomes, the following year 125. Within ten years *all* recognized artists of about forty will have guaranteed minimum incomes of over $6,000 a year.)

The Schein plan for films abolishes entertainment taxes and allocates 10 per cent of all Swedish box-office receipts to a fund which amounts to about $2.5 million a year. Out of this money the Institute was founded, a film school was founded, educational and scientific researches were begun, certain production subsidies were supported. But the chief factor is this: Any Swedish film of quality that incurs a loss, on its domestic receipts alone, within one year of release will have its loss repaid. (The judges of "quality" are a panel of seven critics, two of whom are changed every year.) Thus incentive is necessary; the film must be made. But serious ambition is not penalized; if the film is good but unpopular, the producer is not made to suffer.

Already such directors as Alf Sjöberg and Arne Sucksdorff, who have been handicapped by financial conditions, have been able to resume work. Young directors like Bo Widerberg and Jorn Donner (whose *To Love* was shown at the recent New York Film Festival) have had doors opened to them.

Now Swedish directors may share the same happy problem that Swedes laughingly admit applies generally: the dangers of security.

Copenhagen

Ib Monty, the young director of the Danish Film Museum, says: "A small country has particular problems for an artist—language, finance, and so on. But there's a special one. If he becomes world-famous, for some reason he becomes suspect at home."

Perhaps this is what has shackled Carl Dreyer, who is world-famous and has had to wait nine years for a chance to make a new film. Dreyer, now seventy-five, white-haired, semiangelic, says: "My theme has always been intolerance—the thinking man's troubles with the group. In direction my influences were Sjöström and Griffith. None since. And I have no disciples."

Prague

Vera Uzelac, who looks like an intelligent, slimmer Kim Novak, has acted in eight films in seven years. When I asked her whether she also works in the theater, she says, "No, I am not a professional actress." (Art snobberies die hard.) She is studying film economics and production as a stay against future unemployment.

Warsaw

The organization of the film industries in all the Communist countries is, with the exception of Yugoslavia, more or less the same. Under the Ministry of Culture there are a number of relatively autonomous production groups: in Czechoslovakia five, in Hungary four, in Poland seven. Jerzy Bossak, the head of the Polish group called Camera, is also a distinguished documentary maker and dean of the directing faculty at the film school. (It was in the Camera group that Roman Polanski made the lately successful *Knife in the Water*.) Bossak believes firmly that films must be in the hands of the state, but he is not blind to the dangers of government control. He says that in the West a director's project is weighed by its profit potential, in Poland by its propaganda potential. But just as films are often made in the West that are not blatantly commercial, so films are often made in the East that are not blatantly propagandistic. (Propaganda here means moral pap and praise of the status quo more than outright political preachment.)

A director and/or writer in Bossak's group suggests a theme to him. If he is interested, a script is prepared. If he likes the script, he submits it to a committee consisting of other group heads, critics, "some cultivated politicians." Even if they approve it, the Culture Minister can still veto it. But sometimes Bossak has been turned down on a script, returned with it later, and had it accepted. "Whatever the difficulties," he says, "and they exist, at least here I have a forum to argue in, a jury of my peers."

Boleslav Michaelik, president of the Polish Film Critics Association, is on the committee that selects foreign films for import. Conversation with him suggests that Poland has not made a neat exchange of propaganda motive for profit motive, they have instead added the former to the latter. He says that theaters are owned by the state or municipality or workers' collectives, who are all thoroughly concerned to make money and are resistant to anything out of the ordinary. Michaelik and his colleagues have sometimes had to work for years, buttressing their efforts with critical articles, to gain admission for the exceptional.

Budapest

Istvan Nemeskurty, the head of a Hungarian film group since 1959, has a degree in medieval Hungarian literature. He feels that there is a relation between his education and this post. "Hungarian literature was born in the sixteenth century, films are being born in this century. I am interested in the birth of an art."

Janos Hersko, head of another group, also teaches at the film school. Enthusiasm for the school runs high. One of his students is a young dentist who gave up his profession to study directing. Hersko says that the curriculum includes all the expected cultural and technical subjects—and also sports and Marxism. The former because a director needs health and strength (a point that Pietro Germi firmly underscores later.) The second because, to them, Marxism is not a finalized thesis but a way of looking at reality, not a system of answers but a series of questions.

After this exegesis I am taken downstairs to a big studio where a hundred young dancers are engaged in filming a twist sequence.

Zagreb

Yugoslavia is made up of six federated republics, speaking a total of three languages. Each republic has its own film company, making films in the appropriate language and adding subtitles for shipment to other parts of the country (as in India.) Production here seems much more flexible than in the other Eastern countries. There are some more or less private companies. At the Jadran studios in Zagreb (a suprisingly lovely city reminiscent of Paris and Vienna), I see a huge Roman forum left over from a co-production with Italy. There is much joint effort with Western countries. Welles made *The Trial* here. The studios are large and are equipped with every technical facility. And this in a country where, on railroad trains at nightfall, the conductor comes into a first-class compartment, strikes a match, and lights the kerosene lamp.

As to freedom of thought and action in the Communist countries' films, it seems precise to say that they like to think they are free. A prominent Yugoslav director declares, "There is a very liberal atmosphere in this country today." As he says it, he knocks on wood.

Rome

Vittorio De Sica thinks there are three kinds of directors. First, the cold and intellectual. ("I prefer a good book.") Second, the acrobatic and those interested in novelty for its own sake. Third, those who love humanity, who care only for human problems, who know sorrow but also who know happiness very well and are not embarrassed by this fact.

"And," he adds, "there is a fourth kind, a class in itself. Charles Chaplin."

The Fellini location is like a scene from a Fellini film. The crowd of waiting extras, playing cards, chatting, drinking coffee, staring into space, is a gallery of faces chosen with a Daumier eye. In the midst of the early morning hubbub, as carpenters hammer, electricians yell, lights glare on and off, trucks rumble, Fellini calls for a chair and a small table. With chaos eddying around him, the huge man hunches over a typewriter rewriting the pages that he plans to shoot today. He has a well-prepared script, but he always rewrites a scene on the day he shoots it, guided by what has happened thus far in the making of the film and what the conditions of work are that day (for instance, the sunlight, if they are shooting outdoors).

He rehearses and shoots a short scene over and over. One can see that he is not only refining the performances and camera movement, he is also refining his ideas of what it is that he wants from the scene.

I had expected that dinner with Antonioni and Monica Vitti would be fascinating; the surprise is that it is also delightful. Antonioni has just given the last touches to his new film, *Red Desert,* for the Venice Festival (where it won the Grand Prize), and he and Miss Vitti, who plays the leading role in the picture, are feeling relaxed and happy. After an hour or so of chat as animated as my Italian will permit, I ask, "Well, what about *Red Desert?*" Antonioni smiles broadly, makes a sweeping gesture, and announces with the self-satire of the confident, *"Un film stupendo!"* When I see it subsequently at Venice and am gripped by it, the little joke takes on added charm.

Even those Italian directors who do not like Antonioni's work respect him very much. Germi, no admirer, is quick to point out that Antonioni refused work for several years until he could make films as he wanted to. De Sica, who numbers Antonioni among the "cold," adds in his quaint and taking English: "I consider him."

Paris

Jeanne Moreau, in her dressing room after a day's work, says, "One must have the right to make unsuccessful films; that is essential. But one must choose one's unsuccessful films carefully." She has had considerable experience on the stage but now concentrates on films because she feels she cannot do both. "On the stage one feels extroverted, egotistical. In films one feels personal, private. Acting is more difficult for the screen because it deals in the private mysteries of self and feeling that must nevertheless be revealed."

Philippe de Broca, whose pictures are marvels of *légèreté,* is keenly aware of the difficulty of sustaining a light mood through all the cumbersome mechanics of film-making. "Usually, just before I say 'Action,' I make some kind of joke." He would like to direct a musical comedy in the United States, not in France "because there is no national folklore of dance as there is in America, Russia, and Spain."

Georges Delerue, the gifted composer who has written the scores for, among others, de Broca and Truffaut films, says that de Broca often asks for the principal musical themes before he starts shooting so that he can have their shapes in mind as he plans his camera movements.

Three general observations:

1. The high interest in films everywhere—probably the most vital appetite for art in the world today—is ironically balanced by the difficulties of film-making everywhere.

2. Execution is far ahead of content, East or West, New Wave or Old Current. If I ran a film school, I would ask that each applicant submit a script: not to prove writing talent but as evidence of ability to perceive, imagine, respond.

3. America does not know what is happening in the rest of the film world. It is better the other way around; American films are imported everywhere because they make money. But foreign films are not comparatively profitable here and, in fact, there are signs that the presently insufficient import business will diminish. This is true of features. As for short and animated films, the situation is as ludicrous as the quality of foreign production is high.

One element of Harry Schein's plan is a series of film clubs throughout Sweden for which the Institute imports films. How little money it would take, relatively, for a foundation to set up a similar plan here: to foster clubs and to buy good, unprofitable films for club showings throughout the country. Many deficiencies in the American film world can be improved only by time, talent, social evolution. This is one lack that could be cured virtually overnight.

To repeat: America does not know what is happening in the film world.

Are We Doomed to Festivals?   (October 2, 1965)

Two years ago, after the first New York Film Festival, I commented that "festivals are always imperfect, rationally indefensible, exciting." After the third festival I still think this is true, but the last element—the basal excitement of festival-going—has so diminished (though it still exists) that the two other elements loom larger. I think it is time to examine the very idea of the festival.

First a look—only a look—at the films themselves. There were 25 feature offerings—and more than 25 shorts—shown in twelve days in Philharmonic Hall. Six features, virtually one-quarter of the total, were the latest works of directors already established in the US; Godard's *Alphaville,* Penn's *Mickey One,* Ray's *Charulata,* Dreyer's *Gertrud,* Visconti's *Sandra,* Kurosawa's *Red Beard.* Twelve films were by new or lesser-known directors, including a French anthology film, two pictures written and directed by the young Pole Jerzy Skolimowski in which he played the (same) leading role, and two one-hour television films by a Frenchman and an Englishman. There were seven "revivals." One of these was a Buster Keaton omnibus including the short film *Film,* written by Samuel Beckett and directed by Alan Schneider. Another was a 1915 French serial, *Les Vampires* by Louis Feuillade, all ten chapters of which were strung together to make a six-hour picture with a one-hour intermission.

I offer only a few comments on all three categories. The Beckett film was one of the weaker of his many restatements of his sole theme. Six of the young men's films (including Skolimowski's) were about how tough it is to be young these days and did not demonstrate that it is any less tough to be a young director. Two of the old pictures—Clement's *Knave of Hearts* and Cromwell's *Of Human Bondage*—belong on late-night TV with a décor of commercials, not in festivals. The presentation of the serial as a six-hour work was taffeta toshery at its worst and squashed both the fun and the historical interest that might have attached to a chapter or two. I watched an hour of it, comfortably. Most of the shorts were mere nuisances. An outstanding exception was a nightmare about the letter A—an animated cartoon film by the Pole Jan Lenica. The whole bill again suffered from the program notes of Richard Roud, the Program Director, whose prose is film-journal swill. Examples: One film is "hieratically and soberly photographed." Another is a "breathless mosaic." The serial is a "supreme masterpeice." Mr. Roud writes with a limp mind and wrist.

Concurrently there were thirteen symposiums on various film subjects. I participated in one, attended another and regret both. The fallacy of symposiums in any field, no matter how capable the participants, is now—for me—firmly established. I have never seen one in which the subject was not debased. Here they were used as added attractions to beef up the main event, like sideshows with a circus.

Which brings us to that main event. I am now convinced that the New York Festival is a misconception. The primary purpose of film festivals is as trade fairs. This purpose is blunted in New York because all the films have already been seen at other festivals and importers have had a chance to buy them. It is true that a few previously unsold films have subsequently been bought—presumably as the result of (now permissible) New York newspaper reviews— but their number can hardly be said to justify the huge mechanism at Philharmonic Hall.

Further, in order to sparkle, the bill needs big-name pictures, all of which are going to be seen anyway. To Visconti and Kurosawa, for example, these showings are completely superfluous. (At Cannes and Venice, they have at least the small incentive of prizes.) For the younger men, I am glad to have had a chance to sample their work (even the two or three that I walked out on). For the revivals, I am appreciative. But the festival is not the best place or manner for showings in either of these categories. The over-all hoopla excitement is there, all right; but audiences—and film-makers—are paying too high a price for it.

The situation that has been established is this: There is now a ten- or twelve-day period every September (after Labor Day and before the music season really begins) that must be filled—mostly with new films, whether or not the past year has produced many good ones, whether or not those good ones are available. Scrapings-up and rationalizations, stunts (like *Les Vampires*), are inevitable. Of the good new films, many of them—by the time they get to this affair—are bound for release anyway. As to the merely partially interesting films, they suffer very badly by bearing the implied weight of being major artistic events in an annual harvest of the world's best.

That is precisely what this festival is not. It is only the best that can be done to fill a gap on the Lincoln Center program calendar—a commitment that has been taken on and must now be honored. That, and not artistic celebration, is the first dynamics behind it; and thus it is, in Daniel Boorstin's term, a "pseudoevent." The test is this: Would they call off the festival next year if they could not find sufficient good films? Would they even shorten the program? They brag of their increasing box-office receipts, like the Radio City Music Hall; in the face of this financial rise, would they curtail or abandon next year's festival if they were unhappy about the prospective program? I doubt it. I do not deplore the attendance. I do not think financial success automatically equals mediocrity. But I do think that much of this year's program was tedious, was made to seem more so because of the whooped-up atmosphere around it, and that the circumstances of the festival have taken precedence over the content.

If Lincoln Center and/or the money-men behind it were principally interested in films and not in publicity events, they could make a long stride toward demonstrating it—and toward filling a sorry gap— by effecting a quite different plan; unforced and unfrenetic. What is needed—perhaps including Lincoln Center and certainly throughout the country—is a network of theaters devoted to a dual purpose: the showing of old films that are no longer available from rental services and the showing of more recent films that have not attracted commercial distribution. Most of these latter (of which there are interesting dozens) would come from abroad, simply because most of our good films do come from abroad, but American films, as appropriate, should also be included.

Amos Vogel, the Festival Director in New York, could easily reply that what I propose is simply a continuation and extension of Cinema 16, the society that he founded in New York, ran for a number of years, and had to close as a society (not as a film-rental service) because of mounting expenses. This is only partly true. What I am proposing is the emulation of a plan operating in Sweden under their Film Institute. A series of club theaters has been established, based at universities (here they could also be located in the proliferating cultural centers). Worthy films are imported especially for these theaters if they have not been bought for regular theaters after a reasonable length of time. They are shown around the network for a limited time and are not publicly reviewed. After a tour of some weeks, the rights revert to the owners who are then free to sell them commercially without having had the general audience "spoiled." If the films do not sell, the owners have not lost anything; audiences have gained. The series proceeds on a weekly or biweekly basis—not the 6:30 and 9:30 pace every day for twelve days; but there is never an obligation to put a film in if a worthy one is not available. And the entire enterprise is free of the label of "the cream of the festivals" or any hard sell whatsoever. In the US such a system might well have a stimulating effect on domestic film production.

Import fees would be much smaller than the $15 or $20 thousand which, I am told, is usually needed to bring in and launch the most minor and bedraggled foreign films. Still, such a system might not pay its way and should not be expected to. I presented the idea—without success, so far as I know—to a large foundation last year when I returned from a visit to European film centers convinced that America is ignorant of what is happening abroad. The intensity of American public interest in good films may in time persuade them or another foundation or group. One of the dangers of our festival is that it may beguile them into thinking that the job is already being done.

A festival, compressed in time, fancied up in advertising wrappings, and obliged to try to "succeed," is not the answer. The festival idea may, artistically, be a good way to afford an international sampling in some fields, music and the theater (though even that can be argued). It is not the best method, and may even be a detriment, for film, which badly needs a permanent and independent channel of communication between the American audience and world artists in the art that is the most financially harried of all.

PART IV

THE FILM GENERATION

The Film Generation

Celebration and Concern

Some of the following remarks were included, in differing forms, in talks delivered recently at several universities, colleges, and seminars. In one of the audiences were a distinguished poet and a critic of the graphic arts. Afterward, the critic came up to me and said, "You destroyed us. You wiped out our professions. You rendered my friend and me obsolete." I said that I neither believed nor intended that. Then he said wryly, stroking his chin, "On the other hand, if I were twenty years younger, I know I'd go into films."

His dismal reaction had been prompted by my assertion that film is the art for which there is the greatest spontaneous appetite in America at present, and by my reasons for thinking so. I must be clear that this is not to say that it is the art practiced at the highest level in this country; the film public depends more on imports today than does any other art public. But observation and experience, and the experience of others, make me believe that this uniquely responsive audience exists.

Or, in another phrase, there exists a Film Generation: the first generation that has matured in a culture in which the film has been of accepted serious relevance, however that seriousness is defined. Before 1935 films were proportionately more popular than they are now, but for the huge majority of film-goers they represented a regular weekly or semiweekly bath of escapism. Such an escapist audience still exists in large number, but another audience, most of them born since 1935, exists along with it. This group, this Film Generation, is certainly not exclusively grim, but it is essentially serious. Even its appreciations of sheer entertainment films reflect an over-all serious view.

There are a number of reasons, old and new, intrinsic and extrinsic, why this generation has come into being. Here are some of the older, intrinsic reasons.

1. In an age imbued with technological interest, the film art flowers out of technology. Excepting architecture, film is the one art that can capitalize directly and extensively on this century's luxuriance in applied science. Graphic artists have used mechanical and electronic elements, poets and painters have used computers, composers use electronic tapes. These are matters of choice. The film-maker has no choice: he must use complicated electronic and mechanical equipment. This fact helps to create a strong sense of junction with his society, of membership in the present. American artists have often been ashamed of—sometimes have dreaded—a feeling of difference from the busy "real" American world around them. For the film-maker the very instruments of his art provide communion with the spirit of his age. I think that the audience shares his feeling of union, sometimes consciously (especially when stereophonic sound, special optical effects, or color processes are used). The scientific skills employed are thus in themselves a link between the artist and the audience, and are a further link between them all and the unseen, unheard but apprehended society bustling outside the film theater.

There is a pleasant paradoxical corollary. In an era that is much concerned with the survival of the human being as such, in an increasingly mechanized age, here a complicated technology is used to celebrate the human being.

2. The world of surfaces and physical details has again become material for art. Just as the naturalistic novel seems to be sputtering to a halt, overdescribed down to the last vest button, the film gives some of its virtues new artistic life. A novelist who employs the slow steam-roller apparatus of intense naturalism these days is asking for an extra vote of confidence from the reader, because the method and effects are so familiar that the reader can anticipate by pages. Even when there is the interest of an unusual setting, the reader is conscious that different nouns have been slipped into a worn pattern. The "new" French novel of Robbe-Grillet, Duras, Sarraute attempts to counteract this condition by intensifying it, using surfaces as the last realities, the only dependable objective correlatives. Sometimes, for some readers, this works. But both the old and the latter-day natural-

isms must strain in order to connect. Rolf Hochhuth, the author of *The Deputy,* has said:

When I recently saw Ingmar Bergman's *The Silence,* I left that Hamburg movie house with the question, "What is there left for the novelist today?" Think of what Bergman can do with a single shot of his camera, up a street, down a corridor, into a woman's armpit. Of all he can say with this without saying a word.

Despite Hochhuth's understandable thrill-despair, there is plenty left for the novelist to say, even of armpits, but the essence of his remark rightly strips from fiction the primary function of creating material reality. The film has not only taken over this function but exalted it: it manages to make poetry out of doorknobs, breakfasts, furniture. Trivial details, of which everyone's universe is made, can once again be transmuted into metaphor, contributing to imaginative act.

A complementary, powerful fact is that this principle operates whether the film-maker is concerned with it or not. In any film except those with fantastic settings, whether the director's aim is naturalistic or romantic or symbolic or anything else, the streets and stairways and cigarette lighters are present, the girl's room is at least as real as the girl—often it bolsters her defective reality. Emphasized or not, invited or not, the physical world through the intensifications of photography never stops insisting on its presence and relevance.

This new life of surfaces gives a discrete verity to many mediocre films and gives great vitality to a film by a good artist. Consciously or not, this vitality reassures the audience, tangentially certifying and commenting on its habitat. Indeed, out of this phenomenon, it can be argued that the film discovered pop art years ago, digested this minor achievement, then continued on its way.

3. The film form seems particularly apt for the treatment of many of the pressing questions of our time: inner states of tension or of doubt or apathy—even (as we shall see) doubts about art itself. The film can externalize some psychical matters that, for example, the theater cannot easily deal with; and it can relate them to physical environment in a manner that the theater cannot contain nor the novel quite duplicate. The film can dramatize post-Freudian man, and his habitat—and the relation between the two. One does not need to believe in the death of the theater or the novel—as I do not—in order to see these special graces in the film.

4. Film is the only art besides music that is available to the whole world at once, exactly as it was first made. With subtitles, it is the only art involving language that can be enjoyed in a language of which one is ignorant. (I except opera, where the language rarely needs to be understood precisely.)

The point is not the spreading of information or amity, as in USIA or UNESCO films, useful though they may be. The point is emotional relationship and debt. If one has been moved by, for instance, Japanese actors in Japanese settings, in actions of Japanese life that have resonated against one's own experience, there is a connection with Japan that is deeper than the benefits of propaganda or travelogue. No one who has been moved by *Ikiru* can think of Japan and the Japanese exactly as he thought before.

Obviously similar experience—emotional and spiritual—is available through other arts, but rarely with the imperial ease of the film. As against foreign literature, foreign films have an advantage besides accessibility in the original language. The Japanese novelist invites us to recreate the scene in imagination. The Japanese film-maker provides the scene for us, with a vividness that our minds cannot equal in a foreign setting. Thus our responses can begin at a more advanced point and can more easily (although not more strongly) be stimulated and heightened.

This universality and this relative simultaneity of artistic experience have made us all members of a much larger empathetic community than has been immediately possible before in history.

5. Film has one great benefit by accident: its youth, which means not only vigor but the reach of possibility. The novel, still very much alive, is conscious of having to remain alive. One of its chief handicaps is its history; the novelist is burdened with the achievements of the past. This is also true of poetry. It flourishes certainly; as with fiction, the state of poetry is far better than is often assumed. But poetry, too, is conscious of a struggle for pertinent survival. In painting and sculpture, the desperation is readily apparent; the new fashion in each new season makes it clear. But the film is an infant, only begun. It has already accomplished miracles. Consider that it was only fifty years from Edison's camera to *Citizen Kane,* which is rather as if Stravinsky had written *Petrouchka* fifty years after Guido d'Arezzo developed musical notation. Nevertheless the film continent has only just been discovered, the boundaries are not remotely in

sight. It is this freshness that gives the young generation—what I have called the Film Generation—not only the excitement of its potential but a strong proprietary feeling. The film belongs to them.

These, I think, are some of the reasons for the growth of that new film audience. But they raise a question. As noted, these reasons have been valid to some degree for a long time, yet it is only in about the last twenty years that the Film Generation has emerged. Why didn't this happen sooner? Why have these reasons begun to be strongly operative only since the Second World War?

In that period other elements have risen to galvanize them. Some of these later elements come from outside the film world: the spurt in college education; political and social abrasions and changes; moral, ethical, religious dissolutions and resolutions. All these have made this generation more impatient and more hungry. But, since the Second War, there have also been some important developments within the film world itself.* These developments have been in content, not in form. Three elements are especially evident: increased sexuality, an increase in national flavor, and an increased stress on the individual. The latter two are linked.

As for the first, sex has been important currency in the theater since *The Agamemnon,* and with the first films came the first film idols. In fact there are scenes in many silent films that would have censor trouble today. But apart from sexual display or the sex appeal of any actor or actress, there is now—in many foreign films and some American ones—a sexual attitude that can be respected: an attitude closer to the realities of sexual life than the mythology that is preached by clergy of every faith, by mass media, by parents. This relative sexual freedom, long established in fiction and the theater, has been slower to arrive in films because of their wider availability

---

* These do not include linguistic developments. Nothing has changed the language of film as, for example, electronics has changed music or abstract expressionism has altered the vision of painting. There have been many technical film developments—wide screens, stereophonic sound, color refinements—but so far they have largely been peripheral to the art itself. They, and the improved hand-held camera and recorder, may affect the basic language of film in future; they have not yet markedly done so. This fact can be taken as an implied strength. Experiments in artistic technique are usually a sign that a boundary has been reached with old techniques. In film there is no hint of exhaustion in the techniques that were known to Griffith and Eisenstein forty years ago.

to all ages and mentalities, and the consequent brooding of censors. Now, in a more liberal time, this freedom makes films even more pertinent to this generation. The mythology that still passes for sexual morality is prescriptive, these films are descriptive; but there is more to their merit than verisimilitude. Not by nudity nor bedroom calisthenics nor frank language but by fidelity to the complexities of sexual behavior, these films provide more than recognition. By accepting and exploring complexities, they provide confidence in the fundamental beauty of those complexities, in the desirability of being human, even with all the trouble it involves.

The second element, national flavor, has been described by the English critic Penelope Houston in *The Contemporary Cinema* (1963):

However partial or distorted an image one gets of a society through its cinema, it is still possible to discern the national face behind the screen. It is difficult to conceive of a neorealist idealism [in Italy] without the jubilant preface of the liberation of Rome; or to look at Britain's films of the past few years without reference to our redbrick radicalism; or to ignore the effect of the political climate on a French cinema which declares its awareness of strain in the very insistence with which it puts private before public life and creation for creation's sake before either.

It would be easy to add a similar sentence for almost every major film-producing country. Japanese films are concerned with contemporary unrest, directly and indirectly. Many of their costume pictures about samurai swordsmen are set in the 1860s when the feudal system was crumbling and immense social metamorphosis was taking place. The Soviet film has deepened in lethargy as revolutionary fervor wore off, as Stalinist despotism made it nervous, as some subsequent economic and scientific successes made it smug. It has become, with a few exceptions, either war glory or the ideologic equivalent of the petty bourgeois confection. As for America, the poor boy and rich girl story (or rich boy and poor girl) which was the staple of the popular film before the Second War has disappeared. Money as romance, the Gatsby dream, has receded, not because everyone is now rich but because the middle-class image has replaced both the poor image and the rich image. What American would now relish the ancient compliment "poor but honest"? And what is the difference *in appearance* between the clerk's car and the boss's? The much-mooted ascendancy of the middle class has reached the point where it is strong enough to control cultural forms, to magnify its own image in art.

With this ascendancy we have seen the emergence of a new romantic hero, posed against this bourgeois background, since all such heroes must contrast with their societies. The new romantic is the liberated prole, with a motorcycle or a Texas Cadillac, seeking his life by assaulting convention and morality, rather than by striving for success in accepted modes, either with money or with women. This hero scoffs at ideals of excellence and aspiration at the same time that he wants to dominate. There are signs that this hero may have run his course, but in the last twenty years or so he was pre-eminent.

A lesser companion of his still continues: the Frank Sinatra-Dean Martin figure, the smart, cool operator just inside the law, a philanderer righteously resentful of any claims on him by women. His casual *persona* derives in part from the night-club microphone, which was first a necessity, then became a prop, then a source of power and ease for those who had little power and could achieve nothing but ease. The invisible hand-held microphone accompanies the crooner-as-hero wherever he goes. His oblique, slithering solipsism seems likely to persist after the Brando figure, more directly descended from the proletarian rebel and Byronic individualist, has passed. Mere "coolness" persists; purposeful rebellion fades.

All the national colors described above apply both to popular and serious films. If we concentrate on serious film—film made primarily as personal expression, not as contractual job or money-spinner—then we often find, besides intensified national color, an intensified introspection. This is the third of our elements: a concern with the exploration of the individual as a universe. It is not a novelty in films. No more introspective films have ever been made than Wiene's *The Cabinet of Dr. Caligari* (1919) or Pabst's *Secrets of a Soul* (1926). But merely to mention such names as Bergman, Antonioni, Fellini, Ozu, Torre Nilsson, Olmi, Truffaut is to see that, for many outstanding directors, there has lately been more reliance on inner conflict than on classic confrontation of antagonists. These men and others, including some Americans, have been extending the film into the vast areas of innermost privacy, even of the unconscious, that have been the province of the novel and of metaphysical poetry. Saul Bellow has complained that the modern novelist doesn't tell us what a human being *is* today. Bellow is a notable exception to his own complaint;

but whether we agree or not, we can see that many contemporary film-makers have tried to answer that question, with a more consistent application than ever before in the history of the art.

These two elements—national color and the exploration of the individual—are obviously inseparable. Society and the man affect each other, even if it is in the man's withdrawal. These elements are further linked in a curious contradictory motion against our time. In an age when internationalism is promulgated as a solution to political difficulties, national colors have become more evident in films. In an age when social philosophers have begun to question the durability of individualism—which is, after all, a fairly recent concept in history and almost exclusive to the West—the film is tending to cherish the individual. Does this indicate a time lag between the film and the advances of political and social philosophy? On the contrary, I believe it indicates a perverse penetration to truth. The truth of art sometimes runs counter to what seems politically and intellectually desirable; that is always a risk of art. I think the film is showing us that nationalism, in the purely cultural sense, is becoming more necessary to us as jet plane and Telstar threaten to make us one world. I think that just at the time when technological and power structures challenge individualism, our own minds and souls have become more interesting to us. Up to now, technology has outraced self-discovery. Only now—in this postreligious, self-dependent age—are we beginning to appreciate how rich and dangerous each one of us is.

These elements have led, directly and by implication, to the phenomenon we are examining; the historical moment for the rise of the Film Generation, a surge of somewhat nostalgic revolution; a reluctance to lose what seems to be disappearing, accompanied by an impulse to disaffection, an insistence on an amorphous cosmos. ("Stay loose." "Swing.") Doubtless that nostalgia is sentimental, an unwillingness to be banned from an Eden of individualism that in fact never existed. But much of the revolution is clearheaded; not so much an attempt to halt change as to influence it; a natural and valuable impulse to scratch on the chromium fronts of the advancing tanks of factory-society "Kilroy was here."

The divided attitude toward social change leads to another, crucial polarity. This generation has an ambivalent view of cultural tradition. On the one hand there is a great desire for such tradition, admitted or not. Everyone wants to know that he came from somewhere; it's less lonely. But this desire is often accompanied by a mirror attitude that looks on the past as failure and betrayal. It is of course a familiar indictment, the young accusing the old of having made a mess, but now the accusation is more stringent and more general because of the acceleration of change and the diminutions of choice.

This ambivalence toward tradition—this polarity that both wants and rejects it—has created a hunger for art as assurance of origins together with a preference for art forms that are relatively free of the past. Outstanding among these is film. Even though it has been on hand for sixty-five years or so, the film seems much more of the present and future than other forms. It has its roots—of content and method—in older arts: drama, literature, dance, painting; yet it is very much less entailed by the past than these arts. It satisfies this generation's ambivalent need in tradition.

So far, this inquiry has been almost all celebration; now a concern must be raised. So far, we have discussed certain phenomena as cultural dynamics and social facts: now a word must be said in value judgment of the revolutionary standards involved. Not all the films that the Film Generation venerates seem worth its energy and devotion. It is not my purpose to lay down an artistic credo: I could always think of too many exceptions. Taste is a matter of instances, not precepts. One forms an idea of another's taste—or of one's own—from the perspective of many instances of judgment and preference, and even then, general deductions must be drawn delicately. But, drawing them as delicately as I am able, I am left with a concern to posit against the foregoing celebration.

There are enthusiasms of this Film Generation that I do not share, there are many enthusiasms of mine that they seem not to share. For the most part this is nobody's fault and probably nobody's virtue. But there is one enthusiasm in particular that has taken many members of this generation—not all, but a large proportion—that seems potentially deleterious and therefore to need discussion.

On college campuses around the country, in some film societies and small theaters (there are at least three in New York at this writing), much is being made of certain experimental films. The passion for experiment, as such, is eternal and necessary, but out of disgust with much commercial and fake-serious fare, there is a strong tendency to value experiment for its own sake, to regard it as a value instead of a means to value. And since, at this period in social and political affairs, a passion for these films has been taken to have other significances as well, the phenomenon is especially important.

The films to which I refer are often called underground films. In America a large proportion of them come from a group centered in New York but not confined there, variously called New American Films or the Film-maker's Cooperative. It is an association of dedicated film-makers and dedicated apostles. (The apostles carry the word widely. Two minutes after I met Federico Fellini in Rome, he asked me whether I had seen Jack Smith's *Flaming Creatures.*) The group also has a circle of apostolic critics.

Predictably, this group considers itself the element of poetry in an otherwise prosaic film situation in this country and the world. Also predictably, its works are difficult to describe because it is not a school like neorealism or surrealism. It includes these and many more styles. It welcomes anyone who uses film as a form of personal expression. The most lucid general statement about this group that I know was written by Ken Kelman (*The Nation,* May 11, 1964). He divides their works into three main categories. First, "outright social criticism and protest" (Dan Drasin's *Sunday,* Stan Vanderbeek's *Skullduggery*). Second, "films which suggest, mainly through anarchic fantasy, the possibilities of the human spirit in its socially uncorrupted state" (Jack Smith's *Flaming Creatures* and *Normal Love*). The third group "creates, out of a need to fill our rationalistic void, those actual inner worlds which fall within the realm of myth" (Kenneth Anger's *Scorpio Rising,* Stan Brakhage's *Anticipation of the Night* and *Window Water Baby Moving*).

Kelman's article, like others on the subject, is a ringing statement written with inner consistency and a fire that outstrips mere sincerity. The difficulty is that, when one sees these films (I have seen all those cited and numerous others), one finds small consonance between the descriptions and the works. Not to belabor individual films, one can say that most of them represent the attitudes and intents that Kelman describes but that their acceptance as accomplishment reflects a deliberate disconnection from cultural and social history. For me, most of the "new" techniques are dated, most of the social criticism is facile or vacuous, the mythic content undernourishing, the general quality of inspiration tenuous, strained, trite. Much of the work seems made for a young audience that insists on having its *own* films, at any critical or cultural price.

One of the grave liabilities in the situation is that writing like Kelman's and the attitudes it promotes tend to encourage the symbiotic state that exists today in the graphic arts. There is not much direct relation between film and audience, nothing so simple as the audience coming to the theater and being affected, or not, by what it sees. The audience exists jointly with these films in a highly verbalized critical environment; its preformed attitudes are eager dramatizations of credos and exegeses. Much of modern painting—op, pop, collage, latter-day abstraction—seems to have its life almost as much in what is written about it as on canvas. Indeed many of the paintings seem to have been made to evoke aesthetic disquisition, to exist verbally and in viewers' attitudes. The underground film has entered this territory—of art as "position"—a position sustained as much by the polemic-conscious audience as by the material on the screen. It has long been an indictment of Broadway and Hollywood hits that the audience is preconditioned, whipped into line by newspaper raves. Here is very much the same situation at a higher intellectual altitude.

Another grave liability is the pressure brought to bear by the underground movement for disconnection from cultural history. Generally, as has been noted, the Film Generation has at least an ambivalent attitude toward tradition: this underground movement pushes—by implication and otherwise—for complete rejection of the standards that have been continuingly evolved through some centuries of Western art. They are not to be evolved further, they are to be discarded. It is easy to chuckle patronizingly at this belief as one more instance of the perennial artistic rebellion of the young, but current social upheavals give it a momentum that takes it out of the sphere of mere youthful high spirits—or low spirits. And the morning or the year or the decade after the excitements of rebellion have passed, it may be discovered that a valuable continuum in culture has been seriously injured—to the detriment of the very aims for which the action was taken.

I do not argue against change, including radical change. I do argue against nihilism as a necessary first step for progress. Besides, this film nihilism contains a bitter contradiction. It is often a manifestation in art of discontents elsewhere, of anger at older generations' betrayal of certain ideals. But the best art of the past—in all fields—is expression of those ideals, often despite society's apathy toward them. In discarding that inheritance of art, the rebels discard much of the best work that the human race has done for the very ideals that galvanize this new rebellion.

There is a parallel between this devotion to the underground film in many of the Film Generation and an element in the "new left," the new political radicalism. Some of radical youth are engaged in genuinely creative action: antimilitarism, antidiscrimination, support of various economic programs. But many of them equate radicalism with personal gesture and style—revolt consummated by bizarre hair and dress, unconventional sexual behavior, flirtations with drugs. One who is aware of the valid basis for disaffection can still regret the introversions and futilities of these gestures. Likewise, one hopeful for the invigoration of the American film can doubt the pertinence of comparable gestures in this field: the exaltation of meaninglessness in film as a statement of meaninglessness in the world: the praise of juvenile irreverence—perennial in art—as a new formulation of myth; the approval of a social criticism that is devoid of intellectual foundation and political belief.

I dwell on the partiality to these experimental films not to counterbalance the happy fact of the Film Generation's existence but precisely because of its existence. Art has never been well created for long independently of an audience; in fact, history shows that audience response feeds great eras of art (painting in Renaissance Italy, the drama in Elizabethan England and neoclassic France, the sudden, ravenous world-wide appetite for silent-film comedy).

Speaking in the large, I believe that the Film Generation has the power to evoke the films that it wants, even though that generation is a minority and despite the harsh conditions of production and exhibition around the world. *All* films will not alter, nor should they, but if the dynamics of cultural history still obtains, an insistent group of art takers can—sooner or later, one way or another—have an effect on art makers. The effect is circular. The audience obviously cannot do it alone; there have to be talented artists. But talent is a relative constant in the human race; it is sparked by response and, even at its best, can be dampened by neglect. (Think of Herman Melville's twenty years in the Customs House.)

Thus, by a logical progression, we can see that the Film Generation has extraordinary powers. If it is true (as I have claimed) that film is the most pertinent art at present; if it is true that the young generation is closer to the film than to other arts; if it is also true that audience appetite can evoke art; then, it follows that the Film Generation has the opportunity to help bring forth the best and most relevant art of our age. And it is the possible impediment to this opportunity that makes a devotion to culturally baseless, essentially sterile films seem wasteful.

I am aware that the above puts an almost ludicrously large burden on this Film Generation. In effect, it is almost to ask them to solve the problems of cultural transition, to define what culture will become. The problem is not to be solved in any one locus, even when the locus—film and its audience—has come into being quite naturally. It is never to be solved; it is only to be confronted continually, particularly in an age that is *not* an age, that is a rapid series of continually shifting points. But the size of the conclusion does not diminish the opportunity.

There is not much question among the thoughtful that we live in a time of the most profound cultural change, when the very purposes of art, as well as its content, are being transformed. The New American Cinema is one manifestation of that upheaval. In my view, most of its films that I have seen are of minuscule importance, but the implication in most of them is important: the implication that what's past is quite dead. The art of the future may be divorced from present concepts of humanism; it may find its pertinences in modes that, to most eyes, now look cold or abstract or even antihuman. But they will have been made by men who would not be what they are, whatever that may be, without the precedents of culture; and if that new art, whatever it may be, is to be held to its highest standards, the best of the past needs to be brought forward with us. The real *use* of our inheritance in the contemporary situation would throw a good deal of illumination on much of the new that is now adulated. The Kelmans tell us that an Antonioni is only seemingly free, that he is trapped by attempting to renovate the past. But, to take Antonioni as an example, it is precisely the effort to alter in an altered cosmos without returning Western culture to Year One that may keep a cultural future possible; may sustain us as we travel from a terrain that once was fruitful to one that has not yet been sighted. We don't want to starve en route.

As an important part of this process—this rescue operation, if you like—the Film Generation can demand a new film from the serious film-maker that is more than a gesture of denial. Such a generation, joined with the past and therefore truly equipped to outgrow it, may eventually get in its films what the Kelmans have prematurely claimed: a new social cohesion, a new fertile and reassuring mythos. If these come, they will manifest their presence, not so much by the blown prose of rhapsodists as by an irony: middle-of-the-road art will imitate the new film. That film will certainly not be ignored, as the majority now ignore underground efforts. When the imitation begins, then authentically progressive artists and audiences will know that they have thus far succeeded, and will know it is again time to move forward.

So the Film Generation, flaws and all, represents both a circumstance and an opportunity. On the whole it is, I believe, the most cheering circumstance in contemporary American art. That generation can be a vital force, or it can twiddle its strength and chances away in irrelevant artistic nihilism, in engorged social petulance. One does not ask them to "save" film forever. In the long run, the history of the film will be the same as that of all arts: a few peaks, some plateaus, many chasms; but the present chance—a rare one—could save much time in the development of this young medium. The foreseeable future is all that, reasonably, we can have hopes or anxieties about in art. The Film Generation can help to make the foreseeable future of film interesting and important. Let us see.

Index